Writing a Usable Past

Writing a Usable Past

RUSSIAN LITERARY CULTURE, 1917–1937

Angela Brintlinger

NORTHWESTERN UNIVERSITY PRESS / EVANSTON, ILLINOIS

Northwestern University Press
www.nupress.northwestern.edu

First paperback printing 2008

Printed in the United States of America

10 9 8 7 6 5 4 3 2 1

ISBN 978-0-8101-2523-0

The Library of Congress has cataloged the original, hardcover edition as follows:

Brintlinger, Angela.
Writing a usable past : Russian literary culture, 1917–1937 / Angela Brintlinger.
p. cm.—(Studies in Russian literature and theory)
Includes bibliographical references (p.) and index.
ISBN 0-8101-1768-1 (alk. paper)
1. Russian literature—20th century—History and criticism. 2. Pushkin, Aleksandr Sergeevich, 1799–1837—In literature. 3. Biography as a literary form. 4. Biography in literature. I. Title. II. Series.
PG3026.P87B75 2000
891.7'090042—dc21
00-008691

∞ The paper used in this publication meets the minimum requirements of the American National Standard for Information Sciences—Permanence of Paper for Printed Library Materials, ANSI Z39.48-1992.

For Steven and Olivia

Contents

Acknowledgments

This book could not have been completed without the help and encouragement of many people. My first debt is to the wonderful teachers and mentors with whom I had the pleasure to work on the first stage of this project—Yuri Shcheglov, Judith Kornblatt, Al Senn, Sasha Dolinin, and especially David Bethea, who has taken the role of advisor to the level of a calling. Thanks also to Galina Lapina, Maya Hoptman, and especially Dan Ungurianu, whose own smart work has had a great impact on mine.

I have been fortunate in my colleagues at Ohio State University, many of whom have read and listened to my work, offering comments, criticism, and support—Sara Dickinson, George Kalbouss, and especially Irene Masing-Delic; Lisa Florman and especially David Hoffmann; Stephen Summerhill. The institutional support I have received at Ohio State has also been phenomenal. I'd like to thank in particular Virginia Hull, the Center for Slavic and East European Studies, the Department of Slavic and East European Languages and Literatures, and the College of Humanities for travel and research grants and for that most precious of commodities, time off to read and write. In addition, a travel grant from IREX allowed me to participate in a Griboedov conference in 1995 and to present some of my work to an international audience.

The enterprise of writing owes much to the enterprise of teaching. I had an opportunity to work out some of my ideas with the students of my "Pushkin in the Twentieth Century" seminar in the autumn of 1996, and I am grateful to them, especially Rudi Blaser. Working with graduate students on their projects and on mine over the years has been a rewarding privilege. The research assistance rendered to me by Ona Renner-Fahey in 1998 was invaluable, as were my many consultations with Tatiana Smorodinskaya. Technical assistance by Dianna Murphy was also much appreciated. I feel proud to call these bright, hardworking, and capable women my students and colleagues. I also want to express a special thanks to the members of the Ohio Russian Literary Seminar, who offered useful comments on the first version of my work on Lifar'.

A scholarly community is held together by its most generous members. I'd like to thank Caryl Emerson, Stephanie Sandler, Marcus Levitt, and Sergei Davydov, all of whom have commented on portions of what was once my "Pushkin project." Andrew Walker of the Art Institute of Chicago has also shared his research with me, and I thank him for his magnanimity and enthusiasm. I have benefited from the international nature of our community over the past decade and have cherished the advice and help of such scholars and friends as Sergei Fomichev, Efim Etkind, and Margarita Odesskaia, among others.

Finally, my biggest debt of gratitude I owe to Steven Conn, who read more versions of my manuscript than anyone should have to, who prompted and prodded and took me to the zoo, and whose investment of time, energy, and intellectual effort in me and this book were far above the call of comradeship, friendship, and duty. Thanks.

Chapter One

Writing a Usable Past

Подлинную историю человека пишет
не историк, а художник.

The true history of a person must be written not
by a historian, but by an artist.
—Maksim Gor'kii

Read no history, read nothing but biography, for
that is life without theory.
—Benjamin Disraeli

IN 1918, the American critic Van Wyck Brooks wrote a short essay entitled "On Creating a Usable Past." The essay addressed problems of contemporary American literature, but its tenets ring true in a more universal way. "The spiritual past," wrote Brooks, "has no objective reality; it yields only what we are able to look for in it."[1] For Russians in 1918, this search for meaning in the past, a past that could be used to interpret and understand the present, was just beginning. But the search for a usable past determined the way the Russians saw their history, and the way Russian writers portrayed their history in fiction.

History and literature. In recent years, the boundaries between these two disciplines have become more fluid—literary critics turn to Hayden White and Michel Foucault for ideas and terminology, while historians mine fictional texts for the stories that liven up their narratives and illustrate their analyses. But what is true in the metadisciplines has also been true of their objects of study for some time: history is itself never straight "fact," but relies on various fictions while it is in the making, and literary texts often use historical settings and events to tell their own stories. The relationship between history and literature may well prove to be an enduring theme of twentieth-century intellectual life.

This tension between the enterprises of literature and history lies at the heart of my book in several ways. First of all, the start and end dates of this study, 1917 and 1937, represent historical moments of intense crisis for Russian culture, and Russian literary culture in particular. During these twenty years, vast changes took place on the literary landscape. Certainly one of the most important changes was the emigration and exile of many Russian intellectuals to Europe and beyond. Especially in this period, Russian literature and Russian history are inextricably interwoven, twisted around each other like a double helix. Studying history and the uses to which it was put reveals much about literature; studying literature reveals much about history as well.

But there is an even more compelling reason why history and literature are both central to this study. The authors whose works I intend to examine most closely were engaged in writing literary history or historical literature or both. These literary men were themselves playing the role of historians, sifting through the patches of historical data—characters, events, places—and choosing which patches to piece together into a story.

Let me propose a metaphor to illustrate what I mean. We can think about the enterprise of writing history as a crazy-quilt-making operation where odd-shaped fragments of fabric, rescued and retrieved from a variety of places, are sewn together to form a single textile. Like a quilter, the historian—and the author of fiction who works with historical material—arranges the pieces, culled from incomplete archives and published sources, picking out the best materials to represent their particular design. Stitched together in convincing and coherent ways, the results are displayed as an historical narrative. Each of the authors in my study, in approaching historical material, carefully chose, reworked, and presented a version of the past which seemed to him to be the most tenable, the most "true," and the most usable for his own time. Hayden White has written that it is possible to produce "an imaginary discourse about real events that may not be less 'true' for being imaginary."[2] It is this truth, a usable truth from a usable past, that the authors of my texts envisioned and described.

However, if the enterprise of history-telling is akin to quilt-making, the role of the literary critic reverses this process. Within the pages to follow, I will be "picking apart" the quilts of my authors, pulling out seams and tracing the sources of individual pieces, commenting on the details more than on the overall pattern, and looking at the piles of unstitched patches for clues and answers to the questions I pose. My hope is that through this process of unstitching, the methods and motivations of the original quilters will reveal themselves to us, and we will complete the process by sewing the quilt back together into the literary culture which it depicts.

In his 1932 novel *Glory* (*Podvig*), Vladimir Nabokov gave his hero's rather pompous Cambridge tutor Archibald Moon a very definitive idea of what had happened to Russia with the Bolshevik Revolution:

> Moon . . . saw in the Bolshevist insurrection a certain clear-cut finality. While he willingly allowed that, by-and-by, after the primitive phases, some civi-

> lization might develop in the "Soviet Union," he nevertheless maintained that Russia was concluded and unrepeatable, that you could embrace it like a splendid amphora and put it behind glass. The clay kitchen pot now being baked there had nothing in common with it. The civil war seemed absurd to him: one side fighting for the ghost of the past, the other for the ghost of the future, and meanwhile Archibald Moon quietly had stolen Russia and locked it up in his study. He admired this finality. It was colored by the blue of waters and the transparent porphyry of Pushkin's poetry.[3]

This formulation, of the "old Russia" as the ghost of the past, while the "new Russia" was equally spectral, a phantom of the future, was a neat and convenient way for the practical English scholar of Russia to dismiss the civil war and other serious contemporary events. But for Russians themselves, these ghosts of the past and future were not trivial, and neither were the events "final," as Moon would have it.

In 1917 the Russian world, once whole if not united, began to fragment. Russians had either to embrace or to adjust themselves to the new Bolshevik regime, with the changes that meant in daily life, in artistic creation and appreciation, in intellectual freedom, and in ideological direction, or they had to leave their homeland. Many Russians fled the new regime and the new conditions—or were asked to leave, not always politely—for other parts of the world, creating as a result a far-flung Russian diaspora. That diaspora eventually came to consider itself a new stateless "nation," "Russia Abroad," with its "capital" in Paris and its own set of institutions—literary, cultural, artistic, educational, journalistic. Russia was not merely a museum piece to be placed behind glass, as Nabokov's foreign scholar thought; it was a living entity that had been split in two.

The mere fact of these "two Russias" constituted an enormous shock for Russian literary culture. If throughout the nineteenth century there were at least two "camps" of Russian literary figures on the public scene, the inward-looking Slavophiles and the outward-looking Westernizers, and if Russian writers such as Gogol', Turgenev, and Herzen had lived much of their lives abroad and not in Russia at all, there was nonetheless always only one Russia, one domestic audience, one "given" in Russian literary culture. The new historical and political circumstances in which Russians found themselves seemed like a sudden and complete break with the past. What had been connected to the present and the status quo was now severed from it by the Revolution, but after a brief period of anarchy, the past became for Russians of all ideological casts a source for a new narrative about themselves and their culture.

After 1917, both new Russias needed to constitute themselves culturally, to legitimate their own claims to cultural hegemony and to their cultural patrimony, and to create a "usable past" for their own present and future.[4] A pragmatic approach to the social function of literature has literature doing actual "work in the world"; in Soviet Russia, the doctrine of looking to the future for a picture of what the world should resemble eventually resulted in socialist realist fiction, in which poetry, literature, and art were only to do work in the world, mirroring the Party's image of what the future should be. But many authors insisted that literature should fulfill an aesthetic and a historical as well as a social function, and it is these authors who will interest me in my study. In the texts I examine here, looking to the past and constructing a paradigmatic vision of heroes and programs permitted authors to write about their own times and their own societies. Through visions and revisions of the past, writers found answers for the present. As Brooks has written, "[t]he past is an inexhaustible storehouse of apt attitudes and adaptable ideals; . . . it yields up, now this treasure, now that, to anyone who comes to it armed with a capacity for personal choices."[5] The past also includes an army of potential heroes who can offer models to the searching author.

The year 1937 marks as conveniently as anything the maturation of two distinct Russian cultural worlds. By this time, Soviet society and literary culture were in the process of submitting to the doctrine of socialist realism in art or of paying the price, while émigré communities had become convinced that they alone could be trusted to preserve Russian culture. I have chosen 1937 as the end date of my study for two reasons. Our primary association with this year is with Stalin's Great Purges, which reached their apex in 1937. Certainly for the Russian intelligentsia, the purges loomed ominous during the 1930s. At the same time, official Soviet literary culture was gearing up for an occasion which would reinvent the Russian literary past for the new order of the workers' and peasants' state: in 1937, the Soviet Union commemorated the one hundredth anniversary of the death of the great Russian poet Aleksandr Sergeevich Pushkin.

It would be hard to exaggerate the magnitude of the Pushkin celebrations of 1937. During the years and months leading up to the 1937 "jubilee," Pushkin was brought into the public discourse as a politicized entity, forced to represent a version of his own past which supported the legitimacy of the Soviet state and the cultural hegemony of the proletarian and peasant party. The politicization of Pushkin included rewriting Pushkin's biography and the appropriation of Pushkin activities for the Soviet populace. Pushkin's aristocratic heritage was conveniently erased in the rush to make him more like average Soviet citizens. Clearly the rhetoric of Pushkin as a "people's poet," murdered by enemies, dovetailed nicely with the rhetoric of the Great Purges, according to which the enemies of the people had to be rooted out, arrested, and removed from public space in order to ensure that they would not harm Soviet Russia or her citizens.

The centennial of Pushkin's death was seen as a momentous occasion during which the Soviet Union could lay claim to the "greatest Russian poet." One way to do that was to "popularize" Pushkin. Instead of only commemorating a "Pushkin Day," as émigré communities did each year during their annual celebration of Russian culture, the Soviet Union launched an entire Pushkin year in 1936–37. The All-Union Pushkin Committee, under the chairmanship of official proletarian writer Maksim Gor'kii, was charged with working out a series of measures to commemorate Pushkin's memory among the peoples of the USSR and to promote the broad popularization of his works among the workers. Publication data alone show us just how serious this effort was: during 1936–37 nineteen million copies of Pushkin's works were published in the Soviet Union, of which three million were in languages other than Russian.

The monument to Pushkin in Moscow was rededicated on February 10, 1937, with the uncensored version of a quote from Pushkin's poem about raising a monument to himself replacing the original version. Newspapers celebrated the new Soviet Pushkin: *Izvestiia,* for example, asked in an editorial "How do we value Pushkin?"

> Not one feature of Pushkin's many-sided nature slips by the Soviet reader. He sees farther and deeper than many researchers and many everyday critics. He renders Pushkin his full due, as creator of the Russian literary language, father of new Russian literature, a genius who enriched humanity with his works. But beyond all these attributes the Soviet person seeks Pushkin his contemporary, he seeks in Pushkin for those traits that he thirsts to see in himself and in the daily life of Soviet society. . . . The Soviet reader sees in Pushkin his fellow citizen. He does not want to perceive Pushkin as a thing of the past, as a phenomenon that has receded into history.[6]

Soviet rhetoric and publicity paid lip service to the Pushkin of the nineteenth century. Clichés by writers and critics were trotted out again for the Soviet reader: critic Apollon Grigor'ev's statement that "Pushkin is our all" (*Pushkin—nashe vse*); poet Tiutchev's words that Pushkin was Russia's first love (*Kak pervuiu liubov', / Rossii serdtse ne zabudet*); novelist Dostoevskii's assertion that Pushkin was a universal genius (*vsemirnyi genii Pushkina*). The Soviet Pushkin was made into a friend of the people and an icon for Soviet youth; through careful selection of details from his life and work, Pushkin became a positive hero, part of the Soviet popular version of the "usable past."

Among émigrés, scattered abroad throughout the diaspora, the significance of 1937 was also recognized. For Russia Abroad, the anniversary of Pushkin's birth and the energetic celebration of it in the Soviet Union offered a unique opportunity for cultural warfare. Through its own journals, newspapers, cultural organizations, exhibits, meetings, and editions, the émigré community did its best to "win" Pushkin for itself, to prove that the characteristics given him by Soviet propaganda only masked the lack of respect for the "real Pushkin" that reigned in his homeland.

In a Parisian journal issue dedicated to the 1937 commemorations, one commentator argued that the Soviet events were all politically motivated: "For the Soviet regime, the cult of Pushkin is primarily a political act."[7] For émigrés, or so émigré authors claimed, Pushkin was more than that: he was a living, breathing phenomenon who helped them keep their own faith in Russia and Russian culture. Pavel Miliukov, for example, wrote in his book *The Living Pushkin* that Pushkin was "more contemporary" at the end of the 1930s than he had been in his own time. For Miliukov, Pushkin was "comprehensible," "intimate," "living," and "eternal."[8] Pushkin had become a representative of things Russian, and he was to comfort Russians far from home like a friend or a comrade.

But although émigrés criticized the Soviet rhetoric of Pushkin and politics, they also saw him as a political symbol. For many émigrés, Pushkin was a prophet who had given himself to Russians and who now, in the twentieth century, offered himself as a banner under which they could unite. Dmitrii Merezhkovskii even went so far as to suggest that Pushkin was a symbol of the unity of Russia and a symbol of freedom, and that while acting as a unifying force for the Russian diaspora, Pushkin would inevitably lead the émigrés back to Russia to free their brethren and unite with them in a new Russia.[9]

The contradictions within émigré discourse are not surprising. Proud that it was to a Russian classical author whom the Soviets turned for their own positive hero, émigrés were aggravated by the way Pushkin was being adapted to Soviet needs. The Soviet use of the cultural patrimony seemed almost amoral to émigré observers:

> Wanting to instill in the country patriotism and popular pride (under the threat of external danger), the Soviet regime was forced to turn to the Russian classics, who are the subject of every Russian person's pride and are the strongest stimuli of love for the homeland. At the same time, the Soviet regime is using the study of the classics as a political tool. Pushkin is clothed in the cloak of a revolutionary and is honored primarily as a political poet.[10]

For those who opposed the Bolshevik regime, Pushkin was irrevocably tied to the imperial world, to Russia. By maintaining close ties with the poet Pushkin as the one hundredth anniversary of his death approached, émigrés, too, sought to find a use for this figure from the cultural past and to claim him as their own.

BIOGRAPHY, OR SOMETHING ELSE? RUSSIAN WRITERS CREATE A NEW PAST

Complaining about American literature in 1918, Brooks mused that "the past experience of our people is not so much without elements that might be made to contribute to some common understanding in the present, as that the interpreters of that past experience have put a gloss upon it which renders it sterile for the living mind."[11] In Russian literary culture of 1917 through 1937, the search for a "usable past" often centered around individual historical characters, and thus around biography. Biography, though, in order to be useful, had to strip off what Vladislav Khodasevich called the "anthological gloss" of the "classic," that patina or shellac which history gives its most venerated characters. In search of a usable past, biographers confronted these icons, but they had an easier time constructing a narrative from the lives of lesser-known or less-anthologized characters, from those still living characters whom historians had not made "sterile."

As I have suggested, during these years it was Aleksandr Pushkin who became the most contested literary figure from the past both among émigré communities and in the Soviet Union. But there were other figures who could serve the present in different ways. This book is organized around three authors, each of whom in his own way was attempting to create a "usable past" for himself and his contemporaries, whether in Soviet Russia or in Russia Abroad. All attempted to write biographies of Pushkin, but those works are not what they are known for. Iurii Tynianov, Vladislav Khodasevich, and Mikhail Bulgakov each were involved in other historical projects, all biographies of one kind or another, before approaching Pushkin. Consequently, in the body of my study I look at each author twice, once as he embarked on his biography of a different hero, and a second time as he tried to write the biography of Pushkin.

Chapters 2 ("Science Fiction: Tynianov and *Death of the Vazir-Mukhtar*") and 3 ("Fact or Fiction: Tynianov's Pushkins") center around biographical endeavors in Soviet Russia. With the nineteenth-century poet-diplomat Aleksandr Griboedov—the "other Aleksandr Sergeevich"—Tynianov was able to create a semi-autoreferential portrait of a poet caught in a time of transformation, but when it came to portraying Pushkin, Tynianov had difficulty incarnating in fiction the hero of his scholarly studies. I will examine each of Tynianov's Pushkins and the junctures at which they overlap, and I will suggest that when Tynianov wrote that he preferred his characters to be unfinished and "fuzzy," what he was really saying was that the polished-up literary hero such as Pushkin made for an unsympathetic biographical subject. The "less sterile" ground for creating a new past was to be found in the undertreated characters, or as Brooks has put it:

> Look back and you will see, drifting in and out of the books of history, appearing and vanishing in the memoirs of more aggressive and more acceptable minds, all manner of queer geniuses, wraith-like personalities that have left behind them sometimes a fragment or so that has meaning for us now, more often a mere eccentric name. The creative past of this country is a limbo of the non-elect, the fathers and grandfathers of the talent of today.[12]

Brooks's valuing of the "fathers and grandfathers" has an almost eerie connection with Tynianov's and other formalist theories of literary evolution, which privileged the "uncle," the off-beat forebear over the direct ancestor. The creative past of Russia, too, was filled with *chudaki* like Kiukhel'beker and legends like "Griboed," and it was in them that Tynianov would find his productive characters.

In 1922, the poet and critic Vladislav Khodasevich emigrated to Europe and from there Khodasevich witnessed what he saw as the "twilight" of Russian literature and culture. Chapter 4, "Searching for a Hero: Khodasevich and His Derzhavin," discusses Khodasevich's brilliant literary biography of Derzhavin and leads up to chapter 5, "'Farewell to Pushkin': Khodasevich and His Pushkin." Derzhavin represented for Khodasevich the "active" eighteenth century and the only hope for twentieth-century Russian culture, which in Khodasevich's view was too passive, too willing to observe historical processes, and too afraid to intervene. Derzhavin was also an important predecessor of Pushkin, about whom Khodasevich wrote two versions of collected essays and intended to write a biography. When he admitted that he would never write the Pushkin biography, Khodasevich asserted: "now I have nothing." Chapter 5 looks at the ways in which Khodasevich centered his creative and critical work around Pushkin, and tries to ascertain the reasons why the Pushkin biography was doomed to failure.

The last author to be discussed is both a novelist and a playwright; Bulgakov put Molière between the covers of a biographical novel, *The Life of Monsieur de Molière,* and on stage, in the play originally entitled *A Cabal of Hypocrites.* In chapter 6, "A Playwright in Wolf's Clothing: Bulgakov and His Molière," I explore briefly those two works and through them Bulgakov's way of looking at the literary and political world; in chapter 7, "Pushkin on Stage—or Not: The Curtain Comes Down on Bulgakov's Pushkin," I examine the collaboration between Bulgakov and the scholar Vikentii Veresaev on a play about Pushkin, planned for the 1937 theatrical season and eventually called *Aleksandr Pushkin (Last Days).* In this project, conflict arose from the very start, with Veresaev adamantly opposed to Bulgakov's idea that Pushkin never appear on stage. In the chapter, I look at the attitudes of the two writers toward the myth of Pushkin and the results of their partnership. For Bulgakov, the triangle he found in seventeenth-century France spoke to him of his own era and of Pushkin's.

In calling the concluding chapter "Back to the Future," I am quoting, among others, Anatolii Lunacharskii and his slogan: *Vpered k proshlomu!* The chapter discusses the years leading up to the 1937 commemoration of the centennial of Pushkin's death as they played out on the cultural scenes of the Soviet Union and the Russian émigré diaspora. Materials from the centenary celebration offer a fascinating look at the nexus between the cultural elite, the mass culture, and the scholarly and literary worlds of each of these places in 1937. In the same way that 1917 marked a cultural rupture and the creation of two competing cultural discourses, 1937 represented a watershed in the process of reconfiguring Pushkin; the one hundredth anniversary of Pushkin's death in a duel loomed in the cultural and political imagination of Russians on both sides of the border. It may very well be that all of my authors, and many others besides, felt a cultural pull toward Pushkin and toward re-creating Pushkin for the present, but the task ultimately fell to those cultural players further removed from literary culture, such as the dancer and choreographer Sergei Lifar', to create a usable Pushkin for 1937.

In the years after the Revolution, regardless of where they were living, Russian writers began to turn to biography as a way of understanding the past and their literary predecessors, and as a way of thinking about their own times and themselves as writers. The 1920s were an era of biography worldwide, especially in Europe—England, Germany, France, and Russia.

A quick survey of European biographers and biographical novelists offers up some of the very best and most prolific. In England in 1918, Lytton Strachey published his influential little book *Eminent Victorians*, which represented a new approach to biography. Simple and readable, the four life stories offered a spectrum of English characters from various walks of life: religious, medical, educational, and military. With his work, Strachey demonstrated that biography could be exciting, that the personality of the writer could interact with his subjects, and, perhaps most important, that biographies could sell. Virginia Woolf took the art of biography even further into the world of creativity, refusing in her 1928 *Orlando* to be restricted by the chronological or even physical life of a single human being, instead creating a "fantasy in the form of biography,"[13] loosely based on the personality and life of Vita Sackville-West. In the 1920s and 1930s, theoretical works such as Harold Nicolson's *Development of English Biography* and André Maurois's *Aspects of Biography* were accompanied by a virtual boom of biographies and *biographies romancées*[14] in Western Europe. In Germany, Stefan Zweig was writing his dramatic biographies of Mary Stewart, Marie Antoinette, and Balzac; Maurois was beginning his long career as biographical novelist in France with books on Shelley, Byron, and Disraeli.

Russia was no different, and scholars were tackling similar problems during this time period. Grigorii Vinokur, for example, explored the meaning of biography in his book *Biography and Culture* in 1927, the same year that Nicolson published his *Development of English Biography* and the year before Maurois gave his lectures on biography at Cambridge University.

The biographical novel emerged from nineteenth-century historical fiction, but in the 1920s and 1930s the emphasis had shifted. Instead of merely using the "local color" of a certain historical epoch, the writer now centered his work around the life of a famous historical figure. In contrast to the historical novel à la Walter Scott (a very popular form in nineteenth-century Russia), which often included actual historical figures on the periphery but which focused on the fictional characters, in the new biography historical figures came to the forefront. Thus along with the "decorations" of the time, historical facts and documents were the basis for a re-creation and reinterpretation of the life of a real-life hero, and the creation for the present of a tenable, "usable past."

As some scholars have argued, one reason for the rise of the biographical novel in Russia was that readers had gotten "fed up" with fiction. Boris Eikhenbaum pointed out this trend very early on, in 1913, even before the First World War. He wrote: "If we look carefully at the development of the contemporary European novel, one particular circumstance should jump out at us: *the novel is going toward biography.*"[15] Elsewhere he expanded on this thought: "this is not a coincidental phenomenon. There is something here of the era. . . . We are so tired of 'literature,' that we read and are especially interested in that which is known to be nonliterary, not meant for publication; we are seeking . . . that truth which eludes the pen of the 'creative writer.'"[16] In 1924, Iurii Tynianov commented on a similar interest in nonfiction: "Very recently the reader began somehow to pass over both poetry and prose. This is a reader who is still shy, who still has not admitted this to himself; but nevertheless he is practically the most curious,—he goes directly to the chronicle, the review, the polemic—to those backyards of the journals from which a new type of journal is beginning to appear."[17]

Among Russians, the phenomenon was not limited to the Soviet Union. The literary critic Vladimir Veidle, writing in Paris in 1931, noted a similar situation; interest in biography, he suggested, is fed by the *truth* found therein.

> This interest, this success is linked to a much wider phenomenon: the weakening of such previously influential forms of prose as the novella and the novel, a loss of taste for every kind of narrative. Forms of prose which are loaded with factual or rational material come to the fore more and more . . . such as in memoirs, biography, autobiography, the critical effort, the philosophical dialogue.[18]

These cultural critics in the 1920s and 1930s were arguing that in much the same way as the religious person of earlier centuries looked for a model of behavior in the lives of saints, the modern reader sought a model for his own life in literature, but he now demanded real people and real events. The inventions of the artist no longer fulfilled his requirements; he needed to feel that facts and "truth" were being revealed to him in the process of reading. As Iurii Lotman has written: "The reader's interest in biography is always related to a need to witness an attractive and rich human life. For the reader biography combines two aesthetic experiences . . . : there's a hero, as in a novel, but also a sense of authenticity, as in life."[19] According to Lotman, it is the desire for truth and the need for the sensation of life that underlie a reader's interest in biography.

The development of biography in novel form suggests a change in the way people looked at biography as such, since it is only in the twentieth century that writers began to utilize fully the potential plot inscribed in the life of a historical person. In his essay "The End of the Novel," the Russian poet Osip Mandel'shtam wrote that in the twentieth century people began to lose their own biographies, to become victims of the impersonal forces of history. He explained that the novel could no longer exist, because, as he put it, "the compositional measure of the novel is a human life," and "now Europeans have been ejected from their biographies like billiard balls from the pockets of a table." Their lives were breaking into separate pieces; the *fabula* of life, the connections, began to disappear. Thus the novel, too, in Mandel'shtam's eyes, lost its *fabula*.[20]

In this view, writers were turning to the genre of biography in an attempt to make sense of the lives of others, to find their own biographies again, and to reassert the value of personality in this increasingly depersonalized epoch. The upheavals of World War I and the revolutionary movements throughout Europe affected not only the stability of society, but also the stability of an individual's place in society and history. In Russia this problem was especially acute; after the Revolution people had to rethink themselves, their society, and their history; and since an important part of that history was played by its heroes, its "remarkable people," Russians wanted to reconsider those remarkable people as well.[21]

It is no coincidence that while writers looked to the past to find biographical heroes for their novels, the official doctrine of Soviet literature also had its biographical and autobiographical variants. The socialist realist biographical novel represented a form of exemplary biography that created the saints of Soviet history and mythology, such as Chapaev in Dmitrii Furmanov's novel of that name and Pavel Korchagin of Nikolai Ostrovskii's novelized autobiography *How the Steel Was Tempered.* In the socialist realist tradition, there were two types of biography: biographies of contemporaries, usually heroes of the Revolution, and biographies of historical persons. The interrelationship of contemporary history and the historical model became important in the second type, especially in the 1930s when works suggesting analogies between historical figures and present leaders became possible and indeed encouraged. Through such leader-oriented novels as Aleksei Tolstoi's *Peter the First,* biography gave a stamp of approval to Stalin's reign by affirming the primary role of the autocratic ruler, an important ideological issue for the Soviet Union.

The other model of biography in socialist realism was that of the exemplary biography, which offers an ideal for the masses. Following traditional Marxism, this model suggested that the individual was becoming less significant in the historical process, and consequently the individual of the exemplary biography was maximally generalized. As Lotman noted in reference to the popular series of biographies "Lives of Remarkable People" (*Zhizn' zamechatel'nykh liudei*), "the series founded by Gor'kii is not incidentally named 'The Lives of Remarkable People' rather than 'The Lives of Great People.' The second formula would include within it an opposition of the great man to the ordinary one."[22] Offering an ideal for the "ordinary" man, Gor'kii's model implied that the masses, as if one, could reach this ideal and together sweep in the era of socialism.

In early Soviet times, a particular Marxist ethical code arose, which Lidiia Ginzburg described as combining the historical study of moral standards with the working out of "norms of behavior" that derive from the real interests of man.[23] Such norms of behavior represented an idealized portrayal of man according to this ethical code. But a man without faults was not necessarily everyone's ideal, nor was an exemplary biography of such a man a serious enterprise; Mikhail Bulgakov's reaction to Aleksei Tolstoi's novel is indicative of such friction. Elena Bulgakova passed on his response to *Peter the First:* "I could write a novel like that locked in an empty room without a single book."[24] A lack of respect for history and historical sources and a "rewriting" of history and biography to fit current political scenarios was something Bulgakov, Khodasevich, and Tynianov all contested in their works. This conflict between "official" history and our authors' independent and personal view of the literary past cannot be overemphasized. In addition to their own personal and artistic goals, a polemic with Soviet ideology is always present beneath the surface of the works. If Zhdanov defined socialist realism as "a combination of the most matter-of-fact everyday reality with the most heroic prospects,"[25] the authors I examine sought to define not everyday heroes, but unique subjects from the past who could speak to the present. In reclaiming the uniqueness of their subjects, our authors ultimately rewrote the "exemplary biography" into a paradigm of their own.

Biographies come in all shapes and forms. Scholars often divide biographies into various categories along a spectrum from "facts" to pure fiction.[26] Certainly the nature of a biography entails some organization and interpretation, but not all biographical genres admit that the compiler has shaped his material. The Russian genre of "chronological outline" (*khronologicheskaia kanva*) strives to maintain objectivity by literally presenting a "lifeline" and listing events rather than connecting them with interpretive fabric. One of Tynianov's sources for *Death of the Vazir-Mukhtar* was just such an outline by I. Shliapkin. Another kind of work, V. V. Veresaev's 1926 *Pushkin in Life*, gathered together the comments, stories, and judgments of Pushkin's contemporaries, along with quotes from Pushkin's own papers, to try and present Pushkin "as he was." Claiming to avoid interpretation and subjectivity with this method, Veresaev followed this same formula in 1933 to present Nikolai Gogol', with his subtitle emphasizing the "authenticity" of the data.[27] Like Veresaev's books, an "objective" biography "attempts," in the words of James Clifford, "to assemble everything relating to some person and present it without editorial comment or structure."[28] Clifford's use of the word "attempts" here shows his skepticism at the possibility of such an objective stance.

A second type of biography is the "scholarly-historical" biography, which depends on the prestige of academic work to vouch for its authenticity. Such a work requires "some selection of evidence, but no unacknowledged guesswork, no fictional devices, and no attempts to interpret the subject's personality and actions psychologically."[29] A good Russian example of this would be Iakov Grot's monumental 1880 *Life of Derzhavin*, which in turn served as a source book for Khodasevich's *Derzhavin*. Khodasevich himself wrote an "artistic-scholarly" biography, which involves serious research like the scholarly-historical biography, but which utilizes creative imagination to make it more interesting. Khodasevich's *Derzhavin* recasts information gleaned from Grot's two-volume work in an artistic light, producing what I have called a *literary biography*.

A fourth kind of biography along the "fact-to-fiction" spectrum is the "narrative" biography, which is also based on extensive research, but turns the evidence into a "running narrative, almost fictional in form." In such works, some invented dramatic scenes and conversations can be found, but they are based on documentary evidence. A variant of this type of biography is Bulgakov's *Life of Monsieur de Molière*.

The final category is the fictional biography, which is almost a novel. Tynianov's *Pushkin*, although incomplete, would have fit into this category, while his novel about Griboedov, *Death of the Vazir-Mukhtar*, moved a step further than fictional biography into an experimental realm of fiction, seeming to be a modernist novel rather than a biography or biographical novel. In *Vazir-Mukhtar*, Tynianov used both primary and secondary sources and liberally employed details straight out of the letters of Griboedov, but his stylized text hides the scholarly apparatus beneath the surface of the narrative.

Most biographers would assert that their vision of their subject reveals the "truth" about that person. Tynianov, Khodasevich, and Bulgakov certainly all believed that their images of Griboedov, Derzhavin, Molière, and Pushkin represented truthful renditions of these literary figures. But the nature of truth is difficult to ascertain: how did these authors define truth, and where did it come from? A productive way to look at each author's view of the "truth" of his subject's life is in relation to the most fact- or document-bound Russian biographer, Vikentii Veresaev. Veresaev thought he was avoiding interpretation in his *Pushkin in Life;* he merely collected and published documentary evidence for his reader's edification and judgment, believing that the image that arose from his pages was more true to life than the idealized Pushkin of many biographies:

> once, while I was looking through the excerpts and notes that had piled up, I suddenly saw that before me was a most original and entertaining book, in which Pushkin arose just as if alive. The truly living Pushkin in all the changeability of his moods, in all the contradictions of his complex character, in all the details of his everyday life, his appearance, his clothing, his surroundings. He himself, as he was "when Apollo was not summoning the poet to holy sacrifice"; not the retouched, well-behaved and inspired Pushkin of his biographers, but the "insignificant child of the world," sinful, enthusiastic, often truly insignificant, sometimes even vulgar, and even so at the end of it all an inexpressibly attractive and charming person. A living person, and not the iconic face of the "poet."[30]

In the first edition of the book, Veresaev chose not to identify doubtful statements; only at the request of readers did he decide in the next edition to mark questionable sources. Both these decisions, of course, represent interpretive strategies and editorial decisions; what Veresaev chose to include in his book and how he marked it determined what image of Pushkin arose before his readers.

This method of presenting a character from the past was controversial, to say the least. Khodasevich, writing abroad, was livid that Veresaev could suggest that such a Pushkin seemed "alive":

> Torn from his creative work, consisting only of "character, moods, physical characteristics, clothing," reproduced according to the contradictory, often false, and even more often nearsighted notes of his contemporaries, Pushkin in this book arises not "exactly as if alive," but just the opposite—exactly as if dead. Pushkin without his work is a living corpse.[31]

This reaction reflects Khodasevich's own concerns with the inextricable closeness of life and art for poets and writers, but it also demonstrates the very different approaches to re-creating Pushkin which exist side by side in the 1920s and 1930s.

Veresaev's approach to studying Pushkin is illuminated by his correspondence with Bulgakov as they attempted to co-author a play about Pushkin; Veresaev turned out to be the ultimate text-bound scholar, a truly empiricist historian engaged in searching out the truth through gathering facts. He was unwilling to add anything to the image of Pushkin or his contemporaries for which he could not find documentation; he consciously refused to use any psychological knowledge or imagination that he might have to fill in the blanks in the documents. Veresaev stood firmly behind his convictions of what Pushkin and others were like; having mined the letters and memoirs of Pushkin's contemporaries, Veresaev considered that "his past" was the real past.

Veresaev's arguments with Mikhail Bulgakov during their collaborative work on a play about Pushkin highlight the dissimilarity between these two writers, and I will look more carefully at them in chapter 5. In stark contrast to Veresaev, Bulgakov asserted his right to imagine how his heroes might act. Bulgakov used the eye and ear of a dramatist in portraying D'Anthès and the other characters in his play *Aleksandr Pushkin (Last Days)*, and he utilized the same methods to "see" and "hear" his characters in *The Life of Monsieur de Molière*. Bulgakov, as a man of the theater, felt that he knew instinctively what would sound false from the stage (and from the page) and what would ring true; he found "his truth" about Molière by imagining that he was present and picturing the events and people in his mind. This approach was anathema to Veresaev, who took a much more scholarly and empiricist view of historical events and people.

What, then, would Veresaev have to say about Tynianov's methods of finding the "truth" about Griboedov? After all, it is difficult to find a more meticulous scholar than Tynianov, and he knew the Pushkin era as well as Veresaev did. But Tynianov took a much freer approach to the events and people in Griboedov's life in his novel *Death of the Vazir-Mukhtar* than even Bulgakov did with his Molière. While Bulgakov remained true to chronology as much as he was able, based on the sources he had at hand, Tynianov extracted authentic dialogue from the letters and memoirs of Griboedov and others, reassigned lines, recast the characters and even changed the chronology of events. Tynianov, too, thought that he was creating a "truthful" account of Griboedov's last years, but he used his scholarly talents in a way of which Veresaev would heartily disapprove. Like Bulgakov, he was concerned with the whole picture, with portraying the epoch, but he chose to recombine elements from his sources to make them fit into his picture. In other words, Tynianov was trying to find a model for biography that spoke to him in his own time, and for him this was the essence of a historically accurate portrait.

In *Derzhavin*, Khodasevich was as scrupulous as Veresaev would have been in not putting words into his characters' mouths. He followed Grot and his other sources almost exactly, and was more careful than Tynianov in that he only used dialogue exactly as recorded and always in strict accordance with historical chronology. The artistic quality of his work came into play when he described Derzhavin as a poet; a poet himself, he allowed his narrator to make statements about Derzhavin that, in his mind, are true of all real poets. In fact, these passages are the strongest and, not coincidentally, the most quoted in scholarly literature about Khodasevich; the reader is able to hear the poet's voice coming through the narration at these points. Descriptions of the poet are not the only artistic moments in the book, however. Khodasevich felt very strongly that a biographer is not a novelist and does not have the right to make up scenes and dialogue. Nonetheless, without resorting to fictionalization, Khodasevich managed, through a montage of nonfictional elements, to create a remarkably "artistic" picture of Derzhavin. Khodasevich followed the historical truth of the document, and yet subtly represented it in the light of art. Each of these biographers constructed his work on the basis of his own talents, be they that of a poet, a scholar, or a dramatist, and thereby created a unique biography of another writer that could not have been written by anyone else. This is what Gor'kii meant when he said that the true biography of an artist could only be written by another artist.

In this study, I will be examining three main problems that are inherent to the genre of biography. The first is the usual problem of documentary literature: the question of the reader's preexisting knowledge, be it factual or mythical in nature, about the subject. "Documentary literature," as Lidiia Ginzburg wrote, "is an intermediate stage between the aesthetics of social, historical, and psychological ideas and the specifics of artistic literature." Ginzburg explained further that

> invention, proceeding from experience, creates a "second reality"; documentary literature brings to the reader a double cognition and a doubling emotion, because there exists a feeling of the authenticity of a life event which cannot be replaced by art. In documentary literature it is as if the artistic symbol contains the reader's independent knowledge about the portrayed object. The special tension of documentary literature lies in the incomplete compatibility of the two planes—the plane of life experience and the plane of its aesthetic interpretation.[32]

The author has to accommodate his reader's independent knowledge and work to create a joint character that is both historically and psychologically convincing.

The second issue is the way in which "fact" is transformed and in some ways deformed into "fiction." The problem of myth is something every biographer of famous people, especially of writers and poets, eventually has to address: does he choose to follow the image of his subject as it already exists in the culture, or does he want to adjust that myth through his research, investigation, and intuition? Ginzburg talks about the "double" image that necessarily arises on the border of the artist's image of a historical personage and the reader's previous knowledge, the historical image that he brings to his reading.[33] The author's fidelity to his sources or his revision of them, and the conviction with which he follows through on this choice, affects the final image that the reader carries away; Gor'kii's comment on Tynianov's Griboedov shows that readers can indeed be convinced regardless of their previous image. Gor'kii wrote to Tynianov: "Griboedov is remarkable, although I didn't expect to see him like this. But you showed him so convincingly that he must have been thus. And if he wasn't, he will be now."[34]

The third aspect of this genre is the way in which the writer's own experience is projected onto that of his hero, or the autobiographical aspect of the works. By looking at writers who write the biographies of writers, we can explore more fully this question of why each author selected his particular subject. Scholarship on biography suggests a special relationship between the author and the subject, particularly in the case of biographies by writers about writers. As George Eliot said, "a biography by a writer has a double interest, from the glimpses it gives of the writer as well as his hero."[35] When the biographical novel is not strictly autobiographical, it often benefits from a certain autoreferentiality, a kinship between one writer and another that can serve as the stimulus for the work and add a special dimension to the relationship between the author and subject and to the way the subject is portrayed.

One way to "control" for autobiographical pull in a study of the biographies of authors is to look at how each of several authors examined the same subject, who could not have offered the same degree of autoreferentiality for each author. Since Khodasevich, Tynianov, and Bulgakov each attempted to write biographical works about Pushkin, Pushkin can play just such a role in my study: as a control or a check in determining the ways each author constructed his own version of the Russian literary past. At the same time, Pushkin himself is a charged figure for Russian culture, and the fact that Khodasevich, Tynianov, and Bulgakov all created—artistically speaking—less successful works when they turned to Pushkin suggests that he is inherently difficult to represent in biography. As I will show in the final chapter, other ways of celebrating Pushkin—exhibits, essays, editions of books—offered a different kind of "usable past" than through the purely literary representation.

As important as the "how" of biography is certainly the "why." The question of why a writer chooses a specific subject can have a variety of answers. Works can have a concrete catalyst, such as Chukovskii's suggestion to Tynianov to write *Kiukhlia* for a children's series or Gor'kii's offer that Bulgakov write a biography of Molière for the series "Lives of Remarkable People." In both these cases, the author was already engaged with his subject; Tynianov had been studying Kiukhel'beker and giving lectures on Kiukhel'beker's poetry, and Bulgakov had already written the play *A Cabal of Hypocrites* about Molière. Andrew Wachtel, in explaining his notion of "intergeneric dialogue," has asserted that Tynianov "clearly wanted interested readers to know what he had constructed his fiction from, just as much as he wanted the freedom to construct."[36] Tynianov published his article and materials about Kiukhel'beker *after* he wrote his novel and thus presented readers with "both an overtly fictional perspective and a nonfictional perspective on the same events."[37] I will suggest that Tynianov achieved a "dialogue" between fact and fiction within a single work, the novel *Death of the*

Vazir-Mukhtar, and fostered his own conversation about Pushkin through the three novelistic images of the poet in his three biographical novels.

Although biography necessarily follows the line of its subject's life, the decision of what events to use and what to leave out is, to some extent, at the author's discretion. It is at this juncture that straight biography merges with fiction. In a 1929 lecture, A. J. A. Symons emphasized that "[b]iography *is* the telling of a story—a *life* story." Symons contrasted the biographer to the novelist, suggesting that the novelist is guided by probability, while the biographer is guided by fact. The biographer, Symons argued, also has "a *certain* freedom of choice" allowing for creativity and imagination. Echoing Strachey, Symons added that "books, like rose bushes, are improved by skilful pruning; to omit is as important as to mention."[38]

The biographical novelist is guided by fact (the documents he has on hand), his own image, and the prevailing image of his character in popular myth. In this study I will carefully examine the interaction of source materials, both primary and secondary, with the reflection of those materials in the final works. Each author utilized his sources in his own way. I will show that Khodasevich, the poet turned scholar, was maximally factual and true to his sources, while Tynianov, the scholar turned novelist, maximally fictionalized historical events. Bulgakov offers an interesting compromise between fact and fiction; although his narrative seems extremely subjective, his approach to the Molière scholarship was both a merging and a questioning of the various accounts of Molière's life and work. This is the very blending of history and fiction that defines the biographical novel. Indeed, Bulgakov's method of characterization parallels Tynianov's formulation: "Where the document ends, there I begin."[39] As Ellendea Proffer has commented, "Bulgakov's view, as seen throughout his works, as well as his notes and letters on the play about Pushkin, was that the artist divines a kind of truth which makes use of all the known facts about something, and in this lies real talent."[40] For both Bulgakov and Tynianov, guessing the essence behind the details was what made their works art.

The twentieth-century idea of a "poetic truth" that surpasses the truth of the document is not new for Russian writers; both Dostoevskii and Tolstoi wrote of a deeper *poetic* understanding of history. Tolstoi, in writing *War and Peace*, "was afraid that the necessity of describing the significant people of [18]12 would force [him] to be guided by historical documents rather than by truth," and Dostoevskii asserted that "it is incomparably easier to convey our history through faithfulness to poetic truth than through faithfulness to history *only*."[41] But the focus on a unique individual and the telling of history through that person's biography began to flourish specifically in the 1920s.

The subgenre of the biographical novel in Russia, which is at the center of my book, stands at the intersection of history, biography, and fiction.

Examining where these disciplines meet will help us to understand the place of this genre and these works in Russian literary culture. Whether for Soviet or émigré writers, the question of politics cannot be escaped. Were these writers creating or reinterpreting cultural icons? Why did they choose these particular figures to write about? What did the subject mean for each writer personally? And when the writer chose another writer as his subject, to what extent was he really writing about himself? As I will demonstrate, Tynianov, Khodasevich, and Bulgakov were searching for cyclical patterns and continuity in the writers of the past. Their own self-knowledge depended to a great extent on their knowledge of their forebears. In creating their own versions of the past, these authors followed the formula offered by Leon Edel: "the biographer may be as imaginative as he pleases—the more imaginative the better—in the way in which he brings his materials together. But he must not imagine the materials. He must read himself into the past; but then he must read that past into our present."[42] Each writer was searching for a "usable past," and he found the best method for displaying that past to be the biography.

The émigré critic Veidle gave an insightful definition of the biography of an artist in his 1931 article "On the Art of the Biographer." He wrote:

> The biography of an artist, a poet, will be written for real only when the biographer will be able to include not only the reality of his life, but also the invention born of that life, not only the reality of existence but also the reality of imagination. A true biography of a creative person will be that which both shows his life itself as creative and sees his life transformed in his creative works.[43]

Writing the biography of an artist is indeed a difficult task; as Veidle pointed out, the writer needs to find a way to express *jointly* the life and work of the artist.[44] The fact that Tynianov, Khodasevich, and Bulgakov all chose artists from the past when they were seeking biographical subjects who would speak to the present suggests that this task, of jointly expressing the life and art of a poet, seemed both feasible and crucial to these authors.

HAUNTED BY THE GHOST OF PUSHKIN

As the twentieth century draws to a close, in conjunction with the preparations for the bicentennial of Pushkin's birth in 1999, Russian critics and commentators have again been contemplating the biography/ies of Pushkin. Irina Surat, in an article entitled "The Biography of Pushkin as a Cultural Issue," has examined the two traditions of Pushkin biography in the nineteenth and twentieth centuries: the Annenkov tradition, which sought to find the internal plot of Pushkin's life, and the Bartenev tradition, which endeavored to track down all the facts of Pushkin's life and organize them for

Russian readers.[45] Yet Surat has asserted that there is still no satisfactory biography of Pushkin—and that there is something about the phenomenon of Pushkin himself that makes his biography more difficult to write than that of any other cultural figure. "Pushkin was the very soul of the nation and it was he who determined the paths it was to take," she has argued.[46] By examining the ways in which Khodasevich, Tynianov, and Bulgakov shaped their biographies of other authors and of Pushkin, I will show that the central role of Pushkin in Russian culture really did affect the way these biographers approached their subjects, if not exactly in the ways that one might predict.

Those who wrote biographies of authors, including Pushkin, in the 1920s and 1930s confronted the usual problems of life-writing, but they had a whole host of other cultural and ideological problems to deal with as well. Caught at a time when their readership was changing, when the very conditions under which they created—regardless of whether they had stayed in Russia or emigrated to other lands—were unstable and uncertain, many biographers turned to Pushkin for a subject, one who would attract readers of all kinds. With Pushkin the main cultural icon and central figure both in Soviet Russia and in Russia Abroad, authors on both sides of what was to become the iron curtain felt the magnetic pull of Pushkin as subject. In the project to create a usable past, the creation and codification of the life of Pushkin seemed central and imperative.

In both the Soviet and émigré worlds of the 1930s, in the years leading up to the centennial of Pushkin's death, Pushkin's lines were being quoted regularly from schoolroom to stage, newspaper to cultural festival. The "Pushkin project" of Soviet government and émigrés cast ashore in Europe and elsewhere found its realization in the Soviet "Pushkin Year" of 1937 and in the "Day of Russian Culture" ("Pushkin Day") abroad. With Pushkin in the air, in every museum display, and on every movie screen, his presence in the literary arts came to seem somehow compulsory, but in this situation of Pushkin near-saturation, the act of creating and using Pushkin in a biographical novel or on the stage became even more problematic. What's more, despite his central cultural status and his poetic genius, Pushkin does not seem a likely role model either for youthful readers or for the ideologically pressured Soviet citizens and émigré writers. A carouser and womanizer in his youth, known for his many duels with friends and enemies alike, Pushkin went his own way in the cultural situation of his time. As a poet his behavior may indeed have been close to impeccable, but as a citizen and a moral model his past was checkered, to say the least. Even so, he did function as a building block of writers' re-creations of the Russian past. In Soviet Russia and Russia Abroad, writers were trying to justify their own ownership of Russian culture while searching for "positive heroes" to lead Russians into the postrevolutionary twentieth century; more often than not, that search led them to Pushkin. Whether their finds were successful or not, and why, is the subject of this book.

If, as I have posited, Pushkin was the central figure for Russians throughout the world when they conceived of their own cultural past and cultural future, then in examining the earlier biographical subjects of my authors—Tynianov's Kiukhel'beker and Griboedov, Khodasevich's Derzhavin, Bulgakov's Molière—it is possible to consider these works as trial runs or practice sessions before the authors turned to Pushkin. Another possibility which I will put forth, however, is that having become biographers, Khodasevich, Tynianov, and Bulgakov had little choice in whether they would endeavor to write about Pushkin. It may be that presenting one's own Pushkin, whether in Soviet Russia or in Russia Abroad, had by the 1930s become a cultural imperative that the authors were unable—and unwilling—either to resist or to satisfy.

Chapter Two

Science Fiction: Tynianov and *Death of the Vazir-Mukhtar*

> Как будто жизнь качнется вправо,
> качнувшись влево.
>
> As if life will swing to the right, having swung to the left.
> —Joseph Brodsky, "A Christmas Romance"
>
> Science fiction reflects scientific thought; a fiction of things-to-come based on things-on-hand.
> —Benjamin Appel

MARCH 24, 1929. In a personal letter to Tynianov assessing the novel *Death of the Vazir-Mukhtar,* Maksim Gor'kii wrote: "Griboedov is remarkable, although I didn't expect to find him thus. But you showed him so convincingly that he must have been like that. And if he wasn't—now he will be."

In his search for artistic truth, Tynianov overcame all of Gor'kii's prior convictions about the nineteenth-century poet-ambassador and created a biographical hero who would take the place of those convictions. Griboedov, as re-created by Tynianov, seemed more "true" and "real," despite being "imaginary," to use Hayden White's words, than his previous image in literary history. Tynianov used the power of an artist to create rather than merely to represent. Through his particular method of historical recovery, the author was able to find that truth about Griboedov which would be most useful for his own time.

THE PATH FROM SCHOLAR TO NOVELIST

Iurii Nikolaevich Tynianov was one of the founding members of the school of formalism in Russia and, like his émigré counterpart Vladislav Khodasevich, combined the professions of scholar and critic with those of artist and biographer. Tynianov's path, though, was the mirror image of Khodasevich's. Khodasevich was first and foremost a poet, who ended his life a critic and biographer, while Tynianov was originally a scholar who then moved toward fiction in the mid-1920s and died in 1943 in the Soviet Union more a novelist than a critic.

In fact, originally Tynianov was somewhat reluctant to turn to fiction. The now-famous story told by Kornei Chukovskii of Tynianov's first novel suggests an almost accidental shift. After giving an unappreciated lecture on the poetic style of the nineteenth-century archaist Vil'gel'm Kiukhel'-beker, Tynianov apparently described Kiukhel'beker's life with such empathy and artistry in conversation on the way home that Chukovskii felt compelled to ask: "Why didn't you tell all of this about Kiukhlia to your audience there at the club? Everyone would have become excited. And now, on the street on the way home, you could have told me what you told them there."[1] Within a few days Chukovskii was asked to organize a series of biographies for children for the Kubuch publishing house. He included a novel by Tynianov on Kiukhel'beker, and Tynianov agreed to write it, mostly for financial reasons.

The nascent novelist wrote quickly and for the most part without rough drafts and without consulting any materials; he had studied Kiukhel'-beker since his days at the university, and the poet's archive was already in his head.[2] *Kiukhlia*, the resulting novel, was almost four times longer than the publisher's order and, by one account, was completed in less than three weeks.[3] Of his own reasons for his new endeavor, Tynianov wrote:

> In 1925 I wrote a novel about Kiukhel'beker. The transition from scholarship to literature was not all that simple. Many scholars considered novels and *belles lettres* generally to be hack-work. . . . My fiction arose primarily from a dissatisfaction with the history of literature which tended to skim the surface and present the people, currents and development of Russian literature in a vague way. Such a "universal blur" diminished the works and the old writers. A need to get to know them better and understand them more deeply—that's what fiction was for me. I still think that creative literature differs from history not by its "invention" but by a larger, closer and more vital understanding of people and events, a greater concern for them. A writer never invents anything more beautiful or powerful than the truth. "Invention" is a coincidence which comes not from the matter itself, but from the artist. And when there is necessity, rather than coincidence, that's when a novel begins.[4]

Tynianov believed that in writing fiction he was able to get closer to the "truth." When the artist is decisive, he wrote, the ultimate artistic impression ensues: "the sensation of authentic truth: it could have happened that way, perhaps that is how it happened." Lidiia Ginzburg—who in addition to being an astute literary critic was also one of Tynianov's students—commented that Aristotle had divided the historian and poet into the one who tells what happened and the other who tells what might have happened.[5] Tynianov believed that he was able to combine Aristotle's modes of historian and poet into a synthesized whole, relating both "that which was" and "that which might have been." Indeed, Tynianov anticipated contemporary theoretician of history Hayden White's assertion that imaginary discourse can often be more "true" than historical presentation of the same material.

Tynianov's literary method reflected his first calling as a scholar; he himself "invented" very little of his own fiction. At the base of every novel and story lay real people, real documents, real events. In turning to fiction, Tynianov also tried to work out some of the literary problems he had been studying. As Boris Eikhenbaum commented, "Who should be a writer if not a person who himself has thought through the theoretical problems of literature?"[6] Tynianov's interest in the subjects of his biographical novels dated from his earliest university days, when, in S. A. Vengerov's famous seminar at the University of Petersburg, Tynianov came to study Kiukhel'beker through Aleksandr Griboedov, and from there went on to work on Pushkin. By the time of his death he had written biographical novels about all three poets, as well as novellas (*povesti*) on other historical topics and anecdotes.

The fiction of Iurii Tynianov has most often been examined as a composite body of texts. The Soviet scholarly tradition of the 1960s through 1980s focused on the allegorical quality of Tynianov's fiction; beginning with Arkadii Belinkov, the first scholar to point out the contemporary meaning of Tynianov's historical works, the rhetoric reached a point where that was all scholars sought in him. As another scholar has written: "We can rely on Tynianov's three novels and three stories as a distinctive diary, the pages of which reflect the difficult path traveled by the consciousness of the writer-*intelligent*—a path of thoughts about the societal processes which unfolded over the course of two decades."[7] Tynianov's novels were a particularly popular topic of study in the early 1960s and again in the late 1980s—during the "thaw" periods in the Soviet Union, when scholars felt a mandate to uncover what they saw as the veiled political subtexts of Tynianov's coded historical works.[8]

As with many historically oriented writers, among them Khodasevich and Bulgakov, Tynianov was indeed self-reflexive and autoreferential in his work. Like many of his time, Tynianov saw the historical epochs of Aleksandr I and Nikolai I as being parallel with the eras of Nikolai II and the early Soviet years.[9] But to turn Tynianov's fictional oeuvre into a mere pseudodocumentary project is reductive; the more interesting enterprise is to examine Tynianov and his work as a study in genres, both fictional and scholarly, and to observe their interaction.[10] Tynianov himself saw his work, whether literary or scholarly, as a scientific enterprise, an attempt to discover the past and to present that past to contemporary readers. The interaction of the two modes of writing illuminates both and helps elucidate Tynianov's methodologies.

THE "SCIENTIFIC NOVEL"

Tynianov's novels, and particularly *Death of the Vazir-Mukhtar* (*Smert' Vazir-Mukhtara*, 1929), represent what Boris Eikhenbaum has called a "sui generis scientific novel." Inherent in the concept of a scientific novel are several paradoxes. But Tynianov probably appreciated Eikhenbaum's definition of his fiction as scholarly or scientific (*nauchnyi*), seeing in this an acknowledgment of both his research in the field of literary studies and his careful, deliberate method of presenting his material. In his "scientific novel," Tynianov tried to balance the scholar's penchant for footnoting his sources with a novelist's need for convincing and flowing narrative. Especially in working on Pushkin, but with his other subjects as well, Tynianov had to confront his readers' previous knowledge of the subject of his work. That knowledge differed from reader to reader, and Tynianov had to consider these various previous perceptions of his personages in building his fictional characters. In this sense, while writing fiction, Tynianov was nonetheless confronted with all the problems inherent in the historian's vocation. The "scientific novel" functioned as a hybrid genre which combined in itself literary history and literary biography.

In discussing Tynianov's texts in English, it is essential to translate the genre of *nauchnyi roman* as "scientific novel" rather than "scholarly novel," although in the literary arts we usually consider *nauchnyi* to refer to scholarship. Certainly the concepts in the genre relate to English-language ideas of scholarship in the humanities: research, sources, footnoting. But in Russian generally the words for scholarly pursuits are more closely related to science than they are in English: Russians have not only "natural sciences" and "social sciences" but also the "philological sciences" and "humanitarian sciences." And the linguistic link in Russian between science and scholarship is no coincidence, especially for Tynianov and his time. Living in the age of the "science of history" and of "scientific Marxism," Tynianov thought of his own work as being precise, controlled, and responsible. One critic accused him of "experimenting with history," and in fact that is exactly what he was doing: gathering and analyzing data, running tests on various samples, researching the characters of the past and transforming them into object lessons for the present. In a sense, Tynianov's "scientific novel" is a truly Soviet project; just as the laws of scientific Marxism were supposed to transform Soviet society, the laws of scientific fiction transformed the past.

Tynianov's second novel was *Death of the Vazir-Mukhtar*, a biographical novel about Aleksandr Griboedov, published almost exactly one hundred years after Griboedov's tragic death.[11] In some ways the task of transforming Griboedov into the hero of a novel was a simple one. Indeed, it is hard to imagine a life more similar to the plot of an adventure novel than that of the nineteenth-century poet and diplomat—Griboedov's fame from his comedy *Woe from Wit*, his diplomatic career in such exotic places as Persia, and his tragic demise in a Tehran massacre make for an exciting and dramatic story. Tynianov worked from a detailed outline of Griboedov's life; the editor of the 1889 *Complete Collected Works of A. S. Griboedov* put together a virtually day-by-day "chronological background for studying the biography of A. S. Griboedov," what in the previous chapter I referred to as the specific protobiographical genre of the "chronological outline" (*khronologicheskaia kanva*). However, although a lot of documentation does exist on Griboedov's life, there are still key facts missing and motivations left unexplained in the historical picture. Tynianov may not have considered that he was "inventing" anything, but he was certainly creating a new Griboedov. To use a pseudoscientific metaphor, in his novel Tynianov had to bring the "fuzzy" figure of Griboedov into sharper focus, as if he were looking at him through the lens of a camera or microscope. In the "chronological outline" of Griboedov, the whole was somehow less than the sum of its parts. Despite the many details, the life of Griboedov was missing. In approaching Griboedov as an experimental subject, Tynianov wanted to create a greater whole, a Griboedov who could represent his time and could interact with contemporary times.

In order to present his own ideas about Griboedov, Tynianov chose to place Griboedov's life and work in the context of Russian literature and history as a whole, and he filled his novel with Russian literature through the use of subtexts, which range from the twelfth-century anonymous masterpiece *The Lay of the Host of Igor* to the works of Pushkin, Lermontov, Gogol', Tolstoi, and of course to Griboedov's own major work, the play *Woe from Wit*—creating a work of montage, description, and drama.[12] Of Tynianov's three novels—*Kiukhlia, Death of the Vazir-Mukhtar* and the unfinished *Pushkin*—*Death of the Vazir-Mukhtar* was the most technically innovative and would ultimately be the most definitive example of Tynianov's "scientific novel." One of the most interesting aspects of Tynianov's trilogy of biographical novels is that each of the novels covers approximately the same time period, the first third of the nineteenth century, and contains the same characters—Kiukhel'beker, Griboedov, and Pushkin. The novels *Kiukhlia* and *Pushkin* are similar to each other in their straightforward narrative style as well as in their subject matter; Kiukhel'beker and Pushkin, after all, were students together at the Tsarskoe Selo Lycée, so there was plenty of overlap between the events and settings of the two novels. Since Tynianov left his Pushkin novel incomplete, having followed his subject only as far as Pushkin's youth, I will wait to consider the parts of *Kiukhlia* that parallel *Pushkin* until the next chapter, as components of Tynianov's Pushkin project.

In this chapter I focus on *Death of the Vazir-Mukhtar,* Tynianov's most artistically effective biographical novel. In its staccato rhythms critics have found cinematic techniques of cutting and montage as well as other designs, intricately woven subtexts, and hidden sources.[13] Eikhenbaum has called Tynianov's prose technique "piecemeal composition" (*kuskovaia kompozitsiia*) and asserted that *Vazir-Mukhtar* is the best example of this technique.[14] To use the metaphor from my introduction, Tynianov's novel about Griboedov is a crazy quilt, sewn together from pieces of letters, facts, and archival documents.

Death of the Vazir-Mukhtar is also particularly interesting in terms of Tynianov's contribution to the creation and codification of the Russian biographical novel. In it Tynianov incorporated much of Griboedov's life into the last year of his life, adding the technique of chronological compression to the repository of biographical methodology. In addition, playing off medieval representations of human lives, Tynianov inverted the hagiographical tradition of the "life" of a saint and turned the focus onto the "death" of the ambassador to Persia. Finally, by playfully invoking other texts and other lives, Tynianov enriched the potential content of a biographical novel. These and many other aspects of *Vazir-Mukhtar* represent truly original directions in fictional biography and life-writing.

For Tynianov, the writing of historical fiction created an epistemological dilemma: where does true knowledge come from, documents or intuition, or both? In *Vazir-Mukhtar*, his solution to this dilemma brought the hybrid "scientific novel" into existence. Most scholars who write about Tynianov stress his dependence on documents, his use of actual letters, diaries, and literary works in his prose. His statements in the questionnaire that formed the basis for the collection *How We Write,* however, emphasized a more creative approach. One of Tynianov's most-quoted comments is: "Where the document ends, that's where I begin." He continued: "There are official documents which lie like people. I have no love for 'documents generally' . . . I feel pangs of conscience when I discover that because I didn't have a document, I did not go far enough beyond it or even reach it."[15] The Soviet scholar Arkadii Belinkov interpreted Tynianov's discussion of facts and documents as proving that "in order to understand a historical personage and a historical event, Tynianov needed real things left behind by that personage or that event. . . . For Tynianov an event begins to exist only when it turns from a 'phenomenon' into an object."[16] In his own time, Tynianov's contemporaries often felt that his scholarly background "guaranteed" the truth of historical facts in his work. For example, Konstantin Fedin believed that Tynianov never stopped being a scholar and continued to use a scholar's methods in writing his novels. Within Tynianov's novels, according to Fedin, the documents may be "dissolved" into the text, but they still offer a stamp of the authenticity of Tynianov's historical facts. "It's as if in Tynianov's novel the scholar says: don't worry about the precision of the facts," and for Fedin and readers like him, this added legitimacy to Tynianov's fiction.[17] With many readers, Tynianov did indeed achieve the "sensation of authentic truth" for which he strove. But in *How We Write* Tynianov belied his reputation, insisting that a writer cannot work strictly from documents.[18] He argued that a document is not a fact and that documents cannot be used as a kind of magic transformer of facts into literature; for Tynianov, if there were such a magic device, it would be intuition.

Tynianov used specific examples to prove that often his literary sense refuted existing "documentation." For instance, while working on *Death of the Vazir-Mukhtar*, Tynianov found that according to the historian Berzhe, Samson-khan, the Russian deserter who became the head of the Persian guard, had refused to fight against the Russians during the Russo-Persian war and instead left Tavriz. To Tynianov this seemed like excellent nationalistic propaganda, but only that. He instead wrote of Samson's fighting against the Russians alongside an entire battalion of deserters; and, in fact, he later found the note of a Russian general which confirmed his intuition. Samson had left Tavriz only to rendezvous with his commander, Abbas-Mirza, not to avoid fighting.[19]

Another example of Tynianov's instinct involved Griboedov's servant, Aleksandr Gribov. The son of Griboedov's wet nurse, Gribov serves as a kind of double, or "supplement," to use Tynianov's word, to the poet in the novel; Tynianov claimed not to have noticed the similarity in the two men's names. But when he later added the implication that Gribov was really Griboedov's half-brother (which he still could not prove by documentation), it fit right into his narrative, as if he had subconsciously written this idea into the novel from the first.[20]

Thus in several instances Tynianov's intuition turned out to be "prophetic." But this prophet was progressive. Instead of the nineteenth-century understanding of writer as prophet, which was inherently romantic and superstitious, the prophetic writer in the rational, scientific, modern twentieth-century world combined intuition with a scientifically sound methodological approach which yielded historical data. In *Death of the Vazir-Mukhtar*, Tynianov was a kind of scientific Soviet prophet, and his project was the re-creation of a man through the "scientific novel."

Some readers were amazed at this aspect of Tynianov's gift. For example, one reader exclaimed: "Sometimes he rejected, was forced to reject, what seemed like an indisputable document and—strange as it may seem!—turned out to be right in rejecting the indisputable."[21] But while a healthy disbelief in historical documentation helped Tynianov to create his fiction, he was hardly a prophet. His insights were the "educated guesses" of a historian, based on a critical approach to sources and knowledge of human nature, the "scientific hypotheses" of the laboratory researcher who has run many tests and experiments. Tynianov defined his basic method of "writer's intuition" by saying: "If you have entered into the life of your hero, of your man, then you can sometimes guess about a lot of things yourself."[22]

AUTOREFERENTIALITY IN *DEATH OF THE VAZIR-MUKHTAR*

Tynianov chose the subjects of his biographical novels according to his scholarly interests; he was a specialist in the first third of the nineteenth century and essentially lived with these poets of the Pushkin era, particularly Kiukhel'beker, Griboedov, and Pushkin himself, throughout his own life. But an important element of the novel *Death of the Vazir-Mukhtar* is its intersection with contemporary themes and problems. Along with the epoch that occupied his scholarly interest, Tynianov was portraying his own times. At the end of the 1920s, themes of betrayal of revolutionary ideals and cooperation with the mechanistic state were more than timely. With the disappearance of the literary culture of the prerevolutionary period and the rapid changes in the political structure of Russia, Tynianov was not alone in looking to the past for answers to present predicaments. As Lidiia Ginzburg comments: "Historicism, of course, was typical not of Tynianov only. Tynianov was a person who developed artistically after the Revolution. He absorbed his epoch's passionate desire to figure out the past through the present and the present through the past. Historicism was the air in the 1920s."[23] This "historicism" perhaps best explains Tynianov's search for formulas that would help make sense of his own world; Tynianov went back in time, into history, into his own fiction, but he took the present with him, and then he brought the historical past into his present.

As is common practice for novelists, Tynianov mined his own time for material in order to construct his historical novel. There is evidence that Tynianov modeled the attributes and mannerisms of some of his characters on his contemporaries;[24] and the author himself had much in common with his central hero.[25] While not autobiographical, the novel was certainly autoreferential. Both Tynianov and Griboedov started new careers because of political pressure; Griboedov found himself unable to write poetry after the failure of the Decembrist revolt and turned to a project for transforming the Caucasus as an outlet for his creative instinct, while Tynianov was forced for economic and political reasons to curtail his formalist studies and turn to *belles lettres*.

In their careers, they took antithetical paths, at least nominally: Griboedov left poetry for a more practical, concrete project within government service; and Tynianov left the exactitude of his scholarly work for the intuitive, imaginative realm of fiction. But in many other ways, they were similar. Both men were in ill health and faced an early death. Both were among those whom Tynianov would call "the transformed" in the preface to his novel: despite early opposition to state policy, they both took advantage of opportunities offered them by the state. While his Decembrist friends and acquaintances were executed or languished in prison, Griboedov received the rank of state councillor, the order of St. Anna of the second degree, and four thousand *chervontsy* for his service in securing the Turkmenchai peace treaty; he was appointed ambassador to Persia. Tynianov, in an era when his fellow writers were being exiled or arrested, accepted numerous benefits from the Soviet government: he received membership card number one in the Union of Writers in 1934 and a new apartment in 1936–37; in addition, he traveled abroad to Berlin and Prague (1928) and Paris (1936) for medical treatment. The most important similarity for Tynianov was that both had been forced to forsake their "revolutionary" ideals in order to survive in the new state. Tynianov's advantages must have felt like the fruits of betrayal; certainly he portrayed Griboedov as experiencing such feelings.

In the prologue to the novel, Tynianov's narrator uses the first person and explicitly identifies himself with Griboedov. He asserts that time ferments in the blood and that each age has its own type of fermentation; Pushkin was the fermentation of wine, and Griboedov the fermentation of vinegar. "On this day I pushed aside the scents of perfume and refuse with my hand. Old Asian vinegar runs in my veins, and the blood moves slowly, as if through the wastelands of ruined empires."[26] With Griboedov's Asian, vinegar blood coursing through his body, the narrator accentuates the affinity between himself and his hero. This is the only use of the first person in the novel, but its position in the prologue emphasizes the parallels between Tynianov and Griboedov.

As was the case with Mikhail Bulgakov's novel *Life of Monsieur de Molière,* to which chapter 6 of this book is devoted, Tynianov's narrator tells this story from his own time in the twentieth century. Although the narrator mentions his distance of a century from the events of the novel only once, that is enough for the reader to see Tynianov's analogies between his time and the period of the novel. The prologue of *Death of the Vazir-Mukhtar* begins: "On a very cold square in December of 1825 the people of the 1820s, with their springing step, ceased to exist. Time suddenly broke into two." There is an echo here of Hamlet, who cried that "time is out of joint," but time was not merely out of joint; it was broken, and no one, it seems, could heal it. The failure of the Decembrist revolt ended the decade of the 1820s early, and drew distinct lines between people of the 1820s and those of the 1830s. Men of the 1820s were occupied with women and revolt, poetry and secret societies; men of the 1830s were slaves to factories and plants, caught up in the mechanism of Benkendorf and the tsar's third section. According to the narrator, the men who "lay down like dogs, young and proud dogs" during the 1820s were lucky; the worst fate came to those who survived. "How horrible was the life of the *transformed,* the life of those men of the 1820s whose blood got mixed!"[27] It is into this category that the hero of the story fell, neither accepted nor trusted by the government he was trying to serve, and now rejected by the friends of his youth. An exploration of this category of the "transformed" serves as the main agenda of the novel.

Tynianov used this semitransparent narrator to bring Griboedov closer to contemporary times. Writing at the end of the 1920s, Tynianov was well aware of the "transformed" men walking about in his own era. By connecting Pushkin with wine and Griboedov with vinegar, Tynianov's narrator was already making assumptions about which decade—and which poet—was the happy one, and which the sour one who had to make do as best he could within his historical circumstances. As I will show below, Pushkin plays an important part in this novel about Griboedov, and Tynianov, too, must be considered in the spectrum of men of the 1820s and men of the 1830s. But if Tynianov might have wanted Pushkin to be a model for his own time, his novel about Griboedov showed that the tragic death of the poet-diplomat was a better model, a message from the past which might be used in the 1930s.

READINGS OF *DEATH OF THE VAZIR-MUKHTAR*

The genre of Tynianov's novels has been discussed at great length. Perhaps Eikhenbaum described it best when, writing about Tynianov's first two novels, he said:

> it was not so necessary to describe the life as to reveal the "fate." The traditional genre of the biography was clearly not sufficient for this goal—it was necessary to create the genre anew. . . . Tynianov's goals were better served by the historical novel, but a historical novel which featured one character and, most importantly, which was transferred from the plane of epic tale to the plane of the lyric story, since the main importance lay not in the telling of events and not in the story, but in the creation of an intimate image.[28]

It is the last portion of Eikhenbaum's description that I find most significant. Again, because Tynianov's main characters, Griboedov among them, were known quantities, and their lives were the stuff of historical writing, the story took a backseat to the incarnation of the characters. With Griboedov, Tynianov tried to create a living poet who was authentic and convincing for contemporary readers. Ironically, it was this living character, this intimate image, who would throughout the novel fade into nothingness.

Tynianov began with the man, Griboedov, incarnated him, and then gradually pushed him out of existence, leaving only his title—Vazir-Mukhtar.

Eikhenbaum stressed that there was more to Tynianov's novels than is present in the traditional term "biography." He used the word "fate" to emphasize that difference—essentially describing a historical motive force within the character's life.

> I used the word "fate" in the sense in which it emphasizes the existence of some kind of necessity or pattern and thus adds to the more neutral word—"biography." The feeling of history brings to every biography an element of *fate*—not in a coarse fatalistic sense, but in the sense of the extension of historical laws to the private and even intimate life of a man. The historical novel of our time had to turn to "biography"—in order to turn it into something historically natural, characteristic, significant, happening under the sign not of chance, but of fate. This is already there in *Kiukhlia;* in *Death of the Vazir-Mukhtar* it forms a kind of dominant.[29]

Eikhenbaum's discussion of historical narrative relies on such categories as *fabula* and *siuzhet* and differentiates between the writing of history or biography and the writing of an emplotted life, all categories which have become important in the second half of the century for the theories of Hayden White.[30] For Eikhenbaum, biography implied a mere chronological sequence of events in a person's life, while a description of "fate" (*sud'ba*) required an explanation of these events and a search for their links with the epoch. Another formalist theorist turned novelist, Viktor Shklovskii, hailed Tynianov's creation of a "new genre"—one that combined research with the novel.[31] According to his formalist friends, Tynianov's novel *Death of the Vazir-Mukhtar* was not just a biography; it was a "scientific novel," a search for the "authentic truth" about Griboedov's fate and for the laws that govern fate in every man's life. Ultimately for Eikhenbaum, Tynianov's novel offered another route to historical truth, an alternative scientific method that did not need to follow the rules of socialist realism and the Marxist dialectic in order to discover the laws of fate.

The question of the historical veracity of Tynianov's novel has been hotly disputed in his own time and since. Maksim Gor'kii's reaction, essentially answering the author's goal of the "sensation of authentic truth," is noteworthy in this respect. Gor'kii's assessment of Tynianov's Griboedov goes to the heart of the question of artistic truth: "Griboedov is remarkable, although I didn't expect to find him thus. But you showed him so convincingly that he must have been like that. And if he wasn't—now he will be." There are many other interpretations of *Death of the Vazir-Mukhtar,* most of which are concerned with the authenticity of the hero. In reference to the figure of Griboedov, the scholar S. A. Fomichev writes that "the central hero is just as artistically convincing as he is historically inaccurate."[32] Gor'kii and

Fomichev were essentially writing about the same thing; Tynianov's convincing portrait of Griboedov was extremely influential and essentially took center stage, leaving the Griboedovs created by other writers and historians in the shadows. Tynianov himself, as discussed above, loved to quote examples proving the infallibility of his artistic discoveries, thus contributing to his aura as a prophetic writer, or to his reputation as a skilled historical researcher.

Another explanation of the handling of facts in *Vazir-Mukhtar*, suggested by Arkadii Belinkov, was that Tynianov's main interest was in portraying the spirit of the epoch, and if certain particular truths had to be neglected in order to do so, then so be it. However, Belinkov argued, Tynianov viewed the 1820s through the filter of the 1920s, creating a novel full of political allusions to contemporary circumstances—essentially portraying the spirit of his own epoch along with that of Griboedov's. Belinkov wrote:

> In Tynianov's rendering the problem of "Griboedov and the Decembrists" is transformed from a single incident, from a scholarly debate into the problem of the "intelligentsia and revolution" which so stirred Tynianov and his contemporaries in the first decade after October. . . . Like every writer, Tynianov answered a question from his own time, merely choosing the form of his answer. For Tynianov that form was the historical novel.[33]

Belinkov's interpretation certainly has merit. The prologue to *Vazir-Mukhtar* reads like a thinly veiled analogy between the reign of Nikolai I and that of Stalin.[34] Throughout the novel, themes of betrayal of the old ideals, cooperation with the government, and friendship with agents of the secret police echo the circumstances of Tynianov's times. Tynianov portrayed Griboedov as trying to play the system, to negotiate a victory against his own government on a battlefield filled with land mines, but ultimately Griboedov ends up alone and isolated, friendless and defenseless.

In the past decade a new, revisionist reading of the novel has arisen which asserts that *Vazir-Mukhtar* was neither an exercise in historical intuition nor a political tract in Aesopian language, but rather a reflection of Tynianov's theoretical views about literature. G. A. Levinton has called Gor'kii's reading of the novel "mistaken." He has emphasized instead the vacillating quality of the hero, reading the phrase "nothing had been decided yet" (*eshche nichego ne resheno*), which ends the prologue and begins the novel proper, as Tynianov's assessment of Griboedov, that the image of the hero himself was never "solved" and that there *is* no biographical conception of Griboedov in the novel.[35] He pointed to Tynianov's own idea of the "vacillating" unity of the hero in a literary work to support his claim: "The static unity of the hero . . . turns out to be extraordinarily unstable; it . . . can fluctuate in the course of the work . . . it is enough that there be a sign of unity . . . the sign of the hero, the hero's name, is enough so that we will not look closely in each case at the hero himself."[36] Tynianov illustrated his idea on the basis of Gogol's short story "The Nose," and Levinton has suggested that the same principle is at work in *Vazir-Mukhtar.*

The movement of a pendulum, back and forth, acts as a dominant metaphor in the novel, and elsewhere I have argued that Tynianov's novel mirrors that movement. This interpretation applies on many levels, from the "vacillating" nature of the hero to the movement of the author—from his sources to his creative presentation of those sources. Here, however, I would like to concentrate on the "scientific" aspect of Tynianov's novel. Since this novel acts as the middle of a biographical trilogy, it plays a central role as well in Tynianov's lifelong Pushkin project, and I will look at the Pushkinian subtext in *Vazir-Mukhtar* in conjunction with that project in the next chapter.

"KEYS" TO THE NOVEL: THE USE OF HISTORICAL SOURCES

As mentioned above, Tynianov tried to avoid "inventing" anything while writing this "scientific novel." He preferred to manipulate literary and historical material in order to create a montage with a new effect.[37] Tynianov handled his nonliterary sources in a particularly interesting way. Griboedov's image was based on research; Tynianov used historical documents, the memoirs of the poet's contemporaries and Griboedov's own letters extensively.[38] It is fascinating to examine how Tynianov transformed these documents into fiction. The novelist took many of the facts and direct quotes from other sources and changed them, rearranged them chronologically, reassigned them to other characters. Often authentic remarks lose or utterly alter their meaning when put into a different context or mouth.[39] Some of Tynianov's manipulation of sources was simply for the sake of economy and bears no conceptual significance; for example, Tynianov reduced the number of characters in Griboedov's life so as to form their images more completely. I would call the reasons for such changes purely technical. Looking for thematic justification of such an approach, Levinton has connected Tynianov's method of biographical narration to Griboedov's own work:

> The "compression" of chronology, the "choice" of episodes, personages, finally the very construction of the plot from separate important episodes—all of this recalls that kind of transformation which a narrative story undergoes when being adapted for the stage. It's not unlikely that this is the real constructive principle of *Vazir-Mukhtar,* motivated by the playwright hero.[40]

The technique of "chronological compression" is additionally motivated by Tynianov's choice of time frame. Writing a biographical novel about the last year of the subject's life (and entitled, after all, *DEATH of the Vazir-*

Mukhtar), he managed to include much of Griboedov's life in his last year—thereby extending the plot beyond the time constrictions of the *fabula*—by using episodes and letters not only from 1828 and 1829.[41]

But some holes in Tynianov's version of Griboedov's life are rather gaping; Levinton has pointed out the absence of Zhandr, Viazemskii, and Kiukhel'beker and the virtual absence of Katenin,[42] all close friends and important figures for Griboedov. The character of Begichev in the novel seems incidental, just another old friend who does not understand the new Griboedov, but Griboedov's letters to him presented their relationship in an entirely different light. As the scholar N. K. Piksanov wrote in a prerevolutionary biography of Griboedov, "in letters to [Begichev] there is so much love and tenderness that one could think the poet was writing to a beloved woman."[43] By removing Griboedov's closest friends, Tynianov caused his hero to be even more isolated and thereby furthered his main agenda in the novel—dramatizing the "life of the *transformed*." Midway through the novel, the narrator ceases to refer to Griboedov by name and instead begins to merely call him by his title, Vazir-Mukhtar (ambassador plenipotentiary). By the end of the novel, Griboedov has literally disappeared from life and virtually disappeared from history. When in the famous, if apochryphal, incident Pushkin meets his bodily remains on the road, Griboedov has retained only a portion of his name; the cart haulers refer to him as "Griboed." Having occupied the lofty position of a poet and the honorable position of ambassador, in death Griboedov has vanished. In order to make such a disappearance more believable, Tynianov chose to isolate the character early in the novel.

Some of the chronological changes in the events of Griboedov's life also serve the development of the novel's *fabula*. A rather important chronological shift took place when Tynianov had Griboedov submit his project for transforming the Caucasus into a kind of Russian East India Company, with himself at the head, first to Count Nessel'rode in Petersburg and then again to Count Paskevich in Tiflis, whereas he actually only submitted it to Paskevich. At the time Griboedov was in Petersburg in 1828, the project was not yet written, although Griboedov had certainly begun to envision it. But for Tynianov's purposes, it was important that Griboedov be rejected twice—by the government and by the Decembrist Burtsov, who accused him of betraying his revolutionary friends and their ideals of reform. Isolated from the right and the left, Griboedov was alone and unprotected. Tynianov demonstrated that Griboedov had no place with official Russia and no home with reform-minded friends. Griboedov's dream of escape, which unfolds in various forms throughout the novel, was thus further motivated by his sensation of discomfort and rejection wherever he went.

Levinton has maintained that the reader need only be aware of a certain number of chronological changes, just as he or she must recognize some of the documentable quotes, in order for the constructive principle to become clear. Tynianov, according to Levinton, left clues or "keys" throughout the novel, especially in the form of letters, to stimulate his readers to check the facts for themselves.[44] In his novel, Tynianov offered the data that resulted from his literary scientific experiments. The reader can then take these data and go to his own literary historical laboratory to cook up his own results and compare them with Tynianov's.

This idea of "keys" complements the obvious reason for use of authentic material—to re-create the atmosphere of the late 1820s in describing the events of Griboedov's last year. In fact, there are many different keys that encourage the reader to consult Griboedov's letters and the memoirs of his contemporaries. They include not only letters cited in the text, but also the absence of important friends, the expanded friendship with Bulgarin (which casts a shadow on the idolized historical image of Griboedov as a great poet and Decembrist), the omission of various meetings with Pushkin, specifically Pushkin's reading of *Boris Godunov*, and other inconsistencies which stand out for the careful reader.

One scholar has insisted that "it's hard to say it any other way—Tynianov sadistically rewrote history in *Death of the Vazir-Mukhtar* . . . fiction became for Tynianov a means of experimenting on history."[45] But there is no need for judgment here. Certainly each of Tynianov's changes, omissions, and contradictions of historical fact or documents was made consciously. In "rewriting history" he deliberately left clues—a kind of footnote for the curious, the reader who wants to compare Tynianov's version of events to his sources. In this way Tynianov was able to be a historical writer while creating his own variant of the historical past, a usable past for his own time.

It is the clues that Tynianov left which make *Vazir-Mukhtar* a "scientific novel" and which reveal Tynianov's solution to his epistemological dilemma. Tynianov created his own version of Griboedov, but by leaving bread crumbs along the path, he allowed the reader to trace his way back to the sources, to other versions of history. Having constructed his own Griboedov, his own "intimate image" of the poet-ambassador, Tynianov invited his readers to create their own Griboedovs as well. A closer look at a couple of examples from the novel will help to establish Tynianov's method of treating historical sources: altering facts while dropping a reference to the primary source which offers a different point of view.

In the novel, when Griboedov is in Petersburg he tells Faddei Bulgarin that he is writing a tragedy, *A Georgian Night* (*Gruzinskaia noch'*). Bulgarin reacts immediately.

> ". . . I'll set up a reading. Where do you want to have it? At my place?"
> "No, I don't think so," said Griboedov, and Faddei was offended.
> "Whatever you want. We can do it somewhere else . . . At Grech's, or at Svin'in's," he said frowning.

"Yes, all right, at Grech's," Griboedov said as if giving in, "but not a reading, just a dinner."[46]

Finally, they decide to have the dinner at Bulgarin's, and he promises to invite Krylov and Pushkin. In fact, as K. A. Polevoi attested in his memoirs, such a reading and dinner did occur in Petersburg in 1828, and Krylov, Pushkin, and Grech all attended. However, the event did not take place at Bulgarin's.[47] Here, Tynianov accomplished two tasks in one scene: as he did throughout the novel, he emphasized the friendship between Griboedov and Bulgarin, making the police spy Griboedov's closest ally in his otherwise isolated state. At the same time, Tynianov pointed the reader to the real host, Svin'in, as if saying, "I *know* where the dinner actually took place." Of the three names suggested, only Svin'in is thrown away. Why mention him at all? Here Tynianov was deliberately showing his source. He even footnoted Polevoi's article with the statement: "That dinner later became an event for memoirists."[48]

Tynianov also transformed history in his narrative by avoiding and omitting certain facts and events. Even though Tynianov had Griboedov and Pushkin meet several times, he left out a reading of *Boris Godunov* on May 16, 1828, in Moscow, which Griboedov attended. Both the reading and Griboedov's presence at it were mentioned in Tynianov's first novel, *Kiukhlia,* which readers were likely to be familiar with; and since this date fell within the time frame of *Vazir-Mukhtar,* the exclusion was clearly deliberate. Belinkov has pointed out that most of the literary texts included in the novel were simply bad,[49] and therefore there could be no place for *Boris Godunov.* With his drama, too, Pushkin was intruding on Griboedov's territory; perhaps Tynianov did not want to have the poets compete in Griboedov's one successful area, dramaturgy.[50] But the absence of Pushkin's drama seems particularly conspicuous since throughout the novel Tynianov alluded to other works of Russian literature with similar themes of power, imposture, and betrayal. When in the novel Bulgarin brazenly states, "After all, we don't have a single tragedy right now,"[51] even a layman stops to think: "What year is this? And when was *Boris Godunov* written?" Of course the drama had already been written, and Griboedov was well aware of it.

Another "clue" sends the reader to Pushkin's account of Griboedov's life in "Journey to Arzrum." In *Vazir-Mukhtar* Tynianov used the meeting scene from "Journey," having Pushkin unexpectedly come upon the cart carrying Griboedov's body back from Tehran. In his essay Pushkin had written:

> His return to Moscow in 1824 was a turning point in his fate and marked the beginning of uninterrupted successes. His manuscript comedy *Woe from Wit* made an indescribable impression and suddenly placed him in the ranks of our first poets. Some time later his perfect knowledge of the lands where war was beginning opened a new profession for him; he was appointed ambassador. Having arrived in Georgia, he married the woman he loved . . . I know of nothing more enviable than the final years of his stormy life.

The reader of *Vazir-Mukhtar,* though, experienced Griboedov's last year through Tynianov's eyes, and while it may have been stormy, it was hardly enviable. In Griboedov's wounded literary ego the fruit of incomparable successes was not evident. Griboedov's romance with his sixteen-year-old wife, Nina Chavchavadze, hardly swept the reader away. In other words, Tynianov's account of Griboedov's last year specifically contradicted Pushkin's rendering of that time.

But significantly, by quoting directly such a famous work as "Journey to Arzrum," Tynianov pointed any more or less educated reader back to Pushkin's interpretation of Griboedov's life, which no one, including Tynianov himself, could take lightly. In a way the author was both writing and unwriting his own creation, and Levinton's idea that Tynianov undermined the image of Griboedov in the novel is at least partially correct. This undermining is possible, however, without leaving Griboedov's image unfinished, as Levinton reads the novel. While certain aspects of Tynianov's theory of characterization (as applied to "The Nose") are present, among other things in the epithets which mark the characters, Griboedov's image is nonetheless clearly defined and unforgettable. Reducing the entire novel to political allusion as Belinkov did is not the answer, either. As in his novellas "Second Lieutenant Kizhe" and "The Young Vitushishnikov," Tynianov was searching for archetypes in Russian history, national myths, hoping to find the laws that Joseph Brodsky evoked in his poem "A Christmas Romance": if life has swung to the right, what law will make it swing to the left? With Griboedov Tynianov essentially created his own myth. As Gor'kii argued, Tynianov's powerful portrait of Griboedov replaced previous images of the poet-diplomat.

A myth of Griboedov already existed in the Russian consciousness, but it was dual in nature. On the one hand, his image was fixed as a great poet-martyr, who wrote the immortal comedy *Woe from Wit* but tragically outlived his time and suffered a terrible, if in a way cleansing, death in Tehran. But, on the other hand, Griboedov was the most unclear figure in Russian literature—his date of birth is debatable, his relations with the Decembrists controversial, his talent as a poet (why only one great work?) and as a diplomat (how could he make such a fatal mistake in Persia?) both subject to doubt.[52]

When Griboedov became the subject of a novel, of course, these factors and more came into play. In her study *On the Literary Hero,* Ginzburg contended that in an invented context authentic people differ from invented characters. She gave the example of Napoleon in *War and Peace:* definitely Tolstoi's creation, this Napoleon must live in constant comparison with the real, historical Napoleon. According to Ginzburg, the image of such a character necessarily splits in two.[53] In *Vazir-Mukhtar* Tynianov used this duality, counting on the reader's previous knowledge about Griboedov, while at the same time creating his own concept of the character. The novelist chose to assert the "fixed" part of Griboedov's myth and expressed it in the lead epigraph to the novel, taken from a poem by Evgenii Boratynskii that was long thought to be about Griboedov:

Взгляни на лик холодный сей,
  Взгляни: в нем жизни нет
Но как на нем былых страстей
Еще заметен след!

Так ярый ток, оледенев,
  Над бездною висит,
Утратив прежний грозный рев,
  Храня движенья вид.

Look at this cold face,
  Look: there is no life in it
But how the traces of former passions
Are still evident!

Just so a rapid stream when frozen
  Hangs over an abyss,
Having lost its previous menacing roar,
  The appearance of movement remains.[54]

Tynianov even took this image to the extreme, minimizing the feelings and passions of his hero and showing him to be essentially just going through the motions.[55] But he simultaneously threw this carefully constructed image into doubt by the contradictory sources that he allowed to protrude through the fabric of the narrative.

This duality was emphasized by the very trajectory of the novel, which begins and ends with historical and literary myths. Tynianov started with a general historical and political concept, that of the rift between the men of the 1820s and 1830s and of their metamorphosis, and incarnated it with the physical characteristics of these men. Griboedov himself entered the novel as a shadow and was brought to life by Tynianov's imagination. Quoting from the prologue: "A man, not very tall, sallow and prim, occupies my imagination. He lies motionless. . . . He does not think, does not speak. Nothing is decided yet." Griboedov gradually became a whole man, thinking, speaking, acting, but then began to disappear again, the personality taken over by his position and title of Vazir-Mukhtar. By the end of the novel, he was completely disincarnated and became a mere name. The body that returned home to Russia may or may not be Griboedov's; it was put together from various pieces left by the carnage in Tehran. Not only was his body mutilated, but his name was distorted as well; when Pushkin asked the carters he met on the road from Tehran, "What are you carrying?" he heard in answer, "Griboed."[56]

This return to literary myth may seem to render useless any attempt to see a man behind the name. Yet in his novel Tynianov showed just that man. How can these two sides of Griboedov's myth and these two aspects of Tynianov's novel be reconciled? One possible answer is that there is no reconciliation, that the only thing left is the deformed name and the various truths which posterity is free to concoct. But Tynianov was too interested in determining historical truth to allow such ambiguity in his novel. Instead, by creating his own contribution to Griboedov's myth and simultaneously showing its limits, Tynianov pointed the way to the crux of the myth and the crux of Russian culture. This crux is the immortality of the artist and the significance of the artist's fate for future generations.

In *Death of the Vazir-Mukhtar,* Tynianov immortalized the historical character of Griboedov, just as *Woe from Wit* immortalized the artist. In addition, though, Tynianov was experimenting with various ways of inserting literary history and literary texts into his fictional narrative. One of his main techniques was to emphasize the role of artist as prophet; not only did Tynianov's character Griboedov prophesy the inevitability of his own death in Tehran, but Tynianov's Pushkin contributed to the "truth" which was to ennoble Griboedov's last year. Tynianov incorporated Pushkin's truth into *Death of the Vazir-Mukhtar*, but he also created his own vacillating truth for the twentieth century, introducing a relativity into his portrait of the past which he would expand upon further in his final novel. Griboedov's fame and his tragic fate earned him a place in history. Tynianov brought that historical character to the attention of his contemporaries as a warning (this is what can happen to those who allow themselves to be "transformed") and as a message (it is possible to try and interact with the political system to accomplish something, and while some people perish trying, their fame will outlive their fate).

Chapter Three

Fact or Fiction: Tynianov's Pushkins

Кто знает, что такое слава!
Какой ценой купил он право,
Возможность или благодать
Над всем так мудро и лукаво
Шутить, таинственно молчать
И ногу ножкой называть?

Who knows what fame is!
At what cost did he buy the right,
The opportunity, or the divine gift,
To quip so wisely and so slyly,
About everything, to be mysteriously silent,
And to call a leg a "little leg"?
—Anna Akhmatova

Великим быть желаю,
Люблю России честь,
Я много обещаю—
Исполню ли? Бог весть!

I wish to be great,
I love Russia's honor,
I have much promise—
Will I fulfill it? God knows!
—Pushkin, 1817–19 (II, 491)

LENINGRAD, 1930. Describing his method of writing, Tynianov admitted: "I love rough, unfinished things. I admire rough, unfinished, unlucky people."[1] Griboedov was such an "unfinished" person; the novel *Pushkin* would be an unfinished thing.

In all of his fictional (and much of his scholarly) work, Tynianov's trajectory aimed toward Pushkin. As Monika Greenleaf has argued convincingly, Tynianov's scholarship of the 1910s and 1920s used Pushkin as the given, the background against which to judge other poets of the era: "In his earlier work on the Pushkin period," she writes, "Tynianov had been repeatedly attracted to the underestimated or eccentric careers of Pushkin's contemporaries: Kiukhel'beker, Griboedov, Tiutchev, Katenin, their literary moves *na fone Pushkina.*"[2] In his fiction, too, Pushkin appeared as a foil to Tynianov's other characters. The Lycée friendship between Kiukhel'beker and Pushkin featured prominently in *Kiukhlia,* and, as I discussed in the previous chapter, Pushkin was not only a character but also acted as a subtext throughout *Death of the Vazir-Mukhtar.* This chapter explores the relationship between Tynianov's scholarship and his attempt to write a biography of Pushkin. Comparing the character of Pushkin who emerges from Tynianov's scholarship and his incomplete biography to his "rough, unlucky, unfinished" characters—Griboedov and Kiukhel'beker—may show us why Tynianov's first two novels were more interesting and more successful than his third, as well as help us understand why the novel *Pushkin* remained unfinished. Looking at the contrast between the fictional Pushkins and Pushkin the writer as Tynianov presented him in his scholarly work of the 1920s and 1930s and examining the characters of Pushkin in each of Tynianov's novels—*Death of the Vazir-Mukhtar, Kiukhlia,* and *Pushkin*—will enable me to offer a reading of the juncture between Tynianov's worlds of fiction and of scholarship.

It was in preparation for 1937, the centennial year after Pushkin's death, that Tynianov began to publish the final novel of his trilogy—*Pushkin.* In the earliest stages of his work, Tynianov himself described his plans for the novel: "The entire life of the great poet, from his very birth, will be shown in the novel *Pushkin.* Even the death of the poet does not exhaust the theme . . . I intend to capture the following period too. After all, Pushkin himself as the major literary phenomenon of the last century does not end with his physical death."[3] Tynianov worked on this novel for almost ten years, but the attempt ended with his own death in 1943. It is important to note that Tynianov missed the historical opportunity to answer the Soviet call for a biography of Pushkin by the date of his centennial. In a sense, then, Tynianov's drawn-out biography of the poet was of no use to the Soviet government. The project defeated Tynianov, where his previous biographical novels had triumphed. Instead of offering a new Pushkin to the world, Tynianov would have to rest on the laurels of the endearing Kiukhel'beker from the children's novel and the disappearing Griboedov from the modernist novel.

THE PUSHKINIAN SUBTEXT IN *DEATH OF THE VAZIR-MUKHTAR*

Tynianov did feature a meeting between Pushkin and Griboedov in *Vazir-Mukhtar*—at that same dinner that never took place, hosted by the jester Bulgarin. In the scene, Griboedov and Pushkin entered the room together, almost like Gogol's comical twins Bobchinskii and Dobchinskii.

> When Griboedov and Pushkin appeared, everyone stood. Thank God there were no musicians to beat bass drums, Faddei was capable of organizing such a display. . . .
>
> Grech arose. "Aleksandr Sergeevich," he said to Griboedov, "and Aleksandr Sergeevich," he said to Pushkin. Grech gave a speech about the equal merits of the two poets, and Griboedov responded with a speech of his own: "Two things can be good even if they are in no way alike."[4]

Together, these dissimilar poets formed the heart of *Vazir-Mukhtar*.

Instead of the twins Bobchinskii and Dobchinskii, another literary pair suggests itself in the relationship between Pushkin and Griboedov in *Death of the Vazir-Mukhtar*: that of Pushkin's own Mozart and Salieri. In the personal interactions of the characters Griboedov and Pushkin, Tynianov made Griboedov's jealousy of the other poet evident. Pushkin, who in the novel acted casual, confident, and nonchalant about his own work, parallels his genius character in the little tragedy "Mozart and Salieri" (1830), while Griboedov—frustrated, hardworking, and ultimately unsuccessful in his literary work—watched all the creative projects of the last years of his life, including the Transcaucasian trading company, dissolve around him. Tynianov's "Salieri" did not go to the extreme measures of Pushkin's Salieri in poisoning his rival, but Griboedov's resentment of the other poet bubbled beneath the surface of his disposition, perhaps turning what was wine in Pushkin into vinegar in Griboedov's veins.

While Pushkin's role on the plot level was critical to *Death of the Vazir-Mukhtar*, especially in the ending of the novel, his presence was more than that of a mere character. Tynianov was both working *against* Pushkin's definition of Griboedov—"I know of nothing more enviable than the final years of his stormy life"—and simultaneously including Pushkin's viewpoints in the text. If Pushkin's words from "Journey to Arzrum"—"his death was instantaneous and beautiful"[5]—strike a rather weak note of optimism at the end of the long, seemingly inevitable journey that started with "nothing has been decided yet," the fact that Tynianov included Pushkin's perception of Griboedov in his version forces the reader to consider the meaning of reputation and historical rendering in the life (and death) of a poet.

Pushkin was present in *Vazir-Mukhtar* implicitly as well, through references to his works, opinions, and even hidden references to arguments with friends. For example, in 1828 Katenin, an old friend of both Pushkin and Griboedov, accused Pushkin in the pages of *Ancient Times* (*Staraia byl'*) of flattering the autocrat.[6] In the novel, Pushkin dismissed such gossip as trivial and unimportant. Talking about his military *poema* to Griboedov, he said: "The battle of Poltava. About Peter. Let's not talk about it. A drum-like poem. . . . I had to throw them a bone."[7] Such an interpretation of "Poltava" from Pushkin is suspect, but in the novel Griboedov takes it seriously, frowningly jealous of the ease with which Pushkin can pull off such a concession to the autocracy. On the whole, the relationship between Pushkin and Griboedov in the novel is full of resentment (on Griboedov's part) and rivalry.

The scene where Pushkin meets Griboedov's body on the road is not the only borrowing from "Journey to Arzrum." Chapter 4, part 1, where Griboedov goes to the baths in Tiflis, is more or less directly out of "Journey," with an added touch of estrangement (*ostranenie*) that at first confuses the reader, but in fact foreshadows Griboedov's violent death. Both bathhouse attendants are Tatar, and their bathing rituals are almost identical. But more than that, Tynianov used many of Pushkin's phrases practically word for word. Compare this selection from *Vazir-Mukhtar* with one from "Journey":

Tynianov

> *They bent his arms, legs* . . . The Tatar *beat him* . . . he drummed on his back *with his fists* . . . Then he *stretched* his long legs, and his *joints* cracked. . . . Strange, *there was no pain.* The Tatar, having bent down, *suddenly leapt onto his back* and began to walk *on his back with his feet.* . . . Then the Tatar pulled a wet *linen* sack on his fist . . . and *threw* Griboedov . . . *into the pool.*[8]

Pushkin

> . . . he began to *bend my limbs, pull on my joints, beat me* hard *with his fist; I didn't feel the slightest pain* . . . (Asian bathers sometimes become ecstatic, *leap onto your* shoulders . . . and dance *on your back* in a squatting position . . .) After this he rubbed me for a long time with a wool mitten and . . . began to wash with a soapy *linen* bag. . . . After the bag Hassan *let me go to the bath* . . . (italics mine).[9]

Tynianov added irony to the parallel by having his attendants discuss the bathing.

> "Why are you so red, Ali?" the other Tatar asked Griboedov's attendant.
>
> "When I bathe Russians," answered Ali, "I manipulate them really hard and beat them a lot. I hardly beat my own at all, I mostly wash them. Russians bathe not for cleanliness, but so as to have a story to tell about our baths; it's interesting to them. The boss told me to beat them a lot."[10]

In his bath scene, Tynianov almost directly footnoted not only Pushkin's exoticized version of the experience but also Pushkin's source for his story, the original visit to the bath. The metacommentary on the habits of writers, who like "to have a story to tell about our baths," links Pushkin, Griboedov, and Tynianov in a genealogical line.

In the novel, Griboedov's "quarantine feast"[11] recalls another of Pushkin's little tragedies, "Feast in the Time of Plague." In fact, Tynianov crafted Griboedov's situation in this episode of the novel to virtually mirror Pushkin's own biographical episode. When Pushkin wrote "Feast" in 1830, he was stranded in Boldino, unable to return to Moscow to his fiancée because of a quarantine. Griboedov, in the novel, had also just become engaged, and was prevented from joining Nina due to plague in Paskevich's camps. As in Pushkin's work, in the novel Griboedov made the best of his forced wait, amusing himself with a drunken banquet to while away the time.[12] Tynianov also injected the impiety of Pushkin's piece into the scene: while Pushkin's Val'singam rejected the attempts of a priest to save him from the unholy feast, Griboedov derided a devout German who wanted him to look for the son of God in Persia.

Yet another textual parallel exists between *Vazir-Mukhtar* and Pushkin's work. The element of escape and of the conflict between will and fate (Pushkin's favorite ontological rhyme pair of *volia* and *dolia*),[13] found in an 1834 Pushkin poem, also runs throughout Tynianov's novel. Pushkin wrote:

> Пора, мой друг, пора! покоя сердце просит—
> Летят за днями дни, и каждый час уносит
> Частичку бытия, а мы с тобой вдвоем
> Предполагаем жить, и глядь – как раз умрем.
>
> На свете счастья нет, но есть покой и воля.
> Давно завидная мечтается мне доля –
> Давно, усталый раб, замыслил я побег
> В обитель дальную трудов и чистых нег.
>
> It's time, my friend, it's time! My heart asks for peace—
> Days fly after days, and every hour removes
> A little piece of being, and you and I together
> Assume that we will live, but suddenly we could die.
>
> There is no happiness on earth, but there is peace and freedom.
> I've dreamed a long time of an enviable lot—
> Long ago, tired slave, I devised an escape
> To a far off sanctuary of labor and pure comforts.[14]

The theme of escape was common at this time for Pushkin, who tried on several occasions to get permission to leave the Russian empire. But Tynianov's Griboedov went him one better; he wanted to create his own "abroad" to run to.[15] Griboedov dreamed of two different escapes from his government duty in Persia: he hoped to found a new state where he could still use his creative skills, based on his Transcaucasian project, or he planned for himself a form of Pushkin's "enviable lot"—peaceful retirement at his young wife Nina's estate, Tsinondali.

The novel's narrator seems to sympathize with his character's desire to run, to escape. Griboedov had portrayed a similar desire for refuge in *Woe from Wit*, where Chatskii fled Moscow society, exclaiming:

Вон из Москвы! сюда я больше не ездок.
Бегу, не оглянусь, пойду искать по свету,
Где оскорбленному есть чувству уголок! –
   Карету мне, карету!

Away from Moscow! I shall not come here again.
I'll run, I won't look back, I'll go to search the earth,
A corner for the wounded sensibility!—
   A carriage for me, a carriage![16]

In a sad twist, fate, responding to this call, drove up at the fall of the curtain not in a carriage but in a plain cart pulled by two oxen, the cart that was to carry Griboedov's mutilated body back to Russia.

Of all of Iurii Tynianov's fictional works, the novel *Pushkin* seems the most problematic for critics and readers alike, in part because it is the least experimental. Since Tynianov was an important literary theorist as well as critic and historian of literature, scholars often look to his fiction for practical examples of his theoretical statements.[17] Tynianov's historical stories—"Second Lieutenant Kizhe," "The Young Vitushishnikov," and "The Wax Persona"—were stylized experiments; amusing and insightful, they receive perhaps more attention by scholars than Tynianov's longer works. *Kiukhlia* is usually considered to be a children's novel; written quickly, the novel reads quickly too, and the reader dives into the life of the Lycée's *chudak*-turned-Decembrist and gets lost in that world.[18] This biographical novel covers in broad strokes vast events and territories of Russian history, and perhaps because of this *Kiukhlia* has received a minor share of the critical attention focused on Tynianov's fiction.[19]

While in the Soviet period scholars found it particularly intriguing to investigate the allegorical meanings of Tynianov's fiction, Sandra Rosengrant has argued that Tynianov's novels are much more complex than mere responses to current events. She finds other issues more interesting, particularly the ways in which Tynianov's views on the evolution of Russian literature and his other literary theories are illustrated in the novels. Rosengrant does not treat the novel *Pushkin,* considering that since "he died having completed only the first three parts . . . it is impossible to say what it would have become."[20] Certainly Tynianov had planned to make his final novel a more sweeping portrait of the entire Pushkinian era, and the result would have differed considerably from the novel we have today. It is my contention, however, that by looking more closely at the completed portions of the Pushkin novel and at Tynianov's Pushkin scholarship, we can discover "Tynianov's Pushkin." The question remains as to which part of the past was for Tynianov "usable"; if he, too, was searching for a positive hero in the past, then neither Griboedov nor Kiukhel'beker seem to be that hero. Nor was Pushkin a good candidate, especially as he was portrayed in the unfinished biographical novel. A scholar and scientist above all, Tynianov was mostly intrigued by the process of obtaining a usable past. He had worked out a methodology for retrieving the past through archival excavations and educated hypothetical thinking, but in the end Pushkin thwarted his "scientific" methods.

"THE SHAM PUSHKIN"

As might be expected from a theorist who was so interested in verse language—in language of all kinds—Tynianov entered the debates on Pushkin and Pushkin scholarship in 1922 with an assault on the language of literary scholarship. Tynianov's fear was that careless wording from scholars might contaminate the attribution of various texts. Since Pushkin's works were still being collected, Tynianov's concerns were timely.

In a polemical attack on the Pushkinist N. O. Lerner, Tynianov argued against a "sham Pushkin" (*mnimyi Pushkin*) who was in danger of arising during the period when Pushkin studies were developing in the 1920s. This vehement attack on Pushkinists of one stripe or another was really a more broad-based assault on the direction literary scholarship was taking generally. In his essay, Tynianov advocated a different focus for literary studies a broader interest in literature itself. It seemed to Tynianov that literary scholars had become obsessed with adding to the canon of texts—with attribution rather than analysis. In these years, Tynianov was witness to the creation and entrenchment of the textologically based school of literary studies that still reigns in St. Petersburg today. The irony lies in the fact that Tynianov himself, while arguing against it, contributed to this school of literary studies.[21] Ultimately Tynianov was aware of this contradiction; as his nitpicky argument in the essay "The Sham Pushkin" shows, Tynianov was advocating restraint and prudence. If scholars were going to focus on textological issues, he insisted, they should be very careful not to allow themselves incautious or overly sweeping generalizations.

In the 1922 essay, Tynianov was arguing with Lerner about Pushkin's style and, in truth, about Lerner's style. When Lerner and Pushkinists like him wrote things like: "those lines are worthy of Pushkin in thought and form," argued Tynianov, they were influencing the canon of Pushkinian texts. Even if Lerner were conscientious and qualified his statements, Tynianov argued that a miscommunication was bound to occur sooner or later. Scholars ended up playing what Russians call the game of broken telephone (*isporchennyi telefon*)—two or three references and repetitions away from the original scholar, a text of questionable authorship could enter the collected works with full rights. For example, one of the epigraphs to Pushkin's *Arab of Peter the Great* was to be the following:

Как облака на пебе
Так мысли в нас меняют легкий образ.
Что любим днесь, то завтра ненавидим.

Like clouds in the sky
Thus thoughts in us change their light disguise.
What we love today, we hate tomorrow.

About this epigraph Lerner had written: "As far as this second epigraph, the source of which Pushkin did not name . . . couldn't these lines belong to Pushkin himself?" The result, as Tynianov pointed out, of this "uncertain suggestion," was that the lines ultimately came to be included in the Brokgauz and Efron edition of Pushkin's collected works with the comment: "there is reason to consider these lines to be Pushkin's."

For Tynianov, precision in language and scholarship was everything. In his polemical essay, Tynianov took issue most of all with what he called Lerner's "stylistic technique": Lerner had argued that the lines were "majestic" and "worthy of Pushkin." But, as Tynianov countered, "the lines, perhaps, really are majestic, but Pushkin wasn't the only one to write majestic lines." And in a concluding coup, Tynianov identified the true author of the proposed epigraph: Kiukhel'beker, who had even published the lines in the almanac *Mnemozina.*[22]

On the level of detail, Tynianov was therefore condemning imprecise language and counseling scholars to consider what might happen to their perhaps even innocent conjectures in the hands of others. At the same time, Tynianov had a larger goal in mind in this essay. Why, he asked, must we create a "scholarly discipline about Pushkin" (*nauka o Pushkine*)? It would seem that the future author of the "scientific novel" about Griboedov would welcome scholarly disciplines devoted to Pushkin and Griboedov. But it is at this juncture that we can most clearly see the difference for Tynianov between scholarship and fictional treatments of literary figures. The poet as man was an interesting subject for an "imaginary discourse," to use Hayden White's term. But in literary scholarship, Tynianov condemned the focus on the creators rather than the creations, the authors rather than the works.

Calling the terms *Pushkinovedenie* and *Pushkinovedstvo* "monstrous" and *Pushkinism* "absolutely impossible," Tynianov was arguing a larger point: literary scholars should study works, not personalities, the "literature" (*literatura*) and not the "man of letters" (*literator*). As he was against Pushkin studies, *Pushkinistika,*[23] so he was also against individual author studies and, more broadly, textologically based pseudoscience about literature. "The accumulation of materials has a specific goal—literary study; beyond this goal it turns into either Pliushkin's pile [of rags and trash] or, what is even worse, Chichikov's dead souls."[24] Here Tynianov was criticizing the method that Veresaev would use in his *Pushkin in Life;* not all materials and opinions are of equal value, he contended, and if literary scholars fail to show some discrimination, the stuff of literary study becomes worthless and even dangerous. Literary history and scholarship, Tynianov argued, should be careful to avoid "fetishism"; and in the environment of the 1920s, when *Pushkinistika* was taking hold, it was precisely fetishism that began to flourish.[25]

In Tynianov's opinion, it was through careless scholarship and excessive fetishism that the "sham Pushkin"—or "sham Pushkins"—were born. Texts, words, and opinions that had nothing to do with Pushkin came to be attributed to this shadow poet, this accidental creation of literary scholars. Tynianov objected vehemently to the careless creation of a "sham Pushkin" by professionals, holding literary scholars to a higher standard and requiring them to acknowledge the power over the public that was manifest in their essays, speeches, and books. The individual reader could interpret texts as he liked, but the literary scholar must be cautious and careful in discharging his work according to a high standard of professional ethics.

This notion of the "sham Pushkin" is at the crux of the split between Tynianov the scholar and Tynianov the novelist. When Tynianov came to write fiction several years later, he would begin to create fictional characters from actual literary personages. Because of the rigidity of his theoretical views when he protested the "sham Pushkin," the creation of a *fictional* Pushkin became that much more difficult for him. If in literary scholarship extra care may be taken to avoid misidentification of texts or excessively liberal reading of the author under investigation, in fiction a novelist has no choice but to take that extra step, in Tynianov's words to go "beyond the document," and thus the fictional character—if we are strict about judging him—must needs take on characteristics that parallel, if not repeat, those of the "sham" historical figure in literary studies. The enterprise of fiction seems to preclude following Tynianov's strict rules about what one can and cannot do with literary figures.

Here, though, Tynianov—and many of the critics who study him—would argue that in fiction the writer has the opportunity and right to conjecture, whereas in scholarship he does not.[26] It is the reader's responsibility to know the rules of the genre he has chosen to read; certain expectations that apply for an analytical article fall away for fiction. This may seem to be splitting hairs. But for Tynianov, the distinction was a vital one that allowed him to incarnate the gut feelings he had about the literary and historical figures of the Pushkin era in fictional representations. In the nineteenth century, Alfred de Vigny distinguished between *le vraie* (the true) and *la vérité* (the truth), arguing that in the historical novel, the higher truth be obtained by embellishing the "true" of historical evidence. Whether we think about fictional truth in terms laid out by Hayden White or in de Vigny's romantic terms, the relativity of truth in historical scholarship and fiction gave Tynianov the room he needed to pursue his biographical incarnations.[27] For

Tynianov, there was a continuum of scholarly and literary truth. He was strict about what the limits of scholarly truth were, but when he could not prove something within those limits, he moved into the realm of literary truth in his fiction.

Tynianov's work has traditionally been seen to be in dialogue with itself. Chukovskii's famous story about the genesis for Tynianov's novel on Kiukhel'beker pointed to the potential for swapping storytelling and critical analysis. As I discussed in the previous chapter, Tynianov himself asserted that "the place the document ends is where I begin"—an acknowledgment of the close connection between historical research and the writing of fiction. The writer was accused of writing the novel *Pushkin* primarily to prove in fiction what he could not prove in scholarship—that Katerina Karamzina was Pushkin's mysterious love of the Lycée days. The Soviet scholar N. V. Izmailov has argued that Tynianov did not prove his hypothesis in his article "The Unnamed Love" ("Bezymennaia liubov'") but simply declared it, using the article as a place to work out the theories he planned to include in his novel.[28] In other words, Izmailov—and other scholars with him—suggested that Tynianov was mixing his genres, confusing which rules applied when. In support of the theory of biography and scholarship as autobiography, N. K. Chukovskii has recalled that Tynianov told him the story of Pushkin's love for Karamzina back in the 1920s, two decades before he was to write the article and novel. Chukovskii considered that "Iurii Nikolaevich told this story so often and was so captivated by it that I couldn't help thinking that this story was connected with something personal for him, something out of his own life."[29]

Thus for Izmailov, Tynianov had begun to mix genres, using his scholarship as a dry run for his fiction; for N. K. Chukovskii, Tynianov interpreted events in Pushkin's life through events in his own life, through his understanding of human psychology based on his own experience. For Eikhenbaum, Tynianov's "scientific novels" were a manifestation of the essential unity of Tynianov's careers as a historian of literature, a theorist, a critic and an author of fiction. As he wrote, "For [Tynianov] these areas of creative work do more than exist side by side; they feed and support each other."[30] All three of these views have validity, but they also do not necessarily contradict one another. Tynianov did indeed use his instincts about human nature in creating his fictional characters as well as in trying to understand the history of literature and literary figures. Some of those instincts quite clearly came from his own personal experience as well as from his scholarly knowledge. Again, as in the case of Griboedov and *Death of the Vazir-Mukhtar*, Tynianov was using the facts and hypotheses of literary scholarship to create living characters; and as such he was using the material of one genre, literary scholarship and history, as a source for creation in another genre, fiction. If before he began writing fiction Tynianov was stricter about the boundaries between the genres, by the last decade of his life he was more interested in getting to the heart of his characters and reaching the "authentic truth" about Pushkin and his contemporaries.

X = KIUKHEL'BEKER

In his scholarship, Tynianov used a formula of "Pushkin and x": in 1926 Tynianov published articles on "The Archaists and Pushkin" and "Pushkin and Tiutchev," and in 1934 he published "Pushkin and Kiukhel'beker."[31] This pattern suggests a movement toward and around Pushkin throughout Tynianov's scholarly—and novelistic—career, culminating in the large Pushkin biographical novel project.

In Pushkin Tynianov found approaches and devices that were both useful and interesting to him; for example, in his 1928 article "Pushkin," he vetted ideas that were particularly meaningful for him as an artist. As Tynianov wrote in a personal letter, his work on Pushkin's "Count Nulin" prompted him to think about how a writer experiments with history.[32] The trajectory in Tynianov's scholarly path parallels that of his biographical novels; during his university years he traveled from Kiukhel'beker to Griboedov to Pushkin, and he continued along that trajectory throughout his life.[33] But while Pushkin was critical to Tynianov's literary enterprise, I would suggest that a second, perhaps more significant, uniting factor among the three novels was Kiukhel'beker. Kiukhel'beker was Tynianov's own scholarly discovery. It was Tynianov who resurrected the forgotten poet and Decembrist and forced his contemporaries to consider both Kiukhel'beker's body of literary work and his personal fate through his own two-pronged exploration of Kiukhel'beker. In the previous chapter I argued that Tynianov identified with Griboedov, his frustrations and his tragic fate. Other scholars have suggested that Tynianov's portrait of the late Pushkin also resembled himself.[34] But his affection for "Kiukhlia" as a character—as well as his admiration for the interesting poet in him—are evident both in Kornei Chukovskii's anecdote and in Tynianov's novel about the poet.

The absence of Kiukhel'beker in *Death of the Vazir-Mukhtar* has been noted by scholars.[35] Having just completed his novel about Kiukhel'beker—in which both Griboedov and Pushkin were present—Tynianov must not have felt it necessary to repeat the scenes and characterizations from *Kiukhlia* in *Death of the Vazir-Mukhtar. Death of the Vazir-Mukhtar* was a departure from *Kiukhlia*—stylistically very different, with a different audience and purpose in mind. In addition, if sufficiently different, these two works could be made to talk to each other. After all, Tynianov was engaged not only in inter*generic* dialogue, but was also creating a dialogue between his fictional works, where scenes and characters simultaneously add to and contrast with each other. But if *Vazir-Mukhtar* by design was a departure from *Kiukhlia,* both in style and in content, then the novel *Pushkin* was a return to the days of *Kiukhlia.*

For the admirer of *Death of the Vazir-Mukhtar, Pushkin* at first seems a disappointment. Readers have speculated that the contemporary reaction to *Vazir-Mukhtar* caused Tynianov to back away from his experiments in language and form, that *Pushkin* was a more conventional biographical and historical novel precisely because of the furor over the modernist language and style of Tynianov's previous novel, and because of politically dangerous allegorical interpretations which saw Griboedov's epoch paralleling the early years of Stalinism. Indeed, there may be some truth to this. The design and the slow pace of Tynianov's last novel make one wonder whether he ever intended to complete it.

Clearly, as he began to write, the material took over, expanding and decelerating. In his earliest plans, Tynianov had intended to cover even the period after Pushkin's death, but the amount of detail he used when narrating the first twenty-one years of Pushkin's life set a pattern that would have made for an extremely long novel. Even if we ignore the fact that the remaining seventeen years of Pushkin's life offered more events, more poetry, and even more documentary material from which to work than the first twenty-one had, at the same pace Tynianov would have produced another 500 pages. With the same amount of detail on the rest of Pushkin's life as Tynianov used on three of Pushkin's Lycée years, his novel would have gone on for at least another 750 pages.

In Griboedov's case, Tynianov had emplotted the life using "chronological shifts" (*khronologicheskie sdvigi*) and "compression" (*sgushchenie*) of events. With the Pushkin novel he abandoned such techniques, thereby extending the length, and the life, of the project. This process seems to be a common one with Pushkin biographies. Khodasevich complained that one could never fit Pushkin's life into one volume (and this despite having dealt handily with the long-lived Derzhavin in a mere 260 pages). And Bulgakov, in his play *Last Days (Aleksandr Pushkin),* chose a route similar to Tynianov's one-year time frame for Griboedov, portraying only the final days of Pushkin's life. The pace of Tynianov's plot in the Pushkin novel could have resulted in an epic *War and Peace*–like volume. Indeed, as Tynianov himself said, he had planned to write a many-volumed biography of Pushkin, an "epos about the birth, development, and death of a national poet."[36]

As with all our writers, it was in conjunction with the coming centenary of Pushkin's death that Tynianov began his Pushkin project. The idea dates to 1933, when Tynianov decided to work on a biographical novel about Pushkin. The hardest part of his task he considered to be Pushkin's childhood. Tynianov told a newspaper correspondent in 1934: "there are fewer documentary and historical data about [his childhood], and those which we have offer many unsolved questions. For example, his relations with his father and mother."[37] As another correspondent formulated Tynianov's goal, summing up Tynianov's discussion with readers of the first part of his novel: "[the author was] striving to remove the 'makeup' with which commentators have covered the great poet, to dispel the smoke of legends which surrounds his name. A living Pushkin, and not *Pushkin in Life,*—that's what interests Tynianov."[38] The contrast with Veresaev is not coincidental; in the 1930s all of the Pushkin biographical projects had to come to terms with *Pushkin in Life.* Certainly Tynianov would have put Veresaev in the camp of those who helped to create "sham Pushkins," and he accepted the challenge of trying to counteract those "sham Pushkins" in a couple of ways. His plan included continuing to write polemical articles and literary criticism presenting the real Pushkin and creating the many-volumed Pushkin biography, which would create a legitimate portrait of the poet.

Given his modus operandi, Tynianov needed an archival stimulus to launch into a new fictional project. Tynianov was not a writer who could create a story out of "whole cloth." Instead he needed the patches for his patchwork quilt, and each time he began a new fictional project on his period, the first third of the nineteenth century, Tynianov needed to have a new pile of patches—fresh archival findings that would make up the stuff of his story. In my view, one reason that Tynianov decided to write a novel about Pushkin at all was that he received access to another portion of the Kiukhel'beker archive in 1928 and 1929.[39] This archive, in Tynianov's words, "destroy[ed] the old notion about the Lycée" and shed light on Pushkin's activities during this period of his life.[40] The new documentary evidence which Tynianov uncovered allowed him to return to the world he had described in *Kiukhlia,* and this time write in far greater detail about the first class at the Tsarskoe Selo Lycée. In *Kiukhlia,* as I will show below, Tynianov glossed over most of these six years, unable to make his own mark on the history of the Lycée because he had little actual knowledge of the goings-on at the school. In his own terminology, the Lycée years in *Kiukhlia* would be an example of "not going beyond the document, and not reaching it." His intuition could tell him nothing that would have helped flesh out these scenes. In the 1930s, however, with access to new materials, Tynianov had the "documents" he needed in order to "invent" the rest of the atmosphere at the Lycée in the 1810s. The second reason for the Pushkin novel, as I mentioned above, stems from the Pushkin mood in the 1930s. In these years, no author could escape Pushkin, and the author of novels about two of Pushkin's friends and colleagues was no exception.

Looking at the novel *Pushkin* from a purely schematic point of view, it becomes clear just how important the new archival papers were among Tynianov's sources. Tynianov completed three chapters or parts of his book. "Childhood" ("Detstvo") came out in serialized form in journals in 1935, and "Lycée" was published in 1936–37; together they became a book in

1936 and were republished in 1937 and 1938. The final portion of the novel which Tynianov completed before his death, "Youth" ("Iunost'"),[41] was published in the journal *Znamia* in 1943. In one edition of the novel, the page counts per part—"Childhood," 174; "Lycée," 263; "Youth," 110—demonstrate just how important the Lycée period was for Tynianov's novel. Such a numerical approach to analyzing the novel shows, among other things, that Tynianov was not certain of the scope of his novel as he continued to write and publish it—"Lycée," the second part, is the longest and most detailed, two or three times as long as the other parts. In addition, the time period covered is from 1811, the year the Lycée opened, through the first public examination in 1814—a period of three years, only half of the Lycée period, to which Tynianov devoted almost half of the novel.[42]

One commentator has noted that in writing *Pushkin* Tynianov used a vast quantity of sources: Pushkin's memoirs and letters, both published and unpublished, the surviving lecture notes of the Lycée professors and their published scholarly works, documents from the Lycée archive, and the archives of Kiukhel'beker and Gorchakov, another Lycée student. In addition, Pushkin's own works, including the 1830 plan for his autobiography, played an important role, a topic to which I will return below.[43] Kiukhel'beker was not excessively prominent in this portion of the novel; many of the Lycée students receive detailed attention, as do the professors, staff, course work, and even the grounds of the Tsarskoe Selo Lycée. But by comparing the chapter "Lycée" to Tynianov's 1934 article "Pushkin and Kiukhel'beker" and listening to the dialogue between the pieces, the prominence of the Kiukhel'beker papers in the creation of the novel becomes clear.

Having written an entire novel about Kiukhel'beker's life, Tynianov nonetheless revisited the scene of the Tsarskoe Selo Lycée to portray Vil'gel'm's more famous classmate. And, in truth, in the early portions of the novel Tynianov was more concerned with giving a sense of the epoch and of Pushkin's family and classmates than with focusing on the hero. Contemporary readers even complained that Pushkin was too marginal in both of the first two sections, but Tynianov assured them at author's evenings that he had done this by design.[44] Much less judgmental in "Childhood" in his descriptions of Sergei L'vovich, Nadezhda Osipovna, and Vasilii L'vovich, for example, than is often the case with other writers, Tynianov gave his reader a chance to understand each member of Pushkin's household through the eyes of an omniscient narrator, untainted by the viewpoint of the young Aleksandr Pushkin. In "Lycée," Tynianov was returning to the school he described in *Kiukhlia*, but this time with new information and a new goal.[45]

In the article "Pushkin and Kiukhel'beker," Tynianov used letters between Kiukhlia and his relatives (mother, sister, and others), Kiukhel'beker's diary, and his "Dictionary"—none of which had been previously published or known—to depict the Lycée atmosphere. He was vehement about setting the record straight on the history of the Lycée, which had been misrepresented in the memoirs of later pupils, who imagined that Pushkin and his Decembrist friends attended their alma mater and thus must have had school experiences similar to their own. The early years of the Lycée presented, according to Tynianov, a completely different institution. Tynianov delineated three periods of the Pushkinian Lycée—each different than the other and each important in its own way to Pushkin, Kiukhel'beker, and their classmates.[46] Tynianov wrote:

> The first period lasted from the autumn of 1811 through March 1814—about two and a half years; the second, the "interregnum," or "anarchy"—from March 1814 until February 1816—two years; and finally, the shortest [period]—the "Engel'gardt [period]"—from February 1816 until June 1817, that is, less than a year and a half.[47]

The written histories of the Lycée lead one to believe that the later, "Engel'gardt" period characterized the Lycée as a whole, but Tynianov argued that Engel'gardt had little effect on Pushkin and Kiukhel'beker.[48] Stressing the importance of Malinovskii and Speranskii, and the freer middle period, which lacked official leadership, in the education of Pushkin's Lycée class, he wrote:

> Thus there was no single Lycée; the false unity of the Lycée history of the first class was created by tradition. The Malinovskii period most influenced Val'khovskii and in part Kiukhel'beker and Pushkin; the period of the "interregnum," perhaps, was reflected most of all in Pushkin, Pushchin, Kiukhel'beker—each in his own way; and the Engel'gardt period formed *"cavaliers gallants"* and *"chevaliers servants"*—Gorchakov and Korf.[49]

In this article Tynianov was explicitly correcting an impression he had given in his 1925 novel *Kiukhlia.* In that work, which began with Kiukhel'beker's family's decision to send him to the new institution, the first mention of the new director was not accompanied by a discussion of Malinovskii's death or of the "interregnum" period.[50]

In his first novel, Tynianov had presented the three periods of Lycée life essentially as one, following closely the traditional understanding of the Lycée. He was even careless at times, stating for example that the examinations between the lower three classes and upper three classes "were *always* a big event."[51] Since the 1814 exam of Pushkin's class was the first in Lycée history, it could not be part of a generalized "always."[52] It is clear that in creating the Lycée chapters of *Kiukhlia* Tynianov was relying on the same histories of the Lycée which he later came to criticize for imposing too smooth and uniform a past onto the institution.[53] In the 1934 article "Pushkin and Kiukhel'beker," Tynianov utilized new materials to which he did not have access in the mid-1920s and which shed light on areas of Pushkin and Kiukhel'beker's youth that he earlier had not understood. Consequently, in the novel *Pushkin* Tynianov was able to incarnate scenes of Lycée life that had earlier been mysteriously hidden.

One source for seeking the life and spirit of the Pushkinian Lycée has traditionally been Pushkin's Lycée anniversary poems. The Pushkinist M. A. Tsiavlovskii pointed out to Tynianov a variant stanza from the 1825 "19th of October," which Tynianov was able to put to use in his "Lycée" chapters:

> И черный стол, и бунты вечеров,
> И наш словарь, и плески мирной славы,
> И критики лицейских мудрецов
>
> The black table, and the evening revolts,
> Our dictionary, and the splash of worldly fame,
> And the criticism of Lycée sages.[54]

Several of the details from Pushkin's description of Lycée life were new to Tynianov. The "dictionary," for example, had remained a riddle until Tynianov's 1934 article; it was not even mentioned in the 1925 biographical novel on Kiukhel'beker.[55] Yet once identified and understood, the dictionary would play an important role in characterizing both Vil'gel'm and Aleksandr Pushkin in the novel *Pushkin*.

> Kiukhlia dragged a heavy notebook with him everywhere: this was his famous dictionary. From *A* to *Ia* Kiukhlia patiently copied out every thought which seemed to him remarkable. At first, as always, Aleksandr laughed along with the others, then he stopped poking fun and began to note this and that for Kiukhlia himself, and finally, Kiukhlia's dictionary became his favorite book.[56]

In Tynianov's hands, the dictionary became a device for including philosophical ideas on pride, passion, freedom and so on, "from A to Ia," in his novel, thus giving voice to the otherwise silent thinkers whom the Lycée students read in their spare time.

As Kiukhel'beker and Pushkin each thought about their futures as poets, Tynianov depicted them as virtual opposites: Kiukhlia was a romantic, believing in the trials and martyrdom awaiting him as a poet and seeing the path to poetry strewn with obstacles over which he must rise through inspiration. Pushkin, in contrast, was pragmatic: "when he wrote poetry, there was no ecstasy. Oblivion, sudden cold, rhymes which confirmed the accuracy of it all, the instantaneous happiness of knowledge, dissatisfaction, all sorts of emotions, but not ecstasy."[57] Tynianov used Kiukhel'beker as a foil for Pushkin, while at the same time depicting the two friends with the help of Kiukhel'beker's papers. "Pushkin" and "Kiukhlia" were in Tynianov's mind intimately connected, both during their school days and afterward, as their poetic and personal styles complemented and contrasted with each other. This combination of poets—Pushkin and the Archaists—represented for Tynianov the whole picture of the literary history of the 1810s, 1820s, and 1830s, and he was to stand firmly for the inclusion of the archaist camp along with Pushkin. As he wrote in his theory of literary history, it was essential to include the minor characters along with the major ones, the soldiers along with the generals, to obtain a clear and true picture of the past.

PUSHKIN'S AUTOBIOGRAPHY AND TYNIANOV'S BIOGRAPHY

In *Pushkin* Tynianov's "scientific novel" took a different form than in *Death of the Vazir-Mukhtar,* since in addition to footnoting the works of others, Tynianov had recourse to footnoting himself. The articles about Kiukhel'beker and about Pushkin and the novel *Pushkin* refer the reader back and forth from one to the other, making the Pushkin project an even better example of "intergeneric dialogue," in Wachtel's term, than *Kiukhlia.* One of the more interesting aspects of this dialogue, however, is the way in which it works over the course of time; in a sense, Tynianov created a whole gallery of Pushkins and Kiukhel'bekers during the 1920s and 1930s, always refining his portraits to reflect his newest documentary evidence and to take the place of the previous ones.

The rules of the game of "scientific novel" require the writer to follow his sources. If in *Death of the Vazir-Mukhtar* Tynianov followed the biographical background provided by Shliapkin, then in *Pushkin* he had a more personal approach to the subject. Tynianov used Pushkin's own "autobiographical outline" (*programma avtobiografii*), written in 1830, as a skeleton for his biography. In Pushkin's fragment, the list of events and thoughts he wanted to include in his autobiography only reached 1815 and the famous examination with Derzhavin.[58] But while the genre of "scientific novel" precisely prefers to have such documentary support as this autobiographical outline, it seems to me that in some ways Pushkin's outline interfered with Tynianov's work, dictating both the pace and the content of Tynianov's novel.

Ultimately, it was perhaps Pushkin himself who kept Tynianov from completing the novel. Fully half of Pushkin's "program" consists of the poet's often cryptic notes about his childhood and family, and the notes for 1811 through 1815 are particularly sketchy. Tynianov, as I noted above, considered the "childhood" section of his novel to be the most difficult because of the paucity of documentary evidence. "Where the document ends, that's where I begin," he proclaimed, but for Pushkin's early years much of the plot had to be added by Tynianov, a process which slowed him down and hampered his creative methods.

One of the easiest sections of the Pushkin biography from a documentary point of view should have been the famous Lycée examination of 1815, when the great poet Derzhavin "passed his lyre" on to the young Pushkin. Not only did Tynianov have access to Pushkin's memoirs of the event; he had the reminiscences of others as well for source material. Tynianov could pick and choose details from Pushkin's notes and stitch the scene together himself, just as Khodasevich was to do with the same scene for his literary biography *Derzhavin*. In *Kiukhlia* Tynianov devoted almost five pages to this incident; in *Pushkin* he made do with two. And in each he added something new to the story. In *Kiukhlia* Tynianov described a poem that Kiukhel'beker had written in Derzhavin's honor and insisted on proclaiming during the examination. Kiukhlia and Derzhavin even exchanged a few lines of dialogue in this first novel; it was here that Vil'gel'm gave his passionate defense of poetic ecstasy (which in *Pushkin* came up in connection with the "dictionary") and here also he received praise from Derzhavin: "Resonant. You have movement. It needs more fire. Clearly you have read Derzhavin," the older poet compliments the younger. But in the first rendition of Derzhavin's incursion into Lycée life, Tynianov also had Kiukhlia deliver the important message to Pushkin: "Derzhavin is passing his lyre on to you."[59] In *Pushkin* the narrator focused on Derzhavin.[60] The two poets seemed practically to be alone in the room while Pushkin was declaiming; there was already no room for Kiukhlia.

Hence I can posit two main reasons for Tynianov's inability to finish his biography of Pushkin. On the one hand, in the style of a "scientific novel," Tynianov followed Pushkin's autobiographical schematic, but the outline was only a fragment, and consequently Tynianov's novel remained incomplete; without more documents, Tynianov could not continue. On the other hand, Tynianov developed his character Pushkin in conjunction with his renewed conception of Vil'gel'm Kiukhel'beker, and Kiukhlia was also not an active part of Pushkin's life after his arrest in 1825. Without an outline and without the faithful Kiukhel'beker (and his useful papers) for the remaining portions of the book, Tynianov's novel trailed to a fragmentary and unsatisfactory halt.

Yet another reason for this halt is related to Tynianov's approach to the past. Seeking in that past lessons and models for the present, Tynianov did not find anything "usable" in Pushkin's life and poetic career. Kiukhel'beker was a tragicomic figure who ultimately lived a long and productive life in his Siberian exile, and the enthusiasms he brought to his studies at the Lycée and to the Decembrist uprising were not dampened by his tragic fate. Griboedov was an example of how fame outlives fate, and in representing his last year Tynianov found a man and a methodology for creating a "usable past." But Pushkin, in Tynianov's rendition, would not prove to be a positive hero for Soviet times, nor would the novel about him hone Tynianov's semiscientific tools for excavating the past.

HIDDEN LOVE: *PUSHKIN*, PART III

While the first two sections of Tynianov's novel *Pushkin* are basically completed, the third section has a raw, unfinished feeling to it. Indeed, the conditions under which Tynianov wrote part III of the novel were hardly conducive to polishing; as Tynianov was finishing this part, he had been evacuated to Perm' from Leningrad and was bedridden, in terrible pain, and facing death from multiple sclerosis. Tynianov, like Khodasevich in the 1930s, had neither the time nor the energy nor the health required to finish this final "book of his life."

Regardless of the difficulties involved, Tynianov did publish the third section of the novel in 1943. This section, entitled "Youth," deals with Pushkin's last years at the Lycée through his first exile, approximately 1816 through 1820.[61] Part II ended with the famous Tsarskoe Selo exam at which Derzhavin acknowledged and welcomed his young rival, and part III opens with the arrival of Karamzin, Viazemskii, and Vasilii L'vovich Pushkin at Tsarskoe Selo to crown the young poet with his Arzamas nickname, "Cricket" (*Sverchok*), and to initiate Pushkin into the corps of poets. It is the tools of poetry—love, friendship, history, philosophy, and most important for Pushkin, language—that dominate the third part of the novel.

One scholar has suggested that only in this third part of the novel did Tynianov's style begin to come together; "the flat montage quality of the first two parts is replaced in the third part with a lyrical-philosophical, suggestive metaphorical compression of the text."[62] Others point to this section of the novel in particular for the most convincing evidence of why Tynianov chose to write fiction about Pushkin in the first place; in the novel, he was able to develop his idea about the crush the young Pushkin had on the wife of Nikolai Karamzin, and even of a mutual sexual attraction between Katerina and Aleksandr.[63] In this third section of the novel, Pushkin was to become an adult. In Tynianov's interpretation, as he prepared to embark on life's journey Pushkin took the time to choose a "family" for himself, a group of people who were to be his support system in lieu of his biological family for the rest of his life. Pushkin aligned himself with Pushchin, Del'vig, and Kiukhel'beker—his "brothers" in poetry and in the Lycée family—and Chaadaev, his dashing "older brother" of the hussar guards; he chose the deceased Malinovskii, the first director of the Lycée, as a father figure to replace Sergei L'vovich and Vasilii L'vovich (and as opposed to the new director of the Lycée, Engel'gardt, whose patronage the young poet rejected); and he recalled Arina Rodionovna, his nanny, as his true mother. In summing up, Tynianov reduced Pushkin's young years—which had taken him hundreds of pages to enact—to two things: "There was Arina and there was the Lycée. That's all. Such was life."[64]

The scene with Arina Rodionovna in which Pushkin claims her as his true mother went as follows:

> He saw Arina for the last time. And he parted from her as he should. He embraced her.
>
> "Farewell, mother," he said to her.

And Arina was wonderstruck. She looked at him to see if he was joking. No, he wasn't joking. She looked all around. There was no one, thanks be to the creator.

"What do you mean, Aleksandr Sergeevich," she said, dumbfounded, "You have a mother."

"I do," he said seriously. "You are my mother."[65]

This scene makes Tynianov's point very clearly. The idea was important to Tynianov, who mentioned it again in his jubilee article "Pushkin's Personality." In that piece, a companion to the novels *Kiukhlia* and *Pushkin* in which he used Kiukhel'beker's judgments over and over to clarify the difference between legends about Pushkin and Pushkin himself, Tynianov quoted Kiukhel'beker's reaction to chapter 8 of *Evgenii Onegin:*

> The poet in his eighth chapter himself resembles Tat'iana. For his Lycée comrade, for a person who grew up with him and knows him by heart like I do, the feeling with which Pushkin is filled is always noticeable, even though he, like his Tat'iana, doesn't want the world to know about that feeling.[66]

When in *Evgenii Onegin* Tat'iana speaks of being happy to throw away her social position for a life in the country, for "the humble cemetery, / Where now a cross and the shadow of branches / [Stand] over my poor nanny," Kiukhlia—and Tynianov—read the nanny as Arina Rodionovna as well:

> Of course, here not only Tat'iana and not only her fate [were being described]: his imprisoned friend was not mistaken; here [was] Pushkin's own desire to escape aristocratic society, to throw off the tattered rags of the mascarade, here Pushkin [was] writing not about Tat'iana's nanny, but about his own, about Arina Rodionovna, whom he called his *mama.*[67]

A more subtle instance of the same general idea occurred earlier in the novel, in 1812, when the Pushkin family was fleeing Moscow for Mikhailovskoe during Napoleon's advance. Tynianov had Pushkin's nanny, Arina Rodionovna, try to set off for St. Petersburg to see how Aleksandr Sergeevich was getting along in this time of danger. His real mother, Nadezhda Osipovna, showed no concern for the fate of her eldest son. In a sudden and almost inadvertent new respect for her, Sergei L'vovich began to call his old servant "Irina" and used the formal you (*vy*) with her.[68]

Critics and commentators all note that Tynianov's hypothesis about Katerina Karamzina as Pushkin's one love, the one he will remember and cherish for the rest of his life, is interesting and convincing, if not definitive.[69] It may not be entirely coincidence that this third part, which puts forth the most controversial idea of Tynianov's novel, is also the one which appealed to Sergei Eisenstein as a potential source for a film scenario.[70] The Russian scholar A. L. Grishunin has emphasized Eisenstein's interest in the plot twist; finding Pushkin's love for his wife, Natal'ia Goncharova, absolutely inexplicable, Eisenstein latched onto the psychological motivation in Tynianov's idea that Pushkin's first love was also unrealizable and unrequited.[71] The film was never made, but part three of the novel, with its love intrigue, again emphasizes the dual aspect of Tynianov's Pushkin project and of his "scientific novel"; the article "The Unnamed Love" and the chapters of the novel entitled "Youth" were written virtually simultaneously and were meant to support and footnote each other.

Tynianov had an easier time creating a biographical novel about Griboedov than he did the epic novel about Pushkin. And we can point to several reasons why "Tynianov's Pushkin" did not come to life. With *Pushkin*, Tynianov tried to use the "scientific novel" approach he had used in creating *Death of the Vazir-Mukhtar*. But while with the Griboedov novel he had implemented such techniques as the "chronological shift" and "compression" of events in Griboedov's life into one year, in *Pushkin* he planned a large, sprawling epos about the central poet of Russian culture. In following Pushkin's own plan for his autobiography, Tynianov got bogged down in detail.

The experiment with Griboedov had demonstrated the success of Tynianov's method of historical recovery. But when Tynianov approached the novel about Pushkin without this methodology, with only the Kiukhel'beker archive and Pushkin's autobiographical notes as stepping-off points, his tools were ineffectual and his material sprawled out of control. *Death of the Vazir-Mukhtar* was an immensely controlled novel, with every inflection, word, and detail carefully calibrated and arranged. But Griboedov had been a "fuzzy" character from history who could be brought into focus through Tynianov's experimental methods for use in the present. Pushkin was too celebrated and too large for the same methods to have worked. Where with *Death of the Vazir-Mukhtar* Tynianov had spliced events, characters, and footnotelike references to documentary data and to his own theoretical articles together into an artfully constructed, highly innovative narrative, he wanted *Pushkin* to be more straightforward, more linear, and more conventional.[72] It is conceivable that the emphasis on the realistic novel, which began with the codification of socialist realism as the main method of Soviet art in 1934, caused this new, straightforward, and realistic approach. But by the end of Tynianov's novel (and his life) in 1943, it was clear that the "scientific novel" he had pioneered was not to be a productive genre for the Soviet novel. Tynianov died without creating a biographical portrait of Pushkin.

Chapter Four

Searching for a Hero: Khodasevich and His Derzhavin

Старик Державин нас заметил
И, в гроб сходя, благословил.

The old Derzhavin saw—and blessed us
As he descended to the grave.
—Pushkin, *Evgenii Onegin*, Chapter 8: II[1]

PARIS, JANUARY 13, 1929. Vladislav Khodasevich complained in the pages of the Parisian newspaper *Renaissance* that "for critical and literary historical work the conditions of emigration are exceptionally unfavorable." Nonetheless, Khodasevich's career flourished abroad. It was there that he wrote his excellent biography of the eighteenth-century poet Gavrila Derzhavin, as well as many articles and essays about contemporary literature and about Aleksandr Pushkin. For Khodasevich, emigration brought on a poetic night, but his critical and literary historical work absorbed him, despite the unfavorable conditions.

Finding himself an émigré in the 1920s, Vladislav Khodasevich began to contemplate the cultural and political situation of Russians like himself and of Russians back at home. Russian culture had split in two and, it seemed, would never reunite. Khodasevich and other émigrés asked themselves whether Russian culture could live and prosper as two separate organisms, or whether one part—or both—was fated to deteriorate and die.

In Gavrila Derzhavin, Khodasevich found an answer to these questions. Khodasevich considered Russian culture to be almost dead, to have reached the end of its life cycle, which had begun with Derzhavin. In Khodasevich's formulation, Derzhavin was the "infancy" of Russian literature; Chekhov at the turn of the twentieth century was its dying breath. And if Russian literature was to be reborn, it would have to begin the cycle again, to pass through a new stage of infancy, a new Derzhavinian stage. Using an organic metaphor, Khodasevich saw Russian culture as an entity which passes through a life cycle, but he was not certain if it was fated to be reincarnated. The poet himself, though, had seen the dying breath of the patient and had participated in the posthumous decay and decadence of the Symbolist era. He felt that if Russian culture could be reborn, then it was his duty to revitalize it, to point it in a more healthy direction. Khodasevich could not lead it, but he could coach Russian culture from the sidelines, revealing the fatal qualities to be avoided and the healthy qualities from the past which might be emulated. Hence Khodasevich's quest for a wholesome and energetic "positive hero" from the past who might serve as a model—a quest that, oddly enough, paralleled a similar quest in Soviet Russia, the quest for the socialist realist positive hero in Soviet literature. On both sides of the border, the search was on for a model to lead Russian culture into the next era. As his model, Khodasevich chose not the central figure of Russian literature, Aleksandr Pushkin, but his predecessor Gavrila Derzhavin.

When Khodasevich turned to the writing of his book *Derzhavin* in the late 1920s, he had for the most part ceased to write poetry himself, and though not quite forty-five years of age, like an old man he had begun to look back on his life and assess his era. Like the older Derzhavin, Khodasevich felt himself to be a "poet of a past time."[2] In addition, Derzhavin's search for a successor, a *new Derzhavin*,[3] whom he found in the young Aleksandr Pushkin, was repeated by Khodasevich's fruitless quest in his last years to find a legitimate successor to his own poetic tradition. The younger poets in Russia Abroad were not interested in writing classical poetry, and Khodasevich felt himself to be the last link in his poetic line.

The condition of exile, of living outside one's own culture and on the edges of a foreign culture, along with the significant repercussions of the Russian Revolution for the future of Russian culture, caused Khodasevich, among others, to meditate on the Russian past, and particularly on writers from that past. *Derzhavin* was his first attempt, and the only biography which Khodasevich completed.[4] He also intended to write a biography of Pushkin, although he was never able to complete the project.[5] The fact that Khodasevich chose Derzhavin for his first biography is important. In his 1921 speech at the Petrograd commemorative meetings for the anniversary of Pushkin's death, Khodasevich had named Pushkin as the password for the Russian intelligentsia, a word by which Russians who valued their literary and cultural heritage could know each other in what he identified as the coming darkness of the sun's eclipse.[6] If Pushkin was the code word, the phenomenon that linked Russians at home or abroad, then it is essential to understand why Khodasevich chose Derzhavin instead of Pushkin when creating his "usable past" for the émigré future.

While Pushkin was an important forebear for Khodasevich as a poet, Derzhavin held a special place in Khodasevich's thoughts and affections, and he came to represent a healthy balance of life and art which could be a model for later generations. Khodasevich valued Derzhavin as a poet, tracing his own poetic genealogy to Derzhavin[7] and considering him a major influence on his poetry.[8] But in addition, Derzhavin served as a kind of moral standard of behavior for Khodasevich. From his first 1916 article on the poet, Khodasevich returned to him again and again in essays and articles about Gogol', Chekhov, even about himself. Khodasevich's concern for Derzhavin's place in Russian poetry also contributed to his decision in 1923 to prepare a volume of the selected works of Derzhavin for publication abroad.[9]

Khodasevich's choice of Derzhavin as the subject for his biography was very deliberate, although it may seem somewhat counterintuitive. Derzhavin and Khodasevich were in many ways antipodal. Why would Khodasevich, a dry and archly sophisticated émigré in late 1920s Paris, turn to the naive and straightforward poet/statesman of the eighteenth century? Would it not be more natural for him to re-create the life of such poets as the melancholic Evgenii Boratynskii, whose collection "Twilight" surely struck a note with the author of "European Night," or the pessimistic Konstantin Batiushkov, or even the life of the brilliant philosopher Petr Chaadaev, whose personality was certainly more similar to Khodasevich's than Derzhavin's was? Clearly with Khodasevich and Derzhavin, the situation was one of opposites attracting. Indeed, if biography is often related to autobiography, it might be appropriate to speak of an inverted autobiography when looking at Khodasevich's *Derzhavin.* Khodasevich saw in Derzhavin that which he knew to be necessary to his own era, and that which was missing in himself.

Gavrila Derzhavin was born into an impoverished family in 1743 and orphaned early. A young nobleman from the heart of Russia, he lacked the protection, money, and proper education he needed to get ahead, but with persistence, determination, and hard work he made his way through the ranks of the imperial guards, eventually becoming an officer and later a top government official under three tsars. Throughout his adult life Derzhavin was a very public poet and public figure. He was extremely healthy, living to the age of seventy-three, a gambler and carouser in his youth, a gourmet and perhaps even glutton. Odes celebrating the generals and rulers of Russia were sprinkled throughout his oeuvre, and Derzhavin ended his life as a grand old man of literature, extending his hospitality to young poets and crowds of relatives at his home in Petersburg and at his beautiful country estate Zvanka, on the banks of the Volkhov River.

If Derzhavin was something of an insider, a nobleman at least by birth, a participant in and target of government and court intrigues by career, and an acquaintance of all the main figures in eighteenth-century Russia, then Khodasevich was the ultimate outsider. Vladislav Khodasevich, born in 1886, was the youngest son of a Polish father and a Polish Jewish mother who had converted to Catholicism. He grew up in a virtually all-female household in Moscow and was a loner, preferring to play alone and to observe the world from his window than to play with other children. Khodasevich described himself as being "born too late"; having entered poetry during the twilight of the symbolist movement, he became a loner in literature as well. Always surrounded by other artists in Moscow and Petersburg and after emigrating to Europe, Khodasevich earned his living exclusively by the pen, but he never belonged to any group or trend.

Perhaps it was his status as an outsider and a loner that contributed to Khodasevich's keen powers of observation with regard to literature, for in addition to being a poet, he was also a superb memoirist, critic, and literary historian. By 1929, when Khodasevich began his biography of Derzhavin, he had emigrated to Europe and was living in Paris, eking out an existence by writing articles and essays for newspapers and journals. In stark contrast to Derzhavin, Khodasevich was a very private person and poet, weak and plagued by ill-health all his life, with such poor digestion that he existed mostly on a diet of porridge.

It would seem difficult to find two men with more diverse biographies and inclinations. With unrestrained glee, Khodasevich pointed out one difference between the two in his autobiographical essay "Infancy." According to legend, the first word Derzhavin spoke as a child was "God," when he saw a six-tailed comet burst across the sky. Khodasevich first spoke at the sight of a kitten, saying "here, kitty kitty."[10] Even as children, Derzhavin looked up for inspiration and saw majestic things, while Khodasevich looked down at the small and the mundane.

But perhaps the most important distinction between these two poets is that one stands at the beginning of Russian literature and the other at the end, or what seemed like the end to him. For Khodasevich, the figure of Derzhavin represented the birth of Russian literature, the tradition of which he feared was dying out. When Khodasevich wrote in his 1928 poem "Monument," "in me is the end, in me the beginning," he was writing about the death of Russian literature and culture, but he was hoping that the cycle would begin again, that another beginning was possible. In the late 1920s, Khodasevich looked back to the beginning of it all and relived Russian literature through Derzhavin.

Khodasevich wrote his biography of Derzhavin from January 1929 through January 1931; parts of it appeared in the Paris newspaper *Renaissance* (*Vozrozhdenie*) and parts in the journal *Contemporary Annals* (*Sovremennye zapiski*) before its publication in book form in 1931. Khodasevich had a variety of different impulses for his study of Derzhavin. One reason that he chose Derzhavin as the subject of his biographical investigation stems from what he saw as the faltering of literature after the Revolution. In an effort to prevent the end of the tradition, Khodasevich was looking for a "positive hero," a model for Russian literature and culture to follow. He found that model not in Pushkin or in Chekhov but in Derzhavin. Derzhavin represented both the past of Russian culture and civilization and a hope for its future.

Second, with his biography Khodasevich wanted to counter a specific stereotype of Derzhavin that had prevailed in the nineteenth century and had only begun to be reevaluated at the beginning of the twentieth. Throughout the book the reader feels a polemic surfacing with critics who had relegated Derzhavin to the demeaning category of "court poet." Thus in a way Khodasevich was rehabilitating the older poet, pointing out the merits and achievements of Derzhavin in both civic and poetic arenas.

Finally, and perhaps most important, in *Derzhavin* Khodasevich explored the question of the interrelationship of life and art, whose complementary connection had in his eyes broken down in the romantic era and never been reforged. In Khodasevich's view, Derzhavin knew precisely what his role was in art and in society and strove to fulfill that role to the best of his ability. Beginning with Pushkin—ironically, just at the moment when the poet became a professional in Russia—poets no longer had a specific role in society. Always on the outside, even Khodasevich's favorite poets—Tiutchev, Sluchevskii, Annenskii—faced a split in themselves between the poetic and the everyday world. Khodasevich, in turning to Derzhavin, sought a way to heal that split.

THE BEGINNING AND THE END OF RUSSIAN LITERATURE

Related to Khodasevich's Derzhavin project was his effort to reevaluate the history of Russian literature in light of its present—in light of the splitting of Russian culture into two after the Revolution.[11] Like many others in the 1920s, Khodasevich was unsure of what the future might hold for Russian culture. He very much wanted to believe in the continuation of Russian literature abroad, stating specifically in one essay that "a literature's nationality is created by its language and spirit, and not by either the territory upon which its life flows or the everyday life reflected in it."[12] At the same time, Khodasevich felt that the era of symbolism had had a negative effect on the course of Russian literature and its prospects for the future, and he wasn't certain that the culture could throw off the yoke of attitudes and philosophies born of symbolism.[13] He also, despite attempts at optimism, could not help acknowledging the difficulties of maintaining a readership and an active cultural life under the conditions of diaspora.

The position Khodasevich took in the 1933 essay "Literature in Exile" was a necessary and perhaps inevitable rhetorical step in a world of expatriates separated from Russian soil. The quality of "Russianness," Khodasevich asserted, goes beyond national boundaries and the life lived within those boundaries. Expanding upon the metaphor of the grain, one of the central metaphors of his own poetic oeuvre,[14] Khodasevich advocated nurturing and building on the traditions of Russian literature. He wrote:

> It is necessary for our poetic past to become our present and—in a new form—our future. When Robinson [Crusoe] found a grain in his pocket and planted it on the desert island, good English wheat came up. But what if he hadn't planted it, but merely admired and protected it, so that it didn't, God forbid, fall onto the ground? With tradition, we need to do as we would with a grain. Bring it out, and plant it, and work on it—and create further.[15]

In order to understand Khodasevich's conflicted attitude toward the future of Russian culture, though, we must take into account not only his hopes for nurturing and developing an émigré literature, but also his general melancholy about the twentieth century.

According to Nina Berberova, it was not emigration per se that Khodasevich saw as killing Russian literature, but something more general, "a universal twilight of art" that began in the Chekhovian era. As she wrote in her introduction to Khodasevich's collected *Literary Articles and Memoirs*, "for a person like Khodasevich, emigration was a tragedy. . . . The tragedy, however, arose not from the loss of soil . . . ; it arose from the universal twilight of art which he discerned in the thirties." Berberova also wrote about Khodasevich's "alarm for the present and future of Russian poetry, . . . his fear (which he did not manage to outlive) in the face of the end of our thousand year culture."[16] While the "twilight of art" in the 1930s may have seemed to be a pan-European phenomenon to him, Khodasevich's perception of it was very Russocentric in nature; he was concerned most of all with Russian culture, with the fates of Chekhov, and Derzhavin, and Pushkin. Clearly Khodasevich was old-fashioned in his perceptions of art and culture, and we might even call him antimodernist. Certainly his seeking the future of Russian culture in its past was an antimodernist strategy. While the Futurists in Russia had abandoned the past and devalued its representatives, and the Soviets were seeking to turn the present into the future, Khodasevich held to the out-of-date idea of historical cycles and hoped the wheel would turn again, returning his time to the time of Derzhavin.

It is this feeling of the end that prompted Khodasevich, in his book on Derzhavin, to explore where Russian literature had come from and where it went wrong.[17] As one scholar has commented, "having survived the collapse of his world, [Khodasevich] worked for the history of Russian literature, worked, although he was unsure that such a history was to be a part of its fate." Andrei Zorin connects *Derzhavin* with Khodasevich's feeling of the end:

> Khodasevich found his own stability through his sense of support from the Russian poetic tradition, although it sometimes seemed to him that in this chain he was called to play the role of the last link. But the heavier the feel-

> ing of the end lay upon him, the more insistent became his need to look in the direction where he saw the beginning—toward Derzhavin. In Derzhavin he could understand both himself and that one-and-a-half-century history of national poetry that simultaneously separated and connected them.[18]

Khodasevich reached out to that beginning for answers. As he wrote in an essay on Chekhov, there were things in Derzhavin's life, character, and poetry that could help to keep Russian literature alive. One way to read Khodasevich's continual return to Derzhavin in essays and articles and, finally, the biography would be as a desperate repeating of a refrain that was not being heard. Khodasevich saw in Derzhavin a potential source for the energy needed in the twentieth century, a source that was being ignored.

In the midst of working on the book *Derzhavin,* with his thoughts and, as he himself confessed, his heart full of that poet, Khodasevich wrote an essay for the twenty-fifth anniversary of Chekhov's death. The 1929 essay "About Chekhov" centered on the contrast between two very different writers, two different approaches or tendencies in the history of Russian literature—on Chekhov and Derzhavin. Khodasevich's conclusions illuminate his view of Russian literature. The essay began with an exclamation:

> Chekhov—and Derzhavin! It seems like it would be difficult to find such different Russian writers even on purpose—two people as dissimilar, as foreign to each other as these two.
>
> The fact that one is a poet and the other a prose writer is scarcely the main or the most remarkable difference between them. All the other differences are much more remarkable.[19]

Khodasevich discerned almost directly converse qualities in the two writers. According to Khodasevich, Derzhavin—a fighter and soldier—was healthy, masculine, epic, stubborn, severe and quarrelsome, proud and ambitious, whereas Chekhov—a doctor—was weak, sickly, drawn to the ordinary, earthly and everyday, lyrical, feminine and humble. The key difference was that Derzhavin was a builder and his era a victorious one, while Chekhov was an observer in an era of stagnation and gradual disintegration. "Derzhavin built, Chekhov witnessed the collapse."[20] Derzhavin was healthy, while Chekhov was diseased. Derzhavin contributed to the beginning, while Chekhov experienced the end.

Khodasevich deliberately aligned himself with a renewal of the victorious Derzhavinian tradition. He did not openly lay blame for the destruction of Russia, but he seemed to hold the immediate prerevolutionary epoch at least partially responsible for the split in Russian culture:

> During Chekhov's time we were dying. Now we have died, gone "beyond the border."[21] Chekhov's time is for us like an illness to a dead man. But if we are fated to be reincarnated (and all of our prayers, all of our will urges this), then our future is not in "Chekhovian moods" but in Derzhavinian action. If

> Russia is to rise again, then the pathos of her approaching epoch, the pathos of our tomorrow, will be constructive, not contemplative, epic and not lyric, masculine and not feminine, Derzhavinian and not Chekhovian. Derzhavin must a priori become dearer to us than Chekhov.[22]

In his call for a rebirth of Russian culture, Khodasevich evoked the legacy of Derzhavin. While the present epoch for Khodasevich represented a kind of death in life, Derzhavin's era was a healthy one, an era of action and building. The only path to rebirth in the present for Khodasevich lay in the original birth of Russian literature and culture, in the creative past of the eighteenth century.

Derzhavin was Khodasevich's "positive hero," the man whose approach to life and literature should be an example to his twentieth-century descendants. Political involvement, a naive enthusiasm that more often than not achieved results, an inspirational belief in the power of God and nature, an Enlightenment conviction that men could be educated and reformed through gentle prodding and moral example—Derzhavin's personal qualities, and especially his indefatigable optimism, were missing in Khodasevich's world. And with his biography of Derzhavin, Khodasevich intended to remind his contemporaries of these admirable qualities.

KHODASEVICH'S "NEW" DERZHAVIN

For all these reasons, as the 1920s drew to a close Khodasevich felt unequivocally that a new work on Derzhavin was needed. He stated his reason simply and up front in the introduction to his book: "Our goal was . . . to tell about Derzhavin in a new way and to attempt to bring the image of a great Russian poet, an image that has been partially forgotten, partially eclipsed by widespread and fallacious notions, nearer to the contemporary reader's consciousness."[23] Khodasevich carried on the task begun by B. A. Sadovskoi in 1907,[24] that of dispelling the image of Derzhavin as a "court poet" with questionable talent and rehabilitating him both politically and as an artist. This portrayal of Derzhavin had arisen gradually after his death and may have stemmed in part from some famous comments made by Pushkin. In 1825 Pushkin attacked Derzhavin in letters to friends, mentioning that Derzhavin's "genius thought in Tatar and lacked the leisure time to learn the Russian language," and suggesting that the poet had perfected and personified the art of flattery.[25] By Khodasevich's time, these criticisms of Derzhavin were not only well known, they were taken virtually at face value. A poet from an era long ago, Derzhavin was fair game for the arrow of sarcasm from critics of various schools and persuasions throughout the nineteenth century and into the twentieth.

But Khodasevich was ready to do battle with Pushkin over Derzhavin's oeuvre and reputation. To Pushkin's comment that "of Derzhavin's work, we should save about eight odes and several excerpts and burn everything else,"[26] Khodasevich countered: "if one put together a collection of seventy to a hundred poems from everything Derzhavin wrote, this book would calmly and confidently stand in the same row as Pushkin, Lermontov, Boratynskii, and Tiutchev."[27] Khodasevich also reminded his readers that to some extent Pushkin—just like Maiakovskii and the Futurists in their day—needed to "throw Derzhavin off the ship of contemporaneity."[28] Hence there was no need to take Pushkin's statements literally, but we should instead view them as a game of literary competition. Pushkin's feelings toward Derzhavin were certainly not as one-sided as the quotes above would suggest; one need only recall his famous lines from *Evgenii Onegin*, "The old Derzhavin saw—and blessed us / As he descended to the grave," to be assured of his respect for the older poet.[29]

But Derzhavin's image was permanently tarnished. The efforts of Iakov Grot in his enormous 1880 academic biography of Derzhavin and of early-twentieth-century critics were not enough to reintroduce Derzhavin to the modern reader and to overcome the image of the "court poet." The eighteenth-century system of literary patronage—as symbolized by the *chervontsy*-filled snuffbox which Catherine the Great presented to her poet as "payment" for his verses and which joined Derzhavin's aspirations as poet and statesman—had negative connotations for the independent writers of later centuries, and they were unable to perceive Derzhavin within his own literary context.

Khodasevich attacked this stereotype in *Derzhavin* by reminding his reader of the different mores and traditions that prevailed in the eighteenth century:

> Then all poets served; the profession of writer did not exist. The social significance of literature was already acknowledged, but literary activity was seen to be in the private sphere, not the public one. As far as Derzhavin was concerned, in his mind poetry and service were linked in a unique way.
>
> Of course, he did not consider that rank or decorations would add merit to his poetry; likewise, he did not look at poetry as a method of attaining decorations and ranks; it is time to forget this vulgar notion. The situation was different, much more serious and laudable. By the beginning of the eighties, when Derzhavin had reached a fairly significant position in service and started to be noticed in literature, poetry and service became for him two aspects of one united civic aim.[30]

Khodasevich's interpretation of Derzhavin's motives and system of values added a new element to the image of Derzhavin and in effect countered the conventional stereotype. Before Khodasevich, no one had emphasized the practical reasons for Derzhavin's accepting patronage or the moral and civic aspects of his poetic career.

At the same time Khodasevich strove to avoid creating an idealized portrait of Derzhavin. While writing his first biography, Khodasevich was very conscious of the inherent problems and difficulties of the genre and of readers' expectations of the genre. In Khodasevich's mind, the task of the biographer paralleled that of a memoirist:

> The reader should not expect from me an iconlike, textbook portrait. Such portraits are harmful for history. I am certain that they are also immoral, because only a true and complete portrait of a remarkable person is capable of revealing the best that was in him. The truth cannot be low because there is nothing higher than truth. We have to oppose the *truth which ennobles us* to Pushkin's "ennobling deceit": we should learn to esteem and love a remarkable person with all his weaknesses, and sometimes even for those very weaknesses. Such a person does not need embellishing. He requires something much more difficult from us: fullness of understanding.[31]

Khodasevich had formulated the core of his views already in his 1916 article "Derzhavin (On the Centennial of His Death)," where he tried to argue against the labels Derzhavin had accrued. What Derzhavin wrote was not "false classicism" but something much more vibrant and alive: "in Derzhavin's poetry a spring of creativity is pulsing and frothing—deeply stirring, tense and lively, i.e., precisely not 'false.' Derzhavin's poetry is welded to life with the strongest bond."[32] The poet and the government were on a completely different footing in Derzhavin's time. Not antagonism but mutual respect and even dependence characterized the relationship.

> The eighteenth century, especially its Petrovian beginning and Catherinian ending, was in Russia a constructive and victorious century. Derzhavin was one of Catherine's comrades-in-arms not only in the spread of enlightenment but also in the establishment of government. In Catherine's day these two domains were connected more inextricably than ever before. Any cultural activity, including poetic, became *significant* participation in the construction of government.[33]

For Khodasevich, whose own poetry was personal, private, and reflective, the vision of a constructive poetry was intriguing and appealing.

> Derzhavin-the-poet was the same kind of direct builder of Russia as Derzhavin-the-administrator. Thus we can say that his poetry is not at all a *document* of the era, not a reflection of it, but an actual part of its content; it was not that Derzhavin's time was *reflected* in his poems, but that they themselves, along with various other factors, *created* this time. In those victorious days cannons called out in unison with victorious poetry. Derzhavin was a peaceful warrior while Suvorov was a military one. They were involved in one and the same activity and sometimes even traded weapons. It is doubtful that many people know that not only did Derzhavin dedicate poems to Suvorov, but Suvorov

> also wrote poems to Derzhavin. But then in his day Derzhavin had fought against Pugachev. And, it seems, the difference between the victories of the one and the creative achievements of the other is less than one might think at first glance.[34]

A poet-soldier, a poet-dignitary, a poet-builder. For Khodasevich, this active life offered a totally new perspective on the place of the poet in society, one that seemed appealing to him as he watched his own society faltering.

In Derzhavin the connection between life and literature was seamless, and it was this very integrity that appealed to Khodasevich and that he strove to portray in his book. Petr Bitsilli captured this idea of Khodasevich's in a review of *Derzhavin* in 1931:

> Khodasevich does not separate Derzhavin-the-poet from Derzhavin-the-"man," the soldier, the officer, the governor, the minister, the spouse of "Plenira" and "Milena." This is evidence of the author's tact and his historical perception. The form chosen by Khodasevich is *perfectly appropriate for the material,* i.e., for that concrete person about whom he wrote his book. It seems that it would be an act of violence against the material to write thus about any great artist of a later period. But it would have been falseness, lack of perception of the *main thing* in the subject at hand to write about Derzhavin separately as the governor of Tambov and separately as the "singer of Felitsa."[35]

The relationship between life and art in Derzhavin appealed to Khodasevich. Derzhavin had achieved a unity that Khodasevich could only envy in his own time of alienation. It was this unity that made his hero "positive," and this relationship between life and art that seemed a usable model for the present and future.

THE UNION OF LIFE AND ART

Hence the third main issue in Khodasevich's biography and in his interest in Derzhavin: the organic union of life and art in Derzhavin, which was vital to Khodasevich's image of the poet and was consonant with Khodasevich's own views of poetry. In "On Reading Pushkin (On the 125th Anniversary of His Birth)," Khodasevich wrote:

> Poetry is the transformation of reality at its most concrete. In other words, at the heart of poetic creativity lies the autobiography of the poet. At the last moment of creation, the poet judges himself primarily as a man, for it is from his "human" impressions that poetry is created. The "poet" and the "man" are two hypostases of one personality. Poetry is the extension of the human path.[36]

Art is created from life, from an artist's autobiography, but from autobiography transformed. To use the words of Nabokov, who in this respect was very close to Khodasevich, the artist should take the personal and "so shuffle, twist, mix, rechew and rebelch everything, add such spices of [his] own and impregnate things so much with [him]self, that nothing remains of the autobiography but dust—the kind of dust, of course, which makes the most orange of skies."[37] Thus life should not become a mere realization of an artistic design, nor should art be restricted to a mere borrowing of raw material from life.

These two extremes seem to alternate in the history of Russian literature, and with his *Derzhavin* Khodasevich took issue with them both. The first extreme is represented by the concept of *zhiznetvorchestvo* (life-creation), where romantic writers acted out in their lives certain artistic roles—turning reality into a stage where myths and fantasies are incarnated—and often themselves played leading roles in real-life tragedies.[38] Another result of this unnatural lack of balance was a loss of truth in art, something that Khodasevich was forced to confront when writing about his contemporary and personal friend Maksim Gor'kii. Gor'kii, he wrote, chose to live in a world of self-deceit; "the restoration of truth seemed to him a gray and vulgar exultation of prose over poetry."[39] The similarities between Derzhavin and Gor'kii are as noteworthy as their differences: both Derzhavin and Gor'kii acted as patrons to other writers and were in their respective days the "old men" of Russian literature, but Derzhavin lacked any self-consciousness of creating an autobiographical legend. For Gor'kii in the twentieth century, biographical legend interfered with the course of his life, and even on occasion with his ability to follow his own principles. As Khodasevich remembered:

> A great many times, while taking some sort of step which was not to his liking or went against his conscience, or the other way around—while refraining from that which he wanted to do or which his conscience told him to do, he would say gloomily, with a grimace and a troubled shrugging of his shoulders: "I can't, I'll spoil my biography." Or: "What can I do, I have to, or I'll spoil my biography."[40]

In his study *Biography and Culture*, Grigorii Vinokur defined this phenomenon as a stylization of the biography. He wrote: "Every reflection on one's own behavior, even the smallest, is already a stylization. Stylization takes place every time personal behavior becomes an *event* in private life and is lived through as an event."[41]

This stylization had a profound effect on Khodasevich, who himself witnessed numerous cases of writers turning their whole lives into one all-encompassing stylization, especially among his symbolist friends. Of his own experience in the world of symbolism during the years 1905 through 1914 Khodasevich remembered:

> In the hot, before-the-storm air of those years it was difficult to breathe; everything seemed to us ambiguous and paradoxical; the outlines of objects seemed fuzzy. Reality, dispersing in our consciousness, became transparent.

> We lived in the real world and at the same time in some separate, foggy and complicated reflection of it, where everything was "right, but not quite." It was as if every thing, every step, every gesture was reflected conditionally, projected in another dimension, onto a nearby but intangible screen. Phenomena became visions. Each event, above and beyond its obvious meaning, acquired a second meaning which had to be decoded. This second meaning was not easy to detect, but we knew that it was the real one.
>
> In this way we lived in two worlds. But not knowing how to discover the laws by which events were governed in the second world, which seemed to us more real than the truly real world, we only languished in dark and troubled premonitions.[42]

He continued, "Symbolism [became] for us not only a method but . . . a way of life."[43] Because "symbolism . . . could not and did not want to be incarnated in verbal literary forms only,"[44] it expanded into life, often taking it over completely.

> The symbolists did not want to separate the writer from the man, the literary biography from the personal one. Symbolism did not want to be only a school of art, a literary movement. It always struggled to become a life-creating method, and in that was its deepest and perhaps unembodiable truth, but in such constant striving toward this truth its entire history, essentially, passed. It was a series of attempts, sometimes truly heroic, to find the fusion of life and creativity, a kind of philosopher's stone of art . . . the history of the symbolists turned into the history of broken lives.[45]

Two vivid examples of such destroyed lives were Nina Petrovskaia, who was part of a love triangle with Belyi and Briusov and whose sad fate Khodasevich described in his 1928 essay "The End of Renata," and, among the Acmeists, the young poet and officer Vsevolod Kniazev, who shot himself, torn between his lover Mikhail Kuzmin and his beloved, the ballerina Ol'ga Glebova-Sudeikina.[46]

The second way in which life and art became unbalanced manifested itself in the subordination of art to life. The political pragmatism of certain Soviet writers would be one example of this extreme,[47] although something similar was going on in émigré poetry at the time as well. In Paris Khodasevich engaged in active polemics with Georgii Adamovich, who valued "simplicity" and "humanness" in poetry over purely aesthetic criteria. What for Adamovich and his followers, such as Lidiia Chervinskaia and Anatolii Shteiger,[48] was a "simplifying" of poetry, through the use of intimate, diarylike tones in an effort to become "less literary," was for Khodasevich merely bad verse. The epoch of wars, revolution, and forced emigration gave birth to a memoirlike literature that became known as the "human document" (*chelovecheskii dokument*), but although the experiences chronicled were truly tragic and should not be belittled, in Khodasevich's mind the confessions of the "human document" could not be a substitute for literature.[49] It is indicative that in the polemics of Khodasevich and Adamovich about form and content in poetry, Khodasevich finally conceded—not because Adamovich had won, but because Khodasevich felt that true poets would find their own way, and that if pathos, self-pity, and the "Paris note" were dominating the literary scene, it was only because the present generation of Russian poets in Paris were not worthy or capable of more.

Another aspect of the life/art question was brought to the fore by the formalists, who tried to drive real life out of art. It is interesting to look at Khodasevich's biography of Derzhavin and his choice of Derzhavin as subject in the light of Boris Tomashevskii's 1923 article "Literature and Biography," which Khodasevich may have known and which indeed may have been a specific point of departure for him in his search for a biographical and poetic unity that could influence contemporary poetic and literary culture. Khodasevich, after all, was a firm believer in the organic connection between a poet's work and his biography. In the article, Tomashevskii outlined his concept of writers *with* biographies and writers *without* biographies, that is, the use or nonuse of a writer's own particular biography as an integral component of his body of work. Tomashevskii posed the question for literary historians of whether the actual life of the poet was important in understanding the poet's work.

In some cases, Tomashevskii argued, the writer's biography *is* important for his work, particularly in those cases when writers create an "artificial legendary biography composed of intentionally selected real and imaginary events."[50] We might consider this in light of Vinokur's "stylization"—when a writer chooses an event (whether real or not) and makes that event a part of his stylized life, then the event becomes a part of the writer's mythopoetic world. The way we read writers depends on their own attitudes toward their biographies. In the case of Pushkin, Tomashevskii argued that the poet always kept his "biography" in mind when he wrote poetry:

> The lyricism of Pushkin's long poems is clearly the result of an orientation toward autobiography. The reader had to feel that he was reading, not the words of an abstract author, but those of a living person whose biographical data were at his disposal. Thus the author had to make literary use of his biography.[51]

According to Tomashevskii, during the romantic era "the interrelationships of life and literature became confused" and "biography became an element of literature."[52] Narrators, such as Pushkin's Belkin and Gogol's Rudyi Panko, were a further manifestation of this trend; instead of using their own biographies, writers began to hide behind those of their invented storytellers.

Thus in the romantic era, there sprang up "biographical legends" which served as background for the poet's literary works. Writers and readers had an unspoken contract; they agreed to consider these legends during the creative process and when reading the results of that process. According to Tomashevskii's theory, the next era saw writers without biographies, whose work was a "self-contained unit" and hence did not benefit from biographical details. The biographies of Afanasii Fet, Nikolai Nekrasov, and Nikolai Ostrovskii are interesting for cultural history, Tomashevskii argued, but not for literary history. Moving into the twentieth century to Khodasevich's contemporaries, Tomashevskii pointed out qualities somewhat parallel to those Khodasevich enumerated in *Necropolis:* for Blok, a poet with a lyrical biography, "his biography was a living and necessary commentary to his works";[53] but Gor'kii, agreed Tomashevskii, acted in certain ways knowingly, specifically aware at all times of his biographical legend. In conclusion, Tomashevskii stated: "What the literary historian really needs is the biographical legend created by the author himself. Only such a legend is a *literary fact.*"[54]

Derzhavin, born in the middle of the eighteenth century, fell outside Tomashevskii's schematic. Although he wrote his own biography in the form of his *Notes* (*Zapiski*), Derzhavin's autobiography is a pointedly *nonliterary* biography. This was where Derzhavin differed from the writers who followed him; although Derzhavin's poetry was a synthesized part of his life, he was not conscious of his image in the romantic and postromantic sense, and therefore did not create "biographical legends" about himself according to the Tomashevskiian definition. By Tomashevskii's reasoning, Derzhavin's biography should be merely a cultural fact and hold no interest for the literary historian. But Derzhavin became even more interesting for Khodasevich precisely because of this absence of an overdeveloped self-consciousness. Derzhavin's model represented for his twentieth-century biographer the most harmonious way to combine life and art, avoiding both the extremes of romantic "life-creation" and the formlessness and emotional sloppiness of the "Paris note" and the "human document."

CYCLES OF HISTORY

The image that Khodasevich presented of the poet in the biography was similar to the one that Derzhavin himself emphasized in his *Notes:* obstreperous, difficult, and hotheaded, in Derzhavin's own words "hot-tempered and a real devil," but also excruciatingly honest and sympathetic toward those he perceived to be victims. In Derzhavin there was no irony, no reflection; his personality was healthy and whole as a poet and a man. For Khodasevich, facing the modern malaise of irony in an age of self-absorption, this was an ideal, a heroic stance from the past which might be exemplary in the present.

It is interesting that Khodasevich found this ideal in Derzhavin, even though for him Pushkin was the embodiment of the Russian language, of

Russian literature, and of Russia itself.[55] As Khodasevich expressed this in poetic form:

России – пасынок, а Польше –
Не знаю сам, кто Польше я.
Но: восемь томиков, не больше, –
И в них вся родина моя.

Вам – под ярмо ль подставить выю,
Иль жить в изгнании, в тоске.
А я с собой свою Россию
В дорожном уношу мешке.

Вам нужен прах отчизны грубый,
А я где б ни был шепчут мне
Арапские святые губы
О небывалой стороне.

To Russia—a stepchild, and to Poland—
I myself do not know who I am.
Eight little volumes—nothing more,—
And in them is my entire homeland.

You might place your neck in the yoke,
Or live in exile, in anguish.
But my Russia I take with me
In a traveling sack.

You need crude remains of the fatherland,
But wherever I am—the sacred negro lips
Whisper to me
About a fantastic land.[56]

Those eight volumes of Pushkin's collected works represented Khodasevich's patrimony. For Khodasevich, Pushkin was more than a password for identifying other people of like history and mind; Pushkin was both the meaning of Russia for him and a means of carrying Russia with him even into exile.

But Pushkin was also the founder of the prophetic tradition in Russian literature, which Khodasevich described so strikingly in his essay "Bloody Food."[57] This tradition, which constituted in his view the very heart of Russian culture, flourished during the unhealthy parts of the cycle. Giving this idea an optimistic twist, Khodasevich wrote: "The very purest, best, and precious is always given as a sacrifice. The destruction of poets, by its very nature secret, is mysterious, *ritualistic.* In Russian literature it will cease when the spring of prophesy runs dry. And that will never be."[58] The spring of prophesy might not yet have dried up in these years, but that "spring of creativity . . . pulsing, frothing, deeply stirring, tense and lively,"[59] which Khodasevich found in Derzhavin's poetry, offered the regeneration of poetic currents rather than their destruction. Pushkin, no matter how Khodasevich felt about his poetic legacy, represented the beginning of corruption in Russian culture. That corruption was to find its logical end in the depravity and decadence of the symbolist era.

The "positive hero" who would take Russian émigrés out of the woods of discord and diaspora and into the light of a new Russia had to come from a pre-Pushkinian era. Already Pushkin, according to Khodasevich, had begun to blur art and life.

> He was the first to bind inextricably the tragedy of his human personality with the personality of the artist, subordinating his fate to his poetic experiences. This brought him to a unique biography: the first Russian biography in which the life is organically and consciously merged with the art. It was not by chance that he came to be the first Russian professional writer in the full sense of the term. It is also not by chance that in the history of his death worldly circumstances are not only mechanically, but as if chemically, internally, merged with poetic circumstances. He was the first to live his life as a poet—and only as a poet, and for that he perished.[60]

Khodasevich was devastated by what this confusion of life and art could lead to: by his count, eleven of his own acquaintances had committed suicide by 1932.[61] However much he valued Pushkin, in Derzhavin Khodasevich found a triumphant fate rather than a tragic one. By the 1920s Khodasevich longed to break the tragic cycle he saw being continued all around him and return to a new, triumphant era.

The idea of cycles of Russian history was not uniquely Khodasevich's and was shared by many of his contemporaries. Tynianov's use of the parallels between the epoch of Nikolai I and Stalin's time in his *Death of the Vazir-Mukhtar* is but one example; ultimately Aleksei Tolstoi's *Peter the First* was based on a similar idea, with its comparison of the Soviet era and the reign of Peter the Great, although Tolstoi chose to emphasize the positive nature of this correspondence in the difficult but triumphant building of a new society. Ivan Bunin, in his *Accursed Days*, first published in 1925, also emphasized the cyclical nature of Russian history, which the historian Kliuchevskii had pointed to decades earlier, but which no one had heard or heeded. Writing about 1918, Bunin said: "Kliuchevskii noted the extraordinary 'repetitiveness' of Russian history. To our great misfortune, no one lent an ear to this 'repetitiveness.'"[62] Bunin went on to compare peasant revolts from the Time of Troubles to Stenka Razin with the Revolution, adding: "It is inconceivable that the Lenins did not know all this and take it into consideration!"[63] Tynianov and Bunin, caught in a time that for them was tragic, focused on negative historical parallels to understand the events of their day. Khodasevich, too, was horrified at the prospect of Russian culture dying out, but he sought the answer in a positive historical era.

Interestingly enough, a few years before Khodasevich made the connection between the eighteenth century as the beginning and the twentieth century as the end of the cycle and possible beginning of a new one, one of his contemporaries made the same connection. P. K. Guber, in his 1923 book *Pushkin's Don Juan List,* which Khodasevich the Pushkinist may well have read, contrasted the eighteenth century with the subsequent periods in a manner quite similar to Khodasevich:

> In Russian history the eighteenth century was an age of luck and success, an age of energetic efforts crowned with fortunate achievements, an age of courage, novelty and surface splendor, a primarily aristocratic and noble age, a brutal age. . . . [It] was a sensual epoch, lighthearted, audacious, skeptical, very smart and even in its own way wise. . . . This epoch deafened itself with the thunder of victories and the thunder of kettledrums; it became drunk with delights in total awareness of their fragile and momentary nature; it wasted strength without noticing; it did not fear death, although it loved life to distraction. Next to its predecessor, the nineteenth century seems like some kind of failure.[64]

Guber also suggested that the start of the new cycle of Russian history might resemble the eighteenth century. "[W]e can . . . relatively easily agree that the eighteenth century may also not stand completely isolated in Russian history. Nothing is hindering it from serving as a prototype for new epochs yet to arrive. Is not perhaps the twentieth century destined for such a fate?"[65] Confronted with the apocalypse of Revolution, Khodasevich retreated to the Eden of the eighteenth century, into the state of innocence, before Pushkin's "fall," when categories were simpler and there was no temptation to sin. When Khodasevich went searching for a "positive hero," for a character from the past who could do useful work in the present, he could not use Pushkin and the nineteenth century, the age of failure, but instead went back further to Derzhavin and the age of luck and success. Khodasevich was desperately searching for a means to overcome the epoch in which he found himself, and, all too aware of the fruit of the tree of knowledge, still aspired to become a link to the new cycle.

> В России новой, но великой,
> Поставят идол мой двуликий
> На перекрестке двух дорог,
> Где время, ветер и песок . . .
>
> In a new, but great Russia,
> My two-faced idol will be placed
> On the crossing of two roads,
> Where there is time, and wind, and sand . . .[66]

In a 1937 essay about Nabokov, Khodasevich made the link of Horace's *exegi monumentum* from Horace through Derzhavin and Pushkin;[67] with his own small poem, he encompassed this tradition and became not the last, but a *lasting* link—"Но все же я прочное звено: / Мне это счастие дано"— "But still I am a lasting link: / That happiness has been given me."

THE "POETIC SHAPING" OF A LIFE

Khodasevich claimed that his book *Derzhavin* was by no means a work of fiction, but instead a faithful description of a life: "A biographer is not a novelist. He may explain and clarify, but he may by no means invent. In portraying Derzhavin's life and art (so far as it is connected with his life), we have remained precisely faithful to the information found in Grot and in many other sources."[68] Maintaining a strict methodological discipline, Khodasevich reconstructed Derzhavin's life through retelling and analysis. Khodasevich was working on this project under the difficult conditions of émigré life and hence had no access to new materials; instead, in constructing the biography he utilized Derzhavin's own autobiographical writings, those of his contemporaries, and Iakov Grot's enormous biography of Derzhavin.

But while Khodasevich claimed that "[w]e . . . have not used footnotes, since we would have had to footnote virtually every line,"[69] this was not the only reason for his decision. It is true that much of Khodasevich's material did come straight out of his sources, often almost word for word, which would have made footnoting both cumbersome and awkward. More important, though, was the audience for whom Khodasevich was writing. Not everyone had access to Grot or to Derzhavin, and certainly not every émigré would care to decipher Grot's careful academic style or Derzhavin's eccentric eighteenth-century prose. Indeed, Derzhavin's autobiography must have seemed pretentious even in his own time, written as it was in a self-aggrandizing defensive third-person voice. Khodasevich took that story and transformed it into a measured and charming portrait of the grand old man of Russian letters. In writing the biography, Khodasevich kept to the basic birth-to-death plotline and chronological organization of the life. However, he also had to place a new structure on the life, create a skeleton on which to flesh out his own Derzhavin. If we return to the metaphor of the quilt-making process, we can consider certain historical facts or anecdotes as patches which Khodasevich as biographer needed to stitch together. The biographer also has a choice among which patches of historical truth he wants to use and which he prefers to leave out. The choice of some patches from among others represents a kind of "fabulization" of the life or event. Emplotment into a story is the patching together. We might suppose that Khodasevich would succumb to the temptation to add imaginary events, conversations, or characters to his quilt of Derzhavin's life, as biographical novelists often do. Khodasevich, however, swore that all these elements of his biography were based on historical sources, documents, and letters.

> As far as verbatim quotes go, we have used them only from the memoirs of Derzhavin himself, from his correspondence and from the testimony of his contemporaries. Such quotes are set off with quotation marks. The dialogue which sometimes appears in the narration always reproduces words that were spoken in reality and in the exact form in which they were recorded by Derzhavin or his contemporaries.[70]

Khodasevich acted as he thought a historian might, presenting his subject in accordance with his sources and adding his own judgments and connections.[71] His overt statements about the exactitude of his historical research, however, should give his readers pause. Why was it so important for Khodasevich that we believe his biography to be a "true" biography of Derzhavin?

All the details in the biography were based on historical sources. But it was necessary to connect the details of the life into a coherent narrative, to patch together the overall pattern of the quilt. In constructing this narrative, Khodasevich imposed several overarching ideas onto Derzhavin's life, thus making it his own. I would argue that Khodasevich had three significant ideas in his work. First, he wanted to write a biography that would present "the poet" as a universal character while still being true to what he saw as the historical Derzhavin, the individual poet's life. Second, in searching for an overarching unity in Derzhavin's life, Khodasevich saw two main themes: the presence of God in the poet's life, shaping his understanding of himself in the world, and the role of fate in directing Derzhavin's actions. Khodasevich manipulated Derzhavin's understanding of God and fate and used those categories, the epistemological underpinnings of the eighteenth century, to construct his narrative. And third, while nowhere in the biography does Khodasevich connect Derzhavin to events in twentieth-century Russia, it was precisely in Derzhavin's career that Khodasevich found the roots of the connections between poetry and politics which formed the background of all Russian literature and which determined, perhaps, the situation in which Khodasevich the poet found himself in exile—silent and impotent. Khodasevich implicitly offered the beginning, triumphant moment of the cycle in Derzhavin to his own time, hoping to trigger a new beginning and derail the tragic end.

Zorin has defined the main principle of narrative construction in Khodasevich's *Derzhavin*, in contrast to Grot's work or Derzhavin's own *Notes*, as the principle of "psychological deciphering." Khodasevich worked from the chronology of events in Derzhavin's life but emphasized the internal state of the people he described, focusing on their motives, feelings, and reactions. As is often the case with biographical writing, Khodasevich needed to find his own space between the sources he was using, in this case the marked "apsychologism" of Derzhavin's own autobiographical notes and the "academic cautiousness" of Grot; Zorin sees Khodasevich's writer's intuition filling in that space.[72] Zorin is absolutely correct; Khodasevich did seem to have a certain insight into the character of Derzhavin, his assets and faults, his victories and mistakes. Zorin went on to say that the "psychological decipherings . . . make up only the outer layer of the narrative, its *fabula.* The plot [*siuzhet*] of the book is defined by a deeper stratum of the authorial idea—the conception of Derzhavin's personality which Khodasevich offers."[73] It was this personality, Khodasevich's own Derzhavin, that formed the foundation and motivation for the book. To build on Zorin's thesis, I might add that Khodasevich's psychological explanations for facts that were well grounded in his sources often took the form of "creative decoding." But who is better qualified to penetrate the creative process of a great poet than another great poet?

One of the main purposes of Khodasevich's biography of Derzhavin was to create a kind of archetypal biography of the creative, generative poet, a poet who could stand as a hero and a model for his descendants in all his poetic glory and in all his humanity. Khodasevich wrote of a bond between writers that crossed the obstacles of time and space, creating a mutual history of poets and writers:

> We writers live not only our own lives. Scattered about in various countries and times, we also have a certain superpersonal biography. The events of others' lives we sometimes recall as events of our own life. The history of literature is the *history of our kind,* in a certain conventional sense, the history of each of us.[74]

This principle of connectedness echoes Khodasevich's definition of himself as a "link" in the chain of Russian writers in his poem "Monument." One passage in *Derzhavin* which emphasized that this book was meant to be a more general biography, more than the biography of one concrete historical poet, reads as follows:

> In the life of every poet (if only he is not fated to remain an eternal imitator) there is a moment, when half-consciously, half by feel (but infallibly), he suddenly grasps within himself a stream of images, thoughts, feelings, sounds, which are connected as they have never been connected in anyone else. His future poetry suddenly sends him a signal. He divines that poetry not with his mind, but with his heart. This moment is inexplicable and thrilling, like conception. If it never happened, it is not possible to pretend that it did: the poet either begins with this moment or never begins at all.[75]

In this part of the book, Derzhavin was beginning his poetic career with his "Chitalagai Odes." These odes mark the "inexplicable and thrilling" moment of Derzhavin's birth as a poet. With this moment as the crucial initiation into creativity in young Derzhavin's life, Derzhavin became, in Khodasevich's rendition, the archetypal true poet.

Looking back across the centuries at Derzhavin's life, Khodasevich perceived a pattern that suggested a structure for his biography. One of the main threads in the pattern of Derzhavin's life was his relationship with God:

> From birth he was quite weak, small and skinny. He was subjected to a severe treatment: according to the custom of that time and place, the child was baked into a loaf of bread. He did not die. He was about a year old when a large comet with a six-rayed tail appeared in the sky. There were ominous rumors about it and the people expected great calamities. When they showed the comet to the infant, he spoke his first word:
> "God!"[76]

This first appearance of God in Derzhavin's life offered Khodasevich a category for emplotment. Khodasevich drew a connection between the comet and another prominent being in Derzhavin's life, Catherine.

> It was not in vain that in 1744 that six-tailed comet, which was shown to the infant Derzhavin, appeared in the sky. It promised not calamities, as the people thought, but events, nonetheless, of extreme importance. In that same year, on the ninth of February, the Princess Sophie Friederike Auguste von Anhalt-Zerbst arrived in Moscow. The Empress Elizaveta Petrovna called her to Russia and gave her in marriage to her nephew, the Grand Prince Petr Fedorovich. The Princess became the Grand Princess Catherine Alekseevna, the wife of the successor to the Russian throne.[77]

Only two months before Derzhavin's arrival in Petersburg, Elizaveta Petrovna died and Petr III became emperor, and thus Catherine empress. From this moment in the biography on, Khodasevich emphasized the connection between Catherine and Derzhavin—the empress and the poet who had such a great influence on each other's lives and on the course of Russian political history.

Derzhavin's relationship to the autocracy was equally central to the biography. Although Derzhavin, like most young noblemen, was taught from childhood to believe in the divine nature of the autocracy, Khodasevich suggested that by the time of the "Chitalagai Odes" Derzhavin had relinquished this belief. "To what extent the *Pugachevshchina*[78] was influential here we cannot determine, as there are no direct data,"[79] Khodasevich wrote, hiding his own interpretation behind the guise of an "objective historian." Extracting the poet's views on the monarchy from Derzhavin's poetry itself, Khodasevich found the basis of the tsar's legitimacy to be the *narod*—the people—and not God. Having interpreted how these views were expressed in several of Derzhavin's poems, Khodasevich summed up the argument thus:

> This means, first of all, that a sovereign who is not supported by popular love is, essentially, powerless. Second of all, he is not only not a tsar, but he is a tyrant, a seizer of power, who can be driven from the throne without any sacrilege. Consequently, it is not anointing but the love of the people which distinguishes a tsar from a tyrant. Only this love is the true anointing of a monarch. Thus the people become not only the bulwark but also the very source of tsarist power.

This interpretation of Derzhavin's worldview was Khodasevich's own: "this thought is not in keeping with historically deep-rooted notions of Derzhavin. But it is also not incidental, not uttered in a 'poetic fever': Derzhavin returns to it repeatedly. Henceforth it lies at the foundation of his beliefs, and without it, comprehending Derzhavin is impossible."[80] At this point, Khodasevich's reader in 1930s Europe must have stopped to consider his or her own views of the monarchy as well as of the "people's government" in power in the Soviet Union. Derzhavin's ideas, as Khodasevich presented them, could be useful as a part of contemporary political debate.

If it wasn't God directing the actions of the tsar, there must have been something else to guide him, and, according to Khodasevich, for Derzhavin that higher power was the law. It was Catherine who inspired Derzhavin's secular religion, the driving force behind his actions in poetry and in service; the Enlightenment ideas embodied in her famous "Instruction" ("Nakaz") formed Derzhavin's earthly touchstone and influenced his notion of the nature of the tsar's power. Khodasevich developed his thoughts on law further:

> After the existing code of laws was pronounced from the height of the throne to be imperfect, incapable of protecting the people from arbitrariness and false interpretations; after the dearth of lawfulness was recognized as the primary evil of Russian life; after abiding by the law was declared to be the chief virtue not only of the subject, but of the monarch also,—Derzhavin's eyes, one could say, were opened. The simple word *law* in the Russian air of those days resounded like a revelation. For Derzhavin it became the source of the highest and purest sensations, the object of heartfelt tenderness. It was as if *law* became his new religion; in his poetry the word *law*, like God, was surrounded by love and fear.[81]

This emphasis on law formed part of Khodasevich's rehabilitation of Derzhavin; he was arguing against the idea of Derzhavin as a bowing and scraping servant of the tsars and presenting him instead as a unified personality with one main driving force in service and poetry. Again, for the twentieth century, such an emphasis on law as the basis for government and power would also "resound like a revelation."

Derzhavin had a moral purpose in life: to spread respect for the law throughout the land, through government service or through poetry. And Derzhavin felt that he could have an impact on both fronts. The law became his primary concern: "His governorship . . . would give him access to that which Derzhavin considered his calling: the direct propagation of lawfulness in places where there was hitherto virtually no concept of legality."[82] To Khodasevich, Derzhavin's equation of his poetry and government service was admirable, although perhaps naive and certainly not understood by Derzhavin's peers and sovereign. Indeed, Khodasevich wrote about Catherine and Derzhavin, "the 'incomparably sagacious one' would have been quite surprised if someone suddenly told her that Derzhavin's service was inspired by the same idea as his poetry."[83]

Throughout his life, Khodasevich's Derzhavin was searching for manifestations of God, be they in miracles of nature, the monarch, or the law. But having passed through all these stages, toward the end of his life Derzhavin, in Khodasevich's view, returned to the idea of God in its purest form. A book, and a life, which began with the word "God" and reached its first poetic apex with the ode "God," also ended in the most appropriate manner—with a return to God.

Khodasevich's interpretation of "The River of Time," Derzhavin's last work, supposed that the poet was writing the greatest of his religious odes when he died; "the poem was only begun, but its continuation is not difficult to guess. In refusing historical immortality, Derzhavin must have been turning to thoughts of individual immortality—in God."[84] God, the monarch, and the law were the crucial categories informing Russian life in the eighteenth century, and thus the categories around which Khodasevich built his biography. They were also three of the categories missing, for better or for worse, from his own time.

One of the most powerful passages in all of *Derzhavin* is the description of how Derzhavin composed his masterpiece "God"—the only time in the biography that Khodasevich opened the curtain for his reader onto the poet's workshop. It is interesting to compare Khodasevich's rendition to his primary source, Derzhavin's *Explanations*, and his secondary source, Grot. First, the passage from Khodasevich:

> His heart yearned for isolation, and he decided to run. He suddenly announced to his wife that he was going to inspect his Belorussian lands, which he had never seen, although he had owned them for seven years. It was the worst possible traveling weather, and a long trip was ill-advised. His wife was surprised, but he gave her no time to collect herself. He galloped off to Narva, left his carriage and servants at an inn, rented a wretched little room from an old German woman and locked himself in. He wrote until sleep toppled him onto the bed, and, awaking, took up his work. The old woman brought him food. He worked in the same kind of wild isolation, the same frenzied straining of physical and spiritual strengths as did Cellini when he was pouring his Perseus. Thus it continued for several days. This was again a high ode. With trepidation Derzhavin himself felt the height of his soaring. He again piled up images and words like cliffs, and bringing together sounds,

> he himself reveled in their collision. In these lines it is not difficult to recognize the author of the Chitalagai Odes. But there he stood before us as a desperate apprentice, working at random, having remarkable successes, but in places simply spoiling the material; now this was an absolute master craftsman. It is not difficult to recognize the laconic author of the ode on the death of Meshcherskii in him. But now this laconicism had ceased to be fitful and awkward. In "God" Derzhavin brought into motion huge masses; just as huge was the strength spent in this endeavor, but not a single bit of it is wasted, and nowhere do we see the strain or effort. Such is his mastery over the material this time that from the beginning to the end everything in the ode moves smoothly and harmoniously, despite the fact that during the process of work he gradually leaves the original design. Inspiration possesses him, but he possesses the material.[85]

The main elements of this passage come from Derzhavin's own *Explanations* and *Notes*, sometimes through Grot's retelling of them. For the skeleton of the story, Khodasevich virtually quoted Derzhavin's commentary (the parts Khodasevich used, including the section on which the above passage is based, are italicized):

> The author received the first *inspiration* or idea for writing this ode in the year 1780, being *in the palace* at the night service *before Easter Sunday,* and on that day, *having arrived home, he put the first lines on paper;* but, being occupied with his *duties* and various *worldly activities, however much he tried,* he could not finish it, writing however at various times several couplets. Then in the year 1784, having been discharged from the service, he planned to set about finishing it, but again *because of city life* he was unable to; however he was incessantly impelled by an internal sensation and in order to satisfy it, *having told* his first *wife that he was going to his Polish villages to inspect them,* he set off and, *having arrived at Narva he left his carriage and servants at an inn, rented a small room in town from an old German woman with the understanding that she would also prepare his food;* where, *having locked himself in* he composed this *for several days,* but, not having finished the last couplet of this ode, *which happened already at night, he fell asleep before the dawn; he saw in a dream that light was sparkling in his eyes, he awoke, and indeed his imagination was so heated up, that it seemed to him that the light was racing along the walls,* and along with this *streams of tears poured* from his eyes; he arose and that very moment, in the illumination of the *oil lamp, he wrote this last stanza, finishing up by in fact shedding tears of gratitude for those notions which were given to him.*[86]

The fact that Derzhavin had never seen his lands comes from Derzhavin's description of these same events in his *Notes* ("he took it into his head to travel to his Belorussian lands in order, never having seen them, to inspect them").[87] It is there, too, that Derzhavin explained why he stopped at Narva; the roads were too bad to continue ("the road began to deteriorate"). This is an example of what Khodasevich meant when he wrote that he would have to footnote almost every line of his text. The second part of this description and much of what comes after, especially the interpretation of the ode, is also an example of Zorin's "psychological deciphering."

Khodasevich introduced the category of fate to understand Derzhavin's life when, describing one of Derzhavin's trips to Kazan, he wrote, "it was as if fate itself arranged it so that he again, already for the umpteenth time, proved to be Catherine's inconspicuous traveling companion."[88] In this sense, Derzhavin's life seems "fated." Other invocations of fate in the biography are more direct, as in Khodasevich's explanation for Derzhavin's winning streak at cards after the Pugachev rebellion: "Fortune paid him the extra sum that he was owed by his country."[89] Here Khodasevich was again operating within eighteenth-century categories and ways of interpreting events. *Fortuna* was one of the most popular of such categories, and no doubt Derzhavin and his contemporaries could have made a similar judgment about his sudden gambling successes. At the same time, we must remember that it was Khodasevich who was choosing the details for his crazy quilt, and his use of fate and God was not accidental. In narrating his story, Khodasevich manipulated the "laws" of God and fate to emphasize the heroic nature of his subject and to heighten the dramatic character of Derzhavin's life.

SYMBOLIC "RECASTING"

There are certain pivotal scenes in *Derzhavin* into which Khodasevich wove his own higher, symbolic meaning of events. A close reading of the final pages of the book both demonstrates this technique and ties together the two themes Khodasevich inserted into the pattern—the themes of God and fate. In the last powerful scene, Khodasevich narrated the discovery of Derzhavin's famous last poem and the poet's funeral.

> At three A.M., when the sun was already beginning to rise, and the birds were waking up, and a light fog still covered the fields, and the Volkhov, it seemed, had stopped in its current, Daria Alekseevna and Parasha entered Derzhavin's empty study. There in the daylight a candle lit by his hand still burned, and the clothing he had thrown off in the evening was still lying there. The prayer book was open to the page where he had stopped reading. Parasha took up the slate board—and on it was the beginning of an ode:
>
> Река времен в своем стремленьи
Уносит все дела людей
И топит в пропасти забвенья
Народы, царства и царей.
И если что и остается
Чрез звуки лиры и трубы,
То вечности жерлом пожрется
И общей не уйдет судьбы!

The river of time in its rushing
Carries away all earthly affairs
And drowns in the abyss of oblivion
Peoples, tsardoms and tsars.
And if anything does remain
Through the sounds of the lyre and trumpet,
Then it will be swallowed up in the orifice of eternity
And will not escape the general fate![90]

The poetic quality of Khodasevich's prose passage, with its rhyming pairs (*techenii/chtenie* [current/reading] echoing with Derzhavin's *stremlen'i* [rushing], and *svecha/s vechera* [candle/evening]) added significantly to the richness of the narrative. Following this section, Khodasevich summarized what he saw as Derzhavin's changing attitudes toward life, death, and immortality. In connection with "The River of Time" he remarked:

> Time for him was ending. [Derzhavin] began to think about what would be when it ends altogether, and the Angel, having sworn that *there will be no more time,* will tear the trumpet from Clio's hands and himself sound the horn, and the lyrical voice of Melpomene will no longer be audible.[91]

The book ends with a striking description of Derzhavin's funeral procession: a candlelit cortege with the poet's body sailing along the Volkhov River.

The river is a crucial image here, loaded with extremely rich symbolic meaning. It is the relentless river of time, carrying everything away into oblivion, including the poet's body. And yet, this river appeared to cease flowing: "the Volkhov, it seemed, had stopped in its current." Thus the pessimistic conclusion of Derzhavin's last poem was reversed and turned into an *exegi* (or rather *exegit*) *monumentum.*[92] But perhaps the stopped river was to mean something else, since it resonates with the words about Derzhavin's interest in the Apocalypse, when there will be no time, when the river of time will stop. And, indeed, as I have argued above, the author of *Derzhavin* was himself immersed in thoughts about an apocalypse, the Russian Apocalypse—the end of Russia and its literature.

What was Khodasevich's method for achieving such multidimensional symbolism and what was his purpose? The answer to this question lies in the individual components of the book's finale. Derzhavin's last poem about the river of time is a well-known fact and is certainly the appropriate end to an artistic biography. Khodasevich's words about Derzhavin's preoccupation with the end of time offer an example of a "psychological deciphering" based on sources (in this instance, the poem). The boat carrying Derzhavin's body along the Volkhov comes straight from the accounts of eyewitnesses.[93]

But the opening sentence of the conclusion ("At three A.M. when the sun was already beginning to rise, and the birds were waking up, and a light fog still covered the fields, and *the Volkhov, it seemed, had stopped in its current* . . ." [italics mine]) appears to be Khodasevich's contribution to the scene. And these lines were pivotal to Khodasevich's text, since they introduce the motif of the river. However, even in this instance Khodasevich was utilizing his sources, making almost a direct quotation from the memoirs of Parasha L'vova, Derzhavin's niece. She wrote: "It was three A.M.; the sun was rising in all its magnificence; not a cloud in the sky, everywhere a deep silence, a light fog still covered the fields, it was as if the Volkhov had stopped in its current, from all sides the birds sang and twittered." In Parasha's memoirs, the implication of these words was very different. She portrayed the magnificent morning only to emphasize her anguish: "But I could not enjoy anything: I would have rather that everything answered my grief."[94] And she did not quote Derzhavin's last ode; thus in her writings the stopped river was merely an element of the landscape, devoid of any higher meaning.[95]

In his reworking, Khodasevich released the descriptive potential of the source, but very carefully. He used Derzhavin's poem and the location of his estate and funeral procession on the banks of the Volkhov River to create a montage, a remarkably artistic picture, which, however, was constructed from beginning to end from the words and images of others. Drawing the image of Derzhavin, who in his mind represented a harmonious combination of life and art, Khodasevich tried to echo that combination, quilting the pieces of memoirs into a new textile that was all his own. With this biography of Derzhavin, Khodasevich chose to intervene in the cyclical process of history, even though he had doubts that his intervention could be successful. Interjecting human agency into a process normally governed by God and fate, Khodasevich reversed the pessimistic last ode of Derzhavin and emphasized again that while time had ended for the physical poet Derzhavin, the immortal poet lived on, and perhaps would be able to have an effect on Khodasevich's own time.

In his 1931 review of *Derzhavin*, Petr Bitsilli had written that "[i]t seems that it would be an act of violence against the material to write thus about any great artist of a later period."[96] Khodasevich's method of integrating the life of the poet and the life of the man, in the critic's view, would only work for a preromantic poet. What Bitsilli may not have realized was that he was making a prediction about Khodasevich's future success as a biographer; when Khodasevich finished *Derzhavin*, his contemporaries began to clamor for a similar book on the émigrés' central icon, Pushkin. But Khodasevich's method of biographical investigation was not suited to a work on Pushkin, and Pushkin could not be another hero such as Derzhavin. If Derzhavin could be a medicine for post-Chekhovian Russian society "beyond the border," then Pushkin was more of a poison.

Chapter Five

"Farewell to Pushkin": Khodasevich and His Pushkin

Но: восемь томиков, не больше, —
И в них вся родина моя.

Eight little volumes—nothing more,—
And in them is my entire homeland.
—Vladislav Khodasevich, 1923

Я был резов, ленив и вспыльчив, но чувствителен и честолюбив, и ласкою от меня можно было добиться всего . . .

I was naughty, lazy, and quick-tempered, but at the same time sensitive and ambitious; a kind person could have formed me any way he liked.
—Pushkin, from "A Russian Pelham," 1834–35 (VIII, 416)[1]

PARIS, JANUARY 17, 1935. An announcement in *Renaissance* (*Vozrozhdenie*) entitled "V. F. Khodasevich's *Pushkin*" reminded readers that the one hundredth anniversary of Aleksandr Pushkin's death was fast approaching, and yet no complete, up-to-date biography of the great poet had been written. In Soviet Russia, the authors asserted, no effort was being spared in preparing special editions of *Pushkinistika,* but any biography forthcoming from Russia would necessarily be flawed. The advantages of Soviet scholars with access to libraries and archives would be countermanded by the requisite "Marxist approach": "A biography of Pushkin that is constructed according to the canons of dialectical materialism, however carefully its facts have been checked, can never become the book yearned for by the Russian reader, who for so long and in vain has waited for the life of the great poet to finally be described."[2] There had been no decent book about Pushkin, but, according to this logic, Marxism would pervert any Soviet biography. Such a book, the announcement went on to claim, could only be written abroad, whence the locus of pure Russian culture had been displaced. And the best author for the job was Vladislav Khodasevich, who had studied Pushkin as a poet and a man for many years and who, in fact, had long been working on just such a book.

Like many other poets, critics, and intellectuals of his time, Khodasevich had a long-standing and well-developed relationship with Pushkin. Beyond his poetry, which was often sprinkled with allusions to Pushkin's lyrics and other works, Khodasevich was a teacher, critic, and scholar of Pushkin. His Pushkin activities included a course of lectures and classes on the poet for the Proletkul't organization in Moscow in 1918–19[3] and participation in the Pushkin commemorations in Petrograd in February 1921, at which he read his famous "Shaken Tripod" speech.[4] As David Bethea has pointed out, Khodasevich had plunged himself into Pushkin studies in the mid-1910s, perhaps to find in the order of his literary analyses what the chaotic life of war and Revolution-torn Russia lacked.[5] Khodasevich published a variety of articles and books about Pushkin before leaving Russia in 1922; he was to continue and amend his *Pushkinistika* while living abroad. Khodasevich's close connections with Pushkinists of all flavors—whether his friendship with Mikhail Gershenzon, his outspoken criticism of Vikentii Veresaev,[6] or his vicious literary and even legal disputes with Modest Gofman[7]—kept him in the forefront of the "Pushkinian text" of the 1920s and 1930s.

Khodasevich's long-term "Pushkin project" will be the focus of this chapter. Throughout the mid-1930s, Khodasevich continued to work on his book *Pushkin;* excerpts from the book appeared in the Paris newspaper *Renaissance* in 1932 and 1933, and it was in that paper that the final version was announced in January 1935. Although Khodasevich did not manage to complete the biography by the centennial date, he did publish two more excerpts from it in early 1937 in the Riga newspaper *Today* (*Segodnia*). In the anniversary year, instead of the promised biography, he came out with a reworked version of his 1924 book *Pushkin's Poetic Economy*, adding eight new essays and calling it *About Pushkin* (*O Pushkine* [1937]). In fact, although Pushkin, like Derzhavin, was a through-line in Khodasevich's thinking and writing about Russian poets and poetry throughout his career, Khodasevich never did finish what Zorin called "the book of his life," although he published several sections from it.

Below I will look at Khodasevich's Pushkin essays and consider portions of the fragmentary Pushkin biography, but more important I will address the question of whether Khodasevich or Pushkin was the reason for the "farewell to Pushkin." Was it Khodasevich who ran out of energy toward the end of his life, or who could not find the narrative key to Pushkin's life as he had to Derzhavin's? Or was there something about Pushkin himself that made his biography more difficult to write than any other, especially in the pre-1937 years of "social command"?

As I argued in the previous chapter, Khodasevich admired Derzhavin for the balance he had achieved between his life and his art. Pushkin, on the other hand, while representing the highest achievement of poetry, was not the "best poet." Pushkin's dissipation, slothfulness, rowdiness, and social insecurity, all of which Khodasevich would describe in detail in the portions of the biography which he did complete, kept him from being a successful, organically integrated man and poet as Derzhavin was. For Khodasevich, there was ultimately no usable past to be found in Pushkin. Great poetry was not going to save Russian culture in the twentieth century, but poets, on the model of Derzhavin, just might.

DERZHAVIN AND PUSHKIN

In his biography of Derzhavin, Khodasevich used other texts as intermediaries, most important among them Pushkin's *The Captain's Daughter.*[8] The heroes of the two books, Gavrila Derzhavin and Petrusha Grinev, share many qualities. Both Petrusha and Gavrila had similar upbringings in the provincial gentry, with home-tutored educations straight out of Denis Fonvizin's eighteenth-century play *The Minor* (*Nedorosl'*). In fact, Grinev was in part modeled on Derzhavin, a typical "minor" of his age, and even got his name from one of Derzhavin's comrades-in-arms during the Pugachev rebellion, Lieutenant Colonel Petr Grinev.[9]

Enlisted in the military by their fathers, both Derzhavin and the fictional Grinev ended up fighting in the tsarist army to defeat the Pugachev Rebellion, and their fates seemed tied to Pugachev and Catherine. Ultimately both had their fortunes decided—though Grinev's, to be sure, is the more "novelistic," à la Sir Walter Scott—through the direct intercession of Catherine herself. In fact, Khodasevich reminded his reader of Pushkin's novel and of the similarity between the heroes when discussing Derzhavin's proclivity for gambling:

> In those days, when one often had to await horses at a post station for a long time, even sometimes spend the night, station taverns were breeding-grounds of gambling and swindling. There shady characters lay in wait for travelers. In such a tavern, three years later, Captain Zurin would beat Petrusha Grinev [at billiards].[10]

Given the inherent drama of the age and the opportunity it provided for acts of honor and public heroism, and given the personalities of Derzhavin and Petrusha Grinev, there was no way these two could not have become spiritual brothers or even twins. As Khodasevich said of his hero:

> He grew up in the backwoods, was educated in the barracks and in roadside inns and in the fire of the *Pugachevshchina.* From infancy several hard and simple rules of faith and morality were instilled in him. . . . He could clearly

> distinguish between good and evil; he always knew about himself: this I do well, this I do poorly. In a word, his intellect was honest and his soul simple. Straightforwardness was his chief feature.[11]

Khodasevich's assessment of Derzhavin's character seemed to echo Grinev *père*'s famous words of advice to his departing son:

> "Goodbye, Petr. Serve your superior honestly; obey your commanders; do not chase after their favor; do not thrust yourself forward in service; do not shirk your duties and remember the saying: take care of your clothing while it is new and your honor while you are young."[12]

This typical eighteenth-century code of honor was common both to Derzhavin and to Pushkin's hero. The character of Grinev reproduced a historical type, and Pushkin was highly praised for this character by the prominent Russian historian Kliuchevskii, who felt that it was high time "minors" be rehabilitated after they'd been slandered by Fonvizin.[13] Khodasevich was praised just as highly for his character Derzhavin.

Khodasevich's rearrangement of Grot and Derzhavin created a figure who was both exemplary and typical of his age, just as Pushkin's novel did. But the fact that Khodasevich chose to write his biography of Derzhavin through a Pushkinian text offers an interesting twist on the problem of life and art in biography. According to Vladimir Veidle, a biographer must include the reality of invention along with the reality of existence when writing the life of an artist. What Khodasevich did in his first biographical project was to include Pushkin's art in Derzhavin's life.

The 1935 announcement of Khodasevich's *Pushkin* offered compelling arguments for the superiority of a Pushkin biography penned by Khodasevich: Khodasevich's fine biography of Derzhavin, his pedigree as a poet of the "Pushkin line," and his previous works on Pushkin made him the ideal Pushkin biographer for émigrés in the 1930s. But in addition to advertising the forthcoming book and its author, the announcement had another agenda which identified a major problem in the cultural diaspora:

> The difficult conditions of literary life abroad at the present time are such that the work begun by V. F. Khodasevich can only be completed if at least some portion of its publication will be secured in advance. With this goal in mind, we are announcing a preliminary subscription to the book, which will appear during the year 1936.[14]

Lack of money and of institutional support were yet another condition of émigré life and scholarship with which the émigré writers' Soviet counterparts were not faced. This parameter of literary life was an important one for Khodasevich, although not only for him. Put simply, to write one needs money, and money is hard to come by. In one private letter to his lawyer V. F. Zeeler, Khodasevich complained of his financial troubles, asking for a loan on the security of his wife's fur coat:

> I could explain this in much more detail—forgive me for my haste and my typographical errors: but I have to sit down this very minute to write another article, about the slow suicide of [Boris] Poplavskii and, perhaps, about the fact that suicide is the last refuge of a *writing* writer, that is to say, those who live by their writing and not through advertisements. (In 9 years I have written over 700 articles—*approximately 250,000 newspaper lines*—and the book on Derzhavin.)[15]

Thus the Pushkin biography project had a number of motivations, and Khodasevich had the ideal qualifications to write the book. He was a poet who had studied and been influenced by Pushkin all his life—a follower, disciple, or perhaps in a way successor to Pushkin; he knew biography writing and had produced a lovely and rigorous biography of Pushkin's immediate predecessor, Derzhavin; and, most important, it seems, for those who supported his efforts, he would be not be influenced by the ideological approaches which burdened his Soviet colleagues. If Pushkin was cultural territory over which the two Russian communities—Soviet Russia and the European Russian diaspora—were battling, then Khodasevich seemed to promise a brilliant career as a soldier for the émigré side, wielding his literary skills and creating the definitive Pushkin biography.

KHODASEVICH'S *PUSHKINISTIKA*

Khodasevich first approached Pushkin as a critic. Hence his "Pushkin project," if conceived broadly, began long before his attempts at writing the biography.[16] Indeed, one of Khodasevich's very first scholarly articles was about his poetic ancestor: the article "Pushkin's Petersburg Tales" (about "The Bronze Horseman," "The Queen of Spades" and "The Little House in Kolomna"), published in 1915, launched Khodasevich's friendship with Mikhail Gershenzon, when he sent it to the famous Pushkinist hoping for a response.[17] To Khodasevich, Pushkin's three tales about Petersburg seemed to stand apart from the rest of Pushkin's oeuvre like the islands of the canal-laced city from the center, but none of the attempts to analyze them had been able to actually "throw a bridge" across to the other islands/stories.[18] Khodasevich felt that he had found that bridge, and in his essay he argued that a story by a "Tit Kosmokratov"—"The Secluded Little House on Vasilii [Island]"—was the link between the Petersburg tales, the missing bridge that tied the themes, atmosphere, and style of the tales together.

The episode Khodasevich described, in brief, found Pushkin telling a tale at an evening party and so affecting the young writer V. P. Titov that, "having arrived home, he wrote it down. Then he took it to Pushkin, who looked the draft over,—and as a result the tale was published in Titov's edition, but with Pushkin's corrections, in *Northern Flowers*."[19] This is a familiar story, of Pushkin giving away ideas as he purportedly did to Gogol' with both *The Inspector General* (*Revizor*) and *Dead Souls* (*Mertvye dushi*). But in Khodasevich's rendition, the magnanimity usually associated with such gifts is missing. In his article, Khodasevich implied that Pushkin may not have been entirely pleased to give away his carefully constructed plot. And in restoring this tale to Pushkin as he did with the 1915 publication—in reprinting the tale, he attributed it to "Pushkin-Titov"—Khodasevich also argued that Pushkin took advantage of his inadvertent "gift," subsequently parodying it in his poem "The Little House in Kolomna."[20] The opening essay in the 1915 publication ended with a pronouncement of Khodasevich's future plans for *Pushkinistika:* "Instead of the tenuous connection of lyrical insights and inexplicable 'premonitions,' we propose to establish a direct and durable thematic and textual connection among the cycles of Pushkin's works."[21] Khodasevich's "lucky discovery" of Titov's tale would help him in his scholarly ambitions.[22]

His next book of essays was entitled *Pushkin's Poetic Economy,* which originally came out in two versions. Khodasevich serialized it in the Berlin journal *Colloquium* (*Beseda*) between 1923 and 1925, and in the meantime it was published in Leningrad in 1924. Khodasevich felt compelled to disavow the latter edition, lamenting it as full of errors. Nonetheless, the essays were clearly important to him. In addition, they not only form the basis for much of his Pushkin scholarship, but perhaps help to explain the ultimate failure of his Pushkin biography.

After emigrating Khodasevich embarked on a peripatetic life, staying in various rooms and apartments all over Europe before settling in Paris in 1926. He survived through his writing, publishing some poems and regular articles and reviews in such Russian-language newspapers and journals as *Contemporary Annals, Days, Latest News, Renaissance,* and *Today* (*Sovremennye zapiski, Dni, Poslednie novosti, Vozrozhdenie, Segodnia*), among others. The poet's last collection of poetry, *European Night,* which came out as a part of his 1927 *Collected Poems,* ended with the gloomy spectacle of impotence and night falling over the previously productive sower of grain. Almost exclusively a prose writer by the end of the 1920s, Khodasevich completed and published his literary biography of Derzhavin in 1931. He did not, however, write his dreamed-of biography of Pushkin. Already in mid-1932, as he wrote in a letter to Nina Berberova, Khodasevich felt he had bid his final farewell to Pushkin: "I think that this last flaring up of illness and despair were brought on by the farewell to Pushkin. Now on this, as on poetry, I have placed a cross. Now I have *nothing* left."[23]

The Russian scholar Irina Surat, in her book on Khodasevich as a Pushkinist, has suggested that the reason for the "farewell" is quite simple: she considers that a biography of Pushkin is more difficult to write than one about Derzhavin.

> It is obvious that to write a biography of Pushkin is immeasurably more difficult than Derzhavin's biography. If we add to that the atmosphere of the "European Night" which Khodasevich was breathing, if we remember the deep creative crisis which brought him to reject his poetic gift, then we can only be amazed at the obstinacy with which he returned again and again to this idea.[24]

But while for Khodasevich it does seem to have been true that the Pushkin biography was harder to write than the Derzhavin one, Surat's assumption is too easy. She suggests a cause-and-effect relationship: that Pushkin was a more complex poet than Derzhavin, and thus his life must be harder to write. In fact, the Derzhavin biography took precedence for Khodasevich for other reasons, perhaps mainly because Derzhavin—the strong, secure, confident builder and creator of the victorious eighteenth century—filled the role of a "positive hero" for the 1930s much better than the apolitical Pushkin would have.

ARTICLES ABOUT RUSSIAN POETRY

Articles about Russian Poetry, a little book published in Petersburg in 1922, contains five essays and was Khodasevich's first venture into literary criticism. The first essay, "Countess E. P. Rostopchina," was an early effort devoted to recovering a "once famed, now forgotten poetess,"[25] a project akin to his more serious rehabilitation of Derzhavin years later. In it Khodasevich acted the cavalier, defending the lady against her slandering detractors, among whom the most prominent was Belinskii. Even here, though, in this 1908 essay, Khodasevich was moving toward Pushkin and Derzhavin, moving in the direction of the poets whose lives and oeuvres came to occupy much of his own life and oeuvre. He chose to praise Rostopchina's creative output in the following terms: "Let those [who find such lyricism outmoded] at least now and then be touched by the light wings of holy simplicity and her sister—holy banality."[26] What Khodasevich valued in Derzhavin—the straightforward and often brusque nature of his poetry—and in Pushkin—his laconicism and simplicity—must exist on a flatter, more banal plane as well, and Rostopchina provided that "holy banality."

The second item in this collection was Khodasevich's 1916 article "Derzhavin (On the Centennial of His Death)," which contained the kernel of the later full-length biography to which I devoted my previous chapter. The poetic inspiration Khodasevich described so eloquently in his biography was in his early article subsumed to the laborer's steadiness; it seemed to the young Khodasevich that productivity could be as important as creativity. "Both as an administrator and as a poet, Derzhavin worked indefatigably."[27] But Khodasevich was already honing his skill in resuscitating the old man through descriptive characterization:

> If now, on the one hundredth anniversary of his death, he were to rise again and appear among us,—how angry he would become, that grouchy and restless old man . . . How he would gripe, how irately he would wrap his robe about himself, how he would pull his cap down over his bald pate, seeing what his fame had turned into,—fame, bought with years of work, worries, squabbles, sometimes humiliations—and with years of divine poetic soaring.[28]

In Khodasevich's portrayal the living Derzhavin—in all his grumpiness—stood before the reader as Veresaev's Pushkin, in Khodasevich's opinion, would not. The 1922 collection was rounded out by three more articles: "Pushkin's Petersburg Tales," "About the 'Gavriiliada,'" and "The Shaken Tripod."

Khodasevich turned to the poem "Gavriiliada" in 1917 in connection with its first Russian publication, "eighty-one years after Pushkin's death . . . without abridgement or omissions."[29] But this short essay, more so than the "Petersburg Tales" analysis, was the beginning of Khodasevich's Pushkin biography project. How, he argued, could the Russian reader understand Pushkin if this important poem was removed from the body of works? In Khodasevich's judgment, it was high time for Russian society to read all of Pushkin. And why was it, he wondered, that Pushkin scholars spent so much time seeking out and publishing the most insignificant fragments and letters from archives, when a whole poem such as "Gavriiliada" had until now been left out of the oeuvre?

Khodasevich described Pushkin's "Gavriiliada" as an important poem for Pushkin's work: "over which he toiled with perseverance, which reflected a number of remarkable characteristics of his work, which is so valuable for studying his biography and which, finally, is so wonderful in its spontaneous artistic charm."[30] The fact even this new publication of the poem in 1917 included a caveat ("the book is primarily for people who study Pushkin and not for a wider readership")[31] stirred Khodasevich's blood and prompted him to write the essay contesting the two adjectives traditionally applied to "Gavriiliada": sacrilegious and obscene. Instead, Khodasevich suggested that Pushkin at this stage of his life should be compared to the sixteenth-century Italian painter Veronese.

The spirit of the Italian Renaissance included a pagan joie de vivre and an admiration of the "devilish" charm of the world used to portray biblical themes;[32] Pushkin, in Khodasevich's view, felt these same joys as he wrote his poem.

> If we look a little closer at the "Gavriiliada," then through the shell of sacrilege we will see such a tender glow of love toward the world, toward the earth, such deep feelings for life and for the beautiful, that finally one feels compelled to ask: isn't this love itself religious?[33]

Ultimately, neither the charge of blasphemy nor of indecency should stick. Indeed, argued the critic, those of Pushkin's readers who were able to perceive more than just the plotline would discover the "flame of beauty," of Pushkin's admiration for beauty, by which the obscenities were cleansed from the poem. In this essay on "Gavriiliada" Khodasevich already began to draw his portrait of Pushkin—yes, perhaps Pushkin was throwing out a challenge to the world of Orthodox Christianity and of tsarist censorship, but he was also serious about representing the beauty of the world in poetry. The character whom Khodasevich hoped to feature someday in his biography was already beginning to take form in his critical articles. The problem that Khodasevich would have with that biography, however, was also beginning to take form. If beauty could save the world, then Pushkin might have a place in Khodasevich's usable past. But ultimately Khodasevich would find that "spontaneous artistic charm" was not a strong enough weapon against the forces with which Russian culture had to contend.

PUSHKIN'S POETIC ECONOMY

Khodasevich's second book of essays, *Pushkin's Poetic Economy,* was published in Leningrad in 1924, as Khodasevich wrote: "without my participation and in such an unheard-of, distorted version that I immediately came out in print denying all responsibility for its contents."[34] But while the little volume can be unwieldy (the lack of a table of contents alone makes it aggravating to read), it nonetheless deserves attention and discussion as a part of Khodasevich's Pushkin project.[35] The very title of the book is revealing both of Pushkin's poetic techniques and of Khodasevich's interest in them.

The essays are very uneven, sometimes expressing a whole thought but at other times merely providing a list: of poetic lines, or in one case even of quotes denoting possession of geographical places without commentary.[36] But while the temptation arises to consider the book to be simply unfinished, still in manuscript form, the fact that Khodasevich published it in a very similar form in Berlin proves that he did complete it. If we are discussing the fragmentariness of Khodasevich's Pushkin project throughout his career, then this book can be seen as a microcosm of that very incoherence.

The title of the volume lends a particularly valuable insight into the workings of Pushkin's creative process and Khodasevich's understanding of that process. "Economy," here the Russian word "*khoziaistvo,*" implies a variety of concepts, thus broadening and enriching the term "poetic economy" that Khodasevich coined. "*Khoziaistvo*" also offers room for punning with its synonym from a Latin root, "*ekonomiia.*" "*Khoziaistvo*" on its own implies housekeeping and management. It evokes the terms "*domashnee khoziaistvo,*" domestic economy, and "*sel'skoe khoziaistvo,*" literally village economy, or more commonly agriculture. Thus Khodasevich, in calling his book "Pushkin's '*poeticheskoe khoziaistvo,*'" was underscoring the domestic and management sides of a poetic oeuvre. Along with Khodasevich's assertion that "Pushkin is autobiographical through and through,"[37] an image of a pair of poetic bachelors arises—Pushkin was keeping his house in order, so to speak, through his poetry, and in his book Khodasevich wanted to examine in particular Pushkin's "poetic house" and "poetic household."

As mentioned above, this book underwent another transformation in 1937, when Khodasevich added eight essays and printed the whole thing again under the designation *About Pushkin.* Among other changes, he added titles to each of the essays. One title which sheds light on the discussion is "Berezhlivost," "thrift" or, again, "economy." The 1924 version of the essay began: "He was sometimes economical in the smallest things in his poetic household. Sometimes he kept one line, intonation, technique for ages—and knew exactly how to use it."[38] This poetic habit of Pushkin's does indeed recall the household economy; how long does a piece of string or other potentially useful item lie about the house, waiting for the moment when it will come in handy? In the 1937 version Khodasevich reworked this passage to be even more precise about Pushkin's "economy":

> He was thrifty and retentive of the smallest trifles in his poetic economy [*khoziaistvo*]. At times he kept one line, epithet, rhyme for ages and knew, finally, how to use it. It would be possible to give many examples of such economy [*ekonomiia*]. In most cases they don't say anything about him other than about his thrift [*berezhlivost'*].[39]

Khodasevich, too, turned out to be extraordinarily thrifty in his Pushkin project, reusing and rewriting essays from 1915 through 1939, returning to a theme or an idea over and over. Unfortunately for the twentieth-century critic, the domestic economy—selling a newspaper piece—tended to take precedence over the artistic economy—which would have preferred to save an idea until it was ready for public consumption or, better yet, until Khodasevich could complete his biography of Pushkin. Ultimately the book *Pushkin's Poetic Economy* suffers from the same fragmentariness that doomed his Pushkin biography. Under the conditions of exile abroad—those same conditions which assured Khodasevich's readers that he would be more objective in writing a biography of Pushkin than the Marxists across the border could be—Khodasevich's best work included his newspaper reviews and essays and the short essays of his *Necropolis* (*Nekropol'*). Any longer project suffered and perished in the chaos of émigré life.

"FROM THE BOOK *PUSHKIN*"

The Pushkin biography, when it did see print, of necessity appeared in fragments. Khodasevich published two series of articles "from the book *Push-*

kin": in 1932 through 1935 and in 1937.[40] The first series consisted of three "sections," entitled "The Beginning of Life," "Literature," and "Youth." Clearly Khodasevich was preparing this biography: it was advertised in 1935 as planned for publication in 1936. Although Khodasevich never completed the book, he did reprint two of the earlier sections in the Riga newspaper *Today* in the beginning of 1937: "Black Ancestors" ("Chernye predki," 27 January 1937) was a virtually verbatim reprint of most of "The Beginning of Life"; "My Uncle, the Man of Letters" ("Diadushka-literator," 2 February 1937) repeated "Literature," although it had been lengthened slightly.[41]

These *Today* publications are interesting for a number of reasons: for all practical purposes, Khodasevich seems to have been plagiarizing himself, but the republication of the articles under different titles suggests, first of all, that over the five years since their original publication he had not changed his mind about the narrative of Pushkin's life. This is an important fact in itself. The new versions of the articles, one edited and truncated, the other lengthened, also imply that the author saw the form of a newspaper article as fluid—he seemed willing enough to omit or cut a few "inches" for the sake of the pasteup—which supports the idea that the parts were eventually to fit into a whole, a real book-length biography. The fact that "My Uncle, the Man of Letters" was longer in the 1937 Riga version could mean one of two things: either *Renaissance* cut off the ending upon publication in 1932 or Khodasevich had written more in the intervening five years. The latter scenario would suggest that *Pushkin* did indeed continue to be a work in progress. Finally, the new subtitle to these 1937 articles, "From the book *Pushkin*, being prepared for publication," was even more emphatic than before about future plans for printing the book.[42]

The longest published section of the "book," "Youth" ("Molodost'"), is the one on which I will concentrate. The most finalized section of Khodasevich's biography, it also addressed one of the most important periods of Pushkin's life, the post-Lycée period of his youth. This four-part essay should form the fourth section or "chapter" of Khodasevich's biography, the first two being "The Beginning of Life" and "Literature" and the third, missing in print, being a chapter on Pushkin's Lycée years. The "chapter" of the Pushkin biography that Khodasevich entitled "Youth" was published in four installments over the course of several weeks, in Thursday and Sunday editions of *Renaissance* for March 9, 12, 16, and 19, 1933. The period of Pushkin's life covered in "Youth" runs from the spring or summer of 1817 (graduation from the Lycée) to May of 1820, when Pushkin headed south into "exile." In the following pages I will try to reconstruct a version of Khodasevich's Pushkin biography using the four sections of "Youth," the other two published chapters, and two unpublished manuscript fragments from the M. M. Karpovich papers at Columbia University.

"YOUTH," PART I (9 MARCH 1933)

In choosing the title "Youth" for this chapter of the biography, Khodasevich may very well have had in mind his own first book of poems, which also carried that title. Pushkin, at age eighteen, was making his debut into the world, just as Khodasevich had with the 1908 book of poems, which included his "youthful" output of 1905–7. A draft of a preface to that collection of poems read: "I feel clearly that one period of my life has ended. It did not last long. About four or five years have passed since my existence became deliberate. But these years will always remain in my memory infused with the blue light of the sadness of dusk, the pain of nightfall."[43]

Khodasevich delineated the same period, from about age eighteen, to describe Pushkin's youth—the early years of deliberate living. Khodasevich presented Pushkin's experience as filled with enthusiasm, love, friendship—and yet by the end of part II of "Youth," Pushkin, too, was as sad and filled with pain as the melancholy author of his biography had been.

Khodasevich began this essay with a description of the monarch Aleksandr I. Such a linking of the poet with the tsar seems appropriate for a number of reasons, not the least of which is Khodasevich's own interest in the connection between poets and poetry on the one hand and politics on the other. Aleksandr and his successor Nikolai I played important roles in Pushkin's life and both therefore deserved a place in Pushkin's biography. In addition, the essay was devoted to the year 1817, when Pushkin was completing the Lycée at Tsarskoe Selo—the Lycée originally created to educate the tsar's brothers.[44]

In the previous "chapter" of the biography ("Literature" or "My Uncle, the Man of Letters"), Khodasevich described Pushkin's blood relations. In that second essay, the young Pushkin learned to associate literature with a struggle, as he observed his "dear uncle" Vasilii L'vovich spoiling for a fight with the other camp, the Shishkovites. But it was not only literary lessons that Pushkin was learning; he also was finding his place in his own family. Khodasevich emphasized young Sasha Pushkin's isolation:

> Sasha understood, finally and thoroughly, that he had better keep away both from tutors and his mother. [His father] Sergei L'vovich had no interest in him at all.
>
> It turned out that the best feelings and thoughts should be hidden inside, protected from banal sympathy and rude curiosity.
>
> . . . with disgust and horror [his parents] became convinced (or convinced themselves) that the boy had a *perverse nature,* and perhaps they were only seeking a convenient opportunity to get him as far out of sight as possible.[45]

That opportunity came with the opening of the Lycée outside of St. Petersburg. In the longer, 1937 version of "chapter 2," Khodasevich showed

Vasilii L'vovich agreeing to take his nephew to St. Petersburg to try to get him enrolled in the Lycée. The relationship between the uncle and nephew gains a certain clarity with the lines missing in the published versions: two of Pushkin's aunts had put together a hundred rubles to give him "for nuts"—spending money while he was away at school. "He didn't manage to take those one hundred rubles all the way to Petersburg with him: Vasilii L'vovich borrowed them from him—but forgot to return them."[46] This uncle, who was to facilitate Pushkin's entry into the Lycée and later into the world of literature, would prove something of an embarrassment to Pushkin. Khodasevich used the anecdote about the spending money to suggest a reverse dependency between the two poets. Vasilii L'vovich—self-centered, self-important, and, in Khodasevich's words, a victim of the unrequited love for the muses of literature ("Literature")—would hardly prove the ideal uncle-mentor.

Having depicted a lonely and isolated young Pushkin in "Literature," though, Khodasevich left out the years from 1811 to 1817 by skipping to "Youth" for the next extant section of the biography. It is unfortunate, although perhaps significant, that Khodasevich did not publish what *should* have been chapter 3—the "Lycée" section of his Pushkin biography.[47] It would have been in that section that he could have offered Pushkin a better uncle figure for a poetic mentor—and one whose life he knew in the greatest detail, Gavrila Derzhavin. The examination in 1815 at which Derzhavin "anointed" his successor in Russian poetry is always an important scene in every biography of Pushkin. Khodasevich had dramatized the scene himself—in his biography of Derzhavin:

> A Lycée student of small stature, wearing a blue uniform with a red collar and standing two paces from Derzhavin, began to read his poetry. It is not possible to describe his emotions. When he got to the line where he mentioned the name of Derzhavin, his adolescent voice began to ring out, and his heart started beating with an intoxicating joy . . .
>
> Suddenly Derzhavin rose. His eyes were filled with tears, he raised his hands over the curly head of the boy, he wanted to embrace him—but he had waited too long: the boy had already run away, he was nowhere to be found. Under some mysterious influence, everyone was silent. Derzhavin called for Pushkin. They looked for him, but couldn't find him.[48]

Without the Lycée section of the Pushkin biography, we cannot judge how Khodasevich would have changed his approach in this work. He had already used Pushkin's memoirs—and therefore Pushkin's point of view—to stage the scene in *Derzhavin*, and he did the same in the draft Lycée chapter.[49] The identical elements would no doubt have been included in the next draft; indeed, they are present also in a short biography for a Berlin edition of Pushkin's collected works, where Khodasevich wrote: "On the eighth of January, 1815, at an examination Pushkin read his own poetry in front of the aged Derzhavin, who was touched and enchanted to the point of tears. He predicted a great future for Pushkin."[50] But in the published chapters of the Pushkin biography, Khodasevich stressed the presence of the tsar rather than of Derzhavin in Pushkin's life ("Youth," part I), the importance of 1817 and graduation rather than of 1815 and Pushkin's poetic apprenticeship. The links between Derzhavin and Pushkin were decidedly weakened in the later biography.

During the years that he was at the Lycée, Pushkin changed a lot.[51] He grew up, became a real poet, learned to love his friends and to love women. In the draft of the Lycée chapter Khodasevich emphasized precisely these points. On friendship:

> The Lycée students established a whole little world which lived according to its own anxieties, events, topics of the day, and it's no miracle that the relationships which arose here often lasted to the end of their lives. The love which tied Pushkin to his two comrades, the poet Baron A. A. Del'vig and I. I. Pushchin, subsequently a Decembrist, can serve as the highest model of human friendship, but it is explained not only by the personal qualities of these people: here also a significant role was played by those "Lycée commitments" which were so dear to Pushkin that they shed their light on other people too, considerably less worthy of his love.[52]

On love:

> Love for women, a feeling which was to play such a huge role not only in the life and work of Pushkin but even in his very death, also appeared first on the Lycée bench.[53]

And on poetry:

> But it seems that we will not be mistaken in saying that more and more frequently his thoughts turned to poetry, to which he would give himself so completely and selflessly later on.[54]

The Lycée became the family Pushkin had missed in childhood. But by 1817 Pushkin was ready for something new: "Much united him with the Lycée, and he was sad to part with his comrades. But a thirst for novelty was stronger than sadness in him."[55] So ended the draft Lycée chapter of Khodasevich's manuscript.

The country had also changed considerably between 1811 and 1817,[56] and Khodasevich portrayed that point through the behavior of the tsar. In 1817 Aleksandr Pavlovich attended the Lycée exam *po-semeinomu*—casually, like a member of the family, in contrast with the pomp and ceremony of what Khodasevich called the "before-the-storm days of 1811." At the opening of the Lycée, the emperor had arrived with his entire family as for a formal occasion. Now, six years later, Aleksandr no longer needed the trappings of his position to feel himself an emperor; having grown into his title, he could appear in a more casual way. Over the course of those six years he had not always been attentive to the Lycée, either; the two-year period of "leaderlessness" (*beznachalie*), when the first director of the Lycée had died and a new one had not yet been appointed, featured in Khodasevich's draft chapter as having an irreversible effect on the students.

> The unique life of the Lycée students had already taken shape. Its distinctive characteristic was that the pupils could not leave Tsarskoe Selo, within the confines of which, however, they enjoyed unlimited freedom. They were not conscientious about attending lectures, they engaged in love intrigues, befriended the hussars who lived nearby, organized feasts in the Lycée itself and hardly paid attention to their superiors at all.[57]

Thus the Lycée students, locked up together and secluded from their families, nonetheless experienced a kind of personal freedom which ill suited them for the civil careers they were to take up. And the tsar himself, their ultimate superior, appeared only on official occasions.

In "Youth," Khodasevich described the tsar with a list of adjectives and descriptive phrases, many of which contrasted him with his former self from the beginning of Pushkin's scholastic career at Tsarskoe Selo. Now, in 1817, Aleksandr I was "stout" and "bald," the "conqueror of Napoleon," the "liberator of Europe." He was a solid European ruler, and perhaps for that reason was "merry, gracious, and tender with all." Khodasevich compared Aleksandr Pavlovich to his grandmother Catherine the Great as well, describing him as having inherited from her the dimple in his chin and his "most good-humored, but ambiguous smile." The whole portrait suggests a kinder, gentler tsar, a kind of honorary uncle to the Lycée graduating class—well meaning, but preoccupied, and not entirely interested in the proceedings.

The involvement of the tsar in Pushkin's graduation ceremony seems symbolic of the poet's dual career as literary and government man, a duality that had fascinated Khodasevich in his Derzhavin biography. If Pushkin were to have taken the Derzhavinian path, then Derzhavin, the "patriarch of Russian poetry," would have been his literary father and Aleksandr his civil father. But the end of the 1810s differed greatly from the years of Derzhavin's debut on the literary and civil scene, and Pushkin's path differed as well. Khodasevich had already set up Pushkin's understanding of the literary world as one of conflict, struggle, even battle. Aleksandr I's mild disinterest in Pushkin and his classmates would be matched by a greater disinterest toward the civil service on the part of Pushkin.[58]

In contrast with Derzhavin, Pushkin seemed a poor citizen, if perhaps a greater poet. For Khodasevich, trying to emplot the events of the young Pushkin's life was more difficult than the events of Derzhavin's life, but not because Pushkin was more complex, as Surat has suggested. In contrast to Derzhavin, with his enthusiasm writ large for throwing himself into battle, service, and poetry, Pushkin seemed small and self-absorbed: plagued by indecision, frivolity, and sloth. Khodasevich quite simply found less to admire in the young Pushkin than he had in the young Derzhavin.

In the next scene in "Youth," Khodasevich described the physical act of Pushkin leaving the Lycée, the embarkation point for his journey into life. Khodasevich framed Pushkin in the archway of the school in a portrait-ready stance: "The door of the Lycée slammed shut for the last time—Pushkin walked out under the arch. Life opened out in front of him; he rushed to throw himself into its forceful whirlpool [*krugovorot*]."[59] Khodasevich presented the state of mind of the young Pushkin as he would that of any young man: filled with anticipation, anxious to join the rest of the world, poised to plunge into what he sees as the endless excitement of life. Life is presented as exciting but uncertain. In another draft Khodasevich implicitly compared the "little world" (*mirok*) of the Lycée with the great wide world outside:

> In June of 1817 Pushkin departed the Lycée, leaving it an acknowledged poet, a young man with less than distinguished academic learning but the considerable experience of a passionate heart, with a magnified sense of pride, with glittering hopes, with the beginnings of the poem "Ruslan and Liudmila" and with an indomitable thirst to see the free wide world.[60]

But life was not nearly as exciting as the new graduate had hoped: it was summertime, and Petersburg society had left town for the country.

In the summer of 1817, Pushkin, too, left town. Abandoning his position in the civil service, within a month he departed for a country estate—but, as Khodasevich stressed, the estate of his destination "was already not Zakharovo, so dear to his childhood memories. Zakharovo had been sold long ago."[61] Pushkin was going for the first time to Mikhailovskoe, the estate that would be the site of some of his greatest periods of creativity, but also the site of his exile and his betrayal by his father. It was the latter circumstance, Pushkin's strained relationship with his parents, that Khodasevich chose to focus on here. After six years away from home, Pushkin saw his family again. "The meeting with his parents was rather cold" (*kholodnovata*). The impersonal third-person plural construction, "Zakharovo davno prodali"—"[they] had sold Zakharovo long ago"—helps explain the coldness of reunion between parents and child; incapable of taking care of their household finances, Pushkin's parents were that much more inept at dealing with their eldest son.

Mikhailovskoe belonged to Pushkin's mother, and it was her relations who reintroduced Pushkin to family life after his years at the Lycée. The newness of life in the country, the bathhouse, the peasant girls singing and gathering strawberries, and the strawberries themselves, the habits and ways of the *Gannibalshchina*,[62] the Hannibal relations, who spent all their time visiting each other—all of this was interesting to Pushkin, and he greeted it all joyfully. Of the Hannibals, Khodasevich reported that "the *Gannibalshchina* led a disorderly, turbulent and hospitable life."[63] Khodasevich described the uncles, Petr and Pavel Isaakovich, as a blend of African and Russian characteristics: "African ardor was united in them with the breadth of the Russian nature." The last story of this summer vacation in the country was devoted to another Hannibal relation, Pushkin's grandfather Petr Abramovich, "the last of the black-skinned Hannibals," who seems at the age of seventy-five to have been a habitual drunkard with a tenuous grip on reality. According to Khodasevich, of all Pushkin's Mikhailovskoe impressions, this visit remained most vivid in his memory. Offered some homebrew by his grandfather, Pushkin "drank it without wincing and thence, it seemed, extraordinarily obliged the old Negro."[64]

"Country delights," however, could not entertain Pushkin for long, and he was drawn back to St. Petersburg. And it was Petersburg society upon which Pushkin cut his social teeth. For youth, at least Pushkin's youth as presented by Khodasevich, consisted primarily of these two things in unequal parts: family, the smaller part of one's occupation and impressions, and society, the major occupation, including drinking, dueling and damsels, mysticism and magic, politics and poetry. Khodasevich's chapter covered these two topics as well: in the country, family life, and in the capital, Pushkin's social groupings.

Friendship, love, and poetry: still the three categories into which Khodasevich divided Pushkin's pastimes. He introduced the Princess Golitsyna—"la princesse Nocturne," "la princesse Minuit"—as one of Pushkin's early infatuations. But Khodasevich argued in his Lycée chapter draft that Pushkin was interested in two kinds of women, two kinds of love: "In the history of Pushkin's early passions one can already note two tendencies which correspond to the two main flavors of his love: either spicy-sensual, filled with daring, cynicism and frivolity, or, on the contrary, reverent, ecstatic and shy."[65] Here, in Khodasevich's depiction, the princess is almost mythologized; she was a vessel into which a content was poured, the specific content that society needed. "Rumor ascribed to her an outstanding mind. Perhaps this was not precisely so. Perhaps her mind was primarily passive, that is, like many female minds, it was receptive to ideas which were raised by others."[66] Pushkin, Khodasevich was arguing, was an enthusiast, and Golitsyna a temporary object of that enthusiasm. Throughout this chapter Khodasevich emphasized this side of Pushkin: his ardor and his passion. Indeed, Pushkin visited not only the salon of the princess Nocturne; "rushing to live, hastening to feel, avidly desiring to see, finally, the *beau monde*, he became an ardent visitor of many salons and [even] simple private evenings."[67]

"It is possible to call the state of society of those times feverish," Khodasevich wrote.[68] Pushkin, too, was infected with this fever. However,

Khodasevich introduced a note of seriousness in examining the Pushkin family as an example of how the aristocracy had changed during Aleksandr's generation. Sergei L'vovich and Vasilii L'vovich, Pushkin's father and uncle, were "frivolous and good-humored"; "they . . . did not so much strive for wealth as try to hide their poverty."[69] Aleksandr Sergeevich was a different matter:

> The son of Sergei L'vovich was not frivolous and not good-humored. He expressly remembered that the Pushkin line led back to the times of Aleksandr Nevskii and that when the Romanovs were elected, "6 Pushkins signed the electoral document and two put their hands to it because they knew not how to write." Their literate descendant considered the Romanovs "ungrateful."

Pushkin took his own political rights more seriously than the previous generation had. Poetry and politics were becoming inextricably linked. The circle opposing the government was "widening," wrote Khodasevich, embracing not only the army and not only the young. An epigram which Khodasevich quoted, attributed in a variety of editions over the years to Pushkin, ironically foreshadowed this process:

> Желали прав они—
> права им и даны:
> Из узких сделали
> широкими штаны.
>
> It was rights they desired—rights they acquired:
> Their thin pant legs were changed for wide.[70]

The tsarist government, feeling victorious and strong, did not take the political mood of its citizens seriously, just as Aleksandr I had not taken his Lycée graduates seriously. But, Khodasevich noted, Pushkin's generation was not the fashion-minded frivolous generation to which his father and uncle belonged.

Young officers, of course, formed the core of the "opposition," and Pushkin was quick to give them a nickname: "not delving too deeply into the details of their political thinking, which were still shaky and vague, he called them the 'society of the clever' for the direction of their thoughts."[71] Pushkin was interested in these thoughts, vague though they might have been at first.

> The efforts of "the clever" answered his hidden aristocratic claims, his Europeanism, and finally, his subdued but zealous ambition. They were his teachers in the "rebellious science," and this science at times penetrated his heart more deeply than it did the hearts of the teachers themselves.[72]

In a few succinct phrases, Khodasevich identified the main characteristics of his hero: "he was almost devoid of the instinct of self-preservation"; "he was both slave to and admirer of his own personal passions"; "his soul was open . . . with youthful credulity." This first part of Khodasevich's essay presented to the reader a young man wanting to fit in, searching for his own place, and not finding it in his family or his work (about which Khodasevich wrote virtually nothing). In the social circle he wanted to join, Pushkin was like a younger brother hanging around, tolerated but not taken seriously by those whom he tried to emulate. "They did not pay too much attention to him. They valued his talent and his wit, not attaching much importance to either."[73]

Khodasevich, however, was already ready to make a pronouncement as he ended his first installment, adding a fourth category to his description of the young Pushkin's life—politics: "Let's speak plainly: he was to some degree in love with these people.[74] He was eager to buy their approval and acknowledgment at any price. And this decided his fate for many years to come—perhaps for life."[75] On this important threshold, Khodasevich's Pushkin chose politics along with poetry—perhaps with the wrong reasons, but nonetheless he chose to meld the two, serving politics with his poetic muse. But although the outcome of this juncture resembled the seamless continuum of life and art which Derzhavin represented for Khodasevich, the motivation was not nearly as heroic.

"YOUTH," PART II (12 MARCH 1933)

Having left his readers hanging until Sunday, Khodasevich began the second installment of his essay by introducing the "society of the rowdy." The contrast between the "society of the clever" and "society of the rowdy" makes an amusing linguistic play in Russian: *obshchestvo umnykh* and *obshchestvo shumnykh*—the serious liberal thinkers changed into loud, flighty, drinking, and gallivanting young men by the single sound "sh". But Pushkin by character really belonged neither to "the clever" nor "the rowdy," though he associated with both and was torn by his desire to belong to each group.

Khodasevich presented the young dandies of Petersburg, the "rowdy" crowd, using one of his favorite techniques: the list. Preeminent among these young men was Kaverin, who was included among the "clever" as well.

> Wealthy and attractive, he was famous for knowing neither defeat nor fatigue in his sacrifices to Venus and Bacchus. He treated his French illness with cold champagne, in the morning instead of tea drank a bottle of rum with his bread, and after dinner instead of coffee—a bottle of cognac.[76]

Khodasevich continued down the list, describing various of their characteristics, mainly centering around women and wine (although one young man reputedly loved to exclaim, "The best woman is a boy, and the best wine—vodka!"). Pushkin, Khodasevich asserted, "couldn't take his eyes off the 'clever.' But he joined up with the 'rowdies,' because their company was more accessible to him, and besides, he was drawn to them by temptation. His life became disorderly."[77] Another aspect of the life of the capital was the theater: "the theater was at this time fashionable [and] the plays staged were deemed to be first class, performed by first-class actors."[78] Pushkin was gradually being drawn into a society which did not necessarily answer his spiritual needs and which he definitely could not afford. Khodasevich exploited the contrasts between two "Petersburg dandies," Aleksandr Pushkin and "his friend, Evgenii Onegin":

> Between them was only that truly *devilish* difference (his beloved expression), that Onegin's wealthy relatives, whose only heir he was, kept dying. . . . Pushkin was poor, lived with his parents, argued over kopeks and had to buy his own candles to light his room; when he feasted, as in *Evgenii Onegin*, on "truffles, Strasbourg pie, Limburger cheese and pineapple," "Kaverin and Onegin had to pay."

Khodasevich described Pushkin's early life in Petersburg with irony: "unattractive, poorly dressed, destitute, he lived precisely among the most wealthy, well-dressed, dazzling people of the capital."[79] Pushkin perceived his poverty as humiliating; somehow, to make up for it, he had to drink more, duel more frequently, be wilder and rowdier than anyone. Again, if we contrast this portrait with Khodasevich's portrayal of the impoverished but serious and hardworking young Derzhavin, Pushkin seems the smaller and less heroic man.

As Khodasevich ended part II of the essay, leaving his newspaper readers hanging again until the next Thursday, he painted a picture of Pushkin which constituted a stark contrast with the promising life that had unfolded before the Lycée graduate as he stood beneath the archway in Tsarskoe Selo. His life was now "disorderly," a muddle. And Khodasevich summed up:

> Thus, in pursuit of the sweetness of life, he drank its bitterness; with a smile on his lips he was deeply unhappy; in the circle of his friends he was insulted and humiliated. How can we know? Perhaps this playboy, duelist and swashbuckler sobbed at night in his room from impotent resentment, as he had wept at the Lycée? But now his dear Zhanno Pushchin was no longer just beyond the wall to console him.[80]

This passage, using as in *Derzhavin* Khodasevich's method of historical interpretation, his "psychological decoding" and linking of events, links the essay back to the missing Lycée chapter—familiar to his readers only from their outside knowledge of Pushkin's biography. It also forms a link to another published essay by Khodasevich, "Yard—Snow—Little Bell" ("Dvor—sneg—kolokol'chik," in *Pushkin's Poetic Economy* and *About Pushkin*), about a visit by Pushchin to Pushkin, and to those other collections of essays about Pushkin that ultimately had to take the place of a completed biography. It was certainly possible for readers to piece together a kind of "metabiography" of Pushkin from Khodasevich's many essays, but it remained impossible for Khodasevich to piece that biography together himself.

"YOUTH," PART III (16 MARCH 1933)

Khodasevich began the third installment of his "chapter" "Youth" in media res: "In the beginning of 1818 he caught cold."[81] Khodasevich's sentences often seem to be specifically crafted to have a certain effect, an effect often countered by that of the following sentence. "For about two weeks he was between life and death."[82] Pushkin almost died, here, at the age of eighteen! Suddenly this pronouncement, so casual and matter of fact, seemed important—and, true to his understated style, Khodasevich took his reader in another direction immediately. First, the medical details: he was treated with ice baths. Then the final conclusion: confined to his bed, away from the vanities and superfluous social requirements of life, "now he found time to work again on 'Ruslan and Liudmila.' . . . Perhaps his habit of working in bed dates from this very time."[83]

Here for the first time in this series of essays Khodasevich referred to Pushkin's writing, to his actual creative work. And except for a detailed description of the writing of "Freedom: An Ode" ("Vol'nost'. Oda") and "The Village" ("Derevnia"), this is practically the only "working" Pushkin the reader sees in Khodasevich's biography. Annenkov spent six pages on the publication of "Ruslan and Liudmila" and reactions of critics and friends to the poem.[84] Khodasevich barely mentioned it. In the extant parts of the biography, it seems that Khodasevich was more interested in the experience of youth and youthfulness and in the process by which Pushkin became his own man than he was in the poetry and the poetic process. Pushkin as creative genius was virtually absent. Could Khodasevich simply not figure Pushkin out? Or was this a specific choice, like Bulgakov's choice to leave Pushkin out of his play about Pushkin in 1937?

Perhaps Khodasevich felt that literary criticism had its place elsewhere. In the biography, he presented Pushkin in his relations with others, rather than alone, creating his works. This is an important question faced by all the authors writing about Pushkin in this period: how to present Pushkin's life and his art. Especially in light of Khodasevich's fury over Veresaev's choice—Pushkin in life without any reference to his art—it seems odd that Khodasevich made a similar decision in his Pushkin biography.[85] In his literary criticism, Khodasevich did explore the autobiographical aspects of Pushkin's creative works, plots or motifs whose genesis could be traced to events in Pushkin's life. For example, in the essay "An Argument with His Father" ("Ssora s ottsom") he wrote: "The autobiographical element in 'The Miserly Knight' ['Skupoi rytsar'] has been noted long ago. I simply wanted to show through a concrete example from what angle Pushkin sometimes reflected the real events of his life in his works."[86] Mostly, though, in his Pushkin biography Khodasevich avoided the art. It may be that the literary criticism was one of the reasons Khodasevich did not complete his biography; another outlet for his Pushkin thoughts, his essays kept him from focusing on the biographical project.

According to Khodasevich, Pushkin very much wanted to be invited into the secret society, the Union of Prosperity (Soiuz blagodenstviia)—and was not. When in part III of "Youth" Khodasevich described Ivan Pushchin's membership in the union,[87] he discussed the reasons for Pushkin's rejection as well:

> "But complete trust in him was lacking."[88] They didn't trust Pushkin. Of course, it didn't occur to anyone that he might turn traitor. But they feared his flightiness, his unstable character and—even more bitterly for him—they did not believe in the staunchness and depth of his very views. His intimacy with the rowdies embarrassed and even angered the "clever ones." Oh, if only they knew that they themselves were partially the reason for it![89]

Throughout this section and the previous one, Khodasevich portrayed Pushkin as a young man in search of a circle: his "rowdy" friends were too shallow for him; his serious friends doubted his trustworthiness and sincerity. The most logical group of people, fellow writers, also did not offer Pushkin the "home" he was seeking. Khodasevich quoted a historian about the Arzamas reaction to Pushkin's coming of age:

> "The members of Arzamas regarded the young Pushkin's graduation from the Lycée as a happy occurrence for them, as a celebration. Especially Zhukovskii seemed happy, as though God himself had sent him a dear child . . . The older brothers competed in spoiling the young brother."[90]

Even in the literary society that could have become his home and family, Pushkin was not an equal among equals, but a spoiled and beloved babe and a genius requiring homage. Here also he did not fit in—and Arzamas was practically defunct by this time anyway. Where was he to find the warmth, the intellectual stimulation, and the fun, which he so desperately needed in his youth? His Arzamas "older brothers" tried to influence his behavior; as Khodasevich wrote, "Zhukovskii and Aleksandr Turgenev rejoiced at each of his poetic successes and were horrified at his way of life."[91] Pushkin came to them and to Karamzin to regale them with tales, to tell them "where he had not slept all night long,"[92] but he hardly listened to their remonstrances.

And then, in symbolic "light" and "hope," the circle called the "Green Lamp" arose, growing, according to some, out of semiorgiastic gatherings at one member's home. The green oil lamp in the center of the table shed light on the gathering and offered a rallying point for the young men around it, who read aloud drunken poems about wine and women, and more often lines "against the sovereign and the government."[93] The gatherings were infused with the "spirit of liberalism" and the topic of conversation was potential forms of a new society. Under the guise of drinking and carousing, Khodasevich suggested, a filial of the secret society was forming, a "'free' society, not a direct part of the union, made up of people being prepared for it or 'intended to serve only as instruments.'"[94] These people were, according to the statutes of the Union of Prosperity, not to know "by whom and whence their thoughts and actions were being directed."[95] Khodasevich ended his story here with the irony of Pushkin's belonging and not belonging: "Pushkin, having striven in vain to join the secret society, was drawn into its orbit without knowing it himself. He was not being prepared to be a member, as he was not trusted. But he could be a splendid 'instrument'—and already was one."[96] In his quest for a circle that would match all his interests and appetites—intellectual, spiritual and physical—Pushkin remained on the edge of several groups, but in the "Green Lamp" he found what he was looking for, more so even than he himself knew.

"YOUTH," PART IV (19 MARCH 1933)

In this last Sunday installment of the chapter "Youth," Khodasevich was tying up loose ends before sending Pushkin south to his first exile in the Crimea. Khodasevich touched on all the important themes of previous parts of this "chapter" and of the biography as a whole: Pushkin and his comrades, Pushkin and poetry, Pushkin and society, Pushkin and the tsar, Pushkin and his literary predecessors, Pushkin and his literary mentors.

The chapter began with a reiteration of the "Green Lamp" theme; this circle was precisely what Pushkin had been missing in his life: "the Green Lamp fit his proclivities and his tastes. . . . It was simultaneously clever and rowdy. In its cleverness there was unruliness, and in its unruliness—wit."[97] Mental stimulation, physical distraction, boldness and support: these qualities were what the young Pushkin was seeking, and he in turn played the role into which he had been cast—as an "instrument" of aggression against the status quo.

Two poems especially were effective ammunition, striking a dual blow at the regime. In "Freedom: An Ode," Khodasevich suggested that Pushkin was purposely following Radishchev, finding the inspiration for his subject matter in the eighteenth-century radical reforming thinker, but in his style he was more influenced by another predecessor—Derzhavin, the radical reforming poet. In the summer of 1819 Pushkin retreated to Mikhailovskoe to recover from yet another bout with fever and there wrote "The Village." Called by Khodasevich "the most powerful piece hitherto written against serfdom,"[98] "The Village" underscored Pushkin's debt to and parallel with Derzhavin. Khodasevich pointed out that, just as he had with Derzhavin in the first years of his reign, Aleksandr I thanked the poet for his work and forbade its publication. But Pushkin was already being copied and handed around; he became an underground poet now, and his fame began to build. "This was precisely that propaganda of which he was to be an instrument," wrote Khodasevich.[99] Stories about Pushkin spread, and along with them apocrypha; he himself did nothing to prevent their scope.

More than anything, Khodasevich contended, Pushkin wanted fame, and he was not particular about what kind of fame:

> He wanted fame and did not hide that fact. He knew that it has unpleasant sides—and was prepared to accept them. He called upon others to be amazed at him, in any way they could. Some admired him as the author of "Ruslan and Liudmila," others as a discriminating libertine, still others as the singer of "Freedom," and yet others simply as a drunkard. He himself fostered all these kinds of fame.[100]

This multisided personality was what Pushkin's contemporaries saw, and what Khodasevich was presenting to his readers: not Pushkin the poet-genius, but Pushkin the vainglorious and vulnerable young man. He was an unwitting instrument of the "Union of Prosperity" as he tested the boundaries of public, private, and imperial tastes. "At home he would get scolded. 'No one ever distinguished himself from the crowd without some noise, he would answer.'"[101] He was both intelligent and rowdy, and he was stubborn; he *would* have his effect on society.

If it was distinctiveness that Pushkin strove for, he achieved it. Among rumors about him arose one that insulted him deeply: that he was called into a secret office and whipped for his antigovernment writings. The rumor, Khodasevich noted, was believed by everyone—friend and foe. When it reached Pushkin, he became enraged at his own humiliation. Should he kill himself? kill the tsar? "Then he decided to become as audacious in his compositions and speeches as it would take to force the government to treat him like a criminal. He thirsted for Siberia as a means of redeeming his honor," Khodasevich wrote.[102] Pushkin's personal pride and his pride as an aristocrat could not bear the rumor of whipping, though the rumor lacked any foundation in truth. In characterizing the hero of his piece, Khodasevich spared no paint in portraying Pushkin's highly vulnerable self-esteem.

Tsar Aleksandr himself had already noticed the poet; meeting Engel'gardt, the director of the Lycée, in the gardens at Tsarskoe Selo, the tsar complained: "Pushkin has flooded Russia with outrageous poems."[103] And so Pushkin got what he wanted: a rumor of an impending search, the burning of manuscripts, the search, the arrest. "Pushkin was threatened with Siberia or penitence on the Solovki Islands," Khodasevich reported.[104] Almost immediately, Pushkin's literary mentors and "elder brothers," Karamzin, Zhukovskii, Chaadaev, and Gnedich, began to try in various ways to influence the tsar; and indeed, instead of Siberia or Solovki, Pushkin was allowed to go to the Crimea with the Raevskii family, officially merely transferred to another branch of the Ministry of Foreign Affairs where he served.

Khodasevich was always interested in the relationships between writers, and this exile gave him a chance to explore Pushkin's relationship with Karamzin. He described how Karamzin, the eldest of elder brothers and the one whom Pushkin had offended on several occasions, in person and by epigram, made Pushkin pay for his help. Khodasevich quotes three examples of Karamzin publicizing his coldness and disapproval toward the younger poet; in letters to Dmitriev and Viazemskii he emphasized Pushkin's youth and immaturity ("no doubt in the future he will be more prudent")[105] as well as his cowardice: "Pushkin, who suffered for several days very unpoetic fear due to his poetry about freedom and some of his epigrams, gave me his word that he would quit town."[106] At the same time, Karamzin showed the place in his study that was flooded with Pushkin's tears to another acquaintance. Khodasevich, in emphasizing Karamzin's displeasure, was implying that Pushkin really had been a mad youth, imprudent and even rude.

Khodasevich's chapter "Youth," which began by discussing the familial relationship of the friends at the Lycée, their teachers, and their "uncle" the tsar, ended with another family. Pushkin had severed virtually all ties with his blood family—at one point on the last page of the essay Khodasevich had Pushkin show up at his father's house with a pistol in his hand to defend his own honor against the rumors his father had believed and the disapproval he had expressed. These three years of youth had ended, and Pushkin left for the south prepared to start a new phase of life.

> He was leaving in a mood of deep calm, similar to that pleasant feeling of health that he had felt after his first illness. . . . It seemed to him that youth was over and even that he would no longer write poetry. He was so extremely tired that he imagined that he was escaping Petersburg of his own free will—to the new, unseen lands which beckoned his imagination.[107]

According to Khodasevich, Pushkin was leaving his rowdy friends without a thought, even parting easily with Chaadaev. He had no thought for women ("his heart was empty, or almost empty"),[108] and he was glad to go. So on the fifth of May, 1821, Pushkin received his passport, and on the sixth he was already in his carriage. As the essay ends, Pushkin changed his clothing into a red Russian shirt and a felt cap. "It was a terribly hot time," the biographer added.[109]

The main themes of Pushkin's youth were carried through Khodasevich's four-part essay "Youth": friendship, women, and poetry. The most surprising thing about this poet's biography of a poet was the degree to which Khodasevich did not dramatize the writing Pushkin. But I would argue that his readers might have predicted such an approach from knowing the Derzhavin biography; as a biographer, Khodasevich was more than anything *measured.* In *Derzhavin* Khodasevich saved the creating scene for what he saw as the high point in Derzhavin's poetic career, the ode "God." With the Pushkin biography, he may also have been saving that scene for a more climactic point in the poet's career. It is for his readers to regret that Khodasevich's biography of Pushkin ended with Pushkin's youth. We can only speculate about what the rest of the biography might have contained and about which poetic moment in Pushkin's creative life Khodasevich considered the apex.

NO FINAL FAREWELL

Vladimir Veidle wrote that "Khodasevich is linked with Pushkin as with no other Russian poet, and no other Russian poet is linked with Pushkin as is Khodasevich."[110] Here Veidle was writing of Khodasevich's poetry—but not only. If we follow Khodasevich's career as a *scholar* and *critic,* we see that Pushkin was equally central to those projects as he was to Khodasevich's career as a poet.

Scholars often note the "mythical" connection between Khodasevich and Pushkin through their "muses," their Russian peasant nurses. Arina Rodionovna, Pushkin's nurse, became as essential to Khodasevich as she was to Pushkin. Khodasevich's poem which revealed the connection, "Not by my mother, but by a Tula peasant woman," gave us Khodasevich's "poetic biography"; David Bethea has even interpreted the poem as identifying Khodasevich's poetic parents as Aleksandr Sergeevich Pushkin and the wet nurse Elena Aleksandrovna Kuzina.[111] Thus Khodasevich, the son of a Polish father and Polish Jewish mother, brought up in his mother's adopted Catholic faith to love her national poet, Adam Mickiewicz, found in the breasts of his self-sacrificing simple nurse the milk of his homeland, Russia, to which he had no blood claims.

Не матерью, но тульскою крестьянкой
Еленой Кузиной я выкормлен. Она
Свивальники мне грела над лежанкой,
Крестила на ночь от дурного сна.

. . . .

И вот, Россия, "громкая держава,"
Ее сосцы губами теребя,
Я высосал мучительное право
Тебя любить и проклинать тебя,

В том честном подвиге, в том счастьи песнопений,
Которому служу я в каждый миг,
Учитель мой—твой чудотворный гений,
И поприще—волшебный твой язык.

И пред твоими слабыми сынами
Еще порой гордиться я могу,
Что сей язык, завещанный веками,
Любовней и ревнивей берегу . . .

Not by my mother, but by the Tula peasant woman
Elena Kuzina was I reared. She would
warm my swaddling-clothes above the stove-bench,
ward off bad dreams at bedtime with the sign of the cross.

. . . .

And so Russia, you "renowned power,"
by pulling at her teats with my lips,
I sucked out the agonizing right,
to love and curse you;

in that honorable feat, in that happiness of poetic song,
which I serve each moment,
my teacher has been your wonder-working genius
and my walk of life your magical tongue.

And still at times I can be proud
before your weak sons
that this language, bequeathed through the ages,
I guard more lovingly, more jealously . . .[112]

This poem, begun in 1917 and finished in March of 1922, was one of Khodasevich's two important autobiographical statements. Here, while still in Russia, he seemed to foretell his future exile and need of a refuge, his need to guard jealously the Russia he knew and loved. Khodasevich's identification of the quality of "Russian-ness" with the Russian tongue marked him as a "stepson to Russia" and highlighted one of the tragedies of exile for Russians after 1917.

The poem shares the autobiographical shelf with Khodasevich's essay "Infancy." As I noted in the previous chapter, it was in this essay that Khodasevich ironically connected himself with the Russian poet about whom he was able to complete his work, the other "touchstone" for Khodasevich: the eighteenth-century poet Gavrila Derzhavin. In his obituary for Khodasevich, Georgii Adamovich wrote that Khodasevich "judged all literary phenomena as if 'through Pushkin,'"[113] and Surat, among others, has commented that no matter about whom Khodasevich was writing, whether it be Nabokov, Tsvetaeva, Pasternak, Tolstoi, or Tiutchev, Pushkin turned out to be the point of departure, the measure of truth, depth, and perfection.[114] But there is a difference between judging literary phenomena and judging poets. Pushkin represented the highest achievement of poetry, but not of being a poet. That distinction belonged to Derzhavin.

Irina Paperno has argued that writers of the Silver Age—including Khodasevich—tried to find their own "genealogical" connections to Pushkin.[115] But Khodasevich demonstrated an interest in connecting his own age to Derzhavin's—and throughout the extant chapters of the Pushkin biography, of connecting Pushkin's early career with Derzhavin as well. If Derzhavin was the beginning of Russian literature and Khodasevich was the end, then Pushkin should have been the center that held them together.

It is worth considering, however, that Pushkin was not that center which held Russian culture together, that for Khodasevich Pushkin and his era were already the beginning of the end. That dynamism and energy which Khodasevich sought to renew for his own age through his touting of Derzhavin was in Pushkin directed either toward creative work—which in his biographical fragments Khodasevich was unable to portray—or toward a frivolous attitude to life which was no model for Russians facing the "twilight of art."

In her book *Khodasevich the Pushkinist* Surat set as her goal "to discover the hidden connection between the professional Pushkin studies of Khodasevich and his poetic fate."[116] She began and ended her book with Pushkin's poem "The Prophet." Belief in the mission of the poet, she asserted, allowed Khodasevich to live and create; his loss of faith in Pushkin as prophet and the role of the poet as prophet generally in the twilight of European art signaled his giving up not only on his own poetry, as he had done some years earlier, but on his life as well. One contemporary review of the 1937 book *About Pushkin* lamented that "each of these essays is a chapter of that unwritten creative biography of Pushkin, whose absence we so regret."[117] In praising the new essays added to *About Pushkin*, the critic still felt compelled to push Khodasevich to finish his biography: "Khodasevich could only complete his Pushkin assignment by writing some kind of synthetic work—a creative biography of Pushkin." Mark Aldanov's obituary of Khodasevich two years later sang the same lament:

> How sad that he never wrote the life of Pushkin! . . . He said that he had suddenly found himself without the most necessary sources, that you can't put all of Pushkin's life into one volume, that such a book could only be written in Russia, that he would need two years to write it. All of this was true. But I think that he could have overcome the accidental and outward obstacles. It is more likely that he saw such work as too crucial, requiring too much spiritual exertion. He put it off until better times—as, it seems, did Gershenzon. This loss is irreparable.[118]

Certainly Khodasevich felt a lot of pressure from his contemporaries; everyone expected him to complete "his Pushkin assignment" with the biography of Pushkin. The existence of draft manuscripts from as early as 1921,[119] the publications on Pushkin through the 1920s, the chapters from 1932 and 1933 reprinted in 1937, and such articles as "Pushkin and Nikolai I," published in *Renaissance* on the 101st anniversary after Pushkin's death, when the centenary commemorations had drawn to a close, suggest that Khodasevich was trying to answer the "social command." And even though by gathering together the collection *About Pushkin* to fulfill the terms of the 1935 subscription drive Khodasevich acknowledged a barrier which was preventing him from completing the biography, his publications in 1937 and 1938 argue for his not actually having said his final farewells to the poet or the project.

Khodasevich believed strongly that form and content, like life and art, could and should never be separated. Khodasevich's lifelong frustration with formalists and formalism centered around their attempts to turn literary criticism into a science, using the "exact," "scientific" methods of analysis which together were supposed to make up the "formal method." But surprisingly, Khodasevich's own literary criticism had much in common with formalism. Especially in his *Pushkinistika,* Khodasevich's analyses of sound patterns, recurrent motifs, and syntactic constructions are virtually formalist in nature. The essays of Khodasevich's *Pushkin's Poetic Economy* and the later book *About Pushkin* often represent individual formal observations of one motif or one work. In theory Khodasevich believed that formal analysis was the point "from which every judgment about an author, every account of him, must begin," but that such analysis cannot be the stopping point of the critical act.[120] In practice, he did not always continue to the next step himself, to the "investigation of the artist's outlook." While Khodasevich argued for the importance of author and historical context along with form, he simultaneously questioned the need for biographical commentary in the perception of poetry. "It is not necessary and is even harmful," wrote Khodasevich, "for it transforms a poetic phenomenon into a real-life one."[121]

So Khodasevich found both formal poetic analysis and literary criticism, as practiced in his own essays and articles, and an exploration of the poet and of history, as practiced in his biographical projects, to be vital to literary studies. His hatred of the formalists stemmed from a narrow definition of their work—a definition, it is true, that they themselves provided. As John Malmstad has pointed out, Khodasevich always took extreme examples from formalist studies as targets for his attacks. But while Khodasevich might have reacted as strongly to Tynianov's biographical novels as he did to Veresaev's *Pushkin in Life,* the two men were essentially engaged in the same project: re-presenting Pushkin and other Russian poets to their contemporaries, and in the process searching out a past for themselves and other Russians which would serve them in the new era.

The rocks upon which Khodasevich's Pushkin biographical project went aground were essentially Pushkinian in nature: Khodasevich went afoul of Pushkin's idea of truth. The epigraph to Pushkin's 1830 poem "The Hero" ("Geroi") questions "What is truth?" (*Chto est' istina?*). In his own investigation of truth in biography, Khodasevich came to a conclusion diametrically opposite to that of Pushkin's poet. While the poet in Pushkin's "The Hero" insists that "[t]he deceit which ennobles us is dearer to me than a multitude of low truths" (*T'my nizkikh istin mne dorozhe / Nas vozvyshaiushchii obman*), Khodasevich had to disagree. In his biography of Derzhavin, he had claimed that "the truth cannot be low because there is nothing higher than truth. We have to oppose the *truth which ennobles us* to Pushkin's 'ennobling deceit.'"[122]

Pushkin's magic tricks, his art which elevates while deceiving the reader, did not mesh with Khodasevich's biographical method of integrating the life and art of his subject. And Khodasevich could not figure out how to show the creating Pushkin. Himself a domestic and detail-oriented poet, Khodasevich loved the transformative effect he saw in Pushkin's poetry and which he investigated in quasi-formalistic charts and lists in his Pushkin criticism. But his ambivalence about episodes in Pushkin's life and about the relationship between life and art in his great predecessor kept Khodasevich from continuing his biography past "Ruslan and Liudmila" and into Pushkin's poetic maturity. Pressured from all sides to write the biography of Pushkin, Khodasevich ultimately chose *Derzhavin* as the book which would represent his career as a biographer.

Chapter Six

A Playwright in Wolf's Clothing: Bulgakov and His Molière

Мне на плечи кидается век-волкодав,
Но не волк я по крови своей . . .
И меня только равный убьет.

The wolf-killing century leaps on my shoulders,
But by my blood I'm no wolf . . .
And only an equal can kill me.
—Osip Mandel'shtam, 1931

Я в Париже,
Я начал жить, а не дышать.

I am in Paris;
I have begun to live, not just to breathe.
Dmitriev, "Diary of a Traveler"
Epigraph to Pushkin's *The Blackamoor of Peter the Great* (1827–28)[1]

MOSCOW, FEBRUARY 16, 1936. Bulgakov's play *Molière (A Cabal of Hypocrites)* premiered at the Moscow Art Theater (MKhAT). It closed three weeks later, removed from the repertoire, and was never produced again in his lifetime.

BULGAKOV, MOLIÈRE, AND PUSHKIN

Of the three main authors considered in this book, Mikhail Bulgakov was perhaps the most explicitly autobiographical in his fictional work. Searching not so much for a positive hero as for a place for himself in the world, he conceived of his own life in relation to the social and political forces around him. In his artistic works, Bulgakov consistently explored those relations, trying one or another combination to further refine his theory about the construction of his world. Bulgakov was one of those writers who repeats themes, casts of characters, and situations in his works, using diverse material and playing out various scenarios on that material. Most of his work features a creative personality who is often emblematic of the author himself.

Bulgakov's entire career as a writer unfolded during the Soviet period, from 1920 until his death in 1940, but although he was undoubtedly exceptionally talented, few of his works reached the public in his lifetime. Indeed, his reputation has undergone major renovation in the past three decades, with the publication in the Soviet Union of his last novel, *The Master and Margarita,* in the mid-1960s, and with the rest of his works, both dramatic and fictional, gradually entering the canon of Russian and world literature since then. Bulgakov biographer Lesley Milne has argued that Bulgakov staked his career on immortality. In other words, Bulgakov chose to write about the artist's role in an ideologically foreign environment, and in so doing he knowingly forestalled any opportunities for fame in his own time. In his quest for cultural immortality, Bulgakov chose two writers as role models for his ideal artist, both of whom also found themselves in ideologically alien societies—Molière and Pushkin. Their importance for Bulgakov's understanding of himself and for his creative output cannot be exaggerated.[2]

To represent his world in fiction, Bulgakov used a triangle, the most stable of geometric figures. His triangle consisted of a master (artist, scientist, inventor, or creative personality), a king (or authority figure), and a group of ideologues (be they church fathers, literary critics, society gossips, or party functionaries). Using virtually the same cast of characters, Bulgakov treated the triangle twice in his two Molière works. Both versions of the dynamics among the seventeenth-century French characters would ultimately have an effect on the plot and characters of his Pushkin play.

Mikhail Bulgakov had a clearer idea about how to represent Pushkin in fiction than his fellow writers Iurii Tynianov and Vladislav Khodasevich had. Of the three, Bulgakov was the only one to complete his work about Pushkin—a play about the last days of Pushkin's life—although it was ultimately not to be published or staged in his lifetime. Both Tynianov's novel *Pushkin* and Khodasevich's book *Pushkin* remained works-in-progress, even if parts of them did see publication. If we can measure success by the author's own judgment that his project has been brought to fruition and is ready for public consumption, then Bulgakov's work about Pushkin was the most successful of the three endeavors.

When Bulgakov undertook his play about Pushkin in 1936, his career was at a frustrating standstill. Sixteen years of experience writing for journals and theaters—and almost sixteen years of having his work banned from publication and/or production—had hardened Bulgakov. As I will show in the present chapter, Bulgakov's experiences as a writer, particularly a writer of biographical fiction and drama, shaped his attitudes about history and the place of the writer in society, which in turn shaped his ideas about who Pushkin had been.

Before he considered writing a play about Pushkin to commemorate the centennial of his death in 1937, Bulgakov first honed his skills of character development and historical research on the material of the great seventeenth-century French playwright Jean-Baptiste de Molière. Molière was the model through which Bulgakov understood Pushkin and himself, and he represented a past that Bulgakov hoped to make use of in his own time. For Tynianov, the search for a usable past was rewarded in his development of a critical method and a particular genre, that of the "scientific novel." Khodasevich had been in search of a model from the past who could become a positive hero and who would lead the rejuvenation of Russian culture in the present, and he found that model in Derzhavin. But for Bulgakov, the key to understanding the past and the present was not to be found in a single person, but rather in the relationship between an artist and his patron. It was the tension that held the triangle together which made the seventeenth century usable for Bulgakov.

BEFORE IMMORTALITY—THE SEARCH FOR ORDER

The question of fame in the writer's lifetime remains one of the unsolved questions in Bulgakov's life, despite the many treatments his biography has received over the past several decades.[3] Although it does indeed seem that Bulgakov must have had the proverbial "long desk drawer" (*dolgii iashchik*) in mind as he wrote some of his literary and dramatic works, especially in the 1930s, he nonetheless often worked on commission for theaters and always claimed he planned to publish everything he wrote, including *The Master and Margarita.*

Bulgakov clearly had hopes that his works would reach an audience. And in the first half-decade or so of his career they did. Already in these early works, a longing for order, for an end to chaos, and for a logical construction to the world, appeared. In the 1922–23 feuilleton "The Capital in a Notebook" ("Stolitsa v bloknote"), for instance, Bulgakov demonstrated his desire for the rational, organized life which Moscow of the New Economic Policy years lacked. The story consists of various scenes and descriptions of the NEP-induced chaotic condition of the capital, but asserts that "from the chaos somehow or other order is being born":[4] "Moscow is a cauldron in which is boiling a new life. This is very difficult. We have to be boiled ourselves. Among the Dun'kas and illiterate people a new organizational skeleton, permeating into all the corners of existence, is being born."[5] The piece ends with an odelike passage to the power of a militiaman's red baton and the slogan "give us a foothold and we'll move the earth."[6] In later works as well—in his portrayals of the chaos of the Revolution, civil war period, and NEP in other feuilletons, *White Guard, Zoia's Apartment,* and *Crimson Island*—Bulgakov always sided with order over chaos, with a strong state over the anarchy of life. In another story from 1922, the narrator cries out in the midst of a bloody scene of civil war, "Oh, my dear starry Ukrainian nights. Oh, peace and serene quiet!"—a refrain that would become familiar throughout Bulgakov's works.[7] For Bulgakov the desired "peace and quiet" of the home and hearth were possible only in a country where order reigned over chaos. These two kinds of order, the domestic and the political, were necessarily linked in his mind.

Bulgakov was no apologist for the new regime, but he accepted it as a given and worked to change it, to make it more amenable to artists. His weapon in this effort was satire. "Satire does not allow for second thoughts," he would often say, and he virtually never considered his critics or the censor when he wrote.[8] The Soviet scholar V. Lakshin has written that

> Bulgakov did not consider himself to be an enemy of the new state and moreover believed that he was helping it. Because how could a writer help his country more effectively than with the honest truth? A satirist is a doctor, and Bulgakov knew that a good doctor not only ascertains the nature of the illness and determines where the pain is, but also tries to give a prognosis as to the future course of the disease.[9]

Lakshin depicted a somewhat naive Bulgakov, but his works and letters do suggest that Bulgakov was testing the regime and the censorship, pushing the boundaries of what literature and what behavior could remain acceptable.

In his 1930 letter to the government of the USSR, Bulgakov defined himself as a satirist who had appeared at a time when real satire ("which penetrates into forbidden zones") was absolutely inconceivable.[10] This letter was a kind of manifesto for Bulgakov; after almost a decade of artistic work, he was able to announce his intentions to the highest power, to Stalin, and await the response. In defining his own career as a writer, Bulgakov wrote:

> Taking up the struggle with censorship, of whatever kind and under whatever form of government it exists, is my duty as a writer, just as to call for freedom of speech and press is my duty. I am a faithful devotee of this freedom . . .
>
> . . . [the other characteristics of my work] are the black and mystical colors (I am a MYSTICAL WRITER) in which I portray the innumerable monstrosities of our life; the poison with which my tongue is saturated; a deep skepticism as to the revolutionary process happening in my backward country; and the contrasting to it of my beloved and Great Evolution; and most important, the portrayal of the terrible characteristics of my nation.[11]

In this same letter Bulgakov related that he was repeatedly advised by friends and colleagues to write a "communist play" to bring himself into the good graces of the government and theater world, something that he categorically refused to do. Bulgakov considered himself incapable of such an action: "I was advised to dye my wool. Absurd advice. Whether dyed or clipped, the wolf still doesn't look like a poodle."[12]

Bulgakov's several letters to Stalin and to the Soviet government over the years show that he was not afraid to draw attention to himself. In the letters, he quoted the damaging and, in his mind, unfair reviews that his works received in the press, seeking the leader's protection from the ideological persecution he suffered at the hands of critics. The question "does the Soviet Union need me?" arose again and again as Bulgakov tried to work out what his place was in his homeland.

It is not surprising that Bulgakov identified so strongly with his character Molière, whose situation in seventeenth-century France paralleled his own in Soviet literature; valued and envied by their peers, sought after as playwrights, both Bulgakov and Molière nonetheless repeatedly saw their works censored and forbidden. Bulgakov saw Molière's life reflected in his own in the playwrights' personal relationships with their reigning political leaders as well. Bulgakov was not alone among Soviet writers in having received a phone call from Stalin in 1930. The call seemed to mark the leader's concern for his fate. But Stalin's personal interest in Bulgakov's works, demonstrated vividly by his admiration for *Days of the Turbins* (for the revival of which he was directly responsible in 1932), made their connection more real. Stalin's conversations, reported to Bulgakov by various acquaintances, spoke to a genuine concern on the part of the leader for the playwright.[13]

Thus Bulgakov felt justified in his hunch that his only recourse against the watchdogs who continually tore him to pieces was Stalin himself. And Molière and Louis were not his only historical models; he also had a precedent closer to home. Bulgakov considered the connection between himself and Pushkin as well and thought about how he might negotiate a relationship with the government in the 1930s that would emulate Pushkin's relative freedom in the 1830s. One proof of Bulgakov's autobiographical reading of Pushkin's life is found in a request he apparently made of Stalin; utilizing the historical model of the relationship between Tsar Nikolai and Pushkin, Bulgakov asked Stalin at one point, in a letter which may never have been sent, to be his "first reader," his personal censor, and thus to help his works reach the public.[14] Bulgakov saw the leader as a facilitator, a shortcut through the bureaucratic censorship that could overcome any obstacles to his publications. Lakshin has formulated the issue thus: "One could still hope for support from time to time from the highest power, whether that be Louis XIV for Molière or, in more recent times, Stalin. Tyranny can still allow itself the caprice of patronage. But a daring artist can never find empathy from people with 'ideological eyes.'"[15] In his triangular model of the world, Bulgakov hoped for assistance from its chief point, Stalin. The leader seemed to be his only chance.

The theme of the relationship between art and authority comes up again and again in Bulgakov's biography of Molière, as Bulgakov tried to work out the boundaries of the relationship and the variables of the equation. In an almost incantatory attempt to force the issue, Bulgakov's narrator proclaimed, "Art flourishes under a strong state!"[16] Considering Bulgakov's model adversarial, pitting the writer against everyone else, Lakshin has written that in both the play and the novel about Molière Bulgakov tended to make an exception for Louis XIV, all the while despising the "cabal of hypocrites."[17] But I would argue that throughout his oeuvre Bulgakov was actually very consistent. He and his characters railed against despots and tyrants only in the aftermath of betrayal, but in general preferred to work under the protective force of a powerful government. Expanding on a thought from one of his sources for the Molière biography, Bulgakov explained a defining characteristic of writers, dramatists, and actors:

> One of the thinkers of the seventeenth century used to say that more than anything on earth actors love the monarchy. It seems to me that he expressed himself thus because he didn't think the question through carefully enough. It would be more correct to say that actors passionately love any kind of power. And they cannot not love it! Only under a strong, enduring and wealthy state can the theatrical arts flourish. I could give many examples of this and am not doing so only because it is so obvious.[18]

The ironic tone of this statement notwithstanding, Bulgakov's idea is clear. Having to work and live under a strong autocrat was not the tragedy of Molière's life, nor indeed of Bulgakov's own. The tragedy lay in the fact that autocrats, like ordinary people, can lose interest in their protégés. As Bulgakov dramatized the moment in the biography:

> At this moment Molière felt a cold breeze at his back, and he experienced a sensation as if a huge figure which had been standing behind him had suddenly left. There was no point in fooling himself: the king was abandoning him. How could this be explained? Very simply: everything on earth comes to an end, even the long-term attachment of the world's powerful. Who can discern what goes on in the souls of the rulers of men?[19]

And it is at this moment in an artist's career when the final hunting down of the wolf begins in earnest. While Milne's assertion that Bulgakov was interested in achieving immortality through his works is undoubtedly true, immortality cannot motivate a writer in his daily work. It would have been difficult for Bulgakov to give up hope of reaching an audience, of receiving that return on his creative investment for which every artist longs. In portraying himself as a wolf and choosing the wolf's way, Bulgakov braved the hunters in his efforts to create, even if he knew his end would ultimately be a wolf's demise.[20]

A CABAL OF HYPOCRITES (KABALA SVIATOSH)

Bulgakov was proud of his *A Cabal of Hypocrites*, in his words "a brilliant play."[21] The play was never meant to be a biography per se, although it was consistently mistaken for one. At the first reading of *A Cabal of Hypocrites* to a meeting of the literary repertory committee of MKhAT's Artistic Political Council (Khudpolitsovet) in 1930, Bulgakov had to defend himself against the various plays his listeners had expected him to produce:

> [Bulgakov] explained, that "neither a play about the class struggle in the seventeenth century, nor the creation of a monumental tragedy, nor indeed the creation of an antireligious play" were a part of his plans. He wanted to write a play about the bright, vivid genius of Molière who was crushed by a black cabal of hypocrites with the unconditional consent of the absolute smothering force of the king. The Soviet spectator needed such a play.[22]

It is this triad of artist–king–ideologue that ran throughout Bulgakov's work and most interested him in the case of Molière. The author of *Tartuffe* represented for Bulgakov a historical archetype of the persecuted artist, whose mere existence depended on the whims of an all-powerful monarch and whose works were subject to censure by jealous fellow writers and ideological watchdogs.

In an interview before the premiere of *Molière* in 1936, Bulgakov again felt compelled to explain the genre of his work:

> I wrote a romantic drama, not a historical chronicle.[23] In a romantic drama biographical exactitude is not possible and not necessary. I allowed myself a whole series of shifts to dramatically strengthen and artistically adorn the play. For example, Molière did not actually die on stage but, having felt ill on stage, managed to get home; the coolness of the king toward Molière, which did occur in history, is taken by me in the drama to a level of high conflict, and so on.[24]

Bulgakov's dramatic and artistic decisions were not understood by the leadership of the theater. MKhAT, and especially Stanislavskii, wanted to put on a majestic play showing the genius of Molière, whereas Bulgakov was more interested in the forces leading to the genius's downfall. As Ellendea Proffer has pointed out, Bulgakov "tried at first to satisfy Stanislavskii's desire to have Molière shown 'creating' on the stage—a more conventional *biographie romancée* approach,"[25] but ultimately he could not submit to the reinterpretation of his play and the requested changes in his text. In his novel about Molière, Bulgakov commented that "Molière did not fight as stubbornly for any of his plays as he did for *Tartuffe*";[26] in this sense, *A Cabal of Hypocrites* was Bulgakov's *Tartuffe.*

MKhAT rehearsed the play for four years, over 290 rehearsals, going through several changes of actors, three directors, and two set designers. The final production, although in Elena Bulgakova's words "not the play we had dreamed of,"[27] was a huge success with the audience. Nonetheless, the appearance on March 9 of an unsigned article in *Pravda*, "External Glitter and False Content" ("Vneshnii blesk i fal'shivoe soderzhanie"), portended the death of *Molière.* "In Bulgakov's play," the review read, "the historic Molière is nowhere to be found. A mediocre little actor, caught in the tangles of his family affairs, is offered for the amusement of the spectator."[28] In response to the review, the play was immediately removed from the repertoire.

In the world of Soviet monumental hero-worship, Bulgakov's "living Molière" was unwelcome. Both Bulgakov and the Soviet censorship were searching for a usable past, trying to find characters from the past who might have an influence in the present. But official Soviet practice insisted on the creation of positive heroes who could fulfill a specific function. They should be larger than life and immensely impressive, inspiring Soviet citizens to aspire to great deeds. Bulgakov was not interested in monuments. He was more concerned with the historical past as a model for his present situation. Through the experience of Molière, Bulgakov hoped to understand the role of the artist in society, and he sought an answer that allowed the artist to share power with his protector and patron.

BULGAKOV'S MOLIÈRE

The Soviet enterprise of monumental hero-worship had an institutional home in the series of biographies which would eventually become *Lives of Remarkable People* (*Zhizn' zamechatel'nykh liudei*) and which was to solicit Bulgakov's manuscript on Molière. As early as the beginning of 1917, Maksim Gor'kii had begun approaching writers for a series of biographies that he wanted to publish in Russia. Gor'kii's original idea, loosely based on the prerevolutionary series of the same name, arose in response to the horrors of the First World War; his letters to H. G. Wells and Romain Rolland, written in January 1917, emphasize the need to inspire new generations to feats of greatness through examples from the past. He wrote:

> We adults, who are fated to abandon this world in due time,—we will leave our children a pathetic inheritance, we are bequeathing them a very sad life. This absurd war is a stunning proof of our moral weakness, of the decline of culture. Let's remind our children that people were not always as weak and wicked as—alas!—we are now; let's remind them that all nations had—and have now—great people and noble hearts! It is essential that we do this precisely in our days of victorious cruelty and brutality.[29]

Lives of Remarkable People was intended for school-age children and was to attract the best writers to the cause. Gor'kii's dream finally became a reality in 1933. In the first year of the series, seventeen biographies of famous artists, writers, scientists, and inventors were published, with subjects ranging from Dante, Lomonosov, and George Sand to Surikov, Repin, Gutenberg, Mendeleev, Diesel, and the Wright brothers.

In June of 1932 Mikhail Bulgakov signed a contract with *Lives of Remarkable People* (*ZhZL*) to write a full-length biography of Molière by

February 1933. Bulgakov was uniquely suited to portray the seventeenth-century French playwright and a natural choice for the *ZhZL* series. Gor'kii admired Bulgakov's prose and especially his play about Molière, *A Cabal of Hypocrites*, which Bulgakov had finished in late 1929.[30] In addition to the research on Molière that he had done for the play, Bulgakov again immersed himself in the most authoritative sources available and ended up with a bibliography of some fifty titles for his biographical novel. In the fall of 1932, his work on a play subtitled "Molièriana," based on motifs from Molière, brought him into intimate contact with the playwright's own texts. Between November and March Bulgakov completed the manuscript of the biography and delivered it on March 5, 1933.

The time elapsed between the soliciting of the manuscript and its delivery, however, a mere ten months, saw a substantial change in the direction of Soviet literature. The codification of socialist realist doctrine was only a year in the future, and the epoch of relative permissibility and experimentation that was the 1920s had already come to an end. A. N. Tikhonov, the *ZhZL* series editor, rejected Bulgakov's manuscript out of hand. In a personal letter to Pavel Popov, Bulgakov described his reaction to Tikhonov's rejection in wolfish terms: "I bared my teeth at the form of the review, but didn't bite."[31] He seemed to feel like a lone wolf surrounded by hounds, a writer defenseless among his critics. Speaking metaphorically in his 1931 letter to Stalin, Bulgakov had claimed to be tired of the fight: "The animal has announced that he is no longer a wolf, a writer. He is abandoning his profession. He falls silent."[32] By 1933 Bulgakov had changed his mind again; the wolf continued, but he no longer engaged his enemies. The hope that Gor'kii would save Bulgakov's work, as he had in the past, was dashed with Gor'kii's letter to Tikhonov on April 28, wherein he agreed with the editor and suggested that Bulgakov's "playful" style made the novel about Molière a frivolous work.

Thus the publication of Bulgakov's *Life of Monsieur de Molière* was delayed until 1962. In 1936, however, the *ZhZL* series did publish a biography of Molière—by the Soviet historian of French classicism Stefan Mokul'skii.[33] In his preface, Mokul'skii explained his goal to be the "correct interpretation of Molière's oeuvre as an ideological phenomenon, as a striking manifestation of the class struggle in seventeenth-century France."[34] The publication of Mokul'skii's biography of Molière in 1936 instead of Bulgakov's provided a vivid example of the end of an era in Soviet literature; Bulgakov's "frivolity" would have to remain in his long desk drawer, and his biographical efforts in prose were not to reach the Soviet public for almost three decades. Sergei Ermolinskii noted that Mokul'skii's book delivered a cruel blow to Bulgakov when it hit the bookstores at precisely the same moment as Bulgakov's play *Molière* was banned.[35]

The fact that Gor'kii and Tikhonov trusted Bulgakov to take the Molière commission in the first place was in itself somewhat odd, although it spoke to their belief in his talent. Bulgakov's track record with censorship was hardly good. His first novel, *White Guard,* was never published in its entirety in the Soviet Union during his lifetime; the journal that was serializing it was shut down before the third part was printed. Early good fortune with the novella *Fateful Eggs* and two short-story collections ended in about 1926, after which Bulgakov could get none of his prose work published. His plays, too, held in high esteem by the public, were all taken out of production in 1929; in rapid succession *Days of the Turbins, Zoia's Apartment,* and *Crimson Island* were removed from the repertoires of the Moscow Art Theater, Vakhtangov Theater, and the Moscow Chamber Theater (Kamernyi teatr). Around the same time *Flight,* a play about the tribulations of Russian émigrés after the Revolution, was banned, despite the endorsement of Gor'kii, who had predicted that *Flight* would meet with great success.[36] Stalin's review of the play is interesting both as a gauge of the theatrical and political climate of the time and as a record of Stalin's appreciation of Bulgakov's talent and interest in his work. In 1929 he wrote: "*Flight* is a manifestation of the attempt to create pity, if not sympathy, toward the anti-Soviet emigration,—thus an attempt to justify or partially justify the White Guard cause. In its present form *Flight* is an anti-Soviet phenomenon."[37] In this same letter, Stalin revealed the reasons for his regard for Bulgakov's *Days of the Turbins:*

> As for the play *Days of the Turbins,* it is not all that bad, it's more useful than it is harmful. Don't forget that the main impression which the spectator of this play retains is one favorable to the Bolsheviks: "if even such people as the Turbins are compelled to put down their arms and submit to the will of the people, admitting their own cause to be lost for good,—then the Bolsheviks are unconquerable . . ." *Days of the Turbins* is a demonstration of the all-encompassing strength of Bolshevism.[38]

Apparently Stalin really did like Bulgakov's work: the leader was reported to have seen *Days of the Turbins* no less than fifteen times and *Zoia's Apartment* eight times.[39]

Bulgakov himself saw his relationship with Stalin as very significant. In thinking of Stalin, Bulgakov recalled first of all the humane gestures Stalin had made toward him and the even more humane promises. As Marietta Chudakova has written, "ultimately Stalin was for him . . . yet another incarnation of the Russian state—and he struggled to find for [Stalin] a place in the history of this state."[40] Regardless of Stalin's feelings for Bulgakov, neither *Flight,* nor *Zoia's Apartment,* nor indeed *Days of the Turbins*—which became temporarily unsuitable for the Soviet stage between 1929 and 1932—nor any of Bulgakov's other plays survived the censorship.

To Bulgakov, the authorizations and bannings of his plays seemed random. His words about Molière's *Tartuffe* are equally appropriate for *Flight*, *Days of the Turbins*, and *A Cabal of Hypocrites:* "Who will light the winding paths of the comedian's life? Who will explain to me why a play which couldn't be performed in 1664 and 1667 became permissible in 1669?"[41] Writing to Gor'kii in 1929, Bulgakov complained:

> All of my plays are banned, nowhere will they print a single line of mine, [I have no ready work and no hopes of a single kopek of royalties from anywhere,] not a single institution or person will answer my applications, in a word—everything that I have written over the course of ten years in the USSR has been destroyed. The only remaining task is to destroy that which remains—me myself.[42]

In December of 1931 the Red Theater (Krasnyi teatr) in Leningrad refused *Adam and Eve,* a work they themselves had commissioned. Gor'kii replied to Bulgakov's cry for help with repeated interventions with the Repertory Committee. But Gor'kii could not be Bulgakov's permanent savior; between his frequent absences from Russia and the changing atmosphere of Soviet theater, Bulgakov's plays were destined to remain off the stage. Already in 1927 at a meeting of Agitprop the "end of the experimental period" in theater had been declared and a call for "maximal severity in ideological control" had been made. Bulgakov's name had come up at the meeting as one of the "least loyal" playwrights.[43]

But despite this situation, 1932 and early 1933 seemed to herald a change in Bulgakov's fate as a dramatist. In January of 1932, Bulgakov was suddenly informed that the production of *Days of the Turbins* was to be revived at MKhAT, and at the end of March the theater began rehearsals of *A Cabal of Hypocrites,* renamed *Molière* at the request of the Repertory Committee. The commission that summer from *ZhZL* was a welcome chance to work on a figure who interested Bulgakov greatly and at the same time to alleviate his financial woes. Bulgakov undoubtedly owed this opportunity to Gor'kii's concern for his welfare. In March of 1933, after sending off the manuscript of the biography, Bulgakov also saw rehearsals of *Flight* begin at MKhAT, and things must have seemed to be looking up.

Bulgakov's initial ironic reaction to the commission of the Molière biography—"A biography—10 printers sheets' worth—in this heat—in Moscow!"—belied his interest in the project.[44] The opportunities to finally see a book in print and to receive financial remuneration for his work were important to him, but the subject matter was even more appealing. As discussed above, Molière had interested Bulgakov for years: Molière's genius as a playwright and actor, his tragic conflicts with the church and censorship, and his position as "court poet" all spoke to Bulgakov across the centuries and conjured up an uncanny and productive feeling of kinship.

In the increasingly restrictive atmosphere created by the Main Repertory Committee and revealed in the removal and rejection of Bulgakov's plays in 1929, the fact that Bulgakov turned to seventeenth-century France for material could be interpreted as an easy way out, an attempt to escape the censure his contemporary Civil War and NEP themes seemed to generate. Indeed, a turning to history was in the air, for this reason among others. However, such an explanation would be facile in most cases, and Bulgakov is no exception.[45] In fact, he had a deep personal bond with Molière. Among other things, Molière was proof of Bulgakov's theory that only a theatrical man could be a playwright.[46] During the years of his "Molièriana" Bulgakov lived his working hours in seventeenth-century Paris, immersing himself in Molière's world.[47]

THE LIFE OF MONSIEUR DE MOLIÈRE (ZHIZN' GOSPODINA DE MOL'ERA)

When Bulgakov was starting to work on the biography of Molière, he wrote to his friend Pavel Popov about the contract. Popov thought the idea a magnificent one and considered the key factor to be the common ground between Molière and Bulgakov himself.[48] Having contemplated the figure and fate of Molière for some years, specifically in conjunction with the fate of the artist in general and his own personal destiny in particular, having himself benefited from direct intervention by the "king" and suffered from his own "cabal of hypocrites," Bulgakov had a personal interest in writing the biography of Molière. It is difficult to say whether *ZhZL*'s categorical rejection of his manuscript was a complete surprise to Bulgakov, but certainly his refusal to make any of the suggested changes in order to get the novel published speaks of Bulgakov's commitment to the end result and disagreement with the "ideal" biography the editors wanted him to write. After all, he continued to work on and revise the script of the play about Molière for almost seven years, and while the differences between a book manuscript and a play—which necessarily becomes a joint effort between the author and the director staging the work—are obvious, his obstinacy in this case nonetheless gives one pause.

It is possible to analyze Bulgakov's main creative concepts in *The Life of Monsieur de Molière* by going point by point through Tikhonov's negative review. Bulgakov described Tikhonov's review to his friend Popov:

> Well, my Molière days have begun. They opened with T[ikhonov]'s review, which contains many pleasant things. My narrator, who guides the biography, is called a forward young man who believes in wizardry and deviltry, dabbles

> in the occult, loves alcove stories, uses questionable sources and, worst of all, is prone to royalism![49]

Tikhonov felt that Bulgakov was drawing parallels between seventeenth-century France and the contemporary Soviet Union, and he believed that the book would be far better served by having a "serious Soviet historian" as the narrator. Although Tikhonov, not himself a Molière specialist, simply did not realize just how closely Bulgakov followed his sources, carefully merging and questioning the various extant accounts of Molière's life and work in his text, he was certainly correct about the narrator, whose interests in magic and opaquely drawn parallels with Russia reflect Bulgakov's own approach to Molière.[50]

The narrator in *The Life of Monsieur de Molière* directly addresses certain of Bulgakov's arguments with the state of contemporary literature in the Soviet Union, hence Tikhonov's complaint that "hints at our Soviet reality show through rather clearly." These issues ranged from Soviet publishing policy to Bulgakov's difficulties with his plays and in his life. One example of the contemporaneity of the narration is a digression by the narrator in the prologue which seems to harken back to Bulgakov's own problems in publishing his prose works: "I could name dozens of writers who have been translated into foreign languages although they are not even worthy of being published in their native tongue."[51] Bulgakov was surely aware of the requirements of the era of socialist realism, but he made no concessions to them; indeed, he longed to confront them head on:

> Here I throw down my damned pen in embarrassment! My hero is ideologically unsound. Beyond the fact that he is the son of an obvious bourgeois, the son of a man who in the 1920s in faraway Muscovy would surely have been deprived of his rights, he is also a student of the Jesuits, and on top of that a person who sat at a school desk next to pupils of royal blood.
>
> But in my defense I have something to say.
>
> First of all, I didn't choose my hero. Second of all, unless I want to lie, there is no way that I can make him the son of a worker or the grandson of a peasant. And third of all, as far as the Jesuits go: Voltaire also studied with the Jesuits, which did not prevent him from becoming Voltaire.[52]

This passage is from a rough draft of the novel, but in it we can clearly see the writer's aggravation at the de rigueur biography of Soviet times, which must reread history to fit the categories of the political canon. Of course, as Mokul'skii was to demonstrate, it was entirely possible to create an ideologically correct portrait of Molière—the democratic, almost communist, organization of Molière's troupe alone begged for such an interpretation—but Bulgakov had other goals in mind.[53]

The fact that Bulgakov insisted that he "did not choose his hero" is important for considering his relationship to the usable past. On the most literal level, we can read this statement as a reference to the manuscript order by *ZhZL.* But on a more serious level, it seems that Bulgakov was interested only in the situation, not in the hero himself. He went on to argue that the facts of the case required him to make Molière a bourgeois Jesuit student who had royal acquaintances, all characteristics which in the 1920s would have landed him in prison. Here Bulgakov was straining against the monumental hero-worship of the Soviet 1930s. To make Molière a truly positive hero, Bulgakov would have had to lie, to transform the "ideologically unsound" figure from the past into a hero according to contemporary Soviet standards. But Bulgakov's definition of biographical truth required a fairly close connection with available historical documents and dates. He was not prepared to strap his seventeenth-century hero into a Soviet corset. Indeed, Molière appealed to him precisely as a figure who would not fit the present political climate, but would instead show Bulgakov how he himself might make his own weather.

The similarities in chronology, character, and even small details from the lives of Bulgakov and Molière are striking. The kinship between these two writers was very strong. Writing about Molière's life, Bulgakov was able to draw on similar emotions, frustrations, even situations in his own life. As he shaped his book, Bulgakov mined his psychological affinity with Molière. A typical example of how Bulgakov and his narrator played with this kinship is the description in the book of Molière's first run-in with the censorship:

> On the next day Monsieur Molière received an official notice from the Parisian government that his play *Les Précieuses Ridicules* was banned from further performance.
>
> "Executioners!" muttered Monsieur de Molière, falling into an armchair. "Who could have done this?"
>
> It is necessary to note that Molière was experiencing for the first time something that, one can predict, he will in future be forced to experience often. It's not worth it to describe his state. Those who have not had their plays banned after the first successful performance will never understand this anyway, and those who have had them banned don't need descriptions.[54]

Bulgakov's own frustration and ire show through the narrator's seemingly calm and rational explanation—or lack of explanation. "Those who have had their plays banned" should immediately remind the reader of the scandals associated with Bulgakov's own plays. Well acquainted with the situation in which Molière found himself, Bulgakov was capable of describing it explicitly and vividly when he so chose.

> Molière . . . decided to resort to yet another method of reviving his play.
>
> This method has been known to playwrights for centuries and consists of the author, under pressure from outside forces, purposefully resorting to crippling his work. An extreme method! This is how lizards act when, caught

> by the tail, they break it off and escape. Because every lizard understands that it's better to live without a tail than to lose one's life entirely.[55]

As Bulgakov wrote the biography of his French predecessor, he encoded events and emotions from his own life for the future reader and researcher to decipher. For example, in discussing Molière's play *Tartuffe,* which was banned after the presentation to the king of only the first three acts, Bulgakov wrote: "What did the author of the ill-fated play do? Did he burn it? Hide it? No. Righting himself after the shock at Versailles, the unrepentant playwright sat down to write the fourth and fifth acts of *Tartuffe.*"[56] Bulgakov, like Nikolai Gogol' before him, like the Master in his novel *The Master and Margarita,* had had occasion to burn his own manuscripts, including the first version of the novel about the devil in 1930.[57] In this passage Bulgakov encoded his own faintheartedness and celebrated Molière's audacity. Molière's bravery in continuing his work despite censure earned Bulgakov's respect and admiration.

The book's bittersweet epilogue, entitled "Farewell to the Bronze Comedian," emphasized another of Bulgakov's frustrations with the Soviet state. The description of Molière's monument is precise; Bulgakov wrote specially to his brother in Paris asking for details about the statue, its location, and its condition, and his brother responded promptly, even sending a photograph. Bulgakov's own repeated attempts to receive permission to travel abroad, for reasons of health, literary and dramatic affairs, to see his brothers, from whom he had been separated by the Civil War, and finally just to see the world, all ended in disappointment. The last sentences of the novel about Molière serve to underline Bulgakov's despair at living in a country that had become a prison to him: "There he is! That is he—the king's comedian with bronze bows on his boots! And I, who am fated never to see him, send him my farewell greetings."[58] Bulgakov's prediction came true; he was never to leave the boundaries of the Soviet Union. But his conclusion also formed a segue to his next project, metaphorically re-presenting the creation of another "internal exile," Aleksandr Pushkin. Pushkin's Bronze Horseman, the physical manifestation of Peter the Great's ultimate state power, was now allied with the artist. State power and artistic power were in Bulgakov's mind connected and even, in the long run, equal.

THE TRIANGLE IN BULGAKOV

Both *A Cabal of Hypocrites* and *The Life of Monsieur de Molière* were works about the triangle—the master, the king, and the ideologues. Proffer has identified two levels of evil in Bulgakov's works, consisting of the "fanatics," who are obsessed with doing something for the good of the state, and the "despots," whose work the fanatics do. The despots "rely on informers to stay in power and they prefer to commit crimes at one remove. The key description of a Bulgakovian despot is in the play *Molière;* Molière despairingly compares his king to a golden idol with emerald eyes."[59] But Proffer tended to reject any positive fascination Bulgakov may have had for authority figures and to emphasize the despotic nature of Bulgakov's authoritative characters. Her model implies that the immediate enemy, the fanatic, was less dangerous than the despot in the background. However, in Bulgakov's rendition, the relationships were more complex; for instance, the fanatic might seem to be working toward the monarch's interests, but he often had his own agenda as well and manipulated the monarch into compliance.[60] The relationship between ideologue and king in Bulgakov was tinged with elements of a power struggle. When the king was no longer able or no longer cared to protect his artist, the ideologues were free to destroy his life and work. The image of the idol, instead of demonstrating the human side of the king, showed his helplessness; his emerald eyes were cold, he had become a mere statue or figurehead, and the real power had been usurped by the ideologues.

For Bulgakov, the ideal monarch would be a strong, protective shield who allows the artist to create and is always prepared to step in and defend him from the third force—censors, critics, or jealous writers. In Bulgakov's earlier novellas, the artist figures were the scientists Persikov and Preobrazhenskii, whose experiments were threatened and taken over by the ignorant petty ideologues Rokk and Shvonder. *Heart of a Dog* delivered one of the happiest endings of any of Bulgakov's works because Professor Preobrazhenskii had a protector in the form of a mysteriously powerful person in the government who intervened to keep Shvonder and his ilk away. When confronted with advances on his apartment by the house committee, the professor only needed to make one phone call. The results of his threat were immediate; the mysterious patron offered Professor Preobrazhenskii a document protecting his living space. The professor replied: "Only one condition: by whomever, whatever, whenever, but let this be a paper which guarantees that no Shvonder and no one else can even approach the doors of my apartment. A definitive paper. De facto. Real. *Armor.*"[61] In *A Cabal of Hypocrites*, *The Life of Monsieur de Molière*, and in the play *Aleksandr Pushkin* the monarch figure was not as accommodating of his writer and did not offer him the armor he needed. Bulgakov's Tsar Nikolai was cold toward Pushkin, his character perhaps growing out of the unfeeling and indifferent Louis XIV of the end of *A Cabal of Hypocrites*. And in these works the enemy of the writer was neither ignorant nor petty; the ideologues knew exactly what the consequences of their actions against the artist would be and were merciless in driving him to his death.[62]

In Bulgakov's final novel, *The Master and Margarita*, as in *The Life of Monsieur de Molière*, the immortality of the artist allowed him to triumph.

Bulgakov certainly longed for the power he gave to Ieshua, the power to forgive his king. But despite scholars' insistence on Bulgakov's "wager on immortality," I have argued that at least in the short run, Bulgakov himself was hardly comforted by the thought of immortality. He wrote with irony to his friend Popov: "Some of my well-wishers have chosen a rather strange means of comforting me. I've heard the suspicious unctuous voices more than once: 'don't worry, after your death everything will be published!' Of course, I'm very grateful to them!"[63] Bulgakov was looking not for posthumous triumph and vindication, but for fame and recognition in his own society. Ultimately, of course, he would have to settle for the former.

In *The Life of Monsieur de Molière* the triangle of artist–king–ideologue recedes into the background in comparison with *A Cabal of Hypocrites*, where it was the central conflict. There could be several reasons for this change. With the play in rehearsal and expected to premiere soon, Bulgakov may have assumed that the novel would act as a continuation of images already in the minds of the theater-going public. In addition, having explored the "black cabal" to the fullest extent in his play, Bulgakov chose in the longer work to emphasize the monarch.[64]

When in the novel the archbishop comes to Louis to condemn Molière, the king becomes even more interested in his "favorite poet"—the king and the comedian are allies, fighting against the same repressive force, the church, one for the power to rule and the other for the freedom to write as he pleases. In his rendition, Bulgakov accentuated Louis's protection, which was vital to Molière. The king not only saved the comedian from an auto-da-fé and staved off the worst of his critics, he also offered Molière status and subsidies that kept the playwright writing. But, as Bulgakov noted, "everything on earth ends, even the long-term attachment of the world's powerful." In the novel the reasons for Louis's abandoning Molière at last are much less dramatic than the denunciation-induced confrontation between the two in the play (which ends with Louis's words, "I deprive you of the king's protection").[65] It is the monarch's obsession with ballet that causes him to switch his patronage from Molière to the composer Lully. And though Bulgakov valued the presence of the monarch in Molière's life, he also knew that kings are merely people with earthly power:

> He who ruled the world considered himself to be immortal, but in this, I believe, he was mistaken. He was mortal, like everyone, and consequently blind. If he hadn't been blind, he might have come to the dying man, because he would have seen interesting things in the future and perhaps he might have wanted to become a part of genuine immortality.[66]

Molière died and Louis died, but Molière's plays remained immortal.

In the novel *The Life of Monsieur de Molière* Bulgakov did not pretend, on the whole, to be writing rigorous scholarship; he repeatedly had the narrator assert that he was not a specialist or a historian. Yet Bulgakov did his best to follow the available sources and use them as a historian might. His bibliography included many significant evaluations of Molière's life, including, among others, the first biography of Molière, Grimarest's 1705 *Vie de Monsieur de Molière,* the works of Voltaire (1739), Eugène Despois (1874), the Dane Karl Mantzius (1904), Eugène Rigal (1908), and Jules Patouillet, who wrote the history of Molière in Russia (Russian translation, 1924), along with those of such Russian specialists as Evgenii Anichkov and Aleksei Veselovskii.

Bulgakov's approach to the Molière scholarship was a unique merging and questioning of the various accounts of Molière's life and work. In the tradition of the French *biographie romancée*, Bulgakov included suspicious anecdotes and fictionalized elements to enhance the portrait of his character, but the scarcity of information about Molière's life and the contradictions and myths surrounding what is known made his task a difficult one. The most "incriminating" characteristic of Bulgakov's novel was its autobiographical quality, which cast doubt on his dedication to an objective historical rendition of Molière's life. When he described his hero as a wolf ("clearly our hero felt like a lone wolf, sensing behind him the breathing of fast dogs on a wolf hunt"),[67] he invoked analogous feelings of his own, expressed in his letter to Stalin of May 1931: "In the open field of Russian literature in the USSR I was the one and only literary wolf. . . . And I was treated like a wolf. For several years I was chased in an enclosed yard, according to the rules of the literary hunt."[68] In the biography, Bulgakov's aggravation at his own situation as a playwright who often worked on contract showed through the narrator's comment on this point: "Basically, it seems to me that it would be good if playwrights did not have to take orders from anybody!"[69]

But the similarities between Bulgakov's life and Molière's did exist. Clearly this affinity was what attracted Bulgakov to the figure of Molière in the first place. Bulgakov was looking for an archetypal model of the triangle of which he felt himself to be a part, and even though the theme of such a triangle points to fiction, other nonfiction renditions of Molière's life have presented a similar idea. Molière proved to be an excellent example of the archetype for which Bulgakov was searching, as well as a foreign model according to which Bulgakov could understand his own national poet, Pushkin.

While Bulgakov's indebtedness to his sources is unquestionable, his image of King Louis XIV was his own, as he took advantage of his mythical relationship with his own autocrat to fill in the blanks that history left.[70] If the play about Molière was autobiographical, concentrating as it did on the ideologues who destroy a playwright's life and works, then the novel was even more so. The period of the writing of *The Life of Monsieur de Molière* coincided with several more interventions by Stalin into Bulgakov's fate. And even though the meeting promised during the 1930 phone call never took place, Bulgakov could feel the hand of his protector in the revival of *Days of the Turbins* and the acceptance of *Flight.* In shifting the blame for Molière's downfall away from the autocrat in the prose version, Bulgakov may have been trying to script his own life. Stalin's interest had to be kept, and after all, Bulgakov's works, like Molière's, had a better chance at immortality than did he himself.

PEACE FOR MOLIÈRE AND FOR BULGAKOV

After the initial rejection of *The Life of Monsieur de Molière* in 1933, Bulgakov wrote to Popov: "So, I want to bury Jean-Baptiste Molière. It will be more peaceful for everyone, better for everyone. I am absolutely indifferent to whether my book cover decorates a store window. In essence I am an actor, not a writer. Besides, I love peace and quiet."[71] In Bulgakov's mind, the biographical process necessarily required "stirring up the ashes" of the dead. He had sought a model in Molière, just as he was to seek one in Pushkin, but in reincarnating these characters, he seemed doomed to merely torture them and himself. The fact that he returned to Molière and to biographical subjects several times suggests that Bulgakov's declared love of "peace and quiet" was somewhat coquettish. He was drawn to seek models to help him understand his own life, his fate, his place in society, and he sought them in Molière and Pushkin above all.

The difference between Bulgakov's situation and that of Molière was that for Molière, the triangle relationship among king, comedian, and cabal was a given, the natural course of events in a feudal monarchist state. For Pushkin, too, the relationship with his tsar was a given, although his position in society differed. When Pushkin wrote "I can be a subject, even a slave, but I won't be a lackey and a jester even to the tsar in heaven,"[72] he was expressing the basic dignity due to him as a nobleman; he considered that his social status allowed room for independence. Molière, in his lifetime, *was* merely Louis's jester, forced to bow and scrape and clown for his king's entertainment; only after his death did he gain immortality. In contrast to his two models, Bulgakov in some ways created the triangle situation for himself. He was willing to voluntarily take on the role of comedian to the autocrat, even if that autocrat was not the Sun King or Nikolai Romanov, but Iosif Dzhugoshvili. Bulgakov looked for justification of his role in previous epochs, trying to make his situation seem normal and viable. And in portraying Molière and Pushkin during their "last days" in his two plays, Bulgakov implicitly cast himself in just such a tragic role.

In seeking to invent a usable past for himself, Bulgakov immersed himself in seventeenth-century France. With Molière's fate as a prototype of his own, he hoped to achieve a level of fame within the relative order of a tyrannical state to publish his stories and see his plays performed. The stability of his triangular model of the world, though, depended on each member—the artist, the king, and the cabal—maintaining their roles. When Stalin receded from Bulgakov's life, he could no longer hope to see long runs of his plays. The stability of the triangle suffered, and so did the chance that Bulgakov might win the game on earth. Having identified himself to the government and society as a wolf, Bulgakov received a metaphorical, if not actual, "wolf's ticket"—the *volchii bilet* given in tsarist times to outlaws, criminals, and exiles who had no role to play in the community.[73]

Bulgakov might not have chosen to "bet on immortality," but ultimately that is what Bulgakov would have to do. In the end, Molière was abandoned by his patron Louis XIV, and Bulgakov's Molière was abandoned by the Soviets, who wanted a more monumental hero. Bulgakov's Molière became usable only decades later, after both Bulgakov and Stalin had died. In his lifetime, Bulgakov would try again to achieve a usable past with the play about Pushkin, but that, too, was destined to fail.

Chapter Seven

Pushkin on Stage—or Not: The Curtain Comes Down on Bulgakov's Pushkin

Погиб поэт! – невольник чести –
Пал, оклеветанный молвой,
С свинцом в груди и жаждой мести,
Поникнув гордой головой! . .

Now is the poet dead. Let honor claim
Its votary, though slander smirched his name.
Hot for revenge he met the unworthy foe;
Now is the proud heart pierced, the proud head low.
—Lermontov, "The Death of a Poet," 1837[1]

Я славой был обязен ей –
А может быть и вдохновеньем.

I owed her my fame—
And perhaps also my inspiration.
—Pushkin, 1823 (II, 303)

MOSCOW, MARCH 17, 1936. P. N. Kerzhentsev, the secretary of the Main Repertory Committee, announced in *Soviet Art* that the play *Aleksandr Pushkin* would be banned from production.

If Bulgakov's inspiration for his works on Molière was his own life, it is interesting to consider his relationship with his next biographical subject, Aleksandr Pushkin, about whom he wrote the play *Aleksandr Pushkin*, later staged as *Last Days* (*Poslednie dni*). Clearly, Pushkin's biography differs markedly from Bulgakov's, but the story is essentially another variant of the wolf caught by hunters, of the tragic triangle of artist, king, and ideologues. This theme, which absorbed Bulgakov for much of his life, describes the lives of all three of these writers—Molière, Bulgakov, and Pushkin.

Tsar Nikolai I of Bulgakov's *Aleksandr Pushkin* was no longer Pushkin's "first reader" and certainly not his protector. Bulgakov portrayed him as indifferent to the poet's fate and perhaps even anxious to hasten his death. Bulgakov's three works devoted to Molière and Pushkin—*A Cabal of Hyp-*

ocrites, The Life of Monsieur de Molière, and *Last Days*—seem to document three stages in Bulgakov's own relationship with his autocrat. Stalin's silence on *Days of the Turbins* until 1932, despite the fact that it was one of his favorite plays, was reflected in the denouement of *A Cabal of Hypocrites,* completed in late 1929; the king sacrificed his poet to the church ideologues and did not resurrect *Tartuffe.* But during the writing of *The Life of Monsieur de Molière,* Stalin suddenly recalled Bulgakov's existence, and two of Bulgakov's plays seemed destined for the stage; consequently, in 1932 and 1933 Bulgakov was more inclined to explore the positive aspects of the relationship between artist and king in the novel about Molière.

Bulgakov's Molière projects represented his optimistic attempts to invent a usable past for himself and for other artists, but in his work on Pushkin he was forced to soberly reassess the possibilities for himself as an artist in the Soviet Union. By 1935, completely abandoned by his autocrat and doomed to write work after work that would not see the stage or printed page, Bulgakov began to see again the dangerous consequences of indifference and censure. What's more, the triangular model of the world that Bulgakov constructed for himself and his biographical subjects was collapsing. We cannot forget the events of these years in the Soviet Union as writer after writer disappeared, their absence seemingly condoned by Stalin and by a fourth element, the silent society. Bulgakov's hopes for a benevolent strong leader were by this time a fantastic dream. His triangle, destabilized in the Pushkin play by the addition of society's opinion into the figure, became a shaky quadrilateral, and any hope for order and prosperity in Bulgakov's creative life was gone. He could hope only for peace.

In 1936 Bulgakov wrote to Veresaev: "May God grant peace to Pushkin's ashes and peace to us. I won't disturb [Pushkin] anymore; let him not disturb me either."[2] Having rooted around in the past for many years, Bulgakov finally understood that Pushkin could not become his model for behavior. It was time to let him rest in his grave. Bulgakov would never find his own place in the society in which he lived. In the last years before his death, he understood that Stalin and Soviet society did not need him, and his works would remain in the long desk drawer for many years to come. An engagement with Pushkin in his centennial year might have given Bulgakov the entrée into Soviet Russian literary culture that he craved, but the play about Pushkin was not to see the stage in 1937.

In Russian the word for a contract (*dogovor*) necessarily includes the idea of speaking one's thoughts in full. But Bulgakov was a loner, incapable of that kind of communication. Bulgakov's contracts seemed perennially to suffer from not saying enough (*nedogovorennost'*). In the collaboration between Bulgakov and his longtime friend Vikentii Veresaev on the play *Aleksandr Pushkin,* this same problem of misapprehension arose again. Like Bulgakov's agreement with Tikhonov and the *Lives of Remarkable People* series, the agreement between Bulgakov and Veresaev about their co-authorship of the Pushkin play was not spelled out clearly enough from the start, or perhaps the agreement came to be willfully misinterpreted by each side as the project went on. The problems internal to the collaboration exacerbated even further the difficulty of portraying Pushkin for his centennial.

When Bulgakov took on the task of writing a play about Pushkin, he was already an experienced playwright who felt certain he knew what was legitimate on stage and what was not, what would "sound" from the stage and what would ring false. If there is such a thing as dramatic "truth" in biographical dramaturgy, then Bulgakov was sure that he knew how to achieve it. Bulgakov approached the writing of a play about Pushkin with his own very specific outline of scenes, characters, and personalities. He was familiar with much of the historical material himself and read widely in Pushkin studies; we see the evidence of this in the four large notebooks that make up his materials for the play.[3]

Veresaev, like Tikhonov, considered that his own scholarly understanding of the characters and events was superior to both Bulgakov's historical and scholarly understanding *and* his experienced and instinctual dramatic presentation. Veresaev interpreted his own part in the project to be that of historical consultant, but he did not feel he should be limited to that role.[4] Bulgakov considered Veresaev to be his historical advisor; Veresaev took the "advisor" portion of that job as seriously as the "historical" part and felt that his role included critiquing Bulgakov's characterization and language as well as his usage of the historical material Veresaev supplied him.

The Pushkin project was to strain the two men's friendship, which ultimately would not last through the writing of the play. Over the course of 1934 and 1935 the partnership would cause each of the men to bristle with animosity at the other, as their conflicts over the material and the presentation of Pushkin grew. Their collaboration offers a vivid example of completely different approaches to the question of historical and imaginative truth and to the problem of representing Pushkin. In previous chapters we have seen how Khodasevich and Tynianov each had a difficult time portraying Pushkin in written form. Each of them was overwhelmed with the material about Pushkin's early years and never reached the mature poet's life in their writing. Khodasevich wanted to wrest Pushkin away from Soviet scholars, including Veresaev, and writers, like Tynianov, for Russian émigré culture, to show that the true meaning of Pushkin was to be found abroad, far from Soviet Marxist interference. Tynianov, too, wanted to do his part for Russia, giving Soviet citizens a portrait of their poet a century after his death. As we have seen, neither succeeded in finding a usable past or a positive hero in the great Russian poet Aleksandr Pushkin. And although he had not satisfied the censorship with his portrayal of Molière, Bulgakov thought he could succeed with Pushkin.

But writing a play about Pushkin is necessarily complicated by a number of other factors which do not figure into narrative writing. The most obvious of these factors became a major stumbling block for Bulgakov and Veresaev's collaborative efforts: what were they to do with the physical representation of Pushkin? An actor playing a role before spectators is inherently more visual and confrontational than a description on the page. The first conflict between Bulgakov and Veresaev arose out of Bulgakov's big dramatic idea for solving this difficulty—that Pushkin was to be offstage at all times unless he was already dead. A play about Pushkin without Pushkin: this was to be Bulgakov's contribution to the cultural struggle over the ownership and meaning of Pushkin in his centennial year.

THE BIRTH OF *ALEKSANDR PUSHKIN (LAST YEARS)*

In the novel *The Life of Monsieur de Molière* Bulgakov presented his own biographical vision of his French predecessor. His insights into Molière's character and situation stemmed from his intimate acquaintance with Molière and his era, and even more so from his identification with his hero. And, because he was writing a novel and not a historical work, he could choose to include anecdotes of questionable authenticity in order to complete his portrait. At the same time the novel demonstrates conscientious research and considerable reflection on the conflicting images of Molière over the years. Scholars have called the late 1920s and early 1930s the years of Bulgakov's "Molièriana"—it is clear that the figure of the playwright provided Bulgakov with engrossing material.

Having buried Jean-Baptiste, though, Bulgakov continued to write about writers. It is interesting to speculate about his move toward Pushkin. On the surface of things, it would certainly seem that in turning to a Russian writer, Bulgakov would have preferred Nikolai Gogol', for example. Gogol' had been arguably much more important for Bulgakov's own work than Pushkin. His "literary profile" was more similar to Bulgakov's—both Gogol' and Bulgakov wrote feuilletons, short stories, novels, and plays, no poetry—and Bulgakov had adapted Gogol's novel *Dead Souls* for the stage in 1930. Bulgakov himself stated his partiality for this particular predecessor, saying "Of all writers, I prefer Gogol'. From my point of view, no one can compare to him."[5] But Bulgakov's decision about his next project was not merely an artistic one. Instead, it was almost historically determined by the centennial mood already manifest in the early 1930s. In 1934 Bulgakov turned to a play about Pushkin, hoping to have his Pushkin dominate the theatrical scene during the centennial commemorations.

In preparing to work on the play, he asked Veresaev, a prominent Pushkin scholar and a dear friend, to collaborate with him on the project. It has been suggested that Bulgakov was trying to "pay Veresaev back" for his kindness in years past—during one of Bulgakov's difficult periods Veresaev had gone out of his way to help Bulgakov financially.[6] Indeed, Bulgakov's wife claimed that Bulgakov came to Veresaev and told him the entire play before even beginning their collaboration, which would suggest that he did not really need Veresaev to complete his design. Nonetheless, the partnership did not turn out to be much of a returned favor—rather it was a two-year roller-coaster ride of disagreements, accommodations, frustrations, and exchanged explanations. The partners tried to be good-natured about their different approaches to the material, coming up with a jocular name for their disagreements.[7] But not all was jocularity in the work they shared.

According to the agreement, Veresaev was to provide Bulgakov with the material, and Bulgakov would write the drama which would carry both their names. Financial gains they would divide fifty-fifty.[8] Despite their friendship, the two began to quarrel immediately over contract issues, and the trouble was only beginning. In the summer of 1934 Bulgakov wrote to Veresaev about a book of memoirs that he was reading in which the author reported nicknames of various literary figures based on the names of Moscow streets. Veresaev received the nickname "Stone Bridge [*Kamennyi most*] for the inviolability of his views."[9] Perhaps it is this very intractability in Veresaev, a quality which Bulgakov shared, that caused such irresolvable conflicts over the play. Veresaev had very definite opinions about the historical images of the figures involved, and ultimately he was unable to accept Bulgakov's theatrical versions.

From the start, Bulgakov wanted to write a play about Pushkin without Pushkin. As he considered the idea of this biographical play, the thought of some actor portraying the poet on stage conjured up all sorts of possibilities for vulgarity and banality, for *poshlost';* everything about Pushkin, from the Romantic image attached to his historical personage to his famous sideburns, created too many opportunities for bad taste, for painfully crude interpretations by costumers, makeup artists, and actors themselves. If Tynianov identified a "sham Pushkin" who had arisen in scholarship in the 1920s, in the 1930s the possibility for a "sham Pushkin" on stage was just as real. Veresaev was against the idea of leaving Pushkin out of the play, but after a time he agreed. In truth the concept makes a certain sense. As A. Colin Wright has pointed out, while it was a "bold experiment" to leave the central character out, the decision also showed Bulgakov to be taking a serious problem—what to do about Pushkin—seriously.[10] It is interesting to note that when the play finally began to be produced, Soviet directors have usually put Pushkin back into Bulgakov's play, either having a character dressed as Pushkin appear on stage while a voice reads his poems or indeed even having him physically participate in the action on stage.[11] Bulgakov himself allowed the figure of Pushkin to appear on stage in the background, but kept his "voice" out of the play.

As work on the play progressed, Veresaev objected to a number of dramatic decisions about characters and action. For example, Veresaev wrote: "I find the character of D'Anthès erroneous at its very root and as a Pushkinist I cannot take responsibility for it."[12] Bulgakov responded categorically:

> In answer to you: I, in my turn, find your D'Anthès theatrically impossible. He is so poor, so trivial, so emasculated, that he cannot be put into a serious play. One can't give the tragically perishing Pushkin a little officer from the ball scene of an operetta as a murderer. . . .
>
> D'Anthès cannot cry out "Oo-la-la!" The play is about the life of Pushkin. If we give him lackadaisical partners, it will degrade Pushkin.[13]

Bulgakov pointed out in this same letter that in his view Pushkinists *had* no image of D'Anthès and knew nothing about him. "We need to create D'Anthès ourselves," he wrote.[14] And, in a play about Pushkin in which Pushkin himself was not to appear, the other characters were especially critical. According to Bulgakov, in Veresaev's reworkings, "among living and at the very least complicated characters appear lifeless masks with the labels 'good' and 'evil.'"[15] It is perhaps now not possible to reconstruct which portions of the historical research in Bulgakov's notebooks came to him from Veresaev, but it is clear that Bulgakov himself was a qualified expert on the Pushkin era; on several occasions he was able to point out historical justification for words and expressions which Veresaev had criticized.[16]

In preparing to write the play, Bulgakov composed careful biographical sketches for each character. Now that Bulgakov's notebooks have been published, we can see Bulgakov's process of developing his cast of characters and historical justification for ourselves. Like *A Cabal of Hypocrites*, the play is biographical fiction, with imagined characters alongside historical ones. But in his concern with achieving an authentic "sound," Bulgakov crafted both sets of characters in the spirit of their time, paying special attention to period language and manners.

VERESAEV AND HIS PUSHKIN

In considering Bulgakov's play, it is tempting to discount Veresaev's role. After all, as Elena Bulgakova claimed, and as the notebooks appear to support, Bulgakov had basically planned out the entire play before approaching his friend and collaborator. But Veresaev's contribution to the image of Pushkin in the 1920s and 1930s was not limited to his work with Bulgakov.[17] It has been argued that in seeking to share the credit for *Aleksandr Pushkin* with Veresaev, Bulgakov was recognizing the stamp of ideological firmness that Veresaev carried, especially in comparison to Bulgakov himself, and the drawing power and authoritative status of Veresaev's name in relation to Pushkin, particularly among popular readers and theatergoers. Regardless of Bulgakov's motives, Veresaev threw himself into the project with zeal, even writing his own scenes and trying to persuade Bulgakov to include them. I will look at one of those scenes in detail at the end of the chapter.

Without a doubt, the most famous contribution Veresaev made to *Pushkinistika* was his *Pushkin in Life*, which I discussed in chapter 1. These volumes themselves, with their vast collection of sayings, quotes, rumors, and assessments of the poet, are quite interesting, and they merit contemplation. But the very idea behind the volumes—that idea of the "living Pushkin" outside of Pushkin's work which so enraged Khodasevich—is representative of what I would call Veresaev's own Pushkin. In fact, as I look at Veresaev's "Pushkiniana" in this section, I will demonstrate the way in which each of his Pushkin books and articles fits together into the whole to create a unique character—one who ultimately did not fit into Bulgakov's play.

Pushkin in Life pioneered a completely new genre, a kind of hybrid that combined the results of literary historical scholarship and research with an open indifference to issues of authenticity and reliability. The work was received enthusiastically by casual readers and with skepticism by specialists. This reaction was partially conditioned by the work itself and partially by its author, whose credentials as a scholar were suspect. The fact that Veresaev turned to *Pushkinistika* and wrote his studies in a popular tone has much to do with his background as a novelist. Like the other writers I am examining in this study, Veresaev had a personal stake in creating a usable past from the figures of Russian literary culture, and he chose Pushkin as the most usable embodiment of that culture for contemporary times. Among other things, Veresaev was particularly interested in the fate of the aristocratic Pushkin in the postrevolutionary years of the twentieth century and, as Pushkin became more and more of a symbol of varying groups and tendencies in the years before the centennial of his death, Veresaev felt compelled to state his own position.

Other than *Pushkin in Life*, which has been reprinted many times, Veresaev's works on Pushkin have been difficult to find. A 1996 collection of his "Pushkiniana," which includes several of his smaller books on Pushkin as well as articles and essays from newspapers, remedied this situation.[18] Veresaev wrote numerous books and articles on Pushkin; in fact, most of his work in the 1920s and 1930s was on Pushkin. Iurii Fokht-Babushkin has suggested that Veresaev turned to *Pushkinistika* at a particularly difficult time in his career as a novelist.

> At first glance it might seem strange: why would a widely recognized prose writer—and in the first decades of our century Veresaev really was among the most popular writers; the press called him "a major influence for the Russian

> reader"—suddenly switch to studying Pushkin and to translations of ancient Greek poets, moving the prose which made him famous—novels, tales, stories—into the background?[19]

The titles of Veresaev's novels and stories offer a microcosm of his concerns and philosophical interests. In 1894 he published his first story, "No Road" ("Bez dorogi"), about a generation which "had nothing . . . without a road, without a guiding star, it will perish invisibly and irrevocably." In 1901 he published "Turning Point" ("Na povorote"); in 1908 "Toward Life" ("K zhizni"); in 1909–14 he completed a scholarly work devoted to the philosophies of Dostoevskii, Tolstoi, and Nietszche called "The Living Life" ("Zhivaia zhizn'"), which comprised much of his own philosophy of existence. His first postrevolutionary novel, *Dead End* (*V tupike,* 1920–23), suggests that though a Marxist himself, Veresaev had little hope for the path chosen by the Bolsheviks. In the novel, Veresaev intimated that one of the main sources of difficulties for the Russians might turn out to be the Bolshevik idea that all means are worthy in pursuit of a lofty goal. In one scholar's view:

> Veresaev considered that the main shortcoming in the Bolshevik view of the revolution, that which was capable of killing the people's belief in socialism, was the underestimation of the individual . . . It is impossible to build a just society while disdaining man . . . Lies, lawlessness, the gap between words and deeds, the violation of the individual, lead inevitably to social apathy—the fatal disease of any society.[20]

When Veresaev turned to Pushkin, it seems natural to expect that he was particularly interested in Pushkin as an individual. During the 1920s and 1930s, as the Soviet regime was choosing what icon from the past could become a socialist positive hero, Veresaev, too, was investigating how Pushkin as an individual might fit into a society of the collective.

After the Revolution, Pushkin—or his advocates—had to fight for his place in Russian culture. In 1921, when the first Pushkin Days were taking place in Petersburg, when Khodasevich, Tynianov, Bulgakov, and Blok were all giving their Pushkin speeches, Veresaev gave a lecture entitled "What Is Needed to Be a Writer?" ("Chto nuzhno dlia togo, chtoby byt' pisatelem?") in which he used Pushkin as his main source of examples in trying to teach young proletarian writers. In the 1920s Veresaev's Pushkin was a "positive hero" for the present and future. Veresaev went on to compile *Pushkin in Life,* to write numerous articles, to collect nine of those articles into a full-length book entitled *On Two Planes* (*V dvukh planakh*), and finally to work up his own biography of Pushkin.[21] His was a major voice in *Pushkinistika* in the 1920s and 1930s.

The 1929 *On Two Planes* gives a good basic view of "Veresaev's Pushkin," a Pushkin who offers an interesting contrast to the one resulting from

Khodasevich's *Pushkin's Poetic Economy.* Veresaev's *On Two Planes*, more even than *Pushkin in Life*, provokes Pushkinists to this day. Some would argue that it was this approach of Veresaev's which led to what in Russian circles is often considered to be blasphemy, namely Abram Terts/Andrei Siniavskii's irreverent *Strolls with Pushkin.*[22] In his introduction to *On Two Planes*, Veresaev offered an explanation of what he had been seeking in his examinations of Pushkin: "In him I thought to find the very highest, radiantly bright bearer of 'living life,' the most authentic crowning of that rare human ability to transform life into beauty and happiness in his own consciousness." In the course of his investigations, however, this "crowning" Pushkin eluded Veresaev. Perhaps Veresaev's inability to find what he was looking for was conditioned by nineteenth-century statements about Pushkin. Dostoevskii's 1880 speech about Pushkin as the universal man and Gogol's 1832 statement that Pushkin was "man as he will be in two hundred years" set Veresaev up for disappointment. Veresaev continued: "In the process of my work on Pushkin I became convinced that my approach to him was absolutely incorrect, that I would not find in him that which I sought. In this book, I will describe what I did find in him."[23] The Pushkin Veresaev found was not the beloved poet, the incarnated inspiration he sought.[24] He was instead a lower being, a man with many faults and sins.

Veresaev's idea of "two planes" is a useful one in considering how twentieth-century Russians have reacted to their literary past and in particular to Pushkin. For Veresaev, the easiest means of reconciling the poet and the man was through the vision of a split Pushkinian world. On the "lower plane" of life, which for Veresaev consisted of "political, social, and religious questions," "Pushkin was unstable, he wavered, in various periods he contradicted himself. All of these questions did not concern him very deeply."[25] It was on the "upper plane" of life, the plane of creation, that Pushkin became Veresaev's sought-after artist.

These two planes violate the unity and integrity of the idealized poet.[26] And Veresaev glorified the upper plane, exclaiming:

> But art—art constituted Pushkin's very soul. He lived by it and found the entire purpose of his existence in it. And in the main questions of art Pushkin did not waver, he was always the same. The very foremost question of art for him was the question of the powerful independence of art, its role outside of service to the state.[27]

According to Veresaev, Pushkin could not bear to consider art as having a purpose, a goal. And if the important issues for Pushkin were art and the independence of art, the right of art to do and create anything, the valuing above all of the aesthetic qualities of creation, then this "higher plane" of Veresaev's is not so wrong.

In truth, Veresaev's concept of "two planes" parallels Tomashevskii's idea of "biographical legend": the only biography that is important for studying the art of a writer is that biography which he specifically creates for his reader. His own actual biography, the day-to-day facts and moods that affected him personally, are his own business. This split in Pushkin is part of what Khodasevich was reacting to when he chose Derzhavin as the whole, organic, and positive poet for the twentieth century. Veresaev was following the biographical tradition of P. V. Annenkov, who sought to recreate the portrait of the poet soon after his death by talking with Pushkin's friends and acquaintances. As Veresaev paraphrased Annenkov, "there were two Pushkins: the living Pushkin, the real one, and the ideal, 'created by his genius.'"[28]

In a later section of his book, Veresaev argued that Pushkin was not the happy man he was portrayed to be. Bringing forth the testimony of many of Pushkin's friends and contemporaries about Pushkin's lightheartedness and sunny disposition, Veresaev made the point that Pushkin's famed laughter was really the demonic laughter of the manic-depressive (to utilize the vocabulary of the late twentieth century); in the words of Nietzsche, "the most unhappy and the most melancholy animal is, in all fairness, the most joyful."[29]

> "I said to Pushkin," [Ksenofont] Polevoi relates, "that in his works sometimes one meets with the most authentic joyfulness, a joyfulness which none of our other poets has. He answered that at its core his character is sad and melancholy, and if he sometimes is in a joyful frame of mind, then rarely and not for long. It still seems to me that he was mistaken in describing his character thus."[30]

What should interest us here, of course, is not whether Pushkin the man was happy or sad, lighthearted and filled with joie de vivre or melancholy and depressive. It is important always to separate out *which* Pushkin is under scrutiny at a given moment. Polevoi, in the quote above, was contrasting the Pushkin he knew from poetry and from personal interaction with the Pushkin whom Aleksandr Pushkin himself was presenting to him. But Veresaev found a variety of Pushkins—in this quote, in Pushkin's work and letters, and in the testimony about him of friends, enemies, and acquaintances. The stage had become crowded with Pushkins.

In his article "The Overthrowing of Idols" ("Nizverzhenie kumirov") about Nabokov's *The Gift* and Siniavskii's *Strolls with Pushkin,* Sergei Fomichev has argued that Nabokov and Siniavskii were both somehow wrong in their respective portrayals of Chernyshevskii and Pushkin. He suggested, correctly, in my view, that the "official Chernyshevskii" and "official Pushkin" were never accepted by writers; writers would never embrace "that Pushkin, whose poetic line during the 1937 jubilee (a jubilee celebration of death—isn't this a Stalinist conceit?) met the arriving prisoners at Solovki on a bright red cotton banner: 'Hello, young unknown tribe!'"[31] But the critic, acknowledging that "both Nabokov and Siniavskii chose strong means in order to explode the stereotypes," still found their tactics to be tasteless. A cliché in talking about the "official Pushkin" would suggest that most writers, in creating their own Pushkins, try to remove the "anthological gloss" from their idol. For Siniavskii in the 1960s, this luster had hardened to a thick impenetrable layer of lacquer. Fomichev argued that Siniavskii

> truly loved Pushkin, but his own, another, not that one who had become a consumer good [*shirpotreb*], as a result of the unending Pushkin jubilee which continued without any real breaks from year to year (the anniversaries of his birth and death, of the founding of the Lycée, of his Mikhailovskoe exile, of the Boldino autumn, of the creation of his individual works and so on and so forth . . .).[32]

One more example, I hope, will make my point clear.

Veresaev wanted very much to separate his own two Pushkins so as to understand the man and the genius better. He found the way to do so in Pushkin's own writings. In a letter to Elizaveta Khitrovo in autumn 1828, Pushkin had explained: "Would you like me to be absolutely candid? I may be elegant and well mannered in my writings, but my heart is absolutely vulgar and my inclinations are quite petty bourgeois."[33] Here Pushkin was presenting *himself* as being two very different people in his work and in his art. This was the authentic voice which Veresaev was seeking, and it gave permission to consider Pushkin "on two planes."[34]

In 1936 in advance of the centennial commemoration, Veresaev requested readers' opinions and essays with an article in the newspaper *Izvestiia,* asking: "How is Pushkin dear to you?"[35] The summary of responses offers interesting material for analysis, but the results, I would argue, were influenced in advance by Veresaev's formulation of the problem.

> Not long ago, in answer to my question as to why he loves Pushkin, one worker, with blazing eyes, answered:
>
> —Because he is alive.
>
> This is well said. The incomparable beauty of genuine living life virtually flows from Pushkin's poetry.[36]

The theory of the "living life," *zhivaia zhizn',* which can be traced to Dostoevskii and to Andrei Belyi, was foremost in Veresaev's mind from the beginning of the 1900s.[37] He grafted this theory onto the centrality of Pushkin in Russian culture and began to seek the "living life" in the life of Pushkin.

In inviting Veresaev to collaborate with him, Bulgakov was acknowledging the older man's service to Pushkin studies throughout the 1920s. But Veresaev had more than a detailed knowledge of Pushkin and his contemporaries. He also had definite opinions of how to approach Pushkin as a historical phenomenon and as a contemporary character, and he would prove to be a quarrelsome partner for Bulgakov. It is fair to say, however, that Veresaev's Pushkin, separated into the man on a lower level and the poet on a loftier level, was one of the most influential characterizations for the cultural image of Pushkin in the 1930s Soviet Union. Veresaev's "Pushkin in life" could not have been more different than Bulgakov's Pushkin—but his had a more significant impact.

VERESAEV'S *PUSHKINISTIKA*

Veresaev's first effort at *Pushkinistika*, *Pushkin in Life*, was to determine the shape of virtually everything else he was to write about Pushkin and his contemporaries. In the autumn of 1937 he wrote to Bulgakov, complaining that his biography of Pushkin had been banned.[38] Fokht-Babushkin has called this biography an expository version of *Pushkin in Life;* that is to say, in constructing a biography of Pushkin Veresaev followed the same or very similar categories as he had in his "systematic code of documentary testimony by contemporaries."[39] The pseudodocumentary approach in Veresaev's *Pushkiniana* necessarily resulted in a somewhat awkward style in his writings. One of the author's pieces from 1933, *Pushkin's Relatives*, aptly demonstrates this awkwardness. The little book has a format like an encyclopedia or a "who's who": Veresaev listed the name of each of Pushkin's relatives with their birth and death dates. It is in the expository portion of each "entry" that the unevenness of Veresaev's style is most visible. The entry on Sergei L'vovich Pushkin, for instance, begins: "Father of the poet. Son of a wealthy landowner. Received a secular French upbringing. Under Pavel I served in the light guard of an Eger regiment." Immediately, though, Veresaev fell into the gossipy tone of his informers from *Pushkin in Life:* "But [he] turned out to be poorly suited for service, considering the requirements of the day and his own extreme carelessness and absentmindedness." Veresaev then launched into a series of anecdotes about Sergei L'vovich's service; the use of dialogue, qualifying adverbs (constantly, one time, once, even [*postoianno, odnazhdy, kak-to, dazhe*]), and descriptive authorial remarks (timidly, with a smile [*s robost'iu, s ulybkoiu*]) belie the encyclopedia-like beginning of the description of Pushkin's father and give the reader pause.[40] Veresaev repeated this same odd, awkward format with each section of *Pushkin's Relatives*. Beginning in a fact-oriented, concise style, he then turned to reported speech, extended anecdotes, and a more casual, conversational style in describing each relative further.

In the children's version of Veresaev's biography of Pushkin, Veresaev's vision and method were realized in full. When he and Bulgakov quarreled about how to present Pushkin, Veresaev had suggested that it would be nice to visualize Pushkin talking to his nanny, and Bulgakov reacted in horror. Most of all, Bulgakov feared the kind of "sham Pushkin," to borrow Tynianov's phrase, which would arise from Pushkin's physical presence on stage. The only way Bulgakov was willing to stage a play about Pushkin was by keeping the poet offstage, thereby avoiding possibilities for vulgarity and banality.

In his book on Pushkin, Veresaev followed his instincts, showing what his own version of the play might have looked like:

> At Mikhailovskoe the nanny Arina Rodionovna was in charge of the household. She had a wide face, was totally gray, was slow in her movements. When the opportunity presented itself, she did not refuse a drink.
>
> A winter evening, a storm wails beyond the windows, a tallow candle burns. They sit alone—Pushkin on the stove, the nanny at her spinning wheel. Pushkin is feeling sad.

Veresaev then gave a long quote from "A Winter's Evening":

> Наша ветхая лачужка
> И печальна, и темна.
> Что же ты, моя старушка,
> Приумолкла у окна?
> Или бури завываньем
> Ты, мой друг, утомлена,
> Или дремлешь под жужжаньем
> Своего веретена?
>
> Выпьем, добрая подружка
> Бедной юности моей,
> Выпьем с горя; где же кружка?
> Сердцу будет веселей.
>
> Our frail hut is glum and sullen,
> Dim with twilight and with care.
> Why, dear granny, have you fallen
> Silent by the window there?
> Has the gale's insistent prodding
> Made your drowsing senses numb,
> Are you lured to gentle nodding
> By the whirling spindle's hum?
>
> Let us drink for grief, let's drown it,
> Comrade of my youth so sad,
> Where's the mug? Pour out and down it,
> Wine will make our hearts grow glad.[41]

Bringing the action of the poem to life, Veresaev described biographical scenes as though they served as direct inspiration for Pushkin's poetry. In his biography, he was able to "stage" Pushkin and his nanny at Mikhailovskoe, something Bulgakov had not allowed in their play.

The style in this passage oddly combines those of an encyclopedia or reference style, the author's remarks for a script, and the most typical *biographie romancée.* There is nothing illegitimate about Veresaev's interpretation: "A Winter's Evening" was indeed written at Mikhailovskoe, where Pushkin and his nanny had occasion to sit together and perhaps even drink together to ward off the loneliness and the chill of winter. Certainly by unpacking the poem into a scene Veresaev did not violate any of the rules of biography or of biographical fiction. Yet Bulgakov would not be a party to this kind of novelization of Pushkin's life; he had other uses in mind for Pushkin's poetry. Veresaev, in contrast, used the poetry precisely to get at the life of the poet—a paradoxical approach from the man who separated Pushkin into two planes and who sought in him "living life."

As Veresaev worked out his concept of "two planes" in 1929 in reference to Pushkin, he assigned the poet to the higher plane, literally splitting Pushkin into poet and man: "In life—restless, irritable, frivolous, cynical, blinded to distraction by passion. In poetry—serious, incomparably wise and blindingly bright—'entirely above the world and its passions.'"[42] Thus in life, according to Veresaev, Pushkin was distracted and not at all in touch with the energy-giving springs of "living life." "Nowhere in Pushkin's life do we see or feel a sign of living life, of the celebratory beating of life forces, which tempers and brings into harmony the life chaos that boils around man and within him."[43] Indeed, as Veresaev portrayed Pushkin, the poet was seeking to leave this world, to depart the lower plane—essentially, it seems, to separate himself from his base human twin and maintain only his higher manifestation: "there was one pleasure which Pushkin well knew . . . the *joy of forsaking the living life for the world of bright dreaming.*"[44] The transformative powers which readers and scholars find in Pushkin Veresaev explained thus:

> Pushkin grasps life, pulls it into another plane in one creative burst, and there he transforms everything—bliss and grief, prose and dirt—into divine beauty. . . . and dark, base life with its boredom, depression and hopelessness becomes lit with bright sunlight and everything is equally beautiful. "I feel melancholy and easy; my sadness is light." The most hopeless moods begin to glow with this light,—and then people begin to speak about Pushkin's "sunny love of life," about his acceptance of all the dark sides of life.[45]

But here precisely lies the fault line in *Pushkinistika;* Pushkin himself has no "center," no anchor, and thus each scholar can find in Pushkin whatever and whomever he or she likes.[46] Pushkin, perhaps because of his complexity, his growth in the twenty-some years of his active poetic life, or his canonization beginning in the late nineteenth century, became the subject of more twisting and turning than any other figure in Russian literary history. Veresaev's contribution to this changeable image of Pushkin was significant.[47]

In a rather sharp review of *Pushkin in Life* and *On Two Planes* in *New World* (*Novyi Mir*) in 1937, one critic took Veresaev to task for his approaches in the two works. The separation of Pushkin the man and Pushkin the poet is artificial, Glebov argued, and the tragedy of *Pushkin in Life* was that Veresaev chose to exclude any and all creative aspects of Pushkin's life.[48] The true Pushkin in life should be shown thinking and working. Veresaev, Glebov insisted, left the working, thinking Pushkin out of his portrait, thus giving a version of Pushkin that was not merely a different view but a distorted and erroneous view. Veresaev's goal in his collection of materials about Pushkin—to protest against the "iconic" tradition of memoirs and biographies about Pushkin—was seen by the critic as valid,[49] but his results were just as dangerous as the whitewashing campaigns of well-meaning friends.

In contrast to *Pushkin in Life*, where virtually none of Pushkin's poetry and few of his statements about poetry and creativity were utilized, in the essays in *On Two Planes* Veresaev used the poetry to get closer to Pushkin. He maintained his splitting of Pushkin into two, and here he wanted to approach the poet Pushkin, the being on the higher plane. Veresaev's infatuation with "living life" as a recipe for health and happiness turned into a kind of disdain for those artists who need it:

> Nietszche's description of the distinctive process of artistic "acceptance of life" which stimulates a healthy joie de vivre and spiritual vigor is surprisingly applicable to Pushkin. We don't observe in Pushkin that greedy fascination with base, real, living life, which we see in Homer and the pretragic Greek in general, in Goethe, Lev Tolstoi, Rabindranath Tagore, Walt Whitman. Pushkin did not know how to live in the midst of living life or how to love it, he tried to escape from it into the world of "bright apparitions."[50]

The "living life," one of Veresaev's highest approbations in earlier works, became in these essays a descriptive term for other kinds of writers, but not for Pushkin. It is not surprising, really, that Veresaev's Pushkin and his *Pushkiniana* were the subject of so much controversy and debate: filled with conflicting statements of value themselves, the essays and books annoy and frustrate Pushkinists most of all. Nonetheless, Veresaev's part in creating the language and terminology with which scholars and critics talked about Pushkin in the 1920s and 1930s is indisputable.

VERESAEV, BULGAKOV, AND *ALEKSANDR PUSHKIN*

Veresaev, committed to the "living life" and his own version of a "living Pushkin," was exactly the wrong person to work with Bulgakov on the play *Aleksandr Pushkin*.[51] As many scholars have noted, Veresaev had little experience with the theater. In addition, Veresaev had spent virtually a third of his own life exploring Pushkin's life, and ultimately he could never have agreed to a play without Pushkin. Veresaev wanted the play to be more biographical than Bulgakov would have allowed; he wanted to show Pushkin, or at the very least to take the opportunity to show the characters surrounding the absent Pushkin as weak and evil men. If in *A Cabal of Hypocrites* Bulgakov was not interested in a biographical play, with Pushkin he cared even less. It was characteristic of Bulgakov to choose to dramatize only the final few days of Pushkin's life. To the problem of Pushkin on stage, Pushkin speaking someone else's lines or even his own, Bulgakov found the simplest, most elegant, and perhaps most ironic solution of all: instead of the "living Pushkin" whom Veresaev longed to stage, Bulgakov showed only the deceased Pushkin.

It was equally characteristic of Veresaev to want to follow the letter of the title they had selected and show all of Aleksandr Pushkin, not just his demise. Julie Curtis has argued that for Bulgakov Pushkin represented "a culture which was under threat even in its own time, and which appeared to be being ignored, forgotten and rejected in the modern world."[52] For Veresaev, who has been accused by Bulgakov and by Bulgakov scholars since of excessive "straightforwardness" (*priamolineinost'*), Pushkin was a national treasure, and the spectators of a play, in his mind, needed to be reminded of that fact. As we know, Veresaev was not overly concerned with separating fact from fiction in his collection of memoirs and anecdotes about Pushkin; it was almost as if the act of remembrance was more important than the detail remembered or how that detail fit into the overall scheme of Pushkin's life. Yet, even so, Veresaev turned out to disagree vehemently with Bulgakov's version of the "last days," and their partnership dissolved.

The play *Aleksandr Pushkin* itself consists of four acts, divided into ten scenes. Act I includes a scene at the Pushkin apartment and one at the home of Saltykov, a book lover and the host of a "literary breakfast" at which Pushkin's value as a poet is debated. Act II features a ball at the Vorontsov home—where important tête-à-têtes take place between Natal'ia and Nikolai I, Natal'ia and Heeckeren, Natal'ia and D'Anthès—and a scene at the Third Section, where the various spies and informers discuss Pushkin's latest works and doings. In act III there are three scenes—one at the Heeckeren apartment, the duel itself, and a scene at the Pushkin apartment before the duelists return. The last line of the third act is spoken by Danzas, Pushkin's second, who announces that the poet has been mortally wounded. By act IV, Pushkin's fate is sealed and his posthumous life has begun: in the first scene his body is removed from the apartment, while the second takes place outside the apartment house, on the Moika canal, where students and other well-wishers have gathered—by the count of one fictional guard, over 47,000 of them passed by during this, Pushkin's last day. The final scene of the play is set already at a post station, where those accompanying Pushkin's body to *Sviatye gory* stop in to warm up briefly. According to Irina Erykalova, Bulgakov set down this very plan in the first of his working notebooks, and he never deviated from it.[53]

As the play begins, the first sounds on stage are those of a snowstorm raging outside the window, the absentminded piano playing and singing of Aleksandra Goncharova, Pushkin's sister-in-law, and the chiming of a clock being repaired by the fictional Bitkov, a "clock master" and police spy.[54] These sounds and characters highlight from the very start several important themes of the play: the use of Pushkinian texts, the love and betrayal of friends and foes, and the winding down of Pushkin's last days on earth. Goncharova sings the words to the poem "A Winter's Evening," which evoke the snowstorm and intermingle with its blowing and whistling. She, like Bitkov, loves and appreciates Pushkin's poetry, while Pushkin's wife, Natal'ia Nikolaevna, hates and curses it; society gossips and other poets claim that Pushkin's talent has run dry; and Nikolai I remembers Pushkin's liberal poems of ten years earlier and still holds them against him. Bitkov, who has an excellent memory, appreciates and memorizes Pushkin's lines immediately: "What a marvelous song! . . . A beautiful composition."[55] Some critics have found Bitkov to be an ominous figure, but others, myself included, see him as rather sympathetic.[56]

Among the characters of the play, only the spies—Bogomazov and Bitkov—are fictional. Bulgakov portrays Bogomazov as a willing snitch, but Bitkov lacks malice despite his occupation and finds, perhaps against his will, that the task of reading and memorizing the poetry of Pushkin is a pleasant one indeed.[57] In the last scenes of the play, when Bitkov realizes that he has failed to protect Pushkin from the duel, he goes along to escort the poet's body as a penance for this failure. With a certain symmetry, the same sounds from the opening recur. This time it is Bitkov who recites the lines of "A Winter's Evening" to the station mistress, and the snowstorm rages outside: "Oy, what a storm! . . . He wrote the very best poetry: 'the storm covers the sky with darkness, whirling the snowy eddies. Like a beast the gale is howling, now it's wailing like a child . . .' Do you hear, it's true, like a child? . . . How much for the drink?"[58] Paying the station mistress, Bitkov continues to recite the poem, and the play ends with the police escort, Rakeev, announcing the departure of the funeral cortege: "Let's go!"

Already in the first scene Bulgakov and Veresaev disagreed about a character—Bulgakov wanted to use a woman pawnbroker, and Veresaev insisted on a man. Bulgakov wrote to Veresaev:

> Every time I have made changes in the drafts at your first objection, regardless of whether the point is purely historical or dramaturgical. . . . It is well known that Pushkin owed everyone money. I bring a woman pawnbroker into the first scene. You insist that the woman is no good and we need a male pawnbroker. I change it immediately. What do I think is better? The woman. But I yield.[59]

Veresaev preferred to use the historically accurate character of Aleksei Petrovich Shishkin, with whom Pushkin really did pawn some things for the last time on January 24, 1837. Bulgakov's original character was also mostly historically accurate—he had planned to use Shishkin's wife, changing only her surname (to Kliushkina, an amusing-sounding name which in the eyes of one scholar brought her into the same character gallery with Gogol's Korobochka from *Dead Souls*) but using her real maiden name, Snovidova. The speech of the new pawnbroker, Shishkin, remained virtually identical to Kliushkina née Snovidova's in the draft.[60]

One of Bulgakov's main complaints with Veresaev was that the latter tended to draw out his scenes, adding too much detail to the character's speeches.[61] Another was that Veresaev tended to overcharacterize the roles, leaving the characters seeming too low or petty. An example of both flaws can be found in Veresaev's version of the scene in act III at the Heeckeren apartment. It opens with Heeckeren—the Dutch ambassador and a man of position in society—haggling with a buyer over some lace and velvet he has brought from abroad. When D'Anthès enters, he is annoyed: "Trading again! How can you not find that disgusting, father! After all, they could find out that you, using your diplomatic privileges, import foreign goods duty-free for speculation."[62] The ambassador is a speculator, and his son is embarrassed. The two go on to quarrel, Heeckeren claiming financial need in light of D'Anthès's spendthrift ways, and D'Anthès again accusing his father of being petty in bringing up such issues. Here Veresaev may very well have had in mind similar scenes between Pushkin and his father, but Bulgakov would have balked at using details from Pushkin's biography to characterize the Heeckerens.

In this same scene, Heeckeren receives Pushkin's letter challenging him to a duel. He reacts with typical fear and passion, afraid to fight himself, but not wanting to let his adopted son take his place: "To lose you, my boy. Could I take such a loss?" However, Heeckeren then goes on in a way that Bulgakov must have found unacceptable: "And then, think about it: in wide circles of society here he is exceedingly popular. Of course, he's no Lamartine, no Alfred de Vigny, but for the Russians Pushkin is a great poet too. There could be very many unpleasant complications, for you and for me."[63] Veresaev here clearly wanted to show the disdain Heeckeren and his son D'Anthès had for Russian culture. In fact, Veresaev's manuscript shows marked xenophobia among the Russians. For example, in the Moika scene, the crowd expresses its displeasure that a French citizen is allowed through to see Pushkin's body, while the Russian police prevent any Russians from passing. When Dr. Arendt passes, a "clerk from a good store" protests: "A Frenchman shot him, a German doctored him to death."[64] As D'Anthès, Heeckeren, and Count Stroganov discuss Pushkin's challenge further, Heeckeren continues to doubt, thus "dotting the i and crossing the t" in Veresaev's straightforward way:

> But Count, how will this duel affect my official position? There could be a great deal of unpleasantness. And here is one more complicating factor: they say that Mr. Pushkin is your national poet. If Georges kills him, who knows what accusations the crowd might rain down upon him? Wouldn't it be better to request official satisfaction from Count Nessel'rode?[65]

Bulgakov's reaction? "Drawn out." Veresaev tries to show that D'Anthès also has a sense of honor, as the young man claims "They're already saying that I got married only because I was afraid of a duel. Oo-la-la! I'll show them whether I'm scared of dueling."[66] Here again was one of Bulgakov's complaints: in having D'Anthès make exclamations like "Oo-la-la," he argued, not only D'Anthès, but by association Pushkin becomes low and ordinary.

The contrast in the final scenes of Veresaev's and Bulgakov's plays about Pushkin demonstrates the difference in subtlety between the two men's tactics. In Veresaev's version of the play, a "poorly dressed man" outside of the Pushkin apartment on the Moika shouts, "What is this! They've killed Pushkin,—you could say, the sun of Russia! Where were the authorities looking?"[67] But rather than this awkward mention of Pushkin's posthumous fame as the "sun of Russia"—a quote from Odoevskii's obituary—Bulgakov included another harbinger of Pushkin's fame and his legacy directly into the text, again in poetry. The young man who declaims Lermontov's 1837 "The Death of a Poet" while hanging from a lightpost outside the apartment commemorates both the poet's death and the literature that death would inspire. Veresaev wanted to portray the "living Pushkin," but Bulgakov was more interested in the immortal one.

This marked a change in Bulgakov's use of historical heroes in his works. The differences between Bulgakov's plays *Molière* and *Aleksandr Pushkin* reflect changes in Bulgakov's own character and outlook on life between 1929 and 1934, and also reveal Bulgakov's ideas on whether the past could be usable or not. In Bulgakov's eyes, Molière was willing to bow and to bend to accommodate his king. This model seemed useful to Bulgakov when he still had hope that writers such as himself could function in the Soviet state. By the time he began to write about Pushkin, Bulgakov himself had become as intransigent as his inflexible hero. The past no longer seemed to him a "storehouse of apt attitudes and adaptable ideals," as Van Wyck Brooks would have it, but a place of tragedies for the artist. As Erykalova has written:

> *Aleksandr Pushkin* is a play about departure, about the inescapable tragedy of a conflict between "the artist and the state," about the impossibility of creativity under surveillance, about the preservation of creative freedom even at the price of death. This situation of "the impossibility of existence" was reflected in the unusual structure of Bulgakov's play: in it the eponymous hero is absent.[68]

In the works about Molière, Bulgakov had followed the playwright's life, but in Pushkin, he focused on the death of the poet.

Certainly the main feature of "Bulgakov's Pushkin" is his absence. Bulgakov portrayed Pushkin in the last days of his life, when he was no longer in control of his fate, but had ceded that control to his wife and her flirtations, to the foreigners who frequented Petersburg society, to the pretentious literary men who competed with him, and, most of all, to Nikolai I and his army of police spies. Veresaev continually tried to emphasize Pushkin's importance in his own lifetime by adding lines to the dialogue of the play about the "national poet" and the "considerable popularity" of his verses. But for Bulgakov, who included Pushkin's own verses—from "A Winter's Evening" to *Evgenii Onegin*—in the play as subtexts, Pushkin had gained immortality before his death and did not need the additional advertisements.

In choosing the title *Aleksandr Pushkin* and yet writing only the very end of the life, Bulgakov seems on the surface to be following Tynianov's model from the novel about Griboedov. But while Tynianov included much of Griboedov's life in a novel called *Death of the Vazir-Mukhtar,* Bulgakov reversed the formula, including only Pushkin's death in a biographical play. Here in a sense Bulgakov inverted Tynianov's and Khodasevich's (failed) solutions to the Pushkin problem. While Tynianov and Khodasevich began at the beginning and got bogged down, essentially never reaching Pushkin's life as a poet and an adult, Bulgakov took the last days of Pushkin's life, when it was almost over. Two sets of ironies unfolded with Bulgakov's play. First, he kept the poet offstage and killed him while claiming to show his life. And then the censors killed the play, keeping Bulgakov's *Aleksandr Pushkin* literally offstage for almost a decade.

With *Aleksandr Pushkin,* Bulgakov chronicled the breakdown of his eternal triangle of artist, tsar, and ideologues (in this case played by Nikolai's secret police). The additional scenes at the Saltykov residence and at the Vorontsovs' ball showed the fourth corner which had now been added—society. In this play, the artist remains alone, persecuted by society, the secret police, and the tsar himself. Bulgakov's contribution to the Pushkin myth, like much of his work, was as much about himself as it was about Pushkin. The artist, betrayed by his sovereign, was forced to give in to the hunters and perish like a lone wolf. Bulgakov's ironic resignation over the fate of the artist in a totalitarian society presented an absent Pushkin, already immortalized in his own lines and those of Lermontov. Bulgakov could not impose a happy ending on the poet's life. In the end, he could only protect Pushkin from what he saw as Veresaev's vulgarization. Veresaev had wanted to present a mortal Pushkin. But having seen in his work on Molière that immortality was really what counted, and knowing that immortality could only begin with death, Bulgakov did not bother with the relationship between artist and tsar in his Pushkin play. Recognizing that immortality was the essence of Pushkin, he moved right to immortality in the script. For Bulgakov, Molière and his relationship with Louis XIV was a possible model from the past, while Pushkin was not. The conclusion of Bulgakov's career as a biographical author may be bleak, but he did hold out hope for immortality, both for Pushkin and for himself.

POSTSCRIPT: PUSHKIN AND *PUSHKIN* AT MKHAT

In the agreement between Veresaev and Bulgakov, Bulgakov took on the task of negotiating with theaters to stage the play *Aleksandr Pushkin*. The Vakhtangov Theater in Moscow was very interested in the play; it was there that Bulgakov gave the first full reading of the play on June 2, 1935, which met with great success from the actors. (The following day Veresaev wrote to Bulgakov, offering to take his name off the play's title page. The success was all Bulgakov's.)

Bulgakov was worried that the theater would back out, but in a letter of June 21, B. Zakhava assured the playwright that *Aleksandr Pushkin* would go ahead at Vakhtangov Theater and "be in production by the jubilee days" of early 1937.[69] As further confirmation, a notice appeared in the newspaper *Evening Moscow* on September 5, 1935: "The dramatist M. A. Bulgakov has completed a new play about Pushkin. The play is earmarked for production at the Vakhtangov Theater."[70] By 1936, Bulgakov was certain that the Vakhtangov actors were working on the play, although, as he wrote to his friend Popov, "it will clearly not be produced at MKhAT."[71] Bulgakov had negotiated with theaters in Leningrad, Saratov, Gor'kii, Kiev, Khar'kov, and elsewhere, even discussing a potential opera version with both Shostakovich and Prokof'ev. But after the March 9, 1936, *Pravda* article about *Molière, Aleksandr Pushkin* was doomed as well. Bulgakov's play did not go into rehearsal until after his death in 1940. When the Moscow Art Theater did premiere the play as *Last Days* in 1943, those last days lasted sixteen years.

In 1937, however, without Bulgakov or *Aleksandr Pushkin*, the Moscow Art Theater did host Pushkin festivities. The Pushkinist M. A. Tsiavlovskii was specifically invited to the theater in March of 1936 to give lectures about Pushkin to the actors. According to one scholar, these lectures were originally intended to help prepare the actors for their roles in Bulgakov's play *Aleksandr Pushkin*, which was to be included in the MKhAT repertoire for the 1937 jubilee season.

Only a few days after the first lecture, Bulgakov was summoned to the office of the chairman of the Arts Committee of the Union of People's Commissars of the USSR, P. M. Kerzhentsev. By this time *Molière* had been taken out of production and out of the theater's repertoire. The repercussions of Kerzhentsev's conversation with Bulgakov were clear from the start. When Bulgakov came home, his wife Elena wrote in her diary: "Kerzhentsev criticized *Molière* and *Pushkin.* M. A. understood immediately that rehearsals of *Pushkin* would cease."[72]

Instead of the Pushkin-less play *Aleksandr Pushkin,* MKhAT mounted an "[e]vening dedicated to the memory of Pushkin in commemoration of the one hundredth anniversary of his death," which took place on February 10 and 17, 1937. Thus the efforts of the Pushkinist Tsiavlovskii came in handy for the anniversary, but not for staging Bulgakov. In 1937, both MKhAT and the Vakhtangov Theater remained Bulgakov-less.[73]

Chapter Eight

Back to the Future: Pushkin in the USSR and Abroad

Как славен и велик народ,
Среди которого явился
Великий, истинный поэт,
И с ним впервые засветился
В окошке русском *русский* свет!

How famed and great the people,
Among whom appeared
A great, true poet,
And with him for the first time
A *Russian* light showed in the Russian window!
—D. Minaev, "The Funeral Feast"

SVERDLOVSK, URALS, WARTIME. During the Second World War, the Soviet Pushkin biographer Ivan Novikov had been evacuated to the Urals. He traveled from factory to factory and palace of culture to palace of culture, giving lectures about Pushkin and readings from his novel about Pushkin. Without telling anyone what he was up to, he put aside all of his lecturing fees over the course of a year. When his cache reached 100,000 rubles, he bought an airplane, a "Lavochkin-5" fighter jet, and named it "Aleksandr Pushkin." Novikov never completed the third volume of his biographical trilogy about Pushkin, but he did use the past to address contemporary woes, and he followed the career of the plane and its pilot, Iurii Gorokhov, through the remaining years of the war against Nazi Germany.[1]

Throughout the twenty-year period I have been looking at, authors in Russia and abroad turned to the past and to various figures to seek out for themselves a history they could understand, value, and use in their own times. If by 1937 the ideologues of the Soviet literary establishment had mandated a search for a positive hero from the past to lead Soviet citizens into the future, Tynianov and Bulgakov were still searching for a model for understanding their own situations within a state system which in some ways resembled the autocratic tsarist government of the Golden Age of Russian literature or the religion-influenced monarchy of seventeenth-century France, but in other ways seemed a completely new and strange historical situation. Khodasevich, along with other émigré writers, found himself in a parallel position, creating a usable past for an essentially opposite purpose: to substantiate his claims of cultural legitimacy for his stateless nation, Russia Abroad.

Important writers like the three I have examined in this book do much to shape a literary culture. That they each felt compelled to attempt a biographical project on Aleksandr Pushkin speaks to the way in which the larger culture was shaping them. While Tynianov, Khodasevich, and Bulgakov spread their nets widely, looking to different eras and heroes, they all also looked to Pushkin as they considered what Russian past would merit inclusion in a new Russian future. As individual writers, they felt a need and a desire to shape their own Pushkins to present to the world and to stake their own claims on the territory that Pushkin represented. Each bristled at the Pushkins presented by others and was certain that he alone would be able to create a Pushkin who would accommodate the complexities of that poet's life and work. After the Revolution, Pushkin loomed as the unavoidable shadow on the Russian literary landscape, and whether they wanted to or not, these three writers had to contend with Pushkin's legacy as the dominant inescapable fact of Russian literary life.

And it was not only writers who looked to Pushkin in this era. An entire scholarly discipline, *Pushkinistika,* matured during this period. The personal and public collections of bibliophiles, librarians, and art, artifact, and kitsch collectors all over the world expanded to encompass an ever-growing body of *Pushkiniana.* By 1937, Pushkin was omnipresent in schools, libraries, and factories; on stage, in bookstores, and in exhibition halls; as well as on the front pages of newspapers around the globe. As members of their respective political and cultural communities, Khodasevich, Tynianov, and Bulgakov were all subject to persuasion from their colleagues and friends who believed that they alone were qualified and inspired enough to finally create the definitive biography of Pushkin. Their advocates reminded them that (to recall the *Renaissance* notice on Khodasevich's prospective book) "the Russian reader . . . has been waiting in vain for so long for the life of the great poet to finally be described." Each of these writers was reminded again and again that he owed it to his community to present it with a Pushkin for the present and the future.

And preferably by the deadline, please. The Russian émigré community and Soviet readers alike were preparing to commemorate the tragic death of their national poet one hundred years earlier. Khodasevich, Tynianov, and Bulgakov, along with many of their literary colleagues, were working with a deadline, competing with colleagues and adversaries in their own communities and on the other side of the border to present the definitive Pushkin by 1937. These were hardly the ideal conditions for writing a creative biography of a complex man. As we have seen, only Bulgakov was to complete his work on time—and that portrait, of the absent Pushkin, did not reach the community, stopped by the barrier of Soviet censorship. Neither Tynianov nor Khodasevich was able to produce a completed Pushkin—despite their artistically interesting and imaginative work on previous biographies.

In a collection devoted to memorial moments across the ages and the globe, historian John Gillis has reminded us that

> [c]ommemorative activity is by definition social and political, for it involves the coordination of individual and group memories, whose results may appear consensual when they are in fact the product of processes of intense contest, struggle, and, in some instances, annihilation.[2]

In the absence of truly triumphant biographies by some of the best literary minds of Russia, communities on both sides of the border began to gear up to commemorate Pushkin's centennial on the level of public celebration. And like the writers who strove to create biographies of Pushkin, they saw their celebrations as a competition. The Soviets claimed cultural hegemony over the national poet, and the émigrés professed their own hegemony just as vociferously. If biographers were not going to bring Pushkin back to life, then in 1937 political forces, cultural organizations, ordinary citizens, even the children of Soviet Russia and the émigré diaspora would step in to create their own Pushkin.

DUELING PUSHKINS

In her 1936 teacher's manual entitled *A. S. Pushkin's Jubilee in the Schools*, the Soviet pedagogy specialist S. N. Lunacharskaia instructed elementary and high school teachers how to prepare their students for the big anniversary. The book begins: "In building a communist society, the proletariat of our country is the only direct heir of the best achievements of human thought and culture."[3] According to the author, Soviet schools knew better than anyone else how to commemorate the jubilee dates of great cultural figures—as the jubilees of Beethoven, Tolstoi, Ferdawsi, and Goethe, among others, had already shown. The Soviet Union, in Lunacharskaia's opinion, could be proud of its pedagogical achievements in this area of culture, especially in comparison to other countries. In "Fascist Germany," for example, the centennial of Goethe's death in 1932 featured a "coarse" distortion of that great poet's true character, whereas in Soviet schools "the commemoration . . . revealed to the workers the great significance of Goethe's oeuvre for human culture."[4]

Lunacharskaia's was not the only teaching aid of its kind created in anticipation of the anniversary of Pushkin's death. Preparations for the centennial commemoration began to be mounted in the Soviet Union several years in advance, with the idea of bringing Pushkin's legacy to schoolchildren firmly in the fore. Numerous books appeared explaining how to prepare for the jubilee in various cultural venues—schools, clubs, libraries, et cetera. Other titles of such manuals include: *Materials for the 100-Year Anniversary of A. S. Pushkin's Death (Aid to Folk Art Circles); A. S. Pushkin (1837–1937) Materials for Clubs and Libraries; Pushkin in the Library (Methodological Instructions and Articles toward the Commemoration of A. S. Pushkin's Centenary in Libraries).*[5]

On the eve of the celebration, Russian émigré cultural institutions abroad were also preparing to assert their ownership of Russian culture. Pushkin and *Pushkiniana* were the center for discussions and debates over the true place of Russian culture. Metaphorically speaking, Pushkin became an important piece of cultural and historical territory, and Soviet and émigré Russia formed two political entities fighting for the occupation of this territory. In the words of émigré Nikita Struve,

> by the middle of the thirties political life in emigration had died down almost everywhere . . . the impenetrability of the iron curtain made all direct struggle hopeless. Political debates died down as well; there was no point in continuing them eternally. A number of newspapers and journals (*Rul'*, *Volia naroda*) closed down due to lack of funds. More and more often people spoke about the illusory and doomed nature of émigré existence. *But then culture took over for politics.* The awarding of the Nobel Prize to Bunin in 1933 bolstered the spirits of the émigré community, which had finally been noticed and valued.[6]

Since the émigré celebration of the "Day of Russian Culture" was attached to Pushkin's birthday, all celebrations of Russian culture and poets—whether living, like Bunin, or deceased—were celebrations of Pushkin as well, and by about 1935 Russians abroad were also preparing for the significant one-hundred-year anniversary of Pushkin's death.

Russian émigré communities all over Europe and in China were engaged in discussions about how to increase the quantity and quality of materials about the great poet and how to augment their accessibility to émigrés and especially émigré children. In Harbin, China, in 1934—the year the "Day of Russian Culture" celebrated Bunin as well as Pushkin—V. I. Kolokol'nikov, the secretary of the Harbin "Committee for Aid to Russian Refugees," wrote about the significance of the celebrations for the children of émigrés, "For Russian émigrés, in their state of forced existence in foreign lands, 'Pushkin Day,' the 'Day of Russian Culture,' is not only a day of proud national happiness uniting us, not only a day of great solace and great hopes, but also a day of great national grief."[7] Through learning about Russian culture, Kolokol'nikov asserted, children born in exile would have the chance to acquire the homeland they had never seen and thus to become truly Russian.

The widespread communities of Russians abroad were faced with a daunting task: how were they to preserve Russian language, Russian literary and journalistic endeavors, and Russian culture outside of Russia? Certainly the conditions under which most émigrés left their country contributed to these anxieties; running *from* the Bolsheviks rather than *to* some desired destination, many of these exiles dreamed only of going "home" and of preserving their heritage among themselves and their children until such time as their true homeland would be purged of the Red plague. But twenty years after the Revolution, such an eventuality looked more and more doubtful—thus the "Day of Russian Culture" became for the older generation a day of mourning. In 1937, as the main cultural events were moved to February—to the day of Aleksandr Pushkin's death—the commemorations were doubly sad.

In preparing for the centennial, émigré communities were more than aware of the disadvantages they faced in terms of materials, libraries, archives, and publishing venues. The eminent Dostoevskii scholar A. L. Bem suggested that the émigrés were in need of a "short biography" of Pushkin as an aid to future lecturers during the jubilee celebrations. The conditions in exile, Bem admitted, were such that in his own book of articles about Pushkin he had decided to quote from Pushkin's works liberally and freely, since he imagined that many of his readers lacked access to Pushkin's texts.[8] Attempts to publish a new collected works in Paris in time for the 1937 anniversary failed in the face of financial and organizational complications.[9] Khodasevich did write a short biographical foreword to a one-volume collected works of Pushkin, published in Berlin in 1937. Ten years previously, Khodasevich had still hoped "to facilitate the unity of the émigré community and all of Russia in honoring Pushkin's memory" through the "Day of Russian Culture," but by 1937 all such hopes had vanished in the reigning spirit of animosity and competition.[10]

One of the members of the Parisian Pushkin Committee in 1936 and 1937, M. A. Maklakov, had given a speech a number of years earlier entitled "Russian Culture and A. S. Pushkin," which gave a distinct view of the degree to which Pushkin and Russian culture had, for the émigré community, become one. Discussing the cultural need for "national holidays," Maklakov noted that in other countries, such as the United States and France, national holidays are connected to political events such as the date of independence or of a revolt—the Fourth of July or Bastille Day. In Russia, however, there was never one particular "national holiday." The abundance of Orthodox Church religious holidays, local holidays of one kind and another, and even special tsar's holidays, which changed with each new ruler, did not compensate for having one day that would be a purely Russian holiday.

> In a word, in Russia there was no national holiday; the very idea of such a thing met with no sympathy. And this is understandable: where there is reality, there is no need for symbols; in a house where everyone is still alive there is no need for portraits of family members. . . . The fact that the idea of a national holiday was born in emigration is also a symbol.[11]

Now, in the 1930s, Maklakov wrote, when Russia herself was lost, émigré communities finally felt the need for a national holiday—they needed it "as a symbol that Russia is alive, although her name is forbidden, as a symbol that we are not merely refugees with Dr. Nansen's passports but the citizens of a homeland which has not been and cannot be taken from us by any decrees."[12] Maklakov considered that Russian culture was living on abroad:

> Russian culture turned out to be more powerful and hardy than our Russian state. And we are giving [Russian culture] its just deserts in naming our national holiday after it. After all, could there be a more joyful, meaningful and significant day for this culture than Pushkin's day? . . . Can we possibly think of a better, more indisputable banner for the Russian national holiday [than Pushkin]?[13]

Pushkin was the emotional center of Russia Abroad, and the "Day of Russian Culture," "Pushkin Day," was the yearly evidence of that fervent allegiance.

But even though Pushkin had become the symbol of Russian émigré unity and the preservation of Russian culture abroad, by the mid-1930s an atmosphere of backbiting and strife prevailed among émigré scholars and authors.[14] By the end of the 1930s, as the jubilee date drew closer, there was not even a semblance of harmony among the émigrés. While in rhetoric Pushkin began to be portrayed as a touchstone for the émigré community, as the key to their unification, in fact, the issue of Pushkin's commemoration presented a microcosmic view of the split among the various émigré groups. In Paris, the unofficial capital of Russia Abroad, the Union of Nobility held a separate Pushkin celebration to which the émigré public was not invited. The presence or absence of Soviet representatives at various events divided guests and organizers. The journals and newspapers had to juggle their coverage of Pushkin jubilee events, attempting to suggest a plethora of events rather than competing events happening down the block from each other.

Meanwhile, in the Soviet Union preparations for the centennial celebration began in December 1935, when the Central Committee mandated the formation of a special Pushkin centennial commission. The membership of the official All-Union Pushkin Committee showed that cultural figures, scholars, and politicians alike were being mobilized to promote the jubilee: writers like Veresaev, Tynianov, Chukovskii, Aleksei Tolstoi, Aleksandr Fadeev, Fedor Gladkov, and Aleksandr Serafimovich were to sit down with Pushkinists Tsiavlovskii, Iurii Oksman, and Dmitrii Blagoi, along with theater directors Stanislavskii, Nemirovich-Danchenko, and Meyerhold, and party representatives Voroshilov and Zhdanov, all under the eye of the committee chair Maksim Gor'kii.[15]

The anniversary of Pushkin's death was met in Soviet Russia and abroad with exhibitions, concerts, "one-day newspapers," and special editions of journals. One article summarizing "Pushkin issues of journals" in 1937 Moscow had to admit the impossibility of its task:

> The centenary of the death of A. S. Pushkin gave rise to an enormous quantity of literature about the great Russian poet. Almost all the journals dedicated special issues to Pushkin. An impressive volume of the *Academy of Sciences Herald* was published, including materials from the Pushkin session of the Academy and a series of scholarly articles about Pushkin. The mass "thin" journals—*Ogonek, Young Kolkhoz Worker, Krokodil, Soviet Studenthood*—issued interesting Pushkin editions. Young readers received a special edition of *Murzilka.* The Canal Army of the NKVD Dmitrovskii camp put out a beautifully designed issue of their literary journal *Storming the Road,* made up of works of the canal army men (prose, poetry, painting, music) dedicated to Pushkin. The journal *Anti-Religious Man* printed an article by E. Iaroslavskii entitled "Pushkin's Atheism." The *Red Archive*'s Pushkin issue published very valuable lecture notes from Pushkin's days at the Lycée, along with a previously unpublished article by V. Briusov dedicated to Pushkin's revolutionary lyric poetry.[16]

The article's author, Maslov, summarized the Pushkin issues of the major monthly journals, including *New World, Red Virgin Soil, Star, Literary Critic* (*Novyi mir, Krasnaia nov', Zvezda, Literaturnyi kritik*), among others. He criticized certain of the publications for their immoderate familiarity with Pushkin, others for excessively elaborate approaches to the poet.

Addressing the difficulties of putting Pushkin on the stage—solved, as we have seen, by Bulgakov by keeping him off—Maslov expressed horror at the solution of another playwright, S. Sergeev-Tsenskii, who in the journal *October* published his new play, *At Pushkin's Grave* (*U groba Pushkina*).

> Presenting the living Pushkin on stage is an extremely difficult task for both the dramatist and the actor. S. Sergeev-Tsenskii found a witty means of avoiding the difficulties: in his play he offered the deceased Pushkin. Indeed, according to the author's instruction, the coffin with the body of the poet must stand in the middle of the stage. Another of Sergeev-Tsenskii's ideas is also anti-artistic and inappropriate—forcing the wounded and dying Pushkin to scream aloud. From the poet's apartment "a beastly scream resounds, escaping through an open transom window. . . . The scream becomes stronger, thicker, more unceasing and more unbearable for the ear, like the roar of a huge mortally wounded creature."[17]

Maslov found such a naturalistic effect to be inappropriate in presenting Pushkin to a dramatic audience and thought the editor should have intervened. Sergeev-Tsenskii's was not the only dramatic Pushkin of these years; Ivan Novikov, who later purchased the Pushkin fighter plane, also presented a stage version of Pushkin in 1937 in his play *Pushkin in the South.* In that portrayal, the lonely and friendless Pushkin wanders into an army camp where the soldiers fire a cannon salute and assert that Pushkin need only stay among them. "We all love to recite your ode to freedom," proclaims one soldier; "All of Russia loves you! . . . We are all your friends!"[18] The joyful sharing of baked potatoes around a campfire ends this scene of the affirmation of Pushkin, meant for reading aloud at schools and youth clubs.

There were plenty of other jubilee events in the Soviet Union, from school and library celebrations to Pushkin-themed train trips (from Novosibirsk to Moscow, in two special cars of train number 43, seventy-six of the best railway builders were treated to readings and lectures about Pushkin and his works).[19] On the anniversary of Pushkin's death, asserted one jubilee article, the "sun of Russian poetry" had returned under the Bolsheviks:

> A crisp February sun turned the city's wintry gloom to resplendent lustre yesterday, and crowds paused to watch decorators scale the belfry of the former Strastnoi Monastery on Pushkin Square from which a huge portrait of the poet was suspended. A decorative panel beneath showed his works borne aloft by an advancing army of Soviet readers, symbolizing Pushkin's increasing popularity with a new generation of readers.[20]

Indeed, the editorial of the *Moscow Daily News,* an English-language newspaper published in the capital, focused on the difference between 1837 and 1937:

> Now 100 years later, what a different picture! Millions of people throughout the length and breadth of the Soviet Union join in honoring Pushkin. *The lowering clouds of tsarist tyranny and reaction have been driven from the sky and the sun of a new day, the day of socialism, shines brightly on the Soviet Union.* (italics mine)

Pushkin, the sun of Russian poetry, in the official Soviet view had become one with the sun of socialism.

To mark this union, many Soviet cities, streets, and museums received Pushkin's name. The former Tsarskoe Selo outside of Petersburg, changed to Detskoe Selo, now received a new name in honor of its former pupil—"Pushkin." It was in 1937 that the Moscow Museum of Fine Arts became the Pushkin Museum; streets and embankments, villages and theaters all received Pushkinian appellations.[21] Other types of events in Leningrad were also announced: evening gatherings at plants, factories, houses of culture, universities, and schools; a Pushkin exhibition at the former Winter Palace; operas, ballets, and plays at the Kirov Theater of Opera and Ballet and the

State Theater (including the operas *Tale of the Tsar Sultan*, *Mazepa*, *Ruslan and Liudmila*, and *Evgenii Onegin* and the ballet *Fountain of Bakhchisarai* as well as the little tragedies *Mozart and Salieri*, *The Stone Guest*, and *Feast During the Plague*). Concerts dedicated to Pushkin took place all over the city—at the State Dramatic Theater, Gor'kii Bol'shoi Dramatic Theater, Little Opera House, and the Philharmonic. Pushkin themes even made it into the movies, with new films released by Leningrad Film Studios: *The Poet's Youth* and *Journey to Arzrum*, plus a new documentary, and the old films *Dubrovskii* and *The Stationmaster* were rereleased.[22]

In 1937 Pushkin became a showpiece for the Bolshevik government, still seeking legitimacy on the world political and cultural scene:

> Those who believed that Bolshevism meant discarding the treasures of mankind's cultural heritage have been proved wrong on many occasions. If further evidence were needed, the Pushkin centenary and the work that is being done to collect, study and publish every scrap of information that bears on him or his works are more than sufficient.[23]

The All-Union Pushkin Exhibition saw record attendance, as statistics published in the *Annals of the Pushkin Commission* showed. Over the course of 1937, more than half a million people of all walks of life visited the exhibit.[24] On February 10, shop windows in Moscow and all over the country featured Pushkin portraits, books, and souvenirs, and posters and placards hung in the streets. And in the realms of scholarship and fiction, Pushkin publications came out one after the other.

In Russia Abroad, there were just as many various publications about Pushkin. Articles in special interest magazines detailed any relationship the readership might have with the legacy of Pushkin. *The Sentinel* (*Chasovoi*) emphasized the military poem "Poltava" along with the fairy tales its readers knew from childhood; the *Naval Magazine* (*Morskoi zhurnal*) featured an article on "Pushkin and the Sea."[25] The main event of the Parisian émigré community, especially on a popular level, was the exhibition mounted by Sergei Lifar', "Pushkin and His Epoch," called by one contemporary "if not a miracle, then certainly a heroic feat."[26] This same commentator gave us proof that the Pushkin "holiday" became an excuse for Russian émigrés of all types to gather around their cultural heritage and present that heritage to the rest of the world. He wrote that the exhibits "gave a live approximation of the Pushkin epoch and astonished the foreigners, who visited the exhibition en masse."[27] Here, of course, the "foreigners" the author had in mind were French citizens. The Russian émigré community in France was pleased to have these foreigners acknowledging their great poet during the jubilee year.[28]

In conjunction with the Parisian exhibition and the jubilee, the popular Parisian Russian magazine *Illustrated Russia* put out a special edition devoted to "Pushkin and His Epoch," featuring a long descriptive article by Modest

Gofman (with photographs of the exhibition by E. Markovich).[29] In explanation of the hoopla surrounding this important 1937 date, one author wrote:

> The centennial anniversary of the tragic death of Pushkin was celebrated with extraordinary enthusiasm and unanimity by the Russian émigré community. . . . It is perfectly understandable and acceptable that this jubilee, so sorrowful in character, was transformed into a national Russian holiday, and it was precisely this noteworthy trait that the "Pushkin Days" in all corners of the Russian diaspora had in common.[30]

This edition of *Illustrated Russia* insisted on demonstrating the unity around Pushkin's centennial that all the Russian émigrés desired and that could compete with the Soviet unity of purpose.

One last area of competition between the Soviet Union and the émigré community came in the area of physical monuments. In Moscow, of course, the famous Pushkin monument of 1880 was fixed up for the celebrations, its inscription modernized to the new alphabet and corrected to show Pushkin's own "I have erected a monument to myself . . ." (rather than Zhukovskii's censored version, put forward by the tsarist government at the first dedication of the statue). Leningrad, Odessa, and other cities throughout the Soviet empire received new statues or had their old ones refurbished.

The émigrés had more difficulty raising funds for Pushkin monuments without the institutional resources of the Soviet Union, but some memorials can still be seen.[31] For example, although the French concession in Shanghai, China, is now merely a historical memory, a version of the Shanghai monument to Pushkin, erected at the corners of Gizi and Pishon Streets, stands even today as a peaceful island at a very busy intersection, still the lone Pushkin monument in China.[32] The words spoken at the dedication ceremony for the statue on February 11, 1937, sound ironic in the context of subsequent Chinese, French, and Russian history: "The monument to Pushkin erected here will rise as a symbol of the friendship uniting the French and the Russians,"[33] especially considering the rapid departure of both French and Russians from China by the middle of 1937. Today the monument has inscriptions in Russian and Chinese, but few Russians are around to read them. The Russian émigré schoolchildren who performed a ceremonial march around the statue at its opening in February 1937 fled the country long ago, for France and other destinations.

PUSHKIN AS CULTURAL TERRITORY ABROAD: THE CASE OF SERGEI LIFAR'

For Russians living abroad after the Bolshevik Revolution and the rise of Soviet power, classical Russian culture came to be central to their understanding of themselves. Strangers in a strange land, feeling themselves exiled from the homeland to which most would never return, these Russian émigrés created their own Russian-language shadow cultures in France, Germany, Finland, Lithuania, the United States. Journals, newspapers, lending libraries, concerts, theatrical performances, schools, and clubs existed in the native language throughout the diaspora, allowing these displaced persons to remain culturally and intellectually viable and whole in a foreign environment.

While maintaining a Russian-language culture, the émigrés nonetheless felt a need to build bridges to the dominant cultures within which they lived. For many of them, the validity of Western European cultures was a given. Russians since Peter the Great had looked to the West for new ideas, cultural and otherwise. What they wanted urgently now was some sort of reciprocity, for Western Europeans to recognize the significance of Russian culture and to acknowledge that it belonged rightfully alongside the rest of Western cultural achievement. The cultural task for members of the diaspora, then, was twofold: to refashion Russian cultural history so as to preserve a particular sense of Russian cultural identity, and to present Russian culture to a wider world, so as to legitimize and lay claim to a Russian past that the Soviets were at that very moment rewriting.

The center of that legitimate past was Aleksandr Pushkin. But his literary legacy did not bridge the gap between Russians and their host communities; it seemed that literature was not the best medium for sharing Russian culture and history with foreigners. However, if the literary arts kept Russians separate from the cultures around them and were relatively difficult to share with the non-Russian-speaking natives, there was one Russian art that was eminently translatable and successful in early twentieth-century Europe: the ballet. Through Sergei Diaghilev's *Ballets Russes*, Russian music, set and costume designs, and talented dancers became known throughout the world. Treatments of Russian history and folklore made it to the stage in Monte Carlo, New York, and Paris. More than any other art, perhaps, ballet brought Russian culture to Europe and the rest of the world.

One of the connecting figures between the Russian "shadow culture" in Europe and the general European cultural scene of which Diaghilev's *Ballets Russes* had become a part was Sergei Lifar', a young dancer and choreographer from Kiev. Russian cultural institutions in Europe for the émigré community had existed since the Revolution. But another way of keeping Russian culture alive in exile was to inform and educate the local population about that culture and its icons. For Paris and France, it was Lifar' who took on the role of public relations man for Russian culture and specifically for the main icon of Russian culture in the mid-1930s—for Pushkin.

Lifar' played a surprisingly vital role in the cultural observances surrounding the 1937 commemoration of the centennial of Pushkin's death.

Not only did the dancer mount and preside over the major exhibition of the time in Europe devoted to Pushkin—called "Pushkin and His Epoch," the exhibit ran from March 16 through April 15, 1937, in Paris—he also chose to participate in the celebrations of the literary hero of the Russians through his own literary experiments. It is these literary efforts that I wish to examine in order to shed light on various models for understanding and presenting Pushkin to Russian and French audiences in the 1930s.

Lifar' himself defined his "Pushkinism" as stemming from his reverence for Pushkin's genius, but also from his awareness that

> abroad, the name of Pushkin is not surrounded by that shining aura with which it is surrounded in our homeland and which it deserves. The reason for this is, in the main, foreign society's insufficient knowledge of the true greatness of Pushkin, brought on in turn by the insurmountable difficulty of translating all the power and charm of Pushkin's poetry into a foreign language. . . . This is why I directed my activities as a Pushkinist mainly toward acquainting Western European society with the works of Pushkin.[34]

There is no doubt that Sergei Lifar' played an important role in the Pushkin commemorative celebrations of 1937 in Paris. He was included in the Parisian "Pushkin Committee Abroad," an organization founded in 1934 to prepare for the centennial of Pushkin's death. Lifar's account of his place in Pushkin events, *My Pushkiniana Abroad,* presents a participant's account of the events and intrigues of this portion of Parisian Pushkinian history and the history of Russian Pushkinism generally, and is an invaluable, if biased, source for examining that history.[35]

In a letter to Sergei Lifar' in April of 1937, the Pushkin Committee Abroad addressed the dancer and praised him for his role in Russian émigré culture and in the Pushkin celebrations:

> [F]or a short time you established a real Pushkin House, our Russian Pushkin museum, in the very heart of Paris, and through this effort managed to open to the outside world those brilliant pages of Russian creativity, Russian art, Russian culture authored by the genius of the great Russian poet.[36]

The Pushkin House was mentioned here not coincidentally; members of the Pushkin Committee Abroad deliberately evoked the source of Pushkin studies and exhibits in Soviet Russia—the Pushkin House of the Academy of Sciences in Leningrad. Mimicking Soviet institutions was an intrinsic part of the exiles' commemorations of Pushkin and of Russian culture. Visitors to Lifar's "Pushkin House" shared in more than the rarity and intrinsic interest of the exhibited items. They were also able to share in the triumph of a successful historical and cultural event mounted entirely by émigrés in Russia Abroad.

In putting together the exhibit "Pushkin and His Epoch" in 1937 Paris, Lifar' was in some ways uniquely qualified to represent Pushkin and

Russia to the world of Western Europe. First of all, Lifar' himself had quite a collection of Pushkiniana which he was able to include in the exhibit, including portraits of Pushkin's wife's parents, a miniature of Pushkin himself by the artist Tropinin, Pushkin's seal and his "passport" to Bessarabia, other personal belongings of the poet, and several of Pushkin's manuscripts. The manuscripts essentially led Lifar' to become involved in Pushkin events as well as to launch his own career as a literary man.

As Lifar' related the story, his mentor Diaghilev had in his later years caught the "'microbe' of collectioneering" and collected everything from phonograph records to rare books to manuscripts. In the late 1920s, Diaghilev met Lady Torbi, a patroness of ballet, the wife of the Russian Grand Prince Mikhail Mikhailovich and the daughter of Pushkin's youngest daughter, Natal'ia Aleksandrovna Merenberg. Offended by the Soviet government's treatment of her husband and of his family, Lady Torbi swore that the unique manuscripts she had been treasuring of Pushkin's letters to his fiancée, Natal'ia Nikolaevna Goncharova, would never cross the Soviet border. Torbi promised to leave them to Diaghilev, and when she died some months later, he became obsessed with acquiring the letters. Ultimately Diaghilev did buy the letters from the widower, only to die himself soon afterward. Lifar' acquired the manuscripts and book collection from Diaghilev's estate—and inherited the collecting microbe with them.[37]

A further reason that Lifar' was an ideal candidate to take center stage in promoting commemorations of Pushkin was his status as a European celebrity. As a longtime member of the ballet corps of Diaghilev's *Ballets Russes* and a famous star in his own right, Lifar' had become to the dance world what Fedor Chaliapin was to the world of opera. In fact, in describing to his readers how Miliukov, Fedorov, and Zeeler, the "initiators" of the Pushkin Committee, offered the leadership of the new organization to Lifar', Lifar' explained that it was precisely in his capacity as "the bearer of a famous Russian name, along with Chaliapin and Rakhmaninov" that he was seen to be useful to the cause.[38] Known and valued by Europeans of all sorts, the star dancer, choreographer, and maître de ballet of the Paris Opéra by 1937 was a bridge connecting Russian-speaking and French-speaking Paris. In Lifar's words, as early as 1934 he was "recognized in some measure as the power behind the throne of the international committee and [was] charged with the task of setting up throughout the world branch associations" of the Pushkin Committee Abroad, which were ultimately to number 166.[39]

In addition to his work on the committee and the exhibit, in the 1930s Lifar' launched his own literary and journalistic career of sorts—he might even be seen as another aspiring Pushkinist. Lifar's articles celebrating Pushkin and helping to advertise his Pushkin exhibit reached the welcoming eyes and ears of the Russian diaspora and a larger European audience. Prominent articles written in French for a popular audience were placed in *Figaro Littéraire* (23 January 1937) and *Paris-Soir* (7 February 1937). The headlines emphasized the significance of the centennial celebration not only in European life but in the making of Pushkin's international reputation as well. In *Figaro* Lifar's front-page article proclaimed that "Pushkin is becoming a universal poet," while *Paris-Soir* devoted an entire inner page to Lifar's articles, entitled "The Centennial of a Romantic Genius Is Being Celebrated" and "After a Life of Love Pushkin Died in a Duel to Defend the Honor of His Wife."[40]

However, like authors all over the Russian diaspora and in Soviet Russia, when Lifar' decided to write about Pushkin, he discovered how truly difficult it could be. Even for professional writers and scholars such as Khodasevich and Tynianov, the aura of Pushkin, the iconic value of Pushkin both as poet and as a continually changing mythological figure, defied successful portrayal. Lifar' was becoming interested in Pushkin and Pushkiniana simultaneously with the biographical efforts of Khodasevich, Tynianov, and Bulgakov. It would seem that for Sergei Lifar', who was no professional man of letters despite his cultural prominence, the task ahead would be even more daunting than it had been for our other authors.

Nonetheless, already a star on the stage, Lifar' jumped right into literary life with the publication of Pushkin's "Journey to Arzrum" in 1934 and jubilee editions of Pushkin's letters to Natal'ia Nikolaevna and, in 1937, *Evgenii Onegin.* Lifar' decided to write a preface of his own to the edition of Pushkin's letters, wanting to pour all his feelings about Pushkin into a written vessel. "I wanted to write about Pushkin," he recorded:

> I wanted to concentrate into this preface everything that I feel in relation to this genius, I wanted to convey my admiration of the great Russian genius and of the only artist in the world who can make the most sacred strings of the soul vibrate. Everything that I felt and experienced while reading Pushkin I wanted to express not in a preface, but in a doxology to Pushkin, I wanted my prefacing lines to be a hymn to that beauty which Pushkin expressed so magnificently. I had to write both about Pushkin and about what Pushkin was for me and for millions of other people.[41]

Lifar' offered up to his reader a full-fledged confession and chronicle of the painful process of writing. Finding himself on tour in Rio de Janeiro during the time he hoped to write his preface, Lifar' discovered that he was mute:

> Every word that I wrote onto the page next to the name of Pushkin seemed dead, false, insufficient . . . I fruitlessly sought a beginning. . . . Before me the immortal shades of great people who had in their day uttered fiery words about Pushkin—Lermontov, Dostoevskii—rose up. . . . Thus this month, so horrible for me, continued, and suddenly, after a performance, having returned to my room at dawn and looking through the open window at the ris-

> ing sun, I felt that I had found a solution. Quickly, not stopping to think, I began to fix onto the page the words which jostled each other in my brain.[42]

The images that Lifar' used to describe his experience are telling. First Pushkin himself and his lyricism caused "the most sacred strings of the soul to vibrate," and yet in trying to turn those vibrations into words, Lifar' found himself speechless, silent, mute. In his autobiography, Lifar' referred to his inability to write about Pushkin as "impotence . . . paralysis," both conditions to be overcome by the "joy of creation."[43] In comparing himself to Dostoevskii and Lermontov, Lifar' clearly believed that he lacked the ability and the talent to write about Pushkin. Before the idols of Russian culture, Pushkin, Lermontov, and Dostoevskii, the dancer remained silent in futile awe.

Certainly these are conventional ways to conceive of and describe writer's block. But interestingly, the process of inspiration which Lifar' dramatized for his reader virtually parallels Khodasevich's rendition of Derzhavin writing his famous ode "God." The predawn revelation, the rapid recording of words which flowed as if of their own volition . . . If Khodasevich's Derzhavin had a wonder-filled experience of God himself, then Lifar', too, can be seen to have been filled with the praise of his own doxology until the words spilled out onto the page. In the biography *Derzhavin*, Khodasevich described how the poet was filled with such ecstasy as he wrote his ode about God, such inexpressible happiness at being one with God, that he could write no more:

> This was already at night, not long before dawn. His strength deserted him, he fell asleep and in his dream a light began to shine in his eyes. He awoke and his imagination was so excited that it seemed to him that light was playing on the walls around him. And he burst into tears of love and gratitude to God. He lit an oil lamp and wrote the last stanza. He ended by actually crying grateful tears for the understanding that was given unto him . . . When he finished, it was day.[44]

I am not suggesting, of course, that Lifar' cribbed from Khodasevich. Instead I would assert that Lifar' understood a certain model of what it meant to be inspired and wrote himself and his own experience into that model.

Clearly Lifar' saw himself in the tradition of anointed authors and chose to present the episode of writing about Pushkin in that light. By first referring to the "immortal shadows" of such commentators on Pushkin as Dostoevskii and Lermontov and then documenting the "fiery words" that came to him at last, Lifar' was reading and presenting his own relationship to Pushkin through the lens of a tradition, through his conception of how poetic inspiration is visited upon a supplicant. Derzhavin's God in 1784—or at least Khodasevich's 1930 vision of that God—was not all that different from Lifar's Pushkin in 1937, and the process of inspired writing was virtually identical.[45]

The volume of Pushkin's letters to his fiancée was quite a feather in Lifar's literary cap. Although Lady Torbi's mother had in 1878 entrusted Ivan Turgenev with the task of publishing all of Pushkin's letters to his fiancée and then wife—a total of seventy-five letters—in the *European Herald,* Turgenev had published only the Russian versions of the letters. Ten of the letters, written before the marriage, were composed in French, and it was these manuscripts that had fallen into Lifar's hands. If Turgenev had considered the invitation to handle the publication of the letters as "one of the most honored facts of [his] literary career,"[46] then Lifar', too, felt he needed to take this opportunity seriously.

Although Lifar' charged the commentaries to the letters and the afterword to his friend and fellow Pushkinist Modest Gofman, he himself wrote a long and meandering preface, ending with an explanation of his publishing procedure. The volume included photographic reproductions of the letters on paper similar to that of the originals to facilitate a facsimile of the almost religious experience Lifar' must have had in touching the actual letters.

The themes of Lifar's essay cover a broad range: discussions of whether Pushkin was an optimist—a "sunny poet"—or a pessimist; comparisons of Pushkin with Tolstoi; musings on Pushkin's love lyrics. Lifar' used the by now stock phrases of others to describe Pushkin, as for example in the following statement: "Russia knows and loves her Genius, her 'first love' (as another great poet called Pushkin), her 'All' (as a critic called him)."[47] But one of the most interesting aspects of the publication is Lifar's explanation of what Pushkin means for Russians and why it is necessary to somehow get this across to the "West": "It is necessary for the West to understand that all of Russian culture in both the distant and the recent past and all of Russian contemporaneity are so closely united with Pushkin that without knowledge of him it is not possible to know us."[48] Translations, Lifar' argued—as many have before and since—are not adequate to transmit Pushkin's works. According to Lifar', the only way for a foreigner to understand Pushkin would be, perhaps, through music and painting, two modes of translation that are more successful than words, that indeed obviate the need for language. Pushkin, in Lifar's mind, was all of Russia. In his words: "In all areas of Russian art and Russian culture, everywhere, in everything, the voice of Pushkin is heard, over all is the miraculous wafting of his genius."[49] In the eyes of Lifar', Pushkin was not only analogous to Russian culture, he was explicitly identified with the Russian language. Without the Russian language, the essential Russianness of Pushkin that made him the central symbol of Russian culture, the soul of Pushkin could not be transmitted to the outside world.

In his paean to Pushkin, Lifar' repeated most of the clichés that have accumulated over the years; not only Pushkin as "our All" and Pushkin as "the sun of our poetry," but the idea of "one's own Pushkin" as well:

> There is some kind of genuine miracle in the fact that however much you reread him, however well you know and love him, every time you find in him, "discover" something new which illuminates and enriches. And this is true not only in relation to individual readers, but also for whole generations: in the hundred years which have passed since Pushkin's death, how many times has the spiritual character of his reader changed—and how many times has the spiritual character of the eternally living Pushkin, who does not turn to stone or harden, changed with it; every generation discovered "its own Pushkin" ["*svoi* Pushkin"]—Pushkin turned out to be inexhaustible, the rays of his sun—the serene sun of Russian poetry and Russian culture—to be eternally life-giving, eternally warming.[50]

But for whom was Lifar' writing this appeal—in Russian, no less? He dedicated the publication "To the beautiful and free France—a work about a Russian Genius." The tone of his entire essay is that of a man acting as a bridge between Russian and French cultures. He seemed determined to create a beautiful edition: the paper was lovely, the graphics unique. He also went out of his way to try and convince the reader that the West must be made to understand Pushkin. In the meantime, only the love letters themselves were accessible to the French reader.

"THE GLEAMING LIGHT OF POETRY"

I would like to turn to a different autobiographical essay of Lifar's as yet another—and a contradictory—example of how Lifar' saw his own relationship to Pushkin, and to writing. In this article, "The Gleaming Light of Poetry" ("Siiaiushchii svet poezii"), Lifar' offered a variant model of how one can relate to the poet.[51] His model here was not of the high-culture variety, not in the vein of Dostoevskii or Khodasevich, but represented instead a potential everyman's approach to Pushkin.

Lifar' published this article in Russian in the February 1937 issue of the Riga magazine *For You* (*Dlia Vas*). Thus this piece, like his others in the Parisian press, appeared on the eve of the one hundredth anniversary of Pushkin's duel and death. Despite the general—and exaggeratedly poetic—title, the essay was not so much about poetry or about Pushkin as about Lifar' himself. He began with his school years—according to tradition, he wrote, at school he was "punished" by Pushkin, "our great national poet." Lifar' went on to detail the reading and memorization of Pushkin's works; the rote recitals of thirty schoolboys massacring the lines, rhythm, and rhyme of lyric and narrative poems; the "mortal boredom" wrought by the lines of the classical author. Worse than memorization, commented Lifar', were the "literary analyses" required in the upper forms; worst of all were the compositions.

> "Pushkin, the Great Russian National Poet." "Pushkin and Byron," "Pushkin, the Creator of Russian Literature of the XIX Century," "Russian Society after Pushkin's Novel *Evgenii Onegin*," "An Analysis of the Characters of Onegin and Tat'iana," "What Did Pushkin Think of Poetry and the Poet," "Pushkin's Realism," "Pushkin in the Pleiad of the Greatest Poets of the World," "Russian Might in the Works of Pushkin," "Is Pushkin a World-Class Poet?" and so on and so on.

Reading this list of themes, one cringes at the often schematic nature of literary composition. Such themes, of course, can kill a student's interest in literature. But Lifar' and his schoolmates, back in the 1910s, learned the rote approach to composition well. "[I]t had already become a joke among us," he recalled, "to begin our compositions with one and the same formula: 'Our great national poet, A. S. Pushkin, in his work of genius . . . ,' after which we repeated everything that our teacher taught us, or [copied from] the literary handbook." The formulas are as hackneyed as they are empty: "Before him there was nothing. By the strength of his [desire], he created Russian literature, which now occupies a place worthy of her among the literatures of other peoples." In his article, Lifar' suggested that by making Pushkin obligatory, schoolteachers ruined him for generations of Russians. Never did Lifar' read Pushkin at home, "for himself," although he read Dostoevskii with gusto—an author not taught at school.

"Why read Pushkin?" he asked—"I might as well have read my algebra textbook in my spare time." But after leaving school, Lifar' suddenly—and he asserted in the article that he did not recall why it happened—came to love Pushkin. He picked up a book of poems, read an unfamiliar one, and was hooked. "I reread works that I had known before. They took on a new ring, a freshness, a charming beauty," he exulted.

We might stop to consider why indeed Lifar' changed his attitude about Pushkin. It is possible to speculate that the sounds of Pushkin's poetry and prose were sweeter and plucked the strings of his soul even more when he began to write about Pushkin, by which time he was no longer living in an entirely Russian-language environment. More important, I think, if we consider Lifar' as a representative of his generation of Russians seeking a usable past in the face of the Bolshevik Revolution, this turning to Pushkin, the poet-exile, the aristocratic poet, the martyred poet who died a young and tragic death, marked a general mood of Russian émigrés who themselves were suffering exile and the tragic end of their worlds. Lifar's Pushkin worked at two levels simultaneously, as a particular construction of Pushkin as aristocrat which ran counter to the Soviet Pushkin and as an everyman's Pushkin.

But the process of rediscovering Pushkin, of finding his own Pushkin to replace the one school had crammed down his throat, is not really the unusual part of Lifar's story.[52] What strikes me especially in his essay is the difficulty in writing about Pushkin interestingly. Here, though, in contrast with his confessional style in *My Pushkiniana Abroad,* Lifar' neither detailed the process of finding his own voice to write about Pushkin nor did he seem to realize that he was expressing his newly discovered love of Pushkin in clichés that would have made his teachers at the Kiev Lycée proud.

After narrating the scene of his sudden change of heart, Lifar' continued the essay, writing in trite formulaic phrase after trite formulaic phrase: "Before me the gleaming light of poetry was revealed." "I reread him in his entirety, greedily absorbing into myself the music of his poems which forced me to become mute from delight. The more I read, the more he became for me—'my own.'"

> The "great and genius" Pushkin of the Lycée student had become my dearest and most wonderful comrade, and I saw how much richer and happier life would be with him. Clearly I could never part with him again. And I will remain true to him for my entire life—to Pushkin, my leader and mentor.

Lifar', who had supposedly undergone a life change in realizing that poetry was more important and lasting than algebra, that literature could touch a deep and precious part of the soul and fill a void in everyday life, still wrote about Pushkin and poetry in that saccharine-sweet tonality of museum tour guides and grade-school teachers. In the face of such pathos, the simplicity of Apollon Grigor'ev's adage of 1859 becomes more and more attractive; in his phrase "Pushkin is our all" (*Pushkin—nashe vse*), Grigor'iev avoided adjectives (great, mighty, Russian, genius, world-class) and nouns (leader, mentor, creator, font—even poet) and replaced all praise with a kind of universal appositive—everything.

Lifar', it seems to me, is useful as a representative of several particular styles of writing and thinking about Aleksandr Pushkin. Influenced, to be sure, by his own education and interests, by his amateur status in the literary world, and by the audiences for whom he wrote, Lifar' nonetheless presented in his "Gleaming Light of Poetry" an example of literary *poshlost'* that would have set Vladimir Nabokov's teeth on edge.[53] The intended shape of Lifar's essay is clear; he wanted to make a contrast between the vapid statements about Pushkin which he was taught to make in school and the deeper, truly felt statements he could make in 1937. It is interesting that he was unable to notice that his later statements were equally vapid.

Somehow the almost parenthetical homage to Pushkin that can be found, for example, in the following interview with Nabokov seems both more honest and more genuine. In answer to the question "Why are you so passionately concerned with Pushkin?" Nabokov stated:

> it's not so much caring about Pushkin—I love him dearly of course, he is the greatest Russian poet, there is no doubt about that—but it was again the combination of the excitement of finding the right way of doing things and a certain approach to reality, to the reality of Pushkin, through my own translations.[54]

In this comment, Nabokov showed another way, his own way, of creating Pushkin, through his translations.

Nabokov's approach to Pushkin, while retaining personal affection, was an essentially intellectual endeavor, while Lifar' projected a purely emotive response to Pushkin. In turning Pushkin into a figure for public celebration and everyman's contemplation, Lifar' was not creating a model or a positive hero. His presentations of Pushkin were more hagiographic than biographic, offering a superficial usable past that contrasts with the more meaningful pasts which Tynianov, Khodasevich, and Bulgakov were plumbing. What's more, Lifar' offered a model of self-focus, always keeping himself in the frame of the picture of Pushkin. While others tried to confront Pushkin as a historical figure moved into the historical present, Lifar' related to Pushkin on purely emotional, self-centered, and shallow levels.

In the essay for the Riga glossy magazine *For You* and in the retrospective self-praising narrative of his involvement with the Pushkin Committee and Pushkin events, Lifar' represented two different aspects of understanding the individual's relationship to Pushkin. In the former narrative, he specifically wrote for a general audience in describing his schoolboy hatred of the "great national poet" and cast himself as a normal young man whose normative experience of hating school subjects should and must be replaced by an adult revelation. In contrast, in *My Pushkiniana Abroad* Lifar' tried to ally himself with more authoritative voices of Russian culture, be they Chaliapin, Rakhmaninov, or Khodasevich, in presenting an inspiration-filled model of perceiving Pushkin. The fact that the two literary roles Lifar' chose to play contradict each other should not concern us. Like a good ad man, Lifar' was squarely in the middle of publicizing Pushkin in 1937 Paris and Europe. And as a publicist who saw his client as being in need of "becoming" a universal poet, Lifar' endeavored to loan his own gleam and glamour as a ballet celebrity to his lesser-known comrade.

During the "jubilee year" in the Soviet Union and in the cities and towns of Europe, Egypt, China, and the United States, exhibits were staged, books of and about Pushkin were printed and reviewed, statistics of visitors, readers, numbers of editions were collated. Scholars, writers, and regular people attended concerts, readings, "celebratory meetings" (*torzhestvennye zasedaniia*) to commemorate Pushkin. Another phenomenon of public memory was the "our Pushkin" of the caricature. In *Border* (*Rubezh*), a Harbin publication, a cartoonist offered a full-page comic-strip story entitled "We and Pushkin . . ." with drawings for each of the six panels:

> From infancy the image of Pushkin and his nanny hovered over us . . .
>
> In our early childhood we went to the blue sea, dreaming of a golden fish . . .
>
> As young gymnasium students we raved about Ruslan . . .
>
> In the upper forms we imagined ourselves Onegins . . .
>
> During our student years we completely lost our heads and pontificated about the Decembrists . . .
>
> And so? Isn't it natural that having found ourselves in exile we are again dreaming of the golden fish?

This golden fish, this fondly held hope of wishes that could restore the Russia they so missed, was a constant in émigré publications. Whether dreaming of the extermination of the Soviets or of a miraculous return to a land where both Russias could merge again, émigré authors focused the lens of Pushkin's anniversary squarely on the future of Russia and Russian culture. Pushkin himself became for émigrés the very "golden fish" of his own fairy tale, the means by which wishes were to be granted. More than anything, for the émigré community the Pushkin of 1937 remained a symbol. He was an umbrella for Russian cultural celebrations abroad. He was a sign of the unity of the Russian diaspora. Pushkin was also the territory which had to be won in the cultural war with Soviet power. Most important, through his agency many Russian émigrés were united in spirit with the Russians left on the other side.

In his article about Soviet Pushkin Days, the émigré journalist "P. A." cited letters by Soviet citizens: "Why do we love Pushkin?" "Because Pushkin is life itself." "Because Pushkin is alive." This myth of the "aliveness" of Pushkin was on the one hundredth anniversary of his death exceptionally important for the émigré community—not only in order to win Pushkin from Soviet Russia but also in order to continue to believe, twenty years after the Revolution, that there still existed *something* that was capable of uniting the Russian exiles with the Russians "who remained in captivity."[55]

Oddly enough, in their competition over ownership of Pushkin, the émigrés and the Soviets *were* united. By 1937 Pushkin was the central figure through whom Russians abroad understood their own cultural identity, and he was the main means by which the Soviet Union tried to give itself historical and cultural legitimacy. Both groups ended their search for "their own Pushkin" by creating a Pushkin who simultaneously united and divided Russians around the globe.

Regardless of who won the competition over cultural legitimacy, Russian literary culture was not enriched by the Pushkin commemorations. If Lifar's project of commemoration—including his exhibit, his articles, and his Pushkin publications—succeeded where Bulgakov, Khodasevich, and Tynianov failed, this is because Lifar' skirted, ignored, and otherwise avoided the questions my three writers were asking. Because he himself was not a writer, there was nothing at stake for Lifar' in his engagement with Pushkin. He was able to get away with clichéd emotions and phrases because he had no actual connection to the literary past, but he was therefore not able to enhance that past or his present.

My three main writers searched the past in order to understand their own relationship as writers to the present. Tynianov believed that literary figures from the past could be resurrected and utilized through his scientific and scholarly method, a method he abandoned when confronted with trying to resurrect and utilize Pushkin. Khodasevich searched the past for an exemplary literary hero, and in so doing he found Derzhavin, not Pushkin. Bulgakov chose Molière to explore the complicated relationship between a writer and his patron as a way of modeling his own position in Soviet society, while knowing that whatever else happened, Molière and his works were immortal. By the time of his collaboration with Veresaev on the Pushkin play, he had little faith that such a relationship was possible, and so he could not bring himself to present the living Pushkin on stage.

In the final irony, then, Pushkin would be celebrated in 1937 not by his literary equals but by lesser figures. For serious writers, the issue of literary ownership got in the way; Pushkin was "common property" in a way that Griboedov, Derzhavin, and Molière were not. If Pushkin was all things to all people, as the nineteenth century would have it, then for the biographer he could not be anyone. The cacophony of voices the biographer needed to respond to and engage with was too deafening. Finally, in a literary culture where Pushkin was the greatest writer of all, the definition of literary success changed its parameters, from trying to *become* a new Pushkin to writing about Pushkin. These anxieties and difficulties kept writers like Tynianov, Khodasevich, and Bulgakov from constructing a usable past from Pushkin's life. Writers like these three found themselves on the edges of the 1937 celebrations. Lifar' and others like him, though, could and did respond to the "social command" to commemorate Pushkin. The cacophony of voices is only deafening if you are listening to it, which Lifar' decidedly was not.

POSTSCRIPT: STILL SEEKING A USABLE PAST

In an accidental and ironic coincidence, I was completing the last lines of this book on June 6, 1999, the bicentennial of Aleksandr Pushkin's birth. Even in the United States, radio reports, newspaper articles, and magazine essays punctuated the week leading up to this significant anniversary.[56] Just as the commemorations of 1937 found changed Russian literary and cultural landscapes both in the Soviet Union and in Russia Abroad, the year 1999 saw arguably a more joyous and yet more convoluted set of celebrations of Pushkin and other Russian writers. As the end of the century approached, such jubilees—in the form of concerts, conferences, collections of articles, newspaper features—were myriad in Russia and abroad, with bicentennial and centennial conferences honoring Griboedov, Bakhtin, Zoshchenko, Nabokov, and many others, to the "pre-Pushkin" events leading up to the long-awaited bicentennial of the poet's birth.

In the United States, the *New York Times* and National Public Radio have talked about "Pushkinmania," "Pushkin fever," and the "Pushkin craze," exemplified at the end of our consumer-oriented century above all by the proliferation of "Pushkin kitsch." Pushkin, deemed a "real playboy" by the publishers of Russian *Playboy,* can "add glitz to almost anything," one nightclub owner in Moscow declared. Radio trivia shows, exhibits, concerts, operas, yes, and even a new British film production of *Onegin* starring Ralph Fiennes and Liv Tyler, dominate the Russian scene during this season of Pushkin festivities. But the "official pomp" and "commercial kitsch" have kept the 1999 Pushkin, like his 1937 brother, from representing Russian literary culture. Once again in his anniversary year, the predominant response to Pushkin is emotive, not intellectual.

The political events of the end of the twentieth century reverse those of the period under examination in this book—the Soviet government, founded through Revolution in 1917, perished rather ignominiously of its own weight in the early 1990s, and the Communist Party which so influenced literary and historical events and narratives throughout its reign is now one of several parties in a semidemocratic Russia. The year 1999 is in a way 1937 all over again: similar cultural anxieties and confusion prevail ten years after the collapse of the Soviet regime as did twenty years after its inception. Cultural and historical meaning are presently in flux. And the only statues left standing at the end of the Soviet era are the statues of Pushkin.

But if Pushkin was not central to the "usable past" in 1937, he may not be a part of it for the new century either. It is notable that in constructing a new future, the Russia of émigrés and of those who stayed home are cautiously merging, and the past which joins them is being reconstructed from the "split whole" of the twentieth century into a new union in the twenty-first. What precisely will constitute Russia's "usable past" for the twenty-first century remains to be seen, but unquestionably among the building blocks of that past will be the biographical representations of Tynianov, Khodasevich, and Bulgakov.

Notes

CHAPTER ONE

1. Van Wyck Brooks, "On Creating a Usable Past," *Dial* 64 (1918): 338.

2. Hayden White, *The Content of the Form: Narrative Discourse and Historical Representation* (Baltimore: Johns Hopkins University Press, 1987), 57.

3. Vladimir Nabokov, *Glory*, trans. Dmitri Nabokov and the author (New York: McGraw-Hill, 1971), 64.

4. The term "usable past," coined by Van Wyck Brooks, offers a way to codify one's forebears and to construct a cultural identity in the face of cultural disruption or chaos. As one historian has put it, "legitimacy becomes a subject of discussion only when it is disputed." See Hans Blumenberg, *The Legitimacy of the Modern Age*, trans. Robert Wallace (Cambridge, Mass.: MIT Press, 1983), 97. It was the legitimacy of their own Russian culture over which writers and ideologues in the Soviet Union and in Russia Abroad struggled.

5. Brooks, "Usable Past," 339.

6. "How Do We Value Pushkin?," *Izvestiia*, quoted in Marcus Levitt, *Russian Literary Politics and the Pushkin Celebration of 1880* (Ithaca, N.Y.: Cornell University Press, 1989), 166.

7. P. A., "Pushkinskie dni v Sovetskoi Rossii," *Illiustrirovannaia Rossiia* (Paris, 1937), 141.

8. P. N. Miliukov, *Zhivoi Pushkin* (Paris: Rodnik, 1937), 132, 7.

9. See "O Pushkinskikh dniakh v emigratsii," *Illiustrirovannaia Rossiia* (Paris, 1937), 137.

10. P. A., "Pushkinskie dni," 140. For more on Pushkin as a Soviet saint, see Paul Debreczeny, *Social Functions of Literature: Alexander Pushkin and Russian Culture* (Stanford, Calif.: Stanford University Press, 1997), especially chapter 7.

11. Brooks, "Usable Past," 337.

12. Ibid., 340.

13. Leon Edel, *Literary Biography* (Toronto: University of Toronto Press, 1957), 90.

14. This term, coined in France, refers to novelized versions of biography in which the author uses maximal artistic freedom in portraying the life of his subject for the popular reader.

15. B. M. Eikhenbaum, "Roman ili biografiia?" in *O literature. Raboty raznykh let.* (Moscow: Sovetskii pisatel', 1987), 288.

16. B. M. Eikhenbaum, n.t., *Severnye zapiski* 12 (1913): 195–96; reprinted in *O literature,* 477.

17. Iu. N. Tynianov, "Promezhutok," *Arkhaisty i novatory* (Leningrad: Priboi, 1929), 542.

18. Vladimir Veidle, "Ob iskusstve biografa," *Sovremennye zapiski* 44 (1931): 492–93.

19. Iu. M. Lotman, "Biografiia—zhivoe litso," *Novyi mir* 2 (1985): 228.

20. Osip Mandel'shtam, "Konets romana," reprinted in *Sobranie sochinenii,* 3 vols. (Moscow: Terra, 1991), 2:269. First known publication in *O poezii* (1928).

21. F. Pavlenkov initiated the original Russian series "Lives of Remarkable People" ("Zhizn' zamechatel'nykh liudei"), which published 198 biographies between 1890 and 1907. Maksim Gor'kii founded the Soviet series of the same name in 1933.

22. Lotman, "Biografiia," 228.

23. Lidiia Ginzburg, *O literaturnom geroe* (Leningrad: Sovetskii pisatel', 1979), 133.

24. Mikhail Bulgakov, quoted in Marietta Chudakova, *Zhizneopisanie Mikhaila Bulgakova* (Moscow: Kniga, 1988), 414.

25. Quoted in Katerina Clark, *The Soviet Novel: History as Ritual* (Chicago: University of Chicago Press, 1981), 34.

26. Here I am relying on James Clifford's schematic of five different kinds of biography (see Clifford, *From Puzzles to Portraits: Problems of a Literary Biographer* [Chapel Hill: University of North Carolina Press, 1970], 84–87); other theorists suggest as many as eight different kinds of biographical works (see Paul Murray Kendall, *The Art of Biography* [New York: Norton, 1965], 126–27). In Russia there has been only one work exploring the history of biography in its totality, Dmitrii Zhukov's *Biografiia biografii: razmyshlenie o zhanre* (Moscow: Sovetskaia Rossiia, 1980), which contains a fairly comprehensive summary of biographies worldwide and some discussion of biographical theories.

27. Vikentii Veresaev, *Gogol' v zhizni: sistematicheskii svod podlinnykh svidetel'stv sovremennikov* (Moscow: Academia, 1933).

28. Clifford, *Puzzles to Portraits,* 84.

29. Ibid., 85.

30. Veresaev, *Pushkin v zhizni,* 6th ed. (Moscow: Sovetskii pisatel', 1936), 5.

31. Vladislav Khodasevich, "Pushkin v zhizni," *Poslednie novosti,* no. 2122 (13 January 1927).

32. Ginzburg, *O literaturnom geroe,* 7.

33. Ibid., 8.

34. Maksim Gor'kii, "To Iu. Tynianov," 24 March 1929, quoted in B. Kostelianets, introduction to Iu. N. Tynianov, *Sochineniia v dvukh tomakh* (Leningrad: Khudozhestvennaia literatura, 1985), 25.

35. George Eliot, quoted in Ira Bruce Nadel, *Biography: Fiction, Fact and Form* (New York: St. Martin's, 1984), 131.

36. Andrew Wachtel, *An Obsession with History: Russian Writers Confront the Past* (Stanford, Calif.: Stanford University Press, 1994), 196.

37. Ibid., 224.

38. Symons, quoted in Nadel, *Biography,* 149.

39. Iu. N. Tynianov, n.t., in Andrei Belyi et al., *Kak my pishem* (1930; Benson, Vt.: Chalidze, 1983), 163.

40. Ellendea Proffer, *Bulgakov: Life and Work* (Ann Arbor, Mich.: Ardis, 1984), 636.

41. L. N. Tolstoi, "Vstupleniia, predisloviia i varianty nachal *Voiny i mira,*" in V. G. Chertkov, ed., *Polnoe sobranie sochinenii,* 90 vols. (Moscow: Gosudarstvennoe izdatel'stvo khudozhestvennoi literatury, 1928–53), 13:53; F. M. Dostoevskii, "Zapisi k *Dnevniku pisatelia* 1876 g. iz rabochikh tetradei 1875–1877 gg. Zapisnaia tetrad' 1975-1876 gg.," in V. G. Bazanov, ed., *Polnoe sobranie sochinenii,* 30 vols. (Leningrad: Nauka, 1972–90), 24:312.

42. Edel, *Literary Biography,* 1.

43. Veidle, "Ob iskusstve biografa," 494.

44. Ibid. This problem of life and art is the central one for the biographies of writers. Irina Surat has emphasized that "the life and art of an author present a key to his works and vice versa—the works open up for us the personality and the path of their creator." See Surat, "Biografiia Pushkina kak kul'turnyi vopros," *Novyi mir* 2 (1999): 178.

45. Surat, "Biografiia Pushkina," 179.

46. Ibid., 177.

CHAPTER TWO

1. Kornei Chukovskii, n.t., in Veniamin Kaverin, ed., *Iurii Tynianov: pisatel' i uchenyi. Vospominaniia. Razmyshleniia. Vstrechi* (Moscow: Molodaia gvardiia, 1966), 115.

2. Kornei Chukovskii, "Pervyi roman," in Veniamin Kaverin, ed., *Vospominaniia o Iu. Tynianove: portrety i vstrechi* (Moscow: Sovetskii pisatel', 1983), 142.

3. N. Chukovskii, "Razgovory s Tynianovym," in Kaverin, *Vospominaniia,* 144.

4. Tynianov, "Avtobiografiia," in Kaverin, *Iurii Tynianov,* 19–20.

5. Ginzburg, *O literaturnom geroe,* 8–9.

6. Eikhenbaum, "Tvorchestvo Iu. Tynianova," 187–88.

7. I. G. Volovich, "Istoricheskaia proza Iu. Tynianova," *Izvestiia Akademii Nauk SSSR (Seriia literatury i iazyka)* 48, no. 6 (November–December 1989): 517.

8. On Tynianov and the historical novel, see Iu. A. Andreev, *Russkii sovetskii istoricheskii roman. 20–30-e gody* (Moscow and Leningrad, 1962); T. Khmel'nitskaia, "Issledovatel'skii roman. Istoricheskaia proza Tynianova," in her *Golosa vremeni* (Leningrad: Sovetskii pisatel', 1963), 40–85; Anna Tamarchenko, "U istokov sovetskogo istoricheskogo romana," *Neva* 10 (1974): 179–87; dissertations by G. D. Milekhina (1958) and M. N. Nesterov (1969) on *Pushkin.*

The best Tynianov scholarship has been done by the circle of theoretically and textually oriented scholars who wrote the commentaries to Tynianov's collected articles and who contribute to the *Tynianov Readings* conferences in Latvia. The Tynianov Conference Proceedings (*Tynianovskie chteniia*) often clarify important points and put forth good arguments about Tynianov's texts, both fictional and scholarly. The commentaries and notes to *Poetika. Istoriia literatury. Kino.* (A. P. Chudakov, M. O. Chudakova, E. A. Toddes, 1977) and *Pushkin i ego sovremenniki* (A. L. Grishunin and A. P. Chudakov, 1969), the main collections of Tynianov's scholarship and theoretical work, are also excellent.

9. Volovich concluded that any writer utilizing historical materials and themes is driven by contemporary life, as "it is precisely the present that gives the impulse for such an undertaking." Historical novelists such as Tynianov, he argued, cannot help but sense the potential means of understanding the laws of life and universal foundations which are present in the "strange resemblances" that feed the historical genre. See Volovich, "Istoricheskaia proza," 526.

10. Chudakov, Chudakova, and Toddes have posited four "periods" of Tynianov's scholarly work: 1. his student period; 2. primary interest in poetics and the history of Russian poetry (1919–24); 3. primary interest in theories of literary evolution, along with belles lettres, screenwriting, and film theory (1924–29); and 4. the last period, when he "was occupied predominately with artistic prose and traditional history of literature, biography and textological research" (Chudakov et al., *Poetika,* 399). It was during the last two of these periods that Tynianov intensified his search for a "usable past," in Griboedov and in Pushkin.

11. The novel first appeared in the journal *Zvezda* in 1927 (1–4, 6, 11, 12) and 1928 (1, 2, 4–6). It was published as a book by Priboi publishers in 1929.

12. For an interesting analysis of literary subtexts and allusions, see Andrei Nemzer, "Literatura protiv istorii: Zametki o 'Smerti Vazir-Mukhtara,'" *Druzhba narodov* 6 (1991): 241–52.

13. See Evelyn Jasiulko Harden, "Truth and Design: Technique in Tynjanov's *Smert' Vazir-Muchtara*," in *Mnemozina: Studia litteraria russica in honorem Vsevolod Setchkarev*, ed. Joachim T. Baer and Norman W. Ingham (Munich: Wilhelm Fink Verlag, 1974), 171–84; Dmitri N. Breschinsky and Zinaida A. Breschinsky, "On Tynjanov the Writer and His Use of Cinematic Technique in *The Death of the Wazir Mukhtar*," *Slavic and East European Journal* 29, no. 1 (1985): 1–17; V. V. Poliak, "Pis'ma A. S. Griboedova kak dokumental'nyi istochnik romana Tynianova *Smert' Vazir-Mukhtara*," in *Tynianovskii sbornik: pervye tynianovskie chteniia* (Riga: Zinatne, 1984), 9–17; G. A. Levinton, "Istochniki i podteksty romana *Smert' Vazir-Mukhtara*," in *Tynianovskii sbornik: tret'i tynianovskie chteniia* (Riga: Zinatne, 1988), 6–14; Angela Brintlinger, "Fact and Fiction in Tynjanov's *Smert' Vazir-Muchtara:* Paradoxes of a Scientific Novel," in *Russian Literature* [Amsterdam] 34 (1996): 273–302.

14. Eikhenbaum, "Tvorchestvo Iu. Tynianova," 199–200.

15. Tynianov, n.t., in *Kak my pishem*, 161–64.

16. Arkadii Belinkov, *Iurii Tynianov*, 2d ed. (Moscow: Sovetskii pisatel', 1965), 506. Belinkov based this conclusion on Tynianov's story about a hotel bill; see Tynianov, n.t., in *Kak my pishem*, 160.

17. Konstantin Fedin, in Kaverin, *Vospominaniia*, 309–10.

18. See M. O. Chudakova and V. N. Sazhin, "Arkhivnyi dokument v rabote Tynianova i problema sokhraneniia i izucheniia arkhivov," in *Vtorye tynianovskie chteniia* (Riga: Zinatne, 1986), 141–56. Chudakova and Sazhin suggest that Tynianov's answers to the 1930 survey are a polemic with positions stated by Lef in *Literatura fakta* in 1929. In that collection, N. Chuzhak compared Tynianov and Furmanov and presented them both as "factographers," who work from documents (i.e., facts) and use "invention" only as connective material. See "Literatura zhiznestroeniia," in *Literatura fakta* (1929; Munich: Wilhelm Fink Verlag, 1972), 59.

19. Tynianov, n.t., in *Kak my pishem*, 162–63.

20. Ibid., 164–65.

21. P. G. Antokol'skii, "Znanie i vymysel," in Kaverin, *Vospominaniia*, 253.

22. Tynianov, n.t., in *Kak my pishem*, 163.

23. Ginzburg, n.t., in Kaverin, *Iurii Tynianov*, 90.

24. Nikolai Stepanov, one of Tynianov's students, remembers: "So, portraying Faddei Bulgarin in *Death of the Vazir-Mukhtar*, he gave him the features of one of his acquaintances; I remember how he used to mimic this acquaintance, crossing his short arms on his chest and lowering his head,

overcome with soundless laughter" (Stepanov, "Zamysly i plany," in Kaverin, *Vospominaniia,* 235).

25. Kornei Chukovskii wrote that, without realizing it, Tynianov gave many of his own characteristics, particularly his sarcasm, to his "Vazir-Mukhtar" (Chukovskii, "Pervyi roman," in Kaverin, *Iurii Tynianov,* 146).

26. Tynianov, *Smert' Vazir-Mukhtara,* reprinted in *Sochineniia v dvukh tomakh* (Leningrad: Khudozhestvennaia literatura, 1985), 2:9. Griboedov is portrayed throughout the novel as "Asian," and the color most frequently associated with him is a sallow yellow.

27. Ibid., 2:354, 7, 9.

28. Eikhenbaum, n.t., in Kaverin, *Iurii Tynianov,* 79–80.

29. Eikhenbaum, "Tvorchestvo Iu. Tynianova," 208.

30. White differentiates between the chronicle or annals and the writing of history. For White, the chronicle represents simply the fixation of events and thus is plotless, though it may contain the seeds of a story, whereas in the writing of history the historian, trying to find causal connections for the events of a chronicle, weaves them into a plot.

31. Viktor Shklovskii, n.t., in Kaverin, *Iurii Tynianov,* 67.

32. Sergei Fomichev, introduction to *Griboedov v vospominaniiakh sovremennikov* (Moscow: Khudozhestvennaia literatura, 1980), 14.

33. Belinkov, *Iurii Tynianov,* 188–89.

34. Iu. I. Manin has noted another historical parallel that would have been fresh in the minds of Tynianov's contemporary readers: "In 1918 and 1919 the Russian mission in Iran was attacked twice; the ambassador, I. O. Kolomiitsev, who was saved in 1918, perished in 1919" (Manin, "Tynianov i Griboedov: *Zametki o Smerti Vazir-Mukhtara,*" *Revue des Études slaves* 55, no. 3 [1983]: 513).

35. Related to this is Eikhenbaum's insightful comment that "the novel begins not with Griboedov's childhood or youth (as *Kiukhlia* did), but with the moment when he loses control of his life and his biography, when history takes over. . . . It's no coincidence that the novel's title suggests that it is neither about life nor about Griboedov: *The Death of the Vazir-Mukhtar*" (Eikhenbaum, "Tvorchestvo Iu. Tynianova," 212–13).

36. Tynianov, *Problema stikhotvornogo iazyka* (1924; Moscow: Sovetskii pisatel', 1965), 25–27.

37. On Tynianov's work with film and film theory see Tynianov, "Kino—slovo—muzyka," in Chudakov et al., *Poetika,* 320–45; Herbert Eagle, *Formalist Film Theory* (Ann Arbor: University of Michigan Press, 1985); M. B. Iampol'skii, "'Poruchik Kizhe' kak teoreticheskii fil'm," in *Tynianovskii sbornik. Vtorye Tynianovskie chteniia* (Riga: Zinatne, 1986), 28–43; Jerry Heil, "Jurij Tynjanov's Film Work," *Russian Literature* 21 (1987): 347–58; Monika Frenkel Greenleaf, "Tynianov, Pushkin and the Fragment: Through the Lens of Montage," in *Cultural Mythologies of Russian Mod-*

ernism: From the Golden Age to the Silver Age, ed. Boris Gasparov, Robert P. Hughes, and Irina Paperno (Berkeley: University of California Press, 1992), 264–92; Stephanie Sandler, "Pushkin as a Sign in Contemporary Russian Culture: The Example of Film," in *Structure and Tradition in Russian Society. Papers from an International Conference on the Occasion of the Seventieth Birthday of Yury Mikhailovich Lotman. "Russian Culture: Structure and Tradition,"* ed. Robert Reid, Joe Andrew, and Valentina Polukhina (Helsinki: Slavica Helsingiensia, 1994), especially 139.

38. Griboedov's letters, according to Stepanov, were stylistically particularly suited for weaving into the narrative of a prose work. He wrote:

> In contrast to "business" and "article" style letters, Griboedov's epistolary style could be called the epitome of narrative prose.
>
> Griboedov's letters differ from the general tendency of epistolary style of the beginning of the nineteenth century. It is curious that even his official reports are often just as exemplary as narrative prose as his letters are. In them are detailed descriptions, an exact and even style, and semantic and lexical economy.

Stepanov, "Druzheskaia perepiska 20-x godov," in B. Eikhenbaum and Iu. Tynianov, eds., *Russkaia proza* (1926; The Hague: Mouton, 1963), 81.

39. For examples, see the appendix to Brintlinger, "Fact and Fiction."

40. Levinton, "Istochniki i podteksty," 9.

41. Levinton comments that "in V-M all of the biographical material is 'compacted' into the last 11 months of Griboedov's life, e.g. basically into a 'synchronic slice' (with very few retrospective digressions); the biography is condensed almost into a 'portrait' (which the epigraph from Boratynskii clearly shows)" (ibid., 6).

42. Ibid., 7.

43. N. K. Piksanov, *A. S. Griboedov: Biograficheskii ocherk* (St. Petersburg: Gosudarstvennaia tipografiia, 1911), 108.

44. ". . . the letters inserted in the novel, real and invented, . . . can serve as a kind of key, as a sign of the necessity of consulting the documents or at the very least the letters" (Levinton, "Istochniki i podteksty," 12).

45. M. L. Gasparov, "Nauchnost' i khudozhestvennost' v tvorchestve Tynianova," in Chudakova, ed., *Tynianovskii sbornik: chetvertye tynianovskie chteniia* (Riga: Zinatne, 1990), 17.

46. Tynianov, *Smert' Vazir-Mukhtara,* 125.

47. Ksenofont Polevoi, "Iz stat'i 'O zhizni i sochineniiakh A. S. Griboedova,'" in S. A. Fomichev, ed., *Griboedov v vospominaniiakh sovremennikov* (Moscow: Khudozhestvennaia literatura, 1980), 160–61.

48. Tynianov, *Smert' Vazir-Mukhtara,* 127.

49. See Breschinsky and Breschinsky's comment on this: "Griboedov's spiritual castration—for that is what it is—is the real theme of *The Death of the Wazir Mukhtar* and the reason why relatively little attention is

given in the novel to literary matters" ("On Tynjanov the Writer," 4). Here again Tynianov was portraying the "spirit of the epoch," since the 1830s was a time of mediocrity in literature.

50. Belinkov, *Iurii Tynianov,* 228–30. Belinkov wrote: "Tynianov doesn't forget *Boris Godunov.* He hides it, because *Boris Godunov* gets in the way of his concept." He also noted that nowhere in the extant personal correspondence does Griboedov himself mention this reading, a point which in his eyes functions as further justification of Tynianov's omission (ibid., 231).

51. Tynianov, *Smert' Vazir-Mukhtara,* 124.

52. Tynianov played with the controversy over the year of Griboedov's birth in the novel when Bulgarin hears of Griboedov's death and wants to write an obituary.

> "When was he born? What year was he born?" he began to panic. "Lord!" he hit himself on his bald spot. "What should I write? I can't remember! You could kill me and I still wouldn't remember. How old was he? Oh dear! Thirty-nine," he suddenly decided.
>
> "I remember. No, I don't remember. And not thirty-nine, but thirty . . . thirty-four. How can this be?" And he was afraid. (ibid., 394)

By having Bulgarin hit himself on his bald spot, Tynianov evoked for the reader an earlier scene where the very-much-alive Griboedov, recalling a prank from his youth, slaps a gentleman in the theater on *his* bald spot (ibid., 48). This picture of Griboedov which arises in the reader's mind only serves to enhance the betrayal in the theater scene to follow.

The anecdote about Griboedov applauding on someone's bald spot, incidentally, was mentioned by Shliapkin as having been told to him by Zhandr's wife. I. A. Shliapkin, "Khronologicheskaia kanva dlia izucheniia biografii A. S. Griboedova," in *Polnoe sobranie sochinenii A. S. Griboedova,* 2 vols. (St. Petersburg, 1889), 1:xxxii.

For details of the scholarly debate about Griboedov's date of birth see M. V. Stroganov, "God rozhdeniia Griboedova, ili 'polputi zhizni,'" in S. A. Fomichev, *A. S. Griboedov. Materialy k biografii* (Leningrad: Nauka, 1989), 10–18.

See the summary of the debate about Griboedov and the Decembrists in Fesenko, "Tema 'Griboedov i dekabristy" v rabotakh poslednikh let (nekotorye itogi)," in Fomichev, *A. S. Griboedov,* 92–107.

53. Ginzburg has written: "Actual people put into an imaginary context, such as the historical personages of a novel, have a specific place. They differ from their contextual neighbors because the reader knows something about them regardless of the author. The Napoleon of *War and Peace* is certainly the creation of Tolstoi, Tolstoi's concept, but this image lives in constant comparison with the *real* Napoleon. The structure of the image is

necessarily double, based on the fact that the reader has an idea of Napoleon already" (Ginzburg, *O literaturnom geroe*, 8).

In this regard, we can recall Tolstoi's own comment: "I was afraid that the necessity of describing the significant people of 1812 would force me to depend on historical documents rather than truth" (Tolstoi, "Vstupleniia," 13:53).

54. Tynianov, *Smert' Vazir-Mukhtara*, 7. Piksanov gave the title of the poem as "To a Portrait of Griboedov" (Piksanov, *A. S. Griboedov*, 104).

55. In various memoirs Griboedov is portrayed as lively and even passionate, in contrast to Tynianov's essentially dispassionate character. For a discussion of the "legend" of Griboedov, see Fomichev, *Griboedov v vospominaniiakh sovremennikov*, 5–20.

56. Tynianov, *Smert' Vazir-Mukhtara*, 9, 414. See Pushkin's "Journey to Arzrum."

CHAPTER THREE

1. Tynianov, *Kak my pishem*, 166.

2. Greenleaf, "Tynianov, Pushkin and the Fragment," 280.

3. Tynianov, *Literaturnyi Leningrad* (November 1934).

4. Tynianov, *Smert' Vazir-Mukhtara*, 127–28. Cf. Bestuzhev, who described a conversation with Griboedov about the relative merits of Shakespeare and Goethe. He recalled that Griboedov asserted: "two things can both be beautiful even though they are in no way similar" (Bestuzhev, "Znakomstvo moe s A. S. Griboedovym," in N. K. Piksanov, ed., *Griboedov v vospominaniiakh sovremennikov* [Moscow: Federatsiia, 1929], 136). (In the 1980 edition of *Griboedov v vospominaniiakh sovremennikov*, this line is attributed to Bestuzhev [Bestuzhev, "Znakomstvo," in Fomichev, 99].) The reader reading the "footnotes" has Tynianov's point underlined: Griboedov and Pushkin are the Shakespeare and Goethe of Russia.

5. Tynianov, *Smert' Vazir-Mukhtara*, 416.

6. Tynianov, "O 'Puteshestvii v Arzrum,'" in *Pushkin i ego sovremenniki*, ed. and notes by A. L. Grishunin and A. P. Chudakov (Moscow: Nauka, 1969), 192.

7. Tynianov, *Smert' Vazir-Mukhtara*, 126.

8. Ibid., 157.

9. A. S. Pushkin, "Puteshestvie v Arzrum," in *Polnoe sobranie sochinenii* (Moscow: Academiia nauk, 1937–1949), 8:1, 457.

10. Tynianov, *Smert' Vazir-Mukhtara*, 157–58.

11. Ibid., 245–48.

12. Griboedov's creator, when caught in a similar predicament, did no such thing. In 1918 Tynianov's wife and daughter went to Pskov, and soon the family was separated by the front lines of the Revolution. Tynianov

managed to get through those lines in 1919 and even bring some hard-to-obtain food to his loved ones (Kaverin, "Drug iunosti i vsei zhizni," in *Vospominaniia,* 41–42). Tynianov chose not to draw on his own experience in overcoming comparable frustration when writing this scene.

13. See David Bethea, *Realizing Metaphors: Alexander Pushkin and the Life of the Poet* (Madison: University of Wisconsin Press, 1998), 264 and note 15.

14. Pushkin, *Polnoe sobranie sochinenii,* 3:1, 330.

15. The importance of the theme of refuge was first emphasized by Belinkov. See Belinkov, *Iurii Tynianov,* 302–7.

16. A. S. Griboedov, *Sochineniia v stikhakh* (Leningrad: Sovetskii pisatel', 1967), 171.

17. Even Tynianov's film scenarios are fodder for highly theoretical analyses. See, for example, M. V. Iampol'skii, "'Poruchik Kizhe' kak teoreticheskii fil'm," in *Vtorye tynianovskie chteniia,* ed. M. O. Chudakova (Riga: Zinatne, 1986), 28–43. See also chapter 2, note 37.

18. Support for calling Kiukhel'beker a *chudak,* a "queer bird," is found in a letter written by Evgenii Boratynskii in February 1825: "He's a fascinating person in many ways and sooner or later like Rousseau will be noted among our writers. He has great gifts and his character is much like that of the Geneva *chudak*" (quoted in Tynianov, "Pushkin i Kiukhel'beker," in *Pushkin i ego sovremenniki,* 250). Boris Eikhenbaum, too, noted that the usual characterization of Kiukhel'beker was as "an amusing Lycée student who for some reason ended up among the Decembrists" (Eikhenbaum, "Tvorchestvo Iu. Tynianova," 200). Consider also the "queer geniuses, wraith-like personalities" of Van Wyck Brooks's "usable past" (Brooks, "Usable Past," 340).

19. Andrew Wachtel has treated at least one scene from the novel in his chapter "Literary History, Criticism, and Fiction: The Case of Tynianov," but his focus remained on the chronological appearance of the fictional and literary historical works on Kiukhel'beker and what that sequence says about intergeneric dialogue. See chapter 8 of Wachtel, *An Obsession with History;* on the novel, see 194–96.

20. Sandra Rosengrant, "The Genesis of Tynjanov's Fiction," *Selecta: Journal of the Pacific Northwest Council on Foreign Languages* 8 (1987): 119–20.

21. See, for example, his "New Pages from 'Egyptian Nights,'" read at the 1921 Petrograd Pushkin commemorations. While other lecturers were musing about the poet's mission (Blok, in "Naznachenie poeta") or Pushkin's place in postrevolutionary Russian culture (Khodasevich, in "Koleblemyi trenozhnik"), Tynianov gave a very textological talk.

22. See Tynianov, "Mnimyi Pushkin," in Chudakov et al., *Poetika,* 83–84.

23. Irina Paperno has translated the term *Pushkinistika* as Pushkinistics, according to the model *lingvistika* = linguistics. Throughout my book I have used either the term "Pushkin studies" or the original, *Pushkinistika.*

24. Tynianov, "Mnimyi Pushkin," 79.

25. In this context the issues raised by Stephanie Sandler in her "Remembrance in Mikhailovskoe" seem especially pertinent—in the aftermath of the Civil War, when such cultural sites as Mikhailovskoe had lost most of their original artifacts and even natural surroundings, the tradition of "Pushkin Places" began to take hold: a form of landscape fetishism, perhaps. See Sandler, "Remembrance in Mikhailovskoe," in *Cultural Mythologies,* 231–50.

26. The Russian term for "conjecture" or "supposition" is *domysel.* Tynianov may have been strict with himself and others in scholarship, but in fictional representation he allowed for creative interpretations.

27. Dan Ungurianu has coined the term *dvoepravdie* to talk about the truth of fact and the truth of artistic imagination in the Romantic historical novel. See Ungurianu, "Fact and Fiction in the Romantic Historical Novel," *Russian Review* 57, no. 3 (July 1998): 380–93, especially 386–89.

28. N. V. Izmailov, "Pushkin i semeistvo Karamzinykh," in *Pushkin v pis'makh Karamzinykh 1836–1837 godov* (Moscow, Leningrad: Izdatel'stvo akademii nauk SSSR, 1960), 18.

29. N. Chukovskii, "Razgovory s Tynianovym," 288.

30. See also Eikhenbaum's comment: "these areas of his work do not simply coexist, but they feed and support each other" (Eikhenbaum, "Tvorchestvo Iu. Tynianova," 187). Wachtel goes one further and interprets the "two Tynianovs" in Chukovskii's story as a kind of Dr. Jekyll and Mr. Hyde. See *Obsession with History,* 180–81. Greenleaf has suggested that Tynianov's article "The Unnamed Love" and the novel *Pushkin* can "be seen as an attempt to 'read between the documents,' indeed, to fill in the blanks left by history" (Greenleaf, "Tynianov, Pushkin and the Fragment," 287).

31. See Greenleaf, "Tynianov, Pushkin and the Fragment," 280–81, for the germ of this idea. She has suggested that Tynianov deliberately studied the "underestimated or eccentric" contemporaries of Pushkin against a backdrop of Pushkin himself.

32. Quoted in commentary to Tynianov, *Pushkin i ego sovremenniki,* 393. This type of "experimentation" is precisely what scholars such as M. L. Gasparov considered to have been Tynianov's method in *Death of the Vazir-Mukhtar.* See previous chapter.

33. See letter to V. B. Shklovskii from 1929 quoted in Tynianov, *Pushkin i ego sovremenniki,* 408.

34. See Greenleaf, "Tynianov, Pushkin and the Fragment," 287. She described Tynianov's picture of Pushkin (and himself) as "the writer with an

antipathy to Literature, who retreats to a position of selecting and splicing, editing and recombining documents." Note, though, that this "late Pushkin" did not make it into Tynianov's novel; as I will discuss below, Tynianov's narrative was cut off in 1820, as Pushkin's youth came to an end. Khodasevich's narrative about Pushkin ended around the same date.

35. One could explain this through the time frame of the novel, since in 1828–29 Griboedov had no contact with Kiukhel'beker, but Tynianov's methods of including earlier portions of Griboedov's life and letters would have allowed him to bring in Kiukhlia with ease. One might also argue that Kiukhlia was present through absence—just as Pushkin's *Boris Godunov* was—through related themes such as poetry, archaism, exile. When Tynianov used Pushkin's "Journey to Arzrum" as a subtext and sent his reader to Pushkin's collected works to compare the two renditions of Pushkin's meeting with Griboedov's body, the reader might easily then recall Pushkin's meeting with Kiukhel'beker on the road from Mikhailovskoe to Petersburg ("Vstrecha s Kiukhel'bekerom," 1827; Pushkin, *Polnoe sobranie sochinenii*, 9:458).

36. Tynianov, "Avtobiografiia," in Kaverin, *Iurii Tynianov*, 43.

37. Tynianov, *Literaturnyi Leningrad.*

38. Interview with Tynianov, *Literaturnaia gazeta* 63 (15 November 1935).

39. See notes to "Pushkin i Kiukhel'beker," Tynianov, *Pushkin i ego sovremenniki,* 408. Tynianov had written a literary historical work of this same name while he was in Vengerov's seminar; the manuscript burned in a fire in Iaroslavl' before it could be published. Tynianov made it his mission to collect Kiukhel'beker's unpublished archive, and, as Kaverin recalled, it was in 1928–29 that Tynianov acquired a large collection of Kiukhel'beker's papers from an antique dealer.

40. Tynianov, *Literaturnyi Leningrad.*

41. Note that *iunost'* and *molodost'* both mean "youth" in Russian, so Tynianov and Khodasevich were essentially depicting the same period in Pushkin's life under these two different titles.

42. Perhaps Tynianov ended the "Lycée" section in 1814 precisely because it had already begun to swallow up the entire novel. Other reasons for beginning "Youth" while Pushkin was still at the Lycée might include Pushkin's first publication—of the poem "To a Poet-Friend" ("K drugu-stikhotvortsu"), in Tynianov's opinion dedicated to Kiukhel'beker, in 1814—and the "first real love" Tynianov portrayed in Katerina Karamzina. A published poet paying court to the wife of the tsar's historiographer might no longer be considered a mere student, even if he was still only fifteen years old.

On the addressee of Pushkin's "To a Poet-Friend" see V. E. Vatsuro, ed. *A. S. Pushkin. Stikhotvoreniia litseiskikh let 1813–1817* (St. Petersburg: Nauka, 1994), 521–23.

43. See Kostelianets, in Tynianov, *Pushkin,* in *Sochineniia v trekh tomakh* (Moscow: Terra, 1994), 3:559.

44. Volovich considered that in "Childhood" and "Lycée" the hero is still "only listening to the world"; he is not acting, but merely existing on the edges of life as Tynianov strives to fill him with the passions and petty details of living as well as the sense of history and national culture. See Volovich, "Istoricheskaia proza Iu. Tynianova," 525. In one of his discussions with readers, Tynianov explained the difference between a "historical story" and a "historical novel." The former, he revealed, can focus on the main hero because it is relatively short, but in a historical novel—which will develop slowly over many volumes—it is appropriate to have the hero somewhat silent and marginal during the first parts of the novel. This concern of Tynianov's with the various rules for genres within fiction supports my idea that he kept such dictates in mind as he worked on his fiction and scholarship simultaneously.

45. On *Kiukhlia,* see Eikhenbaum, "Tvorchestvo Iu. Tynianova," 201–5. Eikhenbaum also noted that the Lycée chapters of *Pushkin* are very different than the description of the same time period in *Kiukhlia;* he argued, though, that *Pushkin* differed from *Kiukhlia* in every way. The only similarity he saw was that Tynianov was still writing a "scientific novel" in that the connection between artistic and scholarly thought was still important in Tynianov's Pushkin project. See ibid., 222.

46. See Tynianov, "Pushkin i Kiukhel'beker," 239–43. Tynianov relies on Ivan Pushchin's memoirs about the three Lycée periods: "Our six years in the Lycée can be divided chronologically and historically into three epochs which differed from each other greatly: the period of Malinovskii's directorship, the interregnum (that is to say, the period of rule by professors; they were replaced after each abnormal event) and the directorship of Engel'gardt" (Pushchin, *Zapiski I. I. Pushchina o Pushkine* [St. Petersburg: Sirius, 1907], 25).

47. Tynianov, "Pushkin i Kiukhel'beker," 240.

48. See also Tynianov's "Lichnost' Pushkina," *Pravda,* no. 40 (7006) (10 February 1937), 3, where Tynianov called Engel'gardt "Arakcheev's protégé, with whom Pushkin feuded."

49. Tynianov, "Pushkin i Kiukhel'beker," 243.

50. Tynianov, *Kiukhlia,* in *Sochineniia v trekh tomakh,* 1:34. In *Pushkin* the "interregnum" or "anarchic" period is described as a state of republic: "The Lycée was now a republic, and in this republic chaos ruled" (Tynianov, *Pushkin,* 424).

51. Tynianov, *Kiukhlia,* 36.

52. Note that Tynianov introduced Engel'gardt as the new director a few pages previous to this, i.e., a chronological error of more than two years. Having Engel'gardt preside over the examination which was conceived of by Malinovskii is another error. See the novel: "Steps already rang out on

the stairs—the director was running to greet Derzhavin" (Tynianov, *Kiukhlia*, 37). In Tynianov's later characterizations in *Pushkin*, he would be sure to differentiate between the fatherly but essentially dignified director Malinovskii and the ingratiating Engel'gardt, who might indeed run to make the acquaintance of his honored guest. For the examination, Tynianov gave Derzhavin the task of remembering the director Malinovskii and then, in his elderly senility, remembering that Malinovskii couldn't possibly have gotten offended at him had he not come to the exam, since Malinovskii was dead. See Tynianov, *Pushkin*, 441–42.

53. See his further criticism of the wrongheaded history of the Lycée in Tynianov, "Lichnost' Pushkina."

54. Tynianov, "Pushkin i Kiukhel'beker," 250.

55. See ibid., 247–48. Tynianov described the "Dictionary," which he must have had in his hands, as a "collection of philosophical, moral, political and literary questions which interested Kiukhel'beker (and . . . his comrades) at the Lycée" (ibid., 248). Tynianov suggested that it was not surprising that Kiukhel'beker could have such thoughts so young, and pointed to Pushkin's note in his 1830 plan for an autobiography: "Philosophical thoughts—Martinism."

56. Tynianov, *Pushkin*, 413.

57. Ibid., 418.

58. See Pushkin, *Polnoe sobranie sochinenii*, 12:307–8.

59. See above for the errors in depicting Lycée life which Tynianov corrected in moving from *Kiukhlia* to *Pushkin*.

60. "When Aleksandr finished, only a few people were looking at him; the majority were looking at Derzhavin" (Tynianov, *Pushkin*, 443).

61. Tynianov, *Kiukhlia*, 36–40. Compare the breakdown of Tynianov's novel into three parts (Childhood, Lycée, Youth) to the short newspaper articles which form Khodasevich's Pushkin biography, discussed in chapter 5. Both men stop at about the same point of Pushkin's life, and both, seemingly, for reasons of health.

62. Volovich, "Istoricheskaia proza Iu. Tynianova," 525.

63. See the notes to the article "Bezymennaia liubov'" (1939), in Tynianov, *Pushkin i ego sovremenniki*, 209–32 nn. 401–8.

64. Tynianov, *Pushkin*, 524.

65. Ibid., 546.

66. Quoted in Tynianov, "Lichnost' Pushkina," 3.

67. Ibid.

68. Tynianov, *Pushkin*, 372–73.

69. See Grishunin, Eikhenbaum. Greenleaf has written that "Tynianov's late works, 'Bezymiannaia liubov'' and *Pushkin*, the novel, can also be seen as an attempt to 'read between the documents,' indeed, to fill in the blanks left by history" (Greenleaf, "Tynianov, Pushkin and the Fragment," 287).

70. See Greenleaf, "Tynianov, Pushkin and the Fragment," 264–92; Grishunin, commentary to "Bezymennaia liubov'," in Tynianov, *Pushkin i ego sovremenniki*, 402–3.

71. In Greenleaf's view, it was the possibilities for montage and for synesthetical color-coding that attracted Eisenstein's directorial eye (Greenleaf, "Tynianov, Pushkin and the Fragment," 264–65).

72. "If the novel about Griboedov basically ended with the hero's death, then, as we see, Tynianov was constructing his new novel in a different way," wrote B. Kostelianets (in Tynianov, *Sochineniia*, 3:557). But this new way was not necessarily a productive development for Tynianov or for the "scientific novel."

CHAPTER FOUR

1. James Falen, trans., *Eugene Onegin* (Oxford and New York: Oxford University Press, 1995), 185.

2. And also like Derzhavin, who dictated commentaries of his collected works to his niece, reliving his life through his poetry, Khodasevich wrote notes and explanations in the margins of Nina Berberova's copy of his collected verse. See John Malmstad, "The Historical Sense and Xodasevič's Deržavin," in V. F. Khodasevich, *Derzhavin* (Munich: Wilhelm Fink Verlag, 1975), x; David Bethea, *Khodasevich: His Life and Art* (Princeton, N.J.: Princeton University Press, 1983), 333; Andrei Zorin, "Nachalo," in V. F. Khodasevich, *Derzhavin* (Moscow: Kniga, 1988), 22.

3. Vladislav Khodasevich, *Sobranie sochinenii v chetyrekh tomakh*, ed. Irina Surat (Moscow: Soglasie, 1997), 3:372.

4. The poet had actually conceived of at least two other biographies earlier in his career as a writer. In 1913 Khodasevich sketched out ideas for a biography of Tsar Pavel I, to be centered around a comparison of Pavel and Hamlet, and in 1918 he began a biography of the poet Del'vig, one of Pushkin's schoolmates and closest friends.

5. As Andrei Zorin has commented, "There was no time to write the book of his life"—*Pushkin*. Khodasevich wrote to his wife Nina Berberova (19 July 1932): "I think that this last flaring up of illness and despair were brought on by the farewell to Pushkin. Now on this, as on poetry, I have placed a cross. Now I have *nothing* left." Quoted in David Bethea, ed., "Pis'ma V. Khodasevicha k N. Berberovoi," *Minuvshee: istoricheskii almanakh* 5 (1988): 285. See also page 95 of the present volume.

6. Vladislav Khodasevich, "Koleblemyi trenozhnik," in *Sobranie sochinenii*, 2:85.

7. Nina Berberova wrote in her obituary of Khodasevich, "He himself traced his genealogy from Derzhavin's prosaisms, from some of Tiutchev's more 'severe' lines, through Sluchevskii's 'very strange' poem about the old

woman and the balalaika and Annenskii's 'old-man intonation.'" Berberova, "Pamiati Khodasevicha," *Sovremennye zapiski* 69 (1939): 260. Note that Berberova does not mention any stylistic influence of Pushkin in this characterization of Khodasevich's work.

8. As Zorin notes, "Derzhavin interested Khodasevich throughout his whole life. In a 1915 questionnaire Khodasevich named as 'the writers who had influenced him most' 'above all Pushkin and Derzhavin'" (Zorin, "Nachalo," 12).

9. For several reasons, this edition was never published. According to Zorin, Andrei Belyi had lost part of the manuscript and the prospective publisher, Grzhebin, was forced to close due to financial difficulties before attending to this project (ibid., 14).

10. For the entire story, see note 76 below.

11. See his 1933 article "Literature in Exile," which begins: "Russian literature has been severed in two. Both other halves are still living, suffering torments which are different in form but identical in consequence" (Khodasevich, *Sobranie sochinenii,* 2:256).

12. Ibid., 2:257.

13. On the world of symbolism, see his 1928 essay "The End of Renata" ("Konets Renaty") in Khodasevich, *Koleblemyi trenozhnik: izbrannoe* (Moscow: Sovetskii pisatel', 1991), 269–77. Also see his "About Chekhov" (in ibid., 249–54) and my discussion of that essay below.

14. See his collection of poetry *The Way of the Grain* (*Putem zerna*) in Khodasevich, *Sobranie sochinenii,* 1:137–90.

15. Khodasevich, *Literaturnye stat'i i vospominaniia* (New York: Chekhov, 1954), 10.

16. Berberova, in ibid., 10, 8.

17. Vladimir Nabokov, in his 1937 novel *The Gift,* examined this very question of where Russian literature went wrong. The idea that Russian art and culture had come to an end was in the air; for example, see Vladimir Veidle's *Umiranie iskusstva* (Paris: YMCA Press, 1937). Veidle could very well have influenced Khodasevich on this issue. In fact, Khodasevich reviewed Veidle's book; see Khodasevich, "Umiranie iskusstva," *Vozrozhdenie,* no. 4158 (18 November 1938).

18. Zorin, "Nachalo," 22, 28.

19. Khodasevich, *Koleblemyi trenozhnik,* 249.

20. Ibid., 250. Many of the brush strokes in Khodasevich's description of Chekhov could be applied to a self-portrait, with the exceptions of the medical profession and the quality of kindness usually attributed to Chekhov; Khodasevich himself had more of a venomous personality.

21. The pun here in Russian does not come out in English; the exiles had gone "beyond the border" (*za granitsu*), i.e., abroad, and hence had simultaneously crossed into another world as if they had indeed died.

22. Khodasevich, *Koleblemyi trenozhnik,* 250.

23. Khodasevich, *Sobranie sochinenii,* 3:121.

24. See his article "G. R. Derzhavin," reprinted in Khodasevich, *Derzhavin,* 272–78.

25. Pushkin, *Polnoe sobranie sochinenii,* 13:181–82.

26. Ibid., 13:178.

27. Khodasevich, *Literaturnye stat'i,* 18.

28. This statement from the 1913 Futurist manifesto can be applied retroactively and anachronistically to much of the post-Pushkinian era and to other eras as well. The Futurists, whose statement sounded so loud and radical, were merely reiterating a principle of literary politics whereby newer writers must shake off the influence and reputation of the old in order to make room for themselves.

29. David Bethea explores the relationship between Pushkin and Derzhavin in depth in the second half of his book on Pushkin. See Bethea, *Realizing Metaphors.*

30. Khodasevich, *Sobranie sochinenii,* 3:215.

31. Khodasevich, *Koleblemyi trenozhnik,* 295–96. Here Khodasevich is using and emending Pushkin to interpret Derzhavin. The "truth which ennobles us" is a quote from Pushkin's poem "The Hero."

32. Khodasevich, *Sobranie sochinenii,* 2:39.

33. Ibid., 2:39–40.

34. Ibid., 2:40.

35. P. M. Bitsilli, "Derzhavin," *Rossiia i slavianstvo,* 18 April 1931; reprinted in V. F. Khodasevich, *Derzhavin* (Moscow: Kniga, 1988): 314; italics his.

36. Khodasevich, *Sobranie sochinenii,* 2:118. Irina Paperno has recently interpreted this essay as being a part of Khodasevich's project to "bring about the 'triumph of Orthodoxy.'" While there is much of interest in her argument, I would suggest that Khodasevich was hardly a proponent of Russian Orthodoxy. His usage of church imagery in this passage was more Russian than it was Orthodox. See Paperno's "Nietzscheanism and the Return of Pushkin in Twentieth-Century Russian Culture (1899–1937)," in *Nietzsche and Soviet Culture: Ally and Adversary,* ed. Bernice Glatzer Rosenthal (Cambridge: Cambridge University Press, 1984), 211–32, especially 225.

37. Vladimir Nabokov, *The Gift,* trans. Michael Scammell and the author (1963; New York: Vintage, 1991), 364.

38. Such *zhiznetvorchestvo* was among the main targets of polemics by Khodasevich's younger contemporary and literary ally Nabokov. See Alexander Dolinin's "Nabokov's Time Doubling: From *The Gift* to *Lolita,*" *Nabokov Studies* 2 (1995): 3–40. Bethea has translated this concept as "bioaesthetic plotting." See Bethea, *Khodasevich,* 44–49, for discussion of Khodasevich's view of Briusov, Belyi, Petrovskaia, et al.

39. Khodasevich, *Koleblemyi trenozhnik,* 370.

40. Ibid., 371–72.

41. G. O. Vinokur, *Biografiia i kul'tura* (Moscow: Gosudarstvennaia akademiia khudozhestvennykh nauk, 1927), 51.

42. Khodasevich, *Koleblemyi trenozhnik,* 313–15. This quote is from Khodasevich's essay "Muni," about his close friend, the poet Samuil Kissin, with whom Khodasevich experienced the world of symbolism. Bethea has written: "[d]uring the Symbolist years, as their private lives unfolded on the fringes of literary bohemia and their daily experiences grew to resemble magic-lantern projections of noumenal worlds onto phenomenal ones, Khodasevich and Muni had lived in almost preternatural closeness." Bethea links Khodasevich's severing of ties with the "bio-aesthetic" experience of symbolism to Muni's suicide. See Bethea, *Khodasevich,* 216.

43. Khodasevich, *Koleblemyi trenozhnik,* 315.

44. Khodasevich, *Sobranie sochinenii,* 2:175.

45. Khodasevich, *Koleblemyi trenozhnik,* 269–70.

46. These are two of the most famous such episodes, since both these love triangles served as prototypes for literary works; Briusov's *Fiery Angel* is based on his and Belyi's affair with Petrovskaia, and Akhmatova, a close friend of Glebova-Sudeikina, used her story in "Poem without a Hero."

47. Khodasevich would probably have included Maiakovskii in this group. In an article written after Maiakovskii's death he asserted:

> Until our time, different truths struggled in poetry; one truth conquered another, good was replaced with a different good. It was easy for enemies to respect one another. But in our time truth even here is confronted with falseness itself; our enemies are defending not a *different good,* but the powers of evil. For eighteen years, since the first day he appeared, my literary (and certainly not personal) enmity toward Maiakovskii has endured. And now there is no Maiakovskii. But whence shall I procure respect for his memory? (Khodasevich, *Literaturnye stat'i,* 221)

But perhaps Maiakovskii belonged instead to the category of writers who merge their lives and their poetry. After all, Maiakovskii began his autobiography with the words: "I am a poet. This is what makes me interesting" (Maiakovskii, *Polnoe sobranie sochinenii,* 13 vols. [Moscow: Gosudarstvennoe izdatel'stvo khudozhestvennoi literatury, 1934–38], 13:9).

48. In the first serious attempt to analyze Shteiger's poetry, Aleksey Gibson suggests that although Shteiger has been considered most representative of the elusive "Paris note" in Russian émigré literature, the search for the "Paris note" intonation in his work interferes with analyzing and understanding his poetry. According to Gibson, Shteiger was actually a much better poet than most critics give him credit for being. See Gibson, *Russian Poetry and Criticism in Paris from 1920 to 1940* (The Hague: Leuxenhoff, 1990), 141–64.

49. In these polemics Khodasevich was joined by Nabokov, who lampooned Adamovich in his poems and in *The Gift,* where he is portrayed under the disguise of the literary mogul "Mortus," a critic who has an incurable eye disease and is hopelessly blind aesthetically as well. See Dolinin, "Nabokov's Time Doubling."

50. Boris Tomashevskii, "Literature and Biography," (1923), trans. Herbert Eagle, in *Readings in Russian Poetics: Formalist and Structuralist Views,* ed. Ladislav Matejka and Krystyna Pomorska (Ann Arbor: Michigan Slavic Publications, 1978), 49.

51. Tomashevskii, "Literature and Biography," 50.

52. Ibid., 51.

53. Ibid., 54.

54. Ibid., 55.

55. Veidle wrote that such a feeling was, for him at least, purely instinctive: "What is Russia? If someone woke me up in the middle of the night and asked me that question, I would probably answer: Pushkin" (Veidle, *Umiranie iskusstva,* 5).

56. Khodasevich, *Sobranie sochinenii,* 1:345.

57. For the title of this essay, Khodasevich was quoting Pushkin; in other words, he chose to describe the prophetic streak in Russian literature through its founder himself.

58. Khodasevich, *Koleblemyi trenozhnik,* 466.

59. Khodasevich, *Sobranie sochinenii,* 2:39.

60. Ibid., 2:294.

61. Khodasevich, *Koleblemyi trenozhnik,* 464.

62. Ivan Bunin, *Okaiannye dni* (London: Zaria, 1973), 118–19.

63. Ibid., 121–22.

64. P. K. Guber, "Pushkin i russkaia kul'tura," in *Don-Zhuanskii spisok Pushkina* (1923; St. Petersburg: Petrograd, 1990), 12.

65. Ibid., 14–15.

66. Khodasevich, *Sobranie sochinenii,* 1:362.

67. Khodasevich, *Koleblemyi trenozhnik,* 458–59.

68. Khodasevich, *Sobranie sochinenii,* 3:121.

69. Ibid.

70. Ibid.

71. Khodasevich was also capable of writing brilliant fiction under the guise of historical research as a sort of high-level prank; the splendid "Life of Vasilii Travnikov," a fictitious biography of a fictitious nineteenth-century poet, had his colleagues and peers completely fooled.

72. Zorin, "Nachalo," 17.

73. Ibid., 18.

74. "Tsitaty," *Novyi dom* 2 (1926), reprinted in *Russkaia mysl'* 3505 and 3506 (23 February and 1 March 1984); quoted in Gibson, *Russian*

Poetry, 69. Joseph Brodsky experienced other poets in a similar way; he stated that he sometimes felt he *was* W. H. Auden. See David Montenegro, "An Interview with Joseph Brodsky," *Partisan Review* 54, no. 4 (1987): 538.

75. Khodasevich, *Sobranie sochinenii*, 3:191.

76. Ibid., 3:216. Like Derzhavin, Khodasevich himself was at birth "extremely weak and sickly . . . not long for this world," as he wrote in his autobiographical essay "Infancy" (Khodasevich, *Koleblemyi trenozhnik*, 255–56), and remained weak and sickly all his life. As mentioned above, in this essay Khodasevich contrasted himself and Derzhavin, ending with his familiar wry twist:

> All these events are pre-memory, for me as if prehistoric. The story about the first word I ever spoke was also told to me. My sister Zhenia, who was then twelve, was strolling me like a doll in a wicker pram with wooden wheels. A kitten came into the room. Seeing it, I opened my eyes wide, stretched out my hands and clearly pronounced:
>
> "Here, kitty kitty!"
>
> According to legend, the first word spoken by Derzhavin was "God." This, of course, is incomparably more majestic. I can console myself only with the thought that on the whole:
>
> there is, after all, a difference
> between Derzhavin and me,
>
> and also that ultimately, while speaking my first word I understood what I was saying, whereas Derzhavin did not. (Khodasevich, *Koleblemyi trenozhnik*, 256)

It is interesting that in contrasting himself with Derzhavin, Khodasevich was quoting Pushkin from *Evgenii Onegin* (chapter 1, stanza 56): "Всегда я рад заметить разпость / между Онегиным и мной" (I'm always glad to note the difference / Between Onegin and myself).

77. Khodasevich, *Sobranie sochinenii*, 3:130.

78. That is, the Pugachev rebellion and all of its repercussions.

79. Khodasevich, *Sobranie sochinenii*, 3:216.

80. Ibid., 3:217.

81. Ibid., 3:218; Khodasevich's italics.

82. Ibid., 3:230–31.

83. Ibid., 3:254. Derzhavin went even further in a letter to Dashkova, quoted by Ia. K. Grot in his biography (Grot, *Zhizn' Derzhavina po ego sochineniiam i pis'mam i po istoricheskim dokumentam*, 2 vols. [St. Petersburg, 1880], 1:543–44), saying that he would be happy to continue singing the praises of Felitsa,

> if I were not certain that our actions, in accordance with her divine will, are more pleasant than words . . . if I were to discover that my occasional exercise in poetry would be genuinely welcome and would not be deemed a dis-

> grace to my duties and calling, then, regardless of the malice of my ill-wishers, who cannot tolerate poetry, I would forever dedicate those feeble talents given to me by nature alone to praising the benefactress of the human race. (Derzhavin, *Sochineniia*, ed. Ia. K. Grot, 9 vols. [St. Petersburg, 1864–83], 5:631–32)

The insight this letter offers into Derzhavin's public statements surely influenced Khodasevich's views.

84. Khodasevich, *Sobranie sochinenii,* 3:393.

85. Ibid., 3:227–28.

86. Derzhavin, *Sochineniia,* 3:594; italics mine. Derzhavin, like Khodasevich, saw the connection between the anecdote about his first word and this ode; in the *Explanations* it was at this point that he told the story.

87. Ibid., 6:558–59.

88. Khodasevich, *Sobranie sochinenii,* 3:140.

89. Ibid., 3:197.

90. Ibid., 3:392.

91. Ibid., 3:393.

92. This monument of stopped time anticipates the next significant monument in Russian literary history, Pushkin's "I raised a monument to myself. . . ."

93. See Grot, *Zhizn' Derzhavina,* 1:1004.

94. Quoted in ibid., 1:999.

95. A peculiarity of the Volkhov is that it actually flows both directions in the spring, when the pressure of melting ice from Lake Ladoga overwhelms the current of the river's source, so that Parasha's invocation of the stopped current stemmed from her memories of such an event each spring. But by July, when the funeral took place, the current must have once again been flowing toward Novgorod (or this funeral procession would not have been planned as it was). Even if Khodasevich knew of this natural phenomenon, he certainly used the image for symbolic purposes rather than for geographic precision. I thank George Kalbouss for pointing this out to me.

96. Bitsilli, "Derzhavin," 314.

CHAPTER FIVE

1. See Paul Debreczeny, trans., *Alexander Pushkin: Complete Prose Fiction* (Stanford, Calif.: Stanford University Press, 1983), 463–64.

2. "*Pushkin* V. F. Khodasevicha," *Vozrozhdenie,* no. 3515 (17 January 1935).

3. Proletkul't was the abbreviation for Proletarian Cultural and Educational Organization. On these classes, which covered Pushkin's poetic technique as well as his biography, see Bethea, *Khodasevich,* 123–24.

4. This is the standard translation of *Koleblemyi trenozhnik*, although scholars have tried to introduce others (Brian Horowitz, for example, uses "Swaying Tripod"). On the 1921 commemorations, see Robert P. Hughes, "Pushkin in Petrograd, February 1921," in *Cultural Mythologies*, 204–13. On Khodasevich's *Pushkinistika*, see Irina Surat, *Pushkinist V. F. Khodasevich* (Moscow: Labirint, 1994).

5. Bethea, *Khodasevich*, 119.

6. See chapter 1 for Khodasevich's reaction to Veresaev's *Pushkin in Life*.

7. See Khodasevich's correspondence with his lawyer, V. F. Zeeler, Bakhmeteff Archive, Columbia University, New York. Also Khodasevich, "V sporakh o Pushkine," *Sovremennye zapiski* 37 (1928): 275–94, and "O pis'me g. Gofmana," *Vozrozhdenie* (14 May 1936).

8. Some of the following ideas can be found in David M. Bethea and Angela K. Brintlinger, "Derjavine et Khodassevitch," in *Derjavine: Un poète russe dans l'Europe des Lumières*, ed. Anita Davidenkoff (Paris: Institute d'Études Slaves, 1994), 167–78, and in Bethea, *Realizing Metaphors*.

9. Oksman has argued that Pushkin's hero got his name not from Lieutenant Colonel Petr Grinev, as Grot asserted, but from Lieutenant A. M. Grinev, who was arrested on charges of treason but subsequently acquitted. See Oksman, "Pushkin v rabote nad romanom *Kapitanskaia dochka*," in A. S. Pushkin, *Kapitanskaia dochka* (Leningrad: Nauka, 1985), 165. But this is irrelevant here, as Khodasevich would probably only have been aware of Grot's opinion.

It is not entirely clear whether Pushkin read Derzhavin's *Notes* when working on his *History of the Pugachev Rebellion*. He did mention their existence in a note (*Polnoe sobranie sochinenii*, 7:137), but they were unpublished at the time, and until 1842 Derzhavin's wife had the only copy. The note in *History* can be read either way.

Samuel Schwarzband has suggested that Derzhavin's *Notes* may very well have served as a "historico-literary background" for Pushkin's novel. See Schwarzband, "Les *Carnets* de Derjavine et *La Fille du capitaine* de Pouchkine (Hypothèses)," in Davidenkoff, *Derjavine*, 151.

10. Khodasevich, *Sobranie sochinenii*, 3:147. Khodasevich contradicted Pushkin's assertion, based on Dmitriev's memoirs, that Derzhavin hung men during the Pugachev rebellion more "from poetic curiosity than actual need" (ibid., 3:214). It is intriguing that Lieutenant Colonel Grinev's activities were described within paragraphs of the same chapter (chapter 5) of Pushkin's *History*, where Derzhavin's bravery in quelling a rioting crowd and hanging its ringleaders became a prominent theme. And although he chose to leave this particular scene out of his biography and in fact to contradict some of Pushkin's assertions, Khodasevich did use Pushkin's *History* as a source for his biography. For the argument that *The Captain's Daugh-*

ter is autobiographical, see Irina Reyfman, "Poetic Justice and Injustice: Autobiographical Echoes in Pushkin's *The Captain's Daughter*," *Slavic and East European Journal* 38, no. 3 (1994): 463–78.

11. Khodasevich, *Sobranie sochinenii*, 3:183.

12. Pushkin, *Polnoe sobranie sochinenii*, 8:282.

13. V. O. Kliuchevskii, *Istoricheskie portrety. Deiateli istoricheskoi mysli* (Moscow: Pravda, 1990), 398.

14. "*Pushkin* V. F. Khodasevicha."

15. V. F. Khodasevich, letter to V. F. Zeeler, 12 October 1935, Bakhmeteff Archive, Columbia University, New York (emphasis his). As Nabokov wrote about émigré writers generally:

> Owing to the limited circulation of their works abroad, even the older generation of émigré writers, whose fame had been solidly established in pre-Revolution Russia, could not hope that their books would make a living for them. Writing a weekly column for an émigré paper was never quite sufficient to keep body and pen together. (Nabokov, *Speak, Memory: An Autobiography Revisited* [1967; New York: Vintage, 1989], 283)

Ironic, then, that it was often to Pushkin, the first professional Russian poet, the first to make literature pay and to assert the legitimacy of accepting money for literary art, that Khodasevich and others turned to try and make their own financial way in the world.

16. In her commentary to the three chapters "From the book 'Pushkin'" in the new *Sobranie sochinenii*, Irina Surat has noted the existence of an earlier biographical attempt in 1920–22. Khodasevich apparently wrote three chapters of his draft, starting with Pushkin's ancestors and covering the poet's life almost until his southern exile. Khodasevich also signed a contract to produce such a book by July 1, 1922, but instead he emigrated. See Khodasevich, *Sobranie sochinenii*, 3:527.

17. See Bethea, *Khodasevich*, 119–20, 128 ff.

18. V. F. Khodasevich, *Stat'i o russkoi poezii* (St. Petersburg: Epokha, 1922), 59.

19. Khodasevich, *Sobranie sochinenii* 2:49.

20. V. F. Khodasevich, "Peterburgskie povesti Pushkina," in Pushkin-Titov, *Uedinennyi domik na Vasil'evskom* (Moscow: Universal'naia biblioteka, 1915), 32.

21. Ibid.

22. Khodasevich reprinted this article in his first book of criticism, *Articles about Russian Poetry*, a book in which three of the five essays focused on Pushkin. The 1922 collection concluded with "The Shaken Tripod," a speech that had marked his loss of hope for the possibility of life in Soviet Russia and presaged his ensuing decision to leave his homeland for exile in Europe. On Khodasevich's last year in Russia, see Bethea, *Khodasevich*, 198–206. Bethea, following Berberova's claims, has suggested that

Khodasevich would never have left Russia for Europe if he hadn't fallen in love with Berberova. Certainly it is important to remember that he was not a "political exile," as Brian Horowitz calls him (Horowitz, *The Myth of A. S. Pushkin in Russia's Silver Age: M. O. Gershenzon, Pushkinist* [Evanston, Ill.: Northwestern University Press, 1996], 101).

23. Bethea, "Pis'ma V. Khodasevicha," 285 (letter of 19 July 1932).

24. Surat, *Pushkinist,* 92.

25. Khodasevich, *Sobranie sochinenii,* 2:17.

26. Ibid., 2:38.

27. Ibid., 2:40.

28. Ibid., 2:39.

29. Ibid., 2:71.

30. Ibid.

31. Ibid.

32. Ibid., 2:72.

33. Ibid., 2:75.

34. Ibid., 3:397.

35. For more detail, see Angela Brintlinger, "'Berezhlivost'': Pushkin u Khodasevicha," in *Pushkin i drugie,* ed. V. A. Koshalev (Novgorod: Novgorod University Press, 1997), 142–47.

36. V. F. Khodasevich, *Poeticheskoe khoziaistvo Pushkina* (Leningrad: Mysl', 1924), 48–49, part 27.

37. Ibid., 14.

38. Ibid., 16.

39. V. F. Khodasevich, *O Pushkine* (Berlin: Petropolis, 1937), 39.

40. There are other articles that could also be considered a part of the project; Surat has counted about 150 articles, reviews, and notices between 1913 and 1929 that somehow touch upon the Pushkin theme (Khodasevich, *Sobranie sochinenii,* 3:560; see also Surat, *Pushkinist*). Khodasevich continued to publish on Pushkin after his 1937 *About Pushkin* came out; see, for example, "Pushkin and Nikolai I," published on the 101st anniversary of Pushkin's death (*Vozrozhdenie,* no. 4118 [11 February 1938]).

41. I have used the newspaper publications, but the three chapters ("The Beginning of Life," "My Uncle, the Man of Letters," and "Youth") have now been reprinted in Khodasevich, *Sobranie sochinenii,* 3:54–94. Note that the editors of the *Collected Works* have chosen the 1932 version of "The Beginning of Life," the 1937 Riga version of "My Uncle," and the only (1933) version of "Youth."

42. There are, of course, several potential flaws in the above logic which require an airing. Under the conditions of émigré life, especially in what Bethea has called Khodasevich's "Night Watch" (1927–39), Khodasevich may have been desperate for income and just grabbed a few old pages off his desk and retitled them. He might even have chopped off part of the

essays to stave off accusations of fraud, or added a few paragraphs for the same reason. This scenario seems entirely plausible, especially as the first set of Khodasevich's Pushkin articles was published in Paris and the second in Riga; there would have seemed nothing wrong with selling the same product to two different customers.

Second, the nature of newspaper journalism and editing must be taken into account; the new titles and subtitle and the change in length and form of the articles may have had nothing to do with Khodasevich at all, but be merely the whim of the copy editors and paste-up workers. If the subtitle did come from Khodasevich, it would make a kind of sense; by adding "the book *being prepared for publication*"—it is as if the author were saying, "Yes, I know you've been waiting for this book for years. . . ." Taking into account Khodasevich's jealous attitude toward his own text, as evidenced by his reaction to the Leningrad version of the 1924 *Pushkin's Poetic Economy,* I do think that my argument is convincing. Khodasevich tried to control the details of publication of his works as much as possible. His republishing two sections of his incomplete Pushkin biography had a meaning which we now must try to read.

43. Khodasevich, *Sobranie sochinenii,* 1:496.

44. Recall also Pushkin's own foregrounding of the tsars in his "genealogy" in the poem of that name ("Moia rodoslovnaia"): "The Pushkins were associated with the tsars" (*Vodilis' Pushkiny s tsariami*) (stanza 4). See Pushkin, *Polnoe sobranie sochinenii,* 3:261–63.

45. "Literature"; see Khodasevich, *Sobranie sochinenii,* 3:67–68.

46. "My Uncle . . ."; see ibid., 3:69. In an undated draft manuscript entitled "Praded (Iz knigi: Pushkin)," which is virtually identical to what I am calling chapters 1 and 2 of the Pushkin biography ("The Beginning of Life"/"Black Ancestors" plus "My Uncle, the Man of Letters"), there are two more paragraphs. In them, Vasilii L'vovich rents an apartment on the Moika canal and leaves his nephew in the care of a certain Anna Nikolaevna, Vasilii L'vovich's mistress. The entrance examination is also described, along with Pushkin's first meeting with his future dear friend Ivan Pushchin. See ms. (17–18) at the Bakhmeteff Archive, Columbia University, New York.

47. In chapter 2 of an undated manuscript held at the Bakhmeteff Archive, Khodasevich did indeed describe Pushkin's Lycée period. See "[Biography of Aleksandr Pushkin up to 1820]", M. M. Karpovich Collection, Columbia University, New York, cited as "[Biography . . .]" below.

47. Khodasevich, *Sobranie sochinenii,* 3:377–78. Much of this passage comes straight out of Pushkin's own memoirs of the occasion. See Pushkin, "Derzhavin," in *Polnoe sobranie sochinenii,* 12:158.

49. There the scene reads:

> In the beginning of January of 1815 that historic public exam took place at the Lycée, at which Pushkin, in the presence of Derzhavin—recognized by

all as the patriarch of Russian poetry—read his "Reminiscences in Tsarskoe Selo." "I am incapable of describing my emotions," Pushkin recalled later: "when I reached the line where I mention Derzhavin's name, my adolescent voice began to ring out and broke off, and my heart started beating with an intoxicating joy . . . I don't remember finishing my reading; I don't remember where I ran to. Derzhavin was thrilled: he called for me, wanted to embrace me . . . they looked for me, but couldn't find me." ("[Biography . . .]," 14)

50. Khodasevich, "Aleksandr Sergeevich Pushkin," in *Sochineniia A. S. Pushkina* (Berlin: Petropolis, n.d.), 1–6; 1. This edition seems to date from the 1930s, probably 1936 or 1937.

51. The Lycée changed quite a bit as well. In Khodasevich's draft of the Lycée chapter, he described it thus: "Unfortunately, many of the good beginnings were irretrievably lost during the course of Lycée life. Neither the academic nor the moral education of the Lycée students was stellar. And it seems that precisely the blunders in the former were the main reason for the shortcomings in the latter" (Khodasevich, "[Biography . . .]," 9).

52. Ibid., 11.

53. Ibid., 13.

54. Ibid.

55. Ibid., 15.

56. Khodasevich wrote: "The Lycée opened during fateful days for Russia. The storm of 1812 raged beyond its walls. Like lightning, a surge of patriotism struck all the layers of society and melded them into one mass. . . . The war became that burning interest which from the very beginning brought the Lycée students together" (ibid., 11).

57. Ibid., 10–11.

58. Pavel Annenkov, one of Khodasevich's sources for this material, went ahead and described the Emperor as "fatherly": "His Majesty the Emperor honored the ceremonial act with His presence and commanded that all graduating students be presented to Him. With fatherly tenderness He exhorted them to fulfill their holy obligations to the Monarch and Fatherland and offered them several pieces of advice, which ought to guide them on the path of life" (Annenkov, *Materialy dlia biografii A. S. Pushkina,* 2 vols. [St. Petersburg, 1855], 1:41–42).

59. See Khodasevich, *Sobranie sochinenii,* 3:70.

60. Khodasevich, "[Biography . . .]," 14.

61. See Khodasevich, *Sobranie sochinenii,* 3:70.

62. This collective noun, *Gannibalshchina,* tumbles the family into a generalized group, almost a phenomenon in their own right, parallel to the phenomenon of the *Pugachevshchina.*

63. See Khodasevich, *Sobranie sochinenii,* 3:71.

64. See ibid., 3:72. Annenkov described finding this fragment of Pushkin's on the back of a scrap of paper: ". . . he asked for vodka. They

brought the vodka. Having poured himself a shot, he ordered that I be brought some too; I didn't flinch—and thence, it seemed, pleased the old Arab greatly. Within a quarter of an hour he again asked for vodka and repeated this 5 or 6 times before dinner . . ." (Annenkov, *Materialy*, 1:63).

65. Khodasevich, "[Biography . . .]," 13.

66. See Khodasevich, *Sobranie sochinenii*, 3:72–73.

67. See ibid., 3:73.

68. See ibid.

69. See ibid., 3:74.

70. See ibid., 3:75.

71. Surat has identified "the society of the clever" as a quote from Pushkin's plans for the novel *The Russian Pelham* (*Russkii Pelam* [1834–35]) (ibid., 3:535), in which Pushkin meant to explore characters based on the Decembrists.

72. See ibid., 3:77. See also the fragment from chapter 10 of *Evgenii Onegin*: "И не входила глубоко / В сердца мятежная наука / [Всё это было только] скука / Безделье молодых умов" (And not deeply did rebellious science / Enter into their hearts / [All this was only] boredom / The foolishness of young minds) (Pushkin, *Polnoe sobranie sochinenii*, 6:525).

73. See Khodasevich, *Sobranie sochinenii*, 3:77.

74. Despite Khodasevich's claim to be speaking plainly ("Скажем прямо"), his style belied his wishes; the pronouncement was full of ambiguity. It reads approximately as "it was as if some kind of being-in-love was in him" ("в нем была как бы некоторая влюбленность"). While this passage is full of opinion and marked by the telltale "perhaps" which often signifies Khodasevich's own point of view—the qualifiers undermine the force of the statement, suggesting either a caution not entirely appropriate to this essay or an echoing dramatization of the young Pushkin's own thoughts. Pushkin would never have said to himself, "I am in love with these men," but he might have said it in a vague, roundabout way such as this.

75. See Khodasevich, *Sobranie sochinenii*, 3:77.

76. See ibid., 3:78.

77. See ibid.

78. See ibid., 3:78–79.

79. See ibid., 3:79–80.

80. See ibid., 3:82. Ivan Pushchin's nickname at the Lycée was Zhanno—and he and Pushkin had lived next to each other, with only a partition separating their rooms.

81. See ibid. As reprinted in Khodasevich's 1997 *Sobranie sochinenii*, there is no division at this point in the text—between Zhanno Pushchin and Pushkin's illness—and the effect for the reader is very different. The seri-

alization of the "Youth" chapter added emphasis to certain sections of the work, especially the beginnings and endings of each installment.

82. See Khodasevich, *Sobranie sochinenii,* 3:83.

83. See ibid.

84. Annenkov, *Materialy,* 1:63–69.

85. On the polemics between Veresaev and Khodasevich, see Irina Paperno, "Pushkin v soznanii cheloveka serebrianogo veka," in *Cultural Mythologies,* 26–32.

86. First published in *Sovremennye zapisk*i 20 (1924): 302–8; also in Khodasevich, *Poeticheskoe khoziastvo Pushkina,* 106–13, and Khodasevich, *Sobranie sochinenii,* 3:468.

87. In the *Renaissance* publication of the essay, there is a printer's error here, suggesting that it was Pushkin, not Pushchin, who was invited to join the society; we have to assume that the contemporary reader noticed the mistake as quickly as the modern one does.

88. Here Khodasevich quoted from I. I. Pushchin's "Notes on Pushkin" ("Zapiski o Pushkine" [1858]) (Khodasevich, *Sobranie sochinenii,* 3:537).

89. See Khodasevich, *Sobranie sochinenii,* 3:84–85.

90. See ibid., 3:85. From F. F. Vigel's "Zapiski" (1864–65), quoted in Khodasevich, *Sobranie sochinenii,* 3:537.

91. See Khodasevich, *Sobranie sochinenii,* 3:86.

92. From A. I. Turgenev's 4 September 1818 letter to P. A. Viazemskii (Khodasevich, *Sobranie sochinenii,* 3:537).

93. Khodasevich, *Sobranie sochinenii,* 3:88.

94. Ibid. From a note about the secret societies given to Aleksandr I in 1821 by A. Kh. Benkendorf (ibid., 3:538).

95. Ibid., 3:88.

96. Ibid.

97. Ibid., 3:88–89.

98. Ibid., 3:89.

99. Ibid.

100. See ibid., 3:90.

101. See ibid. These words were reported by Annenkov in his *Aleksandr Sergeevich Pushkin v Aleksandrovskuiu epokhu* (St. Petersburg, 1874).

102. See Khodasevich, *Sobranie sochinenii,* 3:90. Pushkin wrote about this in an unsent letter to Aleksandr I, written sometime between July and September 1825 (ibid., 3:538).

103. Quoted from I. I. Pushchin's "Zapiski o Pushkine" (ibid., 3:538).

104. See Khodasevich, *Sobranie sochinenii,* 3:92.

105. Quoted from N. M. Karamzin's letter to I. I. Dmitriev, 7 June 1820 (Khodasevich, *Sobranie sochinenii,* 3:539).

106. Quoted from N. M. Karamzin's letter to P. A. Viazemskii, 17 May 1820 (Khodasevich, *Sobranie sochinenii,* 3:539).

107. Khodasevich, *Sobranie sochinenii,* 3:93. See commentary to this last sentence in ibid., 3:539.

108. See ibid., 3:93.

109. See ibid., 3:94.

110. Vladimir Veidle, "Poeziia Khodasevicha," *Sovremennye zapiski* 34 (1928): 454.

111. Bethea, *Khodasevich,* 216–17.

112. Khodasevich, *Sobranie sochinenii,* 1: 195–96. Translation by Bethea, *Khodasevich,* 218.

113. Georgii Adamovich, "Pamiat' Khodasevicha, " *Poslednie novosti,* no. 6653 (15 June 1939).

114. Surat, *Pushkinist,* 67.

115. For Khodasevich, Paperno cites as his "unique attempt . . . to 'become a relative' of Pushkin" the passage from "The Beginning of Life" about Pushkin's relative Gannibal; Khodasevich, she writes, ends up being "of the same bloods as Pushkin"—Semitic from Abyssinia and Polish through Gannibal's Polish godmother Queen Kristina (Paperno,"Pushkin v soznanii cheloveka serebriannogo veka," 34).

116. Surat, *Pushkinist,* 5.

117. Iurii Mandel'shtam, "Khodasevich o Pushkine," *Vozrozhdenie,* no. 4077 (8 May 1937).

118. Mark Aldanov, "V. F. Khodasevich," *Russkie zapiski,* no. 19 (1939): 182–83.

119. See Khodasevich, *Sobranie sochinenii,* 3:527, where Surat indicates that a manuscript located in the archive of A. Ivich (I. I. Bernshtein) in Moscow dates to 1920 or 1921.

120. Here I rely on John Malmstad's excellent article "Khodasevich and Formalism: A Poet's Dissent," in *Russian Formalism: A Retrospective Glance. A Festschrift in Honor of Victor Erlich,* ed. Robert Louis Jackson and Stephen Rudy (New Haven, Conn.: Yale Center for International and Area Studies, 1985), 68–81. See also Khodasevich's "Pamiati Gogolia" (1934), in Khodasevich, *Sobranie sochinenii,* 3:290–96.

121. Khodasevich, review of *Rassvety,* a collection of poems by Lidiia Chervinskaia, in *Vozrozhdenie,* no. 4082 (11 June 1937).

122. Khodasevich, *Koleblemyi trenozhnik,* 295–96.

CHAPTER SIX

1. Debreczeny, trans., *Alexander Pushkin: Complete Prose Fiction,* 11.

2. The relationship between Bulgakov and Molière and Pushkin has been explored by a variety of scholars. See, for example, Proffer, *Bulgakov;* Julie Curtis, *Bulgakov's Last Decade: The Writer as Hero* (Cambridge:

Cambridge University Press, 1987); and Lesley Milne, *Mikhail Bulgakov: A Critical Biography* (Cambridge: Cambridge University Press, 1990).

3. The more important biographies of Bulgakov include A. Colin Wright, *Mikhail Bulgakov: Life and Interpretations* (Toronto: University of Toronto Press, 1978); Proffer, *Bulgakov;* Curtis, *Bulgakov's Last Decade;* Marietta Chudakova, *Zhizneopisanie Mikhaila Bulgakova* (Moscow: Kniga, 1988); Milne, *Mikhail Bulgakov.*

4. Mikhail Bulgakov, *Sobranie sochinenii v piati tomakh* (Moscow: Khudozhestvennaia literatura, 1990), 2:261. See also Proffer, *Bulgakov,* 80–82, on this story.

5. In his book on Bulgakov V. V. Novikov identified the "Dun'kas" here as meaning "speculators." See Novikov, *Mikhail Bulgakov: Khudozhnik* (Moscow: Moskovskii rabochii, 1996), 25.

6. Bulgakov, *Sobranie sochinenii,* 2:265.

7. Ibid., 1:514.

8. Quoted in Avgust Iavich, "O bylom," in E. S. Bulgakova and S. A. Liandres, eds. *Vospominaniia o Mikhaile Bulgakove* (Moscow: Sovetskii pisatel', 1988), 162.

9. V. Lakshin, "Mir Mikhaila Bulgakova" (1989), in Bulgakov, *Sobranie sochinenii,* 1:42. Lakshin's argument seems to me correct. Bulgakov felt that by pointing out the dangers of ideological rule (especially by the "uneducated," such as Rokk and Shvonder), by showing the future development of the present situation in the Soviet Union into an absurd dystopia (such as in *Adam and Eve*), he could contribute to the creation of more rational political circumstances that would be more favorable to the artist.

10. Bulgakov, *Sobranie sochinenii,* 5:447.

11. Ibid., 5:446.

12. Ibid., 5:455.

13. For example, Elena Bulgakova wrote in her diary for November 19, 1936:

> By the way, I remembered that soon after *Molière* was taken off, Iakov L[eont'ievich] related to us the words of his friend Mogil'nyi: supposedly Stalin said: "Why have they banned another of Bulgakov's plays? Too bad; he's a talented author."
>
> It's entirely possible. Otherwise it would be hard to explain all these conversations and offers of renewal.

See E. S. Bulgakova, *Dnevnik Eleny Bulgakovoi* (Moscow: Knizhnaia palata, 1990), 125.

14. See Chudakova, "Arkhiv M. A. Bulgakova," in *Zapiski otdela rukopisi,* vyp. 37 (Moscow: Kniga, 1976), 98. She dates the fragment of letter as May 1931.

15. V. Lakshin, "Sud'ba Bulgakova: legenda i byl'," in Bulgakova and Liandres, *Vospominaniia o Mikhaile Bulgakove,* 54.

16. Bulgakov, *Zhizn' gospodina de Mol'era* (Moscow: Molodaia gvardiia, 1991), 55.

17. Lakshin, "Sud'ba Bulgakova," 30.

18. Bulgakov, *Zhizn' gospodina de Mol'era,* 44.

19. Ibid., 162.

20. T. M. Vakhitova also connects Bulgakov's relationship to Stalin with the positions of his literary predecessors Molière and Pushkin vis-à-vis Louis XIV and Nikolai I. She asserts that the play about Stalin would have made a trilogy with the plays about Molière and Pushkin; "Stalin became a hero of Bulgakov's world along with Molière and Pushkin," she writes. Vakhitova, "Pis'ma M. Bulgakova pravitel'stvu kak literaturnyi fakt," in *Tvorchestvo Mikhaila Bulgakova: Issledovaniia. Materialy. Bibliografiia,* ed. N. A. Groznova and A. I. Pavlovskii, kn. 3 (St. Petersburg: Nauka, 1995), 23.

21. Bulgakov, *Sobranie sochinenii,* 5:448. For an interesting analysis of the play's structural and thematic elements, see Gyongi Heltai, "Interludes Leading to *Tartuffe,* of the Dangers of Laughing (Analysis of *The Intrigue of Hypocrites* by Bulgakov)," *Acta Litteraria Academiae Scientarum Hungaricae* 28, nos.1–2 (1986): 119–27.

22. Quoted in Anatolii Smelianskii, *Mikhail Bulgakov v Khudozhestvennom teatre* (Moscow: Iskusstvo, 1986), 265.

23. We can link Bulgakov's "romantic drama" with Pushkin's "romantic tragedy," *Boris Godunov.* Caryl Emerson writes about the specific chronotope of the romantic tragedy:

> Pushkin constricts time and space in the play to the actual world available to any given character at a given historical moment—and then saturates that world with chance, rumor, and the uttered (not the enacted) word. . . . And, in Pushkin's sense of the terms, the chronotope here is both romantic, because utterly unique to the character living it, and tragic, because that character cannot see above, around, or beyond his own situation.

See Emerson, *Boris Godunov: Transpositions of a Russian Theme* (Bloomington: Indiana University Press, 1986), 105. This "intimate perspective, the sort that traps and intimidates," in her words, is certainly present in *A Cabal of Hypocrites.*

24. Quoted in Smelianskii, *Bulgakov v Khudozhestvennom teatre,* 258.

25. Proffer, *Bulgakov,* 393.

26. Bulgakov, *Zhizn' gospodina de Mol'era,* 139.

27. Bulgakova, *Dnevnik,* 111.

28. Quoted in Bulgakova, *Dnevnik,* 367.

29. Maksim Gor'kii, *Sobranie sochinenii v tridtsati tomakh* (Moscow: Gosudarstvennoe izdatel'stvo khudozhestvennoi literatury, 1955), 29: 374–75.

30. Elena Bulgakova reported receiving a copy of a letter in which Gor'kii praised *A Cabal of Hypocrites* (see Bulgakova, *Dnevnik,* 69–70).

Gor'kii was especially struck by Bulgakov's portrait of the aging Molière, exhausted from the double burdens of his complicated personal life and his fame. Bulgakov's Molière spoke directly to Gor'kii at this time in his life; Gor'kii understood too well the weight of fame.

31. Bulgakov, *Sobranie sochinenii,* 5:487–88.

32. Ibid., 5:455.

33. Bulgakov's title (*Zhizn' gospodina de Mol'era*) was apparently given to the novel by Elena Bulgakova on the model of the first Molière biography, Grimarest's 1705 *Vie de Monsieur de Molière,* and possibly to avoid confusion with Mokul'skii's biography in the *ZhZL* series. Bulgakov's working title was simply *Mol'er.* For a discussion of the title and an interesting comparison of the various archival variants of the novel see Irina Erykalova, "Parik, kamzol, gusinoe pero . . . (Rasskazchik v romane M. A. Bulgakova *Mol'er*)," in F. R. Balonov et al., eds., *Mikhail Bulgakov: "Etot mir moi . . . ",* Biblioteka Sankt-Peterburgskogo Bulgakovskogo literaturno-teatral'nogo obshchestva 1 (St. Petersburg: Rossiiskii institut istorii iskusstv, 1993), 147–66.

34. Stefan Mokul'skii, *Mol'er* (Moscow: Zhurnal'no-gazetnoe ob"edinenie, 1936), 12.

35. S. A. Ermolinskii, *Iz zapisok raznykh let: Mikhail Bulgakov. Nikolai Zabolotskii.* (Moscow: Iskusstvo, 1990), 50–51.

36. Quoted in Bulgakov, *Sobranie sochinenii,* 3:643.

37. I. V. Stalin, "Otvet Bill'-Belotserkovskomu," in *Sochineniia,* 13 vols. (Moscow: Gosudarstvennoe izdatel'stvo politicheskoi literatury, 1949), 11:327.

38. Ibid., 11:328.

39. Lakshin, "Sud'ba Bulgakova," 25. Stalin did seem to have a personal interest in the playwright, although Lakshin considers Bulgakov's vision of Stalin's interest in the writer to be a kind of self-hypnosis and misguided self-defense (ibid., 31).

40. Chudakova, *Zhizneopisanie,* 492.

41. Bulgakov, *Zhizn' gospodina de Mol'era,* 146.

42. Bulgakov, *Sobranie sochinenii,* 5:437.

43. Quoted in Bulgakov, *Sobranie sochinenii,* 3:642.

44. Bulgakov, *Sobranie sochinenii,* 5:484.

45. Chudakova has suggested that Bulgakov's original impulse for turning to Molière was related to Maiakovskii and Meyerhold, each in their own way representatives of dramatic schools that were deeply foreign to Bulgakov. On the basis of the play *The Bathhouse,* Meyerhold proclaimed Maiakovskii the "new Molière" (Chudakova, *Zhizneopisanie,* 326).

46. Bulgakova, "Iz dnevnikovykh i memuarnykh zapisei 1933–1970 gg.," in Bulgakova and Liandres, *Vospominaniia,* 405.

47. Bulgakov wrote to his brother in 1933, "I have been living in the ghostly and fairy-tale-like Paris of the seventeenth century already for I

can't remember how many years, counting from the beginning of my work on the play" (Bulgakov, *Sobranie sochinenii,* 5:487).

48. Quoted in Bulgakov, *Sobranie sochinenii,* 5:704.

49. Bulgakov, *Sobranie sochinenii,* 5:487–88.

50. For a detailed analysis of Bulgakov's use of sources, see my dissertation, "The Russian Biographical Novel of the 1920s and 1930s" (University of Wisconsin–Madison, 1994), chapter 3, esp. 174–91.

51. Bulgakov, *Zhizn' gospodina de Mol'era,* 7.

52. Quoted in V. I. Losev, "Bulgakov i Mol'er," in Bulgakov, *Zhizn' gospodina de Mol'era,* 211.

53. One critic's experiment in "computer philology" demonstrated just how similar Bulgakov's and Molière's biographies are, and that of all Bulgakov's heroes Molière is the most similar to his creator. See Leonid Parshin, "Bulgakov i ego geroi glazami komp'iutera," *Literaturnaia gazeta* (26 January 1994), 6. I thank Felix Raskolnikov for bringing this article to my attention.

54. Bulgakov, *Zhizn' gospodina de Mol'era,* 83.

55. Ibid., 84.

56. Ibid., 126.

57. Proffer, *Bulgakov,* 316.

58. Bulgakov, *Zhizn' gospodina de Mol'era,* 174.

59. Proffer, *Bulgakov,* 578–79.

60. Although many scholars rationalize and deemphasize Bulgakov's interest in Stalin, there is no question that he, like Pasternak, Mandel'shtam, and others, for a long time could not believe that Stalin was behind the censorship and eventually the purges. Bulgakov's emphasis on the "cabal," along with his portrayal of the critics in *The Master and Margarita,* revealed his belief that the leader could be manipulated by the evil third force in the triangle.

61. Bulgakov, *Sobranie sochinenii,* 2:138; italics mine.

62. The most sophisticated exploration of the triangle theme was in *The Master and Margarita,* where each section of the novel had its own triangle. In the Moscow scenes, the Master was weak and timid and did not fight for his work, but the critics were punished through the power of Woland. Woland was in some ways the perfect monarch figure, releasing the Master from his earthly sufferings and leading him to the condition that Bulgakov himself often yearned for, peace. But it was in the Jerusalem section and in the ending of the novel that the final solution to the triangle appeared; the persecuted "artist"—the "good man" Ieshua—rose to become all powerful and to forgive Pilate, the authority figure who failed to protect him. This failure was Pilate's only sin; it was cowardice that allowed him to be coerced by the ideologues. Kaifa, the ideologue who pressured Pilate into crucifying Ieshua, was forgotten, and the ruler and artist were reunited on a new footing.

63. Bulgakov, *Sobranie sochinenii,* 5:556–57.

64. At one point Bulgakov's narrator even states that these two men form the core of the novel: "The year 1667 was a significant year and was in no way similar to the preceding year. The two men whose lives I am following, the king of France and the director of the Palais Royale troupe, worked out two thoughts during this year," and he emphasizes the parallel nature of their fates (Bulgakov, *Zhizn' gospodina de Mol'era,* 137). Bulgakov continued to work on ideas along these lines; his last idea for a play was about Richard I and a writer, where "the fall of Richard I was to bring about the fall of the writer as well" (Lakshin, "Sud'ba Bulgakova," 32).

65. Bulgakov, *Sobranie sochinenii,* 3:311.

66. Bulgakov, *Zhizn' gospodina de Mol'era,* 9.

67. Ibid., 116.

68. Bulgakov, *Sobranie sochinenii,* 5:455.

69. Bulgakov, *Zhizn' gospodina de Mol'era,* 153.

70. In his memoirs, Konstantin Paustovskii related: "Deprived of the possibility of publishing, he thought up for his friends and family wonderful stories, both sad and funny." One of these stories involved a relationship with Stalin. In the story, Bulgakov writes Stalin anonymous letters every day, and Stalin, intrigued, orders Beria to find his mysterious correspondent. Stalin dresses Bulgakov literally from the backs of his henchmen. Paustovskii continued: "And thus Bulgakov was clothed, shod, fed, and he begins to visit the Kremlin, and an unexpected friendship springs up between him and Stalin. The image of Stalin is humane, even to some extent likable." The importance of this "friendship" for Bulgakov lay in the fictional Stalin's reaction when he finds out that the theaters will not accept Bulgakov's play: "The theaters are committing an outrage. Don't worry, Misha. Sit down." This "mythical" Stalin was the leader that Bulgakov hoped for: a protector and benefactor of the tormented artist. For the entire story, see Paustovskii, "Bulgakov," in Bulgakova and Liandres, *Vospominaniia,* 107–8.

71. Bulgakov, *Sobranie sochinenii,* 5:488.

72. Pushkin, *Polnoe sobranie sochinenii,* 12:329.

73. See Vladimir Dal', *Tolkovyi slovar' zhivogo velikogo russkogo iazyka,* 4 vols. (Moscow: Russkii iazyk, 1989), 1:233.

CHAPTER SEVEN

1. Robert Hillyer, trans., "The Death of a Poet" by Mikhail Lermontov, in *Centennial Essays for Pushkin,* ed. Samuel H. Cross and Ernest J. Simmons (Cambridge, Mass.: Harvard University Press, 1937), 225–26.

2. Bulgakov, *Sobranie sochinenii,* 5:553.

3. See Irina Erykalova, "Iz istorii rukopisi p'esy M. A. Bulgakova *Aleksandr Pushkin* (po neopublikovannym materialam)," in *Tvorchestvo*

Mikhaila Bulgakova: Issledovaniia i materialy, kn. 2 (St. Petersburg: Nauka, 1994), 184–238.

4. After all, Veresaev had spent many years already delving into the lives of Pushkin and his contemporaries, writing books entitled *Pushkin's Duel and Death* (1927), *Pushkin's Relatives* (1933), and, in the years after his collaboration with Bulgakov, continuing with *Pushkin's Wife* (1935) and *Pushkin's Co-travelers*, volumes 1 and 2 (1937), in addition to the many editions of his *Pushkin in Life*.

5. Quoted in Vakhtin, "Bulgakov i Gogol': Materialy k teme," in A. A. Ninov, ed., *M. A. Bulgakov—Dramaturg i khudozhestvennaia kul'tura ego vremeni* (Moscow: Soiuz teatral'nykh deiatelei, 1988), 334.

6. See Curtis, *Bulgakov's Last Decade*, 83, and Aleksandr Less, "K istorii *Pushkina*," in *Neprochitannye stranitsy* (Moscow: Sovetskii pisatel', 1966), 252–56.

7. As he put the scenes together, Mikhail Afanas'evich would read them to Veresaev. There were arguments and concessions. Once Veresaev said:

> "Sometimes I regret that there is no Pushkin. What a wonderful scene that would be! Pushkin in Mikhailovskoe, with his nanny, sitting in his shabby little house, before him a mug of wine, and he is reading aloud to her: 'Let's have a drink, my dear friend . . .' "
>
> In shock, Bulgakov said:
>
> "Then I might as well let you have D'Anthès's shot at the painting . . . There can be no such scene, Vikentii Vikent'evich!"
>
> From that time on, they called their attempts to come to a compromise "trading mugs for pistols."

See E. S. Bulgakova, "M. Bulgakov—V Veresaev, Perepiska po povodu p'esy *Pushkin* (*Poslednie dni*)," *Voprosy literatury* 3 (1965): 151–52.

8. And indeed, as Elena Sergeevna emphasized, when the play was finally staged after Bulgakov's death, Veresaev always received his half of the royalties, which continued to be paid out to his widow until her death.

9. Bulgakov, *Sobranie sochinenii*, 5:515.

10. Wright, *Mikhail Bulgakov*, 215. A. Gozenpud has suggested that Bulgakov may have chosen to keep Pushkin offstage precisely because of other plays and productions of the 1920s and 1930s. See Gozenpud, "Poslednie dni (Pushkin): Iz tvorcheskoi istorii p'esy," in *M. A. Bulgakov—Dramaturg*, 156.

11. See Wright, *Mikhail Bulgakov*, 215. Note that Wright quotes Konstantin Fedin's opinion (in his 1943 review of the play) that nothing could make up for the absence of Pushkin in the play (ibid., 214); in his conclusion, Wright agrees, stating that "atmosphere cannot replace tragedy, which must be embodied in a living person. The idea of Pushkin is there in all its force but, for the spectator to truly identify with it, it still needs to be personified on stage" (ibid., 222).

12. Quoted in Bulgakov, *Sobranie sochinenii,* 5:539.

13. Bulgakov, *Sobranie sochinenii,* 5:539.

14. Ibid., 5:540. Indeed, Ianina Levkovich has suggested that the literature of *Pushkinistika* usually understood D'Anthès mainly as the blind instrument of Pushkin's enemies at court; the epithets attached to D'Anthès necessarily included "adventurist," "fop," "scoundrel." The main source for characterizations of Pushkin's foe was traditionally the memoirs of the poet's friends; only in 1956, argues Levkovich, with the publication of the Karamzins' letters detailing their admiration of his wit and other good qualities, did the portrait of D'Anthès become more complex. See Ia. L. Levkovich, "Pushkin v sovetskoi khudozhestvennoi proze i dramaturgii," in *Pushkin: Issledovaniia i materialy,* v. 5 ("Pushkin i russkaia kul'tura) (Leningrad: Nauka, 1967), 158.

15. Bulgakov, *Sobranie sochinenii,* 5:547.

16. For example, Veresaev had complained about the religious quotations Bulgakov put into the mouth of his character Dubel't; in response Bulgakov wrote: "Why can't Dubel't cite the holy writ?" and quotes Kostomarov: "Dubel't 'in confirmation of his words readily quoted from the holy writ in which he was apparently *very well-versed*'" (emphasis Bulgakov's). He also justified Saltykov's use of the word "incognito," citing as his source an article in *Russkii arkhiv* from 1878 (Bulgakov, *Sobranie sochinenii,* 5:538).

17. Veresaev has been the subject of at least one lengthy biographical study. See G. Brovman, *V. V. Veresaev: Zhizn' i tvorchestvo* (Moscow: Sovetskii pisatel', 1959). Veresaev was born Vikentii Smidovich in 1867 and had an unusually long literary career. He died in 1945. His choice of pseudonym, which suggests the French *verité,* is characteristic of his didactic manner.

18. See Veresaev, *Zagadochnyi Pushkin* (Moscow: Respublika, 1996).

19. Iurii Fokht-Babushkin, "'Pushkiniana' Veresaeva," in Veresaev, *Zagadochnyi Pushkin,* 4.

20. Ibid., 9.

21. Originally entitled *The Life of Pushkin* (*Zhizn' Pushkina*), this book was first published in Moscow in 1936. Portions of it were published in newspapers and journals throughout 1936 and 1937. The book came out in various formats, sometimes abridged, and under various titles, in the years 1936 and 1937. Veresaev had planned to write a similar biography for children for the publisher Detgiz in 1936; it appears that he published *Zhizn' Pushkina* instead. The last version to come out was indeed addressed to schoolchildren and published by Detgiz in 1945 as *Aleksandr Sergeevich Pushkin;* it is this variant that is included in *Zagadochnyi Pushkin,* with certain sections taken out for the 1945 edition (perhaps in view of the juvenile audience) now reprinted in the commentary. See *Aleksandr Sergeevich Pushkin* (*Zhizn' Pushkina*), 22–148, and commentary, 375–84, in Veresaev, *Zagadochnyi Pushkin.*

22. See Stephanie Sandler, "Sex, Death and Nation in the *Strolls with Pushkin* Controversy," *Slavic Review* 51, no. 2 (Summer 1992): 294–308, and Catherine Nepomnyashchy, introduction to Abram Tertz (Andrei Sinyavsky), *Strolls with Pushkin* (New Haven, Conn.: Yale University Press, 1993), 1–45. Sergei Fomichev pointed out to me that Veresaev and Sinyavsky had very similar ideas about Pushkin the man and Pushkin the artist.

23. V. V. Veresaev, *V dvukh planakh: stat'i o Pushkine* (Moscow: Nedra, 1929), 5.

24. Levkovich considers Veresaev's "living Pushkin" to be a "cynic poisoned by eroticism, the master of a serf harem" (Levkovich, "Pushkin v proze i dramaturgii," 141).

25. Veresaev, *V dvukh planakh,* 110.

26. In describing Veresaev's upper, lofty, poetic plane, Levkovich has written: "the 'thick filth' and 'dark everyday qualities' of Pushkin the man disappear on the 'upper plane'—in the world of creativity, in the process of which the poet rises 'ever higher and higher to the heights of nobility, wisdom and clarity of spirit' " (Levkovich, "Pushkin v proze i dramaturgii," 141; quoting from Veresaev, *V dvukh planakh,* 142, 159).

27. Veresaev, *V dvukh planakh,* 110.

28. Ibid., 43; Annenkov, *Materialy,* 211.

29. Quoted in Veresaev, *V dvukh planakh,* 143.

30. Veresaev, *V dvukh planakh,* 143–44.

31. Fomichev, "Nizverzhenie kumirov," in *Pushkin i sovremennaia kul'tura* (Moscow: Nauka, 1996), 223.

32. Fomichev, "Nizverzhenie kumirov," 223.

33. Pushkin, *Polnoe sobranie sochinenii,* 14:32. I thank David Bethea for directing my attention to this letter in this connection.

34. Indeed, Veresaev commented on this very letter, saying: "Here, perhaps, lies a certain mischievous exaggeration. But nonetheless everyone who knew Pushkin cheerfully notes the extraordinary cynicism which marked his attitude toward women—a cynicism striking even in that rather cynical time" (Veresaev, *V dvukh planakh,* 139). Stephanie Sandler has tried to rehabilitate Pushkin's image on the issue of women somewhat. See Sandler, "The Law, the Body, and the Book: Three Poems on the Death of Pushkin," *Canadian-American Slavic Studies,* 23, no. 3 (Fall 1989), especially 308 n. 47.

35. See Veresaev's article, " 'Za to, chto zhivoi': K sporam o Pushkine," reprinted in Veresaev, *Zagadochnyi Pushkin,* 325–30. See also Fokht-Babushkin's commentary in ibid., 390–96.

36. Ibid., 329.

37. Irina Paperno summarized the phenomenon thus: "For the Symbolist, only life created by art, that is, life as a product of the incarnation of the spirit, was 'the living life' (Bely, using Dostoevsky's phrase)." See Paperno, "The Meaning of Art: Symbolist Theories," in *Creating Life: The*

Aesthetic Utopia of Russian Modernism, ed. Irina Paperno and Joan Delaney Grossman (Stanford, Calif.: Stanford University Press, 1994), 23.

38. Quoted in Curtis, *Bulgakov's Last Decade*, 90.

39. In the book *Pushkin in Life* the accent was on the poet's life. In the articles, essays, sketches, primary attention is focused on his work. But the monograph *Aleksandr Sergeevich Pushkin (Zhizn' Pushkina)* appears to be a kind of authorial explanation of *Pushkin in Life.* As Fokht-Babushkin writes, "[T]hese two books . . . often simply repeat each other word for word" (Fokht-Babushkin, *Zagadochnyi Pushkin,* 19).

40. V. V. Veresaev, *Rodstvenniki Pushkina* (Moscow: Biblioteka Ogonek, 1933), 3–4.

41. Veresaev, *Zagadochnyi Pushkin,* 71; Walter Arndt, trans., *Alexander Pushkin: Collected Narrative and Lyrical Poetry* (Ann Arbor, Mich.: Ardis, 1984), 68 (slightly modified).

42. Veresaev, *V dvukh planakh,* 140.

43. Ibid., 146.

44. Ibid., 151.

45. Ibid., 159.

46. Ibid., 169. By the time of the 1937 Pushkin centennial, especially in Europe, Pushkin becomes even more of a banner for all sorts of groups. See Angela Brintlinger, "A. S. Pushkin v Parizhskoi emigratsii 1937-go goda," in *"Ot zapadnykh morei do samykh vrat vostochnykh . . .": A. S. Pushkin za rubezhom* (Moscow: Pushkin Institute, 1999), 305–15, and Sergei Denisenko, "Posmertnaia maska Pushkina. (Zametki po materialam russkoi emigrantskoi pechati 1937 goda)," in *Pushkin i drugie,* 148–52.

47. For more on Pushkin in Soviet culture, see Debreczeny, *Social Functions of Literature.*

48. See Gl. Glebov, "O mnimom i deistvitel'nom Pushkine," *Novyi mir* 6 (1937): 230–47. It is perhaps not entirely coincidental that Glebov uses the same term—"sham Pushkin"—as Tynianov did in his 1922 essay.

49. Ibid., 233.

50. Veresaev, *V dvukh planakh,* 172.

51. Julie Curtis has detailed the to's and fro's of Veresaev and Bulgakov's correspondence and work on the play and has suggested that Bulgakov was "a man fascinated by the detail rather than the broad outlines of history" (Curtis, *Bulgakov's Last Decade,* 25). She argued that this should have made him and Veresaev ideal partners, based on the detail-filled volumes of *Pushkin in Life,* but I disagree. They were both fascinated by details, but their approach to them and their ideas about how to use them were cardinally different. (Curtis translates Veresaev's book as *Pushkin in His Lifetime.* I have used the translation *Pushkin in Life,* as it seems to me that it reflects more clearly Veresaev's ideas of the living poet, the man as he appeared in life.)

52. Ibid., 77.

53. Bulgakov, *Sobranie sochinenii,* 3:681.

54. The most frequent reference to Pushkin throughout Bulgakov's works, and indeed the most pertinent to the play about Pushkin, was to snowstorms; Pushkin's poem "A Winter's Evening" ("Zimnyi vecher"), in particular, appears in *Days of the Turbins, The Master and Margarita,* and as an important leitmotif in *Aleksandr Pushkin,* in addition to acting as an epigraph to Bulgakov's story "The Snowstorm" ("V'iuga"). Bulgakov also used the snowstorm scene in *The Captain's Daughter* as an epigraph to *The White Guard.* On Pushkin motifs in Bulgakov see Curtis, *Bulgakov's Last Decade,* 75–80. It is ironic that "A Winter's Evening" is the same poem that Veresaev "staged" in his Pushkin biography, but this irony is also indicative of how Bulgakov's and Veresaev's methods differed.

55. Bulgakov, *Sobranie sochinenii,* 3:464.

56. Some of the characterization of Bitkov as a reprehensible, sneaky police informer was left on the cutting room floor. In Veresaev's version of the Moika scene, for example, Bitkov is everywhere, sticking his nose in, eavesdropping on conversations of the students and university professor who have come to pay their respects. The professor notices Bitkov and nervously looks him over; one student addresses Bitkov directly, exclaiming angrily: "Get out of here! If I see you again, I'll maim you!" See Veresaev, "Avtograf p'esy *Pushkin* (1935)" (Moscow: RGALI fond 1041, op. 1, ed. khr. 22), 13–15.

57. On these characters and their historical prototypes, see Erykalova, "Iz istorii rukopisi p'esy M. A. Bulgakova *Aleksandr Pushkin.*"

58. Bulgakov, *Sobranie sochinenii,* 3:511.

59. Ibid., 5:537.

60. See Erykalova, "Iz istorii rukopisi," 200–202.

61. Erykalova has noted that on some of Veresaev's typed drafts, Bulgakov wrote "drawn out" ("*rastianuto*") in the margins (ibid., 235). This is also visible in the manuscript from which I am citing, for example Veresaev, "Avtograf," 9, a "drawn out" passage which I examine in detail.

62. Veresaev, "Avtograf," 8.

63. Ibid., 9.

64. Ibid., 14.

65. Ibid., 10.

66. Ibid.

67. Ibid., 15.

68. Erykalova, "Iz istorii rukopisi," 187.

69. See Bulgakov, *Sobranie sochinenii,* 3:687.

70. Ibid.

71. Ibid., 5:551.

72. Bulgakova, *Dnevnik,* 117.

73. Here I rely on Alla Rabiniants, "M. A. Bulgakov i pushkinisty," in I. Belobrovtseva and S. Kul'ius, eds., *Bulgakovskii sbornik II: Materialy po istorii russkoi literatury XX veka* (Tallinn: Tallinn Pedagogical Institute, 1994), 101.

CHAPTER EIGHT

1. See Less, "K istorii *Pushkina*," 104–6, and Iu. A. Kozlovskii, "O tvorchestve I. A. Novikova," in I. A. Novikov, *Povesti i rasskazy* (Moscow: Khudozhestvennaia literatura, 1981), 12.

2. John Gillis, "Memory and Identity: The History of a Relationship," in *Commemorations: The Politics of National Identity* (Princeton, N.J.: Princeton University Press, 1994), 5.

3. S. N. Lunacharskaia, *Iubilei A.S. Pushkina v shkole* (Moscow: Gosudarstvennoe uchebnoe pedagogicheskoe izdatel'stvo, 1936), 3.

4. Ibid.

5. Shkola FZU tresta "Poligrafkniga," Moscow, 1937; M. A. Tsiavlovskii and G. A. Volkov, eds., Moscow, 1937; D. N. Nikolich, B. V. Bank, N. I. Malyi, eds., Leningrad, 1936, respectively.

6. Nikita Struve, "Russkaia emigratsiia i Pushkin," *Vestnik russkogo khristianskogo dvizheniia* 149, no. 1 (1987): 232–36.

7. V. I. Kolokol'nikov, *Den' russkoi kul'tury (odnodnevnyi vypusk, posviashchennyi prazdnovaniiu "Dnia Russkoi Kul'tury" v Kharbine 11 iiulia 1934 g.)* (Harbin, 11 July 1934), 2–4.

8. A. L. Bem, *O Pushkine. Stat'i.* (Uzhgorod: Pis'mena, 1937), 5.

9. See minutes of the Day of Russian Culture Committee from 1935 and 1936, Zeeler archive, Box 11, folder "Komitet po ustroistvu dnia russkoi kul'tury, Minutes and Financial Records," Bakhmeteff Archive, Columbia University, New York. Nikita Struve also discusses the desirability of a "pocket Pushkin"—a book which all Russians could keep on their desks or at their bedsides. Struve claims that the Parisian Pushkin Committee did publish a one-volume collected works, edited by Modest Gofman, for the jubilee, but the print run must have been very small. Struve admits that it is now a "bibliographic rarity," and I have seen no trace of it. See Struve, "Russkaia emigratsiia i Pushkin," 235. Carol Ueland mentioned a seven-volume collected works published in China for the anniversary, which is also a bibliographic rarity. Ueland, "Pushkin and the Russian Émigré Community in China," paper presented at the "Pushkin Beyond Europe" conference at Pennsylvania State University, 23 October 1999.

10. In this particular article Khodasevich was reminding his compatriots that "Pushkin Day" should be celebrated on June 6, not June 8. "K istorii 'Dnei russkoi kul'tury,'" *Vozrozhdenie*, no. 736 (8 June 1927), supplement. The confusion in dates was due to the shifting correspondence of

the Julian and Gregorian calendars. "Old style" Russian dates differ by thirteen days in the twentieth century but by twelve in the nineteenth century and by eleven in the eighteenth century; Pushkin was born in the eighteenth century, on May 26, 1799.

11. V. A. Maklakov, "Russkaia kul'tura i A. S. Pushkin," *Mir i iskusstvo (Le Monde et l'art)*, no. 4 (1 June 1930): 2–5; 3.

12. Ibid., 3. For Maklakov in 1930, as for Khodasevich in the late 1920s, the need was still for unity with all Russians—this holiday was to "unite us amongst ourselves and with those who stayed in Russia." Pushkin's birthday became the obvious choice for the "Day of Russian Culture." Here Maklakov seemed unaware of Khodasevich's version of the genesis of the holiday as going back to 1921 Petrograd. Nikita Struve also marked emigration as the birthplace of the "Pushkin Day"—in Estonia the first holiday of a "Day of Russian Enlightenment" was celebrated in conjunction with the 125th anniversary of Pushkin's birth (Struve, "Russkaia emigratsiia i Pushkin," 232).

13. As Sergei Denisenko has argued, it is precisely as a symbol that Pushkin was used on banners of all colors in the various émigré communities and in Soviet Russia of 1937, whether brown fascist banners or red communist banners. In print he has referred to the "death mask" of Pushkin fitting all kinds of faces; see Denisenko, "Posmertnaia maska Pushkina."

14. See the violent polemics between Khodasevich and M. L. Gofman, the author of several books about Pushkin including *Pushkin. Psikhologiia tvorchestva* (Paris: J. V. Povolozky, 1928). These polemics even reached the state of legal skirmishes; see the correspondence between V. F. Zeeler, Khodasevich's lawyer, and the poet, Zeeler fond, Bakhmeteff Archive, Columbia University Library, New York. See also V. F. Khodasevich, "O pis'me g. Gofmana," *Vozrozhdenie*, no. 3998 (14 May 1936).

15. Gor'kii died in 1936, before the official commemorations began.

16. Z. Maslov, "Pushkinskie nomera zhurnalov," in *Kniga i proletarskaia revoliutsiia*, vol. 5 (Moscow, 1937), 59–66.

17. Ibid., 61.

18. Ivan Novikov, *Pushkin na iuge* (Moscow: Khudozhestvennaia literatura, 1937), 83–87.

19. See "Most Distant Points Join Central Cities in Marking Day," *Moscow Daily News*, 10 February 1937, 1.

20. Ibid.

21. See "Towns, Institutions, Streets Named after Pushkin," *Moscow Daily News*, 10 February 1937, 1.

22. See "Leningrad to Hold Many Pushkin Events," *Moscow Daily News*, 10 February 1937, 4.

23. *Moscow Daily News*, 10 February 1937, 1.

24. By February 1, 1938, the All-Union Pushkin Exhibition had been visited by 641,026 people, including workers, peasants, soldiers, students,

civil servants, specialists, and performing artists. See K. Bogaevskaia, "Posetiteli Vsesoiuznoi Pushkinskoi vystavki," *Vremennik Pushkinskoi komissii,* vyp. 4–5 (1938): 579–83.

25. See G. Ia. Troshin, "Pushkin i more," *Morskoi zhurnal* 101, no. 9 (January 1937): 3–13, complete with a lithograph of Pushkin gazing from a cliff and the Pushkinian caption "Farewell, free element" ("Proshchai, svobodnaia stikhiia").

26. Kul'man, *Sovremennye zapiski* 65 (1937): 460. On Lifar's exhibition "Pushkin and His Epoch," see *Centenaire de Pouchkine. 1837–1937. Exposition Pouchkine et son époque.* (Paris, 1937); Kul'man's review of this catalogue (*Sovremennye zapiski* 65 [1937]: 460–61); and also F. Naval, "Pushkin vo Frantsii," *Pushkin i sovremennaia kul'tura,* ed. E. P. Chelyshev et al. (Moscow: Nauka, 1996), 271.

27. *Centenaire de Pouchkine,* 406.

28. Every émigré edition found its equal number in Russia. The Pushkin Jubilee Exhibit catalogue in France was matched by a similar catalogue published in the Soviet Union: *A Short Guide to the Exhibition Dedicated to the Centenary of the Death of the Great Russian Poet Aleksandr Sergeevich Pushkin* was published in Moscow by the All-Union Pushkin Committee in 1937.

29. A. S. *Pushkin i ego epokha (A.S. Pouchkine et son époque),* numéro spécial, a publication of the magazine *Illiustrirovannaia Rossiia* (Paris: Les éditions "La Russie Illustreé," 1937). Gofman's article runs from page 114 through 131, with many photos of the various rooms and exhibits. Other interesting articles in the issue include: "Pushkin Days in Emigration," which named all the countries of the Russian diaspora and described their commemorative events; "Pushkin Days in Soviet Russia"; and Sergei Lifar's short article entitled "The French Press on the Pushkin Exhibition."

30. "Pushkinskie dni v emigratsii," *Pushkin i ego epokha,* 132. Later in the year the émigré community continued this trend of connecting Pushkinian events with general preservation of Russian culture; May 9, the Parisian "Day of Russian Culture" for youth, was "dedicated to the young Pushkin" and included such events as "declamation, skits, singing, music, dances, rhythmic gymnastics"—in other words, the day was a folk festival at which Pushkin served as a uniting force and stood in for Russian culture generally.

31. Efforts were made to erect a Pushkin monument in Paris; in fact, according to V. F. Zeeler, an entire separate Pushkin Committee was formed at *Illustrated Russia* in April 1935 for the express purpose of funding such a monument. The committee engaged the sculptor Gudzhan and the architect Fidler, who agreed to work for free. It is not clear whether the committee ever succeeded in their goal. See V. F. Zeeler Collection at the

Bakhmeteff Archive, Box 11, "Komitet po ustroistvu Dnia russkoi kul'-tury—Minutes and Financial Records," 20 April 1936 [*sic;* probably 1935].

32. My thanks to Steven Conn, who searched out the monument for me in the summer of 1997. Chuan Tefu, who wrote the first Chinese biography of Pushkin (published 1997), confirmed for me that this statue is the only one of Pushkin in China. For further description of the monument and its complicated history, see Ueland, "Pushkin and the Russian Émigré Community in China."

33. "Pushkinskie dni v emigratsii," 133.

34. Sergei Lifar', *Moia zarubezhnaia Pushkiniana* (Paris: Éditions Bérisniak, 1966), 23.

35. For a slightly different version of my argument on Lifar', see Angela Brintlinger, "Pushkinist or P.R. Man: Sergei Lifar in 1930s Europe," *Pushkin Review* 2 (1999): 45–65.

36. Lifar', *Moia zarubezhnaia Pushkiniana,* 25. The Pushkin Committee Abroad included V. Maklakov, I. Bunin, M. Fedorov, and others.

37. See ibid., 26–31. On attempts to acquire Lifar's Pushkiniana for the Soviet Union, see I. Zil'bershtein, "'Pushkiniana' Sergeia Lifaria," in M. I. Samoilova and Iu. I. Osipov, eds., *"Solntse nashei poezii" (iz sovremennoi Pushkiniany)* (Moscow: Izd. Pravda, 1989), 266–76. The authenticity of some items on exhibit has been called into question. See T. I. Krasnoborod'ko, "'Tret'i litseiskii risunok': Pushkin ili psevdo-Pushkin?" in *Pushkin i drugie,* 120–26.

38. Lifar', *Moia zarubezhnaia Pushkiniana,* 32.

39. Sergei Lifar', *Ma Vie from Kiev to Kiev,* trans. James Holman Mason (Cleveland: World Publishing Company, 1979), 140.

40. Lifar', *Moia zarubezhnaia Pushkiniana,* 73, 87.

41. Ibid., 43.

42. Ibid., 43–44; see also Lifar', *Ma Vie from Kiev to Kiev,* 140–41.

43. Lifar', *Ma Vie from Kiev to Kiev,* 141.

44. Khodasevich, *Sobranie sochinenii,* 3:229.

45. Andrei Zorin has written about this passage in Khodasevich's biography of Derzhavin—the one time when Khodasevich "opens the door" of the poet's studio—as being particularly autobiographical. He also cited Mark Aldanov as pointing to these very paragraphs and identifying them as important enough to "enter into the classical canon" of Russian literature. See Zorin's afterword in Khodasevich, *Derzhavin* (Moscow: Mysl', 1988), 281.

46. Quoted in Lifar', introduction to *Pis'ma Pushkina k N. N. Goncharovoi* (Paris: S. Lifar, 1937), 25.

47. Lifar', *Pis'ma Pushkina,* 10.

48. Ibid.

49. Ibid., 11.

50. Ibid., 9.

51. Sergei Lifar', "Siiaiushchii svet poezii," *Dlia Vas*, no. 6 (164) (7 February 1937), 13.

52. In his essay "Geroi *Evgeniia Onegina*," in *Evgenii Onegin* (Paris: Étoile, 1937), 293–305, Lifar' also referred to his days as a schoolboy.

> When I think of Pushkin's Onegin, of Eugene Onegin . . . I am always grateful that I am a gymnasium student no longer, and that no one is forcing me to write a "characterization of Eugene Onegin" (I will note in parentheses that since I graduated from gymnasium I have had the opportunity to speak about friends, associates and acquaintances, but I have never given a "characterization" and I have never heard two identical opinions about the same person). (Ibid., 294)

His essay was, in essence, a response to the question, "Who are the main heroes of the novel *Evgenii Onegin*?" He gave a fairly predictable explanation:

> Pushkin drew in *Eugene Onegin* a full and extensive portrait of contemporary Russia, the Russia of the twenties, but there are only two true heroes, in the full sense of that word, in the novel: Onegin and Tat'iana. But both Onegin and Tat'iana are not fully completed, and in their portraits the facial features change imperceptibly to such an extent that the following statement is absolutely indubitable: the story of the novel, the development of its plot with its character-heroes were only the necessary canvas for the lyrical digressions, for the "diverse stanzas" of the novel. (Ibid., 305)

In other ways, though, his essay, amateurish and meandering as it was, seemed to presage better scholarly explorations of Tat'iana and Evgenii, which would be written much later. Lifar' defended Onegin from the attacks of nineteenth-century critics (ibid., 295) and pointed out that the Onegin of the "Decembrist" chapter was not at all like the Onegin of chapter 1, or even chapter 8 (ibid., 296). He even argued that the "ideal Russian woman" Tat'iana was hardly that (ibid., 297–98) and that the main reason the reader finds her attractive is that Pushkin was so in love with her (and here he quoted many lines where the poet called her "my dear Tatiana"; see ibid., 300–301). Compare with Caryl Emerson's "Tat'iana," *Vestnik Moskovskogo universiteta* [*Seriia 9: Filologiia*], no. 6 (November–December 1995): 31–47.

53. *Poshlost'*, translated as "vulgarity," "banality," "the pettiness of everyday life and existence," is perhaps best explained by Nabokov's essay on the phenomenon (see Nabokov, "Philistines and Philistinism," in *Lectures on Literature*). For the sake of American audiences, Nabokov frequently insisted on spelling the word *poshlust* in English, to gain additional connotational resonance from the stressed second syllable. In his *Strong Opinions* Nabokov noted: "Hack reviews are frequently *poshlost*, but it also lurks in certain highbrow essays. *Poshlost* calls Mr. Blank a great poet, and

Mr. Bluff a great novelist" (Nabokov, *Strong Opinions* [New York: Vintage, 1990], 101).

54. Nabokov, *Strong Opinions*, 13.

55. Quoted in "Pushkinskie dni v emigratsii," 137.

56. See Celestine Bohlen, "Nobody Doesn't Like Aleksandr Sergeyevich," *New York Times*, 2 June 1999; Sophia Kishkovsky, "For Everyone, Non-Russians, Too, There's a Personal Pushkin," *New York Times*, 5 June 1999; Ralph Fiennes, "Shooting Pushkin," New Yorker (7 June 1999), 44–50; also National Public Radio's *Morning Edition*, 6 June 1999.

Selected Bibliography

Adamovich, Georgii. "Pamiat' Khodasevicha." *Poslednie novosti*, no. 6653 (15 June 1939).

Aldanov, Mark. "V. F. Khodasevich." *Russkie zapiski*, no. 19 (1939): 182–183.

Andreev, Iu. A. *Russkii sovetskii istoricheskii roman. 20–30-e gody*. Moscow and Leningrad, 1962.

Annenkov, P. V. *Materialy dlia biografii A. S. Pushkina*. 2 vols. St. Petersburg, 1855.

———. *Pushkin v Aleksandrovskuiu epokhu*. St. Petersburg, 1874.

Antokol'skii, P. G. "Znanie i vymysel." In *Vospominaniia o Iu. Tynianove: portrety i vstrechi*, ed. Veniamin Kaverin, 248 56. Moscow: Sovetskii pisatel', 1983.

Arndt, Walter, trans. *Alexander Pushkin: Collected Narrative and Lyrical Poetry*. Ann Arbor, Mich.: Ardis, 1984.

Baskakov, V. A. *Pushkinskii dom*. Leningrad: Nauka, 1988.

Belinkov, Arkadii. *Iurii Tynianov*. 2d ed. Moscow: Sovetskii pisatel', 1965.

Bem, A. L. *O Pushkine. Stat'i*. Uzhgorod: Pis'mena, 1937.

Berberova, Nina. "Pamiati Khodasevicha." *Sovremennye zapiski* 69 (1939): 256–61.

Bestuzhev, A. A. "Znakomstvo moe s A. S. Griboedovym." In *Griboedov v vospominaniiakh sovremennikov*, ed. N. K. Piksanov. Moscow: Federatsiia, 1929. Reprinted in *Griboedov v vospominaniiakh sovremennikov*, ed. S. A. Fomichev. Moscow: Khudozhestvennaia literatura, 1980.

Bethea, David M. *Khodasevich: His Life and Art*. Princeton, N.J.: Princeton University Press, 1983.

———, ed. "Pis'ma V. Khodasevicha k N. Berberovoi." *Minuvshee: istoricheskii almanakh* 5 (1988): 228–327.

———. *Realizing Metaphors: Alexander Pushkin and the Life of the Poet*. Madison: University of Wisconsin Press, 1998.

———. "Slavic Gift-Giving, The Poet in History, and Pushkin's *The Captain's Daughter*." In *Russian Subjects: Empire, Nation, and the Culture of the Golden Age*, ed. Monika Greenleaf and Stephen Moeller-Sally, 259–73. Evanston, Ill.: Northwestern University Press, 1998.

Bethea, David M., and Angela K. Brintlinger. "Derjavine et Khodassevitch." In *Derjavine: un poète russe dans l'Europe des Lumières,* ed. A. Davidenkoff, 167–78. Paris: Institute d'Études Slaves, 1994.

Bitsilli, P. M. "Derzhavin." *Rossiia i slavianstvo,* 18 April 1931. Reprinted in V. F. Khodasevich. *Derzhavin.* Moscow: Kniga, 1988. 314–16.

Bogaevskaia, K. "Posetiteli Vsesoiuznoi Pushkinskoi vystavki." *Vremennik Pushkinskoi komissii,* vyp. 4–5 (1938): 579–83.

Bohlen, Celestine. "Nobody Doesn't Like Aleksandr Sergeyevich." *New York Times,* 2 June 1999.

Breschinsky, Dmitri N., and Zinaida A. Breschinsky. "On Tynjanov the Writer and His Use of Cinematic Technique in *The Death of the Wazir Mukhtar.*" *Slavic and East European Journal* 29, no. 1 (1985): 1–17.

Brintlinger, Angela. "A. S. Pushkin v Parizhskoi emigratsii 1937-go goda." In *"Ot zapadnykh morei do samykh vrat vostochnykh . . .": A. S. Pushkin za rubezhom,* 305–15. Moscow: Pushkin Institute, 1999.

———. "'Berezhlivost'': Pushkin u Khodasevicha." In *Pushkin i drugie,* ed. V. A. Koshelev, 142–47. Novgorod: Novgorod University Press, 1997.

———. "Fact and Fiction in Tynjanov's *Smert' Vazir-Muchtara:* Paradoxes of a Scientific Novel." *Russian Literature* [Amsterdam] 34 (1996): 273–302.

———. "The Russian Biographical Novel of the 1920s and 1930s." Ph.D. diss., University of Wisconsin–Madison, 1994.

———. "*Smert' Vazir-Mukhtara.*" In *Reference Guide to Russian Literature,* ed. Neil Cornwell, 856–57. London and Chicago: Fitzroy Dearborn, 1998.

Brooks, Van Wyck. "On Creating a Usable Past." *Dial* 64 (1918): 337–41.

Brovman, G. *V. V. Veresaev: Zhizn' i tvorchestvo.* Moscow: Sovetskii pisatel', 1959.

Bulgakov, Mikhail. "Aleksandr Pushkin. Podgotovitel'nye materialy k p'ese." In *Tvorchestvo Mikhaila Bulgakova: Issledovaniia i materialy,* vol. 2, 239–82. St. Petersburg: Nauka, 1994.

———. *Sobranie sochinenii v piati tomakh.* Moscow: Khudozhestvennaia literatura, 1990.

———. *Zhizn' gospodina de Mol'era.* Moscow: Molodaia gvardiia, 1991.

Bulgakova, E. S. *Dnevnik Eleny Bulgakovoi.* Moscow: Knizhnaia palata, 1990.

———. "Iz dnevnikovykh i memuarnykh zapisei 1933–1970 gg." In *Vospominaniia o Mikhaile Bulgakove,* ed. E. S. Bulgakova and S. A. Liandres, 391–411. Moscow: Sovetskii pisatel', 1988.

———. "M. Bulgakov–V. Veresaev. Perepiska po povodu p'esy *Pushkin (Poslednie dni).*" *Voprosy literatury* 3 (1965): 151–52.

Bulgakova, E. S., and S. A. Liandres. *Vospominaniia o Mikhaile Bulgakove.* Moscow: Sovetskii pisatel', 1988.

Bunin, Ivan. *Okaiannye dni.* London: Zaria, 1973.

Chudakova, M. O. "Arkhiv M. A. Bulgakova." In *Zapiski otdela rukopisi,* vyp. 37, 25–151. Moscow: Kniga, 1976.

———. *Zhizneopisanie Mikhaila Bulgakova.* Moscow: Kniga, 1988.

Chudakova, M. O., and V. N. Sazhin, "Arkhivnyi dokument v rabote Tynianova i problema sokhraneniia i izucheniia arkhivov." In *Vtorye tynianovskie chteniia,* 141–56. Riga: Zinatne, 1986.

Chukovskii, Kornei. N.t. In *Iurii Tynianov: pisatel' i uchenyi. Vospominaniia. Razmyshleniia. Vstrechi,* ed. Veniamin Kaverin, 111–20. Moscow: Molodaia gvardiia, 1966.

———. "Pervyi roman." In *Vospominaniia o Iu. Tynianove: portrety i vstrechi,* ed. Veniamin Kaverin, 138–46. Moscow: Sovetskii pisatel', 1983.

Chukovskii, N. "Razgovory s Tynianovym." In *Iurii Tynianov: pisatel' i uchenyi. Vospominaniia. Razmyshleniia. Vstrechi,* ed. Veniamin Kaverin, 285–93. Moscow: Molodaia gvardiia, 1966.

Chuzhak, N. "Literatura zhiznestroeniia." In *Literatura fakta,* 34–65. 1929; Munich: Wilhelm Fink Verlag, 1972.

Clark, Katerina. *The Soviet Novel: History as Ritual.* Chicago: University of Chicago Press, 1981.

Clifford, James L. *From Puzzles to Portraits: Problems of a Literary Biographer.* Chapel Hill: University of North Carolina Press, 1970.

Curtis, J. A. E. *Bulgakov's Last Decade: The Writer as Hero.* Cambridge: Cambridge University Press, 1987.

Dal', Vladimir. *Tolkovyi slovar' zhivogo velikogo russkogo iazyka.* 4 vols. Moscow: Russkii iazyk, 1989.

Debreczeny, Paul, trans. *Alexander Pushkin: Complete Prose Fiction.* Stanford, Calif.: Stanford University Press, 1983.

———. *Social Functions of Literature: Alexander Pushkin and Russian Culture.* Stanford, Calif.: Stanford University Press, 1997.

Denisenko, S. V. "Posmertnaia maska Pushkina. (Zametki po materialam russkoi emigrantskoi pechati 1937 goda)." In *Pushkin i drugie,* ed. V. A. Koshelev, 148–52. Novgorod: Novgorod University Press, 1997.

Derzhavin, G. R. *Sochineniia.* Ed. Ia. K. Grot. 9 vols. St. Petersburg, 1864–83.

Dolinin, Alexander. "Nabokov's Time Doubling: From *The Gift* to *Lolita.*" *Nabokov Studies* 2 (1995): 3–40.

Dostoevskii, F. M. "Zapisi k *Dnevniku pisatelia* 1876 g. iz rabochikh tetradei 1875–1877 gg. Zapisnaia tetrad' 1975–1876 gg." In *Polnoe sobranie sochinenii,* ed. V. G. Bazanov, 30 vols., 24:66–186. Leningrad: Nauka, 1972–90.

Edel, Leon. *Literary Biography.* Toronto: University of Toronto Press, 1957.

Eikhenbaum, B. M. "Roman ili biografiia?" *Russkaia molva,* 18 February 1913. Reprinted in *O literature. Raboty raznykh let,* 288–89. Moscow: Sovetskii pisatel', 1987.

———. N.t. In *Iurii Tynianov: pisatel' i uchenyi. Vospominaniia. Razmyshleniia. Vstrechi,* ed. Veniamin Kaverin, 73–85. Moscow: Molodaia gvardiia, 1966.

———. "Tvorchestvo Iu. Tynianova." In *O proze. O poezii,* 186–223. Leningrad: Khudozhestvennaia literatura, 1986.

Emerson, Caryl. *Boris Godunov: Transpositions of a Russian Theme.* Bloomington: Indiana University Press, 1986.

———. "Tat'iana." *Vestnik Moskovskogo universiteta* [Seriia 9: Filologiia], no. 6 (November–December 1995): 31–47.

Ermolinskii, S. A. *Iz zapisok raznykh let: Mikhail Bulgakov. Nikolai Zabolotskii.* Moscow: Iskusstvo, 1990.

Erykalova, I. E. "Iz istorii rukopisi p'esy M.A. Bulgakova *Aleksandr Pushkin* (po neopublikovannym materialam)." In *Tvorchestvo Mikhaila Bulgakova: Issledovaniia i materialy,* kn. 2, 184–238. St. Petersburg: Nauka, 1994.

———. "Parik, kamzol, gusinoe pero . . . (Rasskazchik v romane M. A. Bulgakova *Mol'er*)." In *Mikhail Bulgakov: "Etot mir moi . . .,"* Biblioteka Sankt-Peterburgskogo Bulgakovskogo literaturno-teatral'nogo obshchestva 1, ed. F. R. Balonov et al., 147–66. St. Petersburg: Rossiiskii institut istorii iskusstv, 1993.

Falen, James, trans. *Eugene Onegin.* Oxford and New York: Oxford University Press, 1995.

Fedin, Konstantin. "Virtuoznyi master." In *Vospominaniia o Iu. Tynianove: Portrety i vstrechi,* ed. Veniamin Kaverin, 307–10. Moscow: Sovetskii pisatel', 1983.

Fesenko, Iu. P. "Tema 'Griboedov i dekabristy" v rabotakh poslednikh let (nekotorye itogi)," In *A. S. Griboedov: Materialy k biografii,* ed. S. A. Fomichev, 92–107. Leningrad: Nauka, 1989.

Fiennes, Ralph. "Shooting Pushkin." *New Yorker* (7 June 1999): 44–50.

Fokht-Babushkin, Iurii. "'Pushkiniana' Veresaeva." In V. V. Veresaev, *Zagadochnyi Pushkin,* 3–20. Moscow: Respublika, 1996.

Fomichev, S. A., ed. *A. S. Griboedov: Materialy k biografii.* Leningrad: Nauka, 1989.

———, ed. *Griboedov v vospominaniiakh sovremennikov.* Moscow: Khudozhestvennaia literatura, 1980.

———. "Nizverzhenie kumirov." In *Pushkin i sovremennaia kul'tura,* 220–25. Moscow: Nauka, 1996.

Gasparov, M. L. "Nauchnost' i khudozhestvennost' v tvorchestve Tynianova." In *Tynianovskii sbornik: chetvertye tynianovskie chteniia,* ed. M. O. Chudakova, 12–20. Riga: Zinatne, 1990.

Gibson, Alexey. *Russian Poetry and Criticism in Paris from 1920 to 1940.* The Hague: Leuxenhoff, 1990.

Gillis, John R. "Memory and Identity: The History of a Relationship." Introduction to *Commemorations: The Politics of National Identity,* 3–24. Princeton, N.J.: Princeton University Press, 1994.

Ginzburg, L. M. N.t. In *Iurii Tynianov: pisatel' i uchenyi. Vospominaniia. Razmyshleniia. Vstrechi*, ed. Veniamin Kaverin, 86–110. Moscow: Molodaia gvardiia, 1966.

———. *O literaturnom geroe.* Leningrad: Sovetskii pisatel', 1979.

Glebov, Gl. "O mnimom i deistvitel'nom Pushkine." *Novyi mir* 6 (1937): 230–47.

Gor'kii, A. M. *Sobranie sochinenii v tridtsati tomakh.* Moscow: Gosudarstvennoe izdatel'stvo khudozhestvennoi literatury, 1955.

Gozenpud, A. A. "Poslednie dni (Pushkin): Iz tvorcheskoi istorii p'esy." In *M. A. Bulgakov—dramaturg i khudozhestvennaia kul'tura ego vremeni*, 154–67. Moscow: Soiuz teatral'nykh deiatelei, 1988.

Greenleaf, Monika, "Tynianov, Pushkin and the Fragment: Through the Lens of Montage," In *Cultural Mythologies of Russian Modernism: From the Golden Age to the Silver Age*, ed. Boris Gasparov, Robert P. Hughes, and Irina Paperno, 264–92. Berkeley: University of California Press, 1992.

Griboedov, A. S. *Sochineniia v stikhakh.* Leningrad: Sovetskii pisatel', 1967.

Grot, Ia. K. *Zhizn' Derzhavina po ego sochineniiam i pis'mam i po istoricheskim dokumentam.* 2 vols. St. Petersburg, 1880.

Guber, P. K. "Pushkin i russkaia kul'tura." In *Don-Zhuanskii spisok Pushkina*, 5–18. 1923; St. Petersburg: Petrograd, 1990.

Harden, Evelyn Jasiulko. "Truth and Design: Technique in Tynjanov's *Smert' Vazir-Muchtara.*" In *Mnemozina: Studia litteraria russica in honorem Vsevolod Setchkarev*, ed. Joachim T. Baer and Norman W. Ingham, 171–84. Munich: Wilhelm Fink Verlag, 1974.

Heltai, Gyongyi. "Interludes Leading to *Tartuffe*, of the Dangers of Laughing (Analysis of *The Intrigue of Hypocrites* by Bulgakov)." *Acta Litteraria Academiae Scienturum Hungaricae* 28, no. 1–2 (1986): 119–27.

Hillyer, Robert, trans. "The Death of a Poet" by Mikhail Lermontov. In *Centennial Essays for Pushkin*, ed. Samuel H. Cross and Ernest J. Simmons, 225–26. Cambridge, Mass.: Harvard University Press, 1937.

Horowitz, Brian. *The Myth of A. S. Pushkin in Russia's Silver Age: M. O. Gershenzon, Pushkinist.* Evanston, Ill.: Northwestern University Press, 1996.

Hughes, Robert P. "Pushkin in Petrograd, February 1921." In *Cultural Mythologies of Russian Modernism: From the Golden Age to the Silver Age*, ed. Boris Gasparov, Robert P. Hughes, and Irina Paperno, 204–13. Berkeley: University of California Press, 1992.

Iampol'skii, M. V. "'Poruchik Kizhe' kak teoreticheskii fil'm." In *Vtorye tynianovskie chteniia*, ed. M. O. Chudakova, 28–43. Riga: Zinatne, 1986.

Iavich, Avgust. "O bylom." In *Vospominaniia o Mikhaile Bulgakove*, ed. E. S. Bulgakova and S. A. Liandres, 157–63. Moscow: Sovetskii pisatel', 1988.

Izmailov, N. V. "Pushkin i semeistvo Karamzinykh." In *Pushkin v pis'makh Karamzinykh 1836–1837 godov*, 11–49. Moscow, Leningrad, 1960.

Kaverin, Veniamin. "Drug iunosti i vsei zhizni." In *Vospominaniia o Iu. Tynianove: portrety i vstrechi,* ed. Veniamin Kaverin, 38–58. Moscow: Sovetskii pisatel', 1983.

———, ed., *Iurii Tynianov: pisatel' i uchenyi. Vospominaniia. Razmyshleniia. Vstrechi.* Moscow: Molodaia gvardiia, 1966.

———. *Vospominaniia o Iu. Tynianove: portrety i vstrechi.* Moscow: Sovetskii pisatel', 1983.

Kendall, Paul Murray. *The Art of Biography.* New York: Norton, 1965.

Khmel'nitskaia, T. "Issledovatel'skii roman. Istoricheskaia proza Tynianova." In *Golosa vremeni,* 40–85. Leningrad: Sovetskii pisatel', 1963.

Khodasevich, V. F. *Derzhavin.* Moscow: Mysl', 1988.

———. *Derzhavin.* Moscow: Kniga, 1988.

———. *Koleblemyi trenozhnik: izbrannoe.* Moscow: Sovetskii pisatel', 1991.

———. *Literaturnye stat'i i vospominaniia.* New York: Chekhov, 1954.

———. "O pis'me g. Gofmana." *Vozrozhdenie,* no. 3998 (14 May 1936).

———. *O Pushkine.* Berlin: Petropolis, 1937.

———. "Peterburgskie povesti Pushkina." In Pushkin-Titov, *Uedinennyi domik na Vasil'evskom,* 3–33. Moscow: Universal'naia biblioteka, 1915.

———. *Poeticheskoe khoziaistvo Pushkina.* Leningrad: Mysl', 1924.

———. "Pushkin i Nikolai I." *Vozrozhdenie,* no. 4118 (11 February 1938).

———. "*Pushkin v zhizni,*" *Poslednie novosti,* no. 2122 (13 January 1927).

———. Review of *Rassvety,* a collection of poems by Lidiia Chervinskaia. *Vozrozhdenie,* no. 4082 (11 June 1937).

———. *Sobranie sochinenii v chetyrekh tomakh,* ed. Irina Surat (Moscow: Soglasie, 1996–97).

———. *Stat'i o russkoi poezii.* St. Petersburg: Epokha, 1922.

———. "Umiranie iskusstva." *Vozrozhdenie,* no. 4158 (18 November 1938).

———. "V sporakh o Pushkine." *Sovremennye zapiski* 37 (1928): 275–94.

Kishkovsky, Sophie. "For Everyone, Non-Russians, Too, There's a Personal Pushkin." *New York Times,* 5 June 1999.

Kliuchevskii, V. O. *Istoricheskie portrety. Deiateli istoricheskoi mysli.* Moscow: Pravda, 1990.

Kolokol'nikov, V. I. *Den' russkoi kul'tury (odnodnevnyi vypusk, posviashchennyi prazdnovaniiu "Dnia Russkoi Kul'tury" v Kharbine 11 iiulia 1934 g.* (Harbin, 11 July 1934), 2–4.

Kostelianets, B. Introduction to Iu. N. Tynianov, *Sochineniia v dvukh tomakh,* vol. 1, 5–30. Leningrad: Khudozhestvennaia literatura, 1985.

Kozlovskii, Iu. A. "O tvorchestve I. A. Novikova." In I. A. Novikov, *Povesti i rasskazy,* 3–14. Moscow: Khudozhestvennaia literatura, 1981.

Lakshin, V. "Mir Mikhaila Bulgakova" (1989). In M. A. Bulgakov, *Sobranie sochinenii v piati tomakh,* 1:5–68. Moscow: Khudozhestvennaia literatura, 1990.

———. "Sud'ba Bulgakova: legenda i byl'." In *Vospominaniia o Mikhaile Bulgakove,* ed. E. S. Bulgakova and S. A. Liandres, 7–37. Moscow: Sovetskii pisatel', 1988.

Less, Aleksandr. "K istorii *Pushkina.*" In *Neprochitannye stranitsy,* 104–6. Moscow: Sovetskii pisatel', 1966.

Levinton, G. A. "Istochniki i podteksty romana *Smert' Vazir-Mukhtara.*" In *Tynianovskii sbornik: tret'i tynianovskie chteniia,* 6–14. Riga: Zinatne, 1988.

Levitt, Marcus. *Russian Literary Politics and the Pushkin Celebration of 1880.* Ithaca, N.Y.: Cornell University Press, 1989.

Levkovich, Ia. L. "Pushkin v sovetskoi khudozhestvennoi proze i dramaturgii." In *Pushkin: Issledovaniia i materialy,* vol. 5: *Pushkin i russkaia kul'tura,* 140–78. Leningrad: Nauka, 1967.

Lifar', Sergei. "Geroi *Evgeniia Onegina.*" In *Evgenii Onegin,* 293–305. Paris: Étoile, 1937.

———. *Ma Vie from Kiev to Kiev.* Trans. James Holman Mason. Cleveland: World Publishing Company, 1979.

———. *Moia zarubezhnaia Pushkiniana.* Paris: Éditions Bérisniak, 1966.

———, ed. and intro. *Pis'ma Pushkina k N. N. Goncharovoi.* Paris: S. Lifar, 1937.

———. "Siiaiushchii svet poezii." *Dlia Vas,* no. 6 (164) (7 February 1937), 13.

Losev, V. I. "Bulgakov i Mol'er." In M. A. Bulgakov, *Zhizn' gospodina de Mol'era,* 175–215. Moscow: Molodaia gvardiia, 1991.

Lotman, Iu. M. "Biografiia—zhivoe litso." *Novyi mir* 2 (1985): 227–36.

Lunacharskaia, S. N. *Iubilei A. S. Pushkina v shkole.* Moscow: Gosudarstvennoe uchebnoe pedagogicheskoe izdatel'stvo, 1936.

Maiakovskii, V. V. *Polnoe sobranie sochinenii.* 13 vols. Moscow: Gosudarstvennoe izdatel'stvo khudozhestvennoi literatury, 1934–38.

Maklakov, V. A. "Russkaia kul'tura i A. S. Pushkin." *Mir i iskusstvo (Le Monde et l'art),* no. 4 (1 June 1930), 2–5.

Malmstad, John, "The Historical Sense and Xodasevič's Deržavin." In V. F. Khodasevich, *Derzhavin,* v–xviii. Munich: Wilhelm Fink Verlag, 1975.

———. "Khodasevich and Formalism: A Poet's Dissent." In *Russian Formalism: A Retrospective Glance. A Festschrift in honor of Victor Erlich,* ed. Robert Louis Jackson and Stephen Rudy, 68–81. New Haven, Conn.: Yale Center for International and Area Studies, 1985.

Mandel'shtam, Iurii. "Khodasevich o Pushkine." *Vozrozhdenie,* no. 4077 (8 May 1937).

Mandel'shtam, Osip. "Konets romana" (1928). In *Sobranie sochinenii,* 3 vols., 2:266–69. Moscow: Terra, 1991.

Manin, Iu. I. "Tynianov i Griboedov: Zametki o *Smerti Vazir-Mukhtara.*" *Revue des Études slaves* 55, no. 3 (1983): 507–21.

Maslov, Z. "Pushkinskie nomera zhurnalov." In *Kniga i proletarskaia revoliutsiia,* vol. 5, 59–66. Moscow, 1937.

Milne, Lesley. "Mikhail Bulgakov." In *Reference Guide to Russian Literature,* ed. Neil Cornwell, 199–200. Chicago: Fitzroy Dearborn, 1998.

———. *Mikhail Bulgakov: A Critical Biography.* Cambridge: Cambridge University Press, 1990.

Miliukov, P. N. *Zhivoi Pushkin.* Paris: Rodnik, 1937.

Mokul'skii, S. S. *Mol'er.* Moscow: Zhurnal'no-gazetnoe ob"edinenie, 1936.

Montenegro, David. "An Interview with Joseph Brodsky." *Partisan Review* 54, no. 4 (1987): 527–40.

Nabokov, Vladimir. *The Gift.* Trans. Michael Scammell and the author. 1963; New York: Vintage, 1991.

———. *Glory.* Trans. Dmitri Nabokov and the author. New York: McGraw-Hill, 1971.

———. "Philistines and Philistinism." In *Lectures on Russian Literature,* 309–14. New York: Harcourt Brace Jovanovich, 1981.

———. *Speak, Memory: An Autobiography Revisited.* 1967; New York: Vintage, 1989.

———. *Strong Opinions.* New York: Vintage, 1990.

Nadel, Ira Bruce. *Biography: Fiction, Fact and Form.* New York: St. Martin's, 1984.

Nemzer, Andrei. "Literatura protiv istorii: Zametki o 'Smerti Vazir-Mukhtara.'" *Druzhba narodov* 6 (1991): 241–52.

Nepomnyashchy, Catharine Theimer. Introduction to Abram Tertz (Andrei Sinyavsky), *Strolls with Pushkin,* 1–45. New Haven, Conn.: Yale University Press, 1993.

Novikov, Ivan. *Pushkin na iuge. Dramaticheskie stseny v 4-x deistviiakh dlia chteniia.* Moscow: Khudozhestvennaia literatura, 1937.

Novikov, V. V. *Mikhail Bulgakov: Khudozhnik.* Moscow: Moskovskii rabochii, 1996.

Oksman, Iu. G. "Pushkin v rabote nad romanom *Kapitanskaia dochka.*" In A. S. Pushkin, *Kapitanskaia dochka,* 145–99. Leningrad: Nauka, 1985.

P. A. "Pushkinskie dni v Sovetskoi Rossii." *Illiustrirovannaia Rossiia,* 140–41. Paris, 1937.

Paperno, Irina. "The Meaning of Art: Symbolist Theories." In *Creating Life: The Aesthetic Utopia of Russian Modernism,* ed. Irina Paperno and Joan Delaney Grossman, 13–23. Stanford, Calif.: Stanford University Press, 1994.

———. "Nietzscheanism and the Return of Pushkin in Twentieth-Century Russian Culture." In *Nietzsche and Soviet Culture: Ally and Adversary,* ed. Bernice Glatzer Rosenthal, 211–32. Cambridge: Cambridge University Press, 1994.

———. "Pushkin v soznanii cheloveka serebriannogo veka." In *Cultural Mythologies of Russian Modernism: From the Golden Age to the Silver Age*, ed. Boris Gasparov, Robert P. Hughes, and Irina Paperno, 19–51. Berkeley: University of California Press, 1992.

Parshin, Leonid. "Bulgakov i ego geroi glazami komp'iutera." *Literaturnaia gazeta* (26 January 1994), 6.

Paustovskii, K. "Bulgakov." In *Vospominaniia o Mikhaile Bulgakove*, ed. E. S. Bulgakova and S. A. Liandres, 93–108. Moscow: Sovetskii pisatel', 1988.

Pechkovskii, M. I. "Pushkin i Amerikanskaia Rus'." *Russkii Vestnik*, no. 48 (1 July 1936): 4–5.

Piksanov, N. K. *A. S. Griboedov: Biograficheskii ocherk.* St. Petersburg: Gosudarstvennaia tipografiia, 1911.

Polevoi, K. "Iz stat'i 'O zhizni i sochineniiakh A. S. Griboedova.'" In *Griboedov v vospominaniiakh sovremennikov*, ed. S. A. Fomichev, 160–67. Moscow: Khudozhestvennaia literatura, 1980.

Poliak, V. V. "Pis'ma A.S. Griboedova kak dokumental'nyi istochnik romana Tynianova *Smert' Vazir-Mukhtara.*" In *Tynianovskii sbornik: pervye tynianovskie chteniia*, 9–17. Riga: Zinatne, 1984.

Proffer, Ellendea. *Bulgakov: Life and Work.* Ann Arbor, Mich.: Ardis, 1984.

Pushchin, I. I. *Zapiski I. I. Pushchina o Pushkine.* St. Petersburg: Sirius, 1907.

Pushkin, A. S. *Polnoe sobranie sochinenii.* Moscow: Akademii nauk, 1937–49.

Rabiniants, Alla. "M. A. Bulgakov i pushkinisty." In *Bulgakovskii sbornik II: Materialy po istorii russkoi literatury XX veka*, ed. I. Belobrovtseva and S. Kul'ius, 96–102. Tallinn: Tallinn Pedagogical Institute, 1994.

Rosengrant, Sandra. "The Genesis of Tynjanov's Fiction." *Selecta: Journal of the Pacific Northwest Council on Foreign Languages* 8 (1987): 115–20.

Sadovskoi, B. A. "G. R. Derzhavin" (1907). Reprinted in V. F. Khodasevich, *Derzhavin*, 272–78. Moscow: Kniga, 1988.

Sandler, Stephanie. "The Law, the Body, and the Book: Three Poems on the Death of Pushkin." *Canadian-American Slavic Studies* 23, no. 3 (Fall 1989): 281–311.

———. "Pushkin as a Sign in Contemporary Russian Culture: The Example of Film." In *Structure and Tradition in Russian Society. Papers from an International Conference on the Occasion of the Seventieth Birthday of Yury Mikhailovich Lotman "Russian Culture: Structure and Tradition,"* ed. Robert Reid, Joe Andrew, and Valentina Polukhina, 138–52. Helsinki: Slavica Helsingiensia, 1994.

———. "Remembrance in Mikhailovskoe." In *Cultural Mythologies of Russian Modernism: From the Golden Age to the Silver Age*, ed. Boris

Gasparov, Robert P. Hughes, and Irina Paperno, 231–50. Berkeley: University of California Press, 1992.

———. "Sex, Death and Nation in the *Strolls with Pushkin* Controversy." *Slavic Review* 51, no. 2 (Summer 1992): 294–308.

Schwarzband, Samuel. "Les Carnets de Derjavine et *La Fille du capitaine* de Pouchkine (Hypothèses)," in *Derjavine: un poète russe dans l'Europe des Lumières,* 149–58. Paris: Institute d'Études Slaves, 1994.

Shklovskii, Viktor. N.t. In *Iurii Tynianov: pisatel' i uchenyi. Vospominaniia. Razmyshleniia. Vstrechi,* ed. Veniamin Kaverin, 48–72. Moscow: Molodaia gvardiia, 1966.

Shliapkin, I. A. "Khronologicheskaia kanva dlia izucheniia biografii A. S. Griboedova." In *Polnoe sobranie sochinenii A. S. Griboedova,* 2 vols., 1:xxxii. St. Petersburg, 1889.

Smelianskii, A. *Mikhail Bulgakov v Khudozhestvennom teatre.* Moscow: Iskusstvo, 1986.

Stalin, I. V. "Otvet Bill'-Belotserkovskomu." In *Sochineniia,* 11:326–29. Moscow: Gosudarstvennoe izdatel'stvo politicheskoi literatury, 1949.

Stepanov, Nikolai. "Druzheskaia perepiska 20-x godov." In *Russkaia proza,* ed. B. Eikhenbaum and Iu. Tynianov, 74–101. 1926; The Hague: Mouton, 1963.

———. "Zamysly i plany." In *Vospominaniia o Iu. Tynianove: Portrety i vstrechi,* ed. Veniamin Kaverin, 231–47. Moscow: Sovetskii pisatel', 1983.

Strachey, Lytton. *Eminent Victorians.* London: Chatto and Windus, 1918.

Stroganov, M. V. "God rozhdeniia Griboedova, ili 'polputi zhizni.'" In *A. S. Griboedov. Materialy k biografii,* ed. S. A. Fomichev, 10–18. Leningrad: Nauka, 1989.

Struve, Nikita. "Russkaia emigratsiia i Pushkin." *Vestnik russkogo khristianskogo dvizheniia* 149, no. 1 (1987): 232–36.

Surat, Irina. "Biografiia Pushkina kak kul'turnyi vopros." *Novyi mir* 2 (1999): 177–95.

———. *Pushkinist V. F. Khodasevich.* Moscow: Labirint, 1994.

Tamarchenko, Anna. "U istokov sovetskogo istoricheskogo romana." *Neva* 10 (1974): 179–87.

Tertz, Abram (Andrei Sinyavsky). "On Socialist Realism" (1960), trans. George Dennis. In *The Trial Begins and On Socialist Realism,* 127–219. Berkeley: University of California Press, 1982.

Tolstoi, L. N. "Vstupleniia, predisloviia i varianty nachal *Voiny i mira.*" in *Polnoe sobranie sochinenii,* ed. V. G. Chertkov, 90 vols., 13:53–197. Moscow: Gosudarstvennoe izdatel'stvo khudozhestvennoi literatury, 1928–53.

Tomashevskii, Boris. "Literature and Biography" (1923), trans. Herbert Eagle. In *Readings in Russian Poetics: Formalist and Structuralist Views,* ed. Ladislav Matejka and Krystyna Pomorska, 47–55. Ann Arbor: Michigan Slavic Publications, 1978.

Troshin, G. Ia. "Pushkin i more." *Morskoi zhurnal* 109, no. 1 (January 1937): 3–13.
Tynianov, Iu. N. "Avtobiografiia." In *Iurii Tynianov: pisatel' i uchenyi. Vospominaniia. Razmyshleniia. Vstrechi*, ed. Veniamin Kaverin, 9–20. Moscow: Molodaia gvardiia, 1966.
———. *Kiukhlia*, in *Sochineniia v trekh tomakh*, vol. 1. Moscow: Terra, 1994.
———. "Lichnost' Pushkina," *Pravda*, no. 40 (7006) (10 February 1937), 3.
———. *Poetika. Istoriia literatury. Kino.*, ed. and notes by A. P. Chudakov, M. O. Chudakova, and E. A. Toddes. Moscow: Nauka, 1977.
———. "Promezhutok" (1924). In *Arkhaisty i novatory*, 541–80. Leningrad: Priboi, 1929.
———. "Proza Pushkina," *Literaturnaia gazeta*, no. 10 (646) (20 February 1937), 3–4.
———. *Pushkin*, in *Sochineniia v trekh tomakh*, vol. 3. Moscow: Terra, 1994.
———. *Pushkin i ego sovremenniki*, ed. A. L. Grishunin and A. P. Chudakov. Moscow: Nauka, 1969.
———. *Smert' Vazir-Mukhtara*. In *Sochineniia v dvukh tomakh*, vol. 2. Leningrad: Khudozhestvennaia literatura, 1985.
———. "Tvorcheskie plany," *Literaturnaia gazeta*, no. 7 (786) (5 February 1939), 6.
———. N.t. In Andrei Belyi, M. Gor'kii, et al., *Kak my pishem*, 158–68. 1930; Benson, Vt.: Chalidze, 1983.
Ungurianu, Dan. "Fact and Fiction in the Romantic Historical Novel." *Russian Review* 57, no. 3 (July 1998): 380–93.
"V. F. Khodasevich's *Pushkin*," *Vozrozhdenie*, no. 3515.
Vakhitova, T. M. "Pis'ma M. Bulgakova pravitel'stvu kak literaturnyi fakt." In *Tvorchestvo Mikhaila Bulgakova: Issledovaniia. Materialy. Bibliografiia*, ed. N. A. Groznova and A. I. Pavlovskii, kn. 3, 5–24. St. Petersburg: Nauka, 1995.
Vakhtin, B. "Bulgakov i Gogol': Materialy k teme." In *M. A. Bulgakov—Dramaturg i khudozhestvennaia kul'tura ego vremeni*, ed. A. A. Ninov, 334–42. Moscow: Soiuz teatral'nykh deiatelei, 1988.
Vatsuro, V. E., ed. *A. S. Pushkin. Stikhotvoreniia litseiskikh let 1813–1817*. St. Petersburg: Nauka, 1994.
Veidle, Vladimir. "Ob iskusstve biografa." *Sovremennye zapiski* 44 (1931): 491–95.
———. "Poeziia Khodasevicha." *Sovremennye zapiski* 34 (1928): 454.
———. *Umiranie iskusstva*. Paris: YMCA Press, 1937.
Veresaev, V. V. "Avtograf p'esy *Pushkin* (1935)." Moscow: RGALI fond 1041, op. 1, ed. khr. 22.
———. *Pushkin v zhizni*. 6th ed. Moscow: Sovetskii pisatel', 1936.

———. *Rodstvenniki Pushkina.* Moscow: Biblioteka Ogonek, 1933.
———. *V dvukh planakh: stat'i o Pushkine.* Moscow: Nedra, 1929.
———. *Zagadochnyi Pushkin.* Moscow: Respublika, 1996.
Vinokur, G. O. *Biografiia i kul'tura.* Moscow: Gosudarstvennaia akademiia khudozhestvennykh nauk, 1927.
Volovich, I. G. "Istoricheskaia proza Iu. Tynianova." *Izvestiia Akademii Nauk SSSR (Seriia literatury i iazyka)* 48, no. 6 (November–December 1989): 517–27.
Wachtel, Andrew. *An Obsession with History: Russian Writers Confront the Past.* Stanford, Calif.: Stanford University Press, 1994.
White, Hayden. *The Content of the Form: Narrative Discourse and Historical Representation.* Baltimore: Johns Hopkins University Press, 1987.
Wright, A. Colin. *Mikhail Bulgakov: Life and Interpretations.* Toronto: University of Toronto Press, 1978.
Zhukov, D. A. *Biografiia biografii: razmyshlenie o zhanre.* Moscow: Sovetskaia Rossiia, 1980.
Zorin, Andrei. "Nachalo." In V. F. Khodasevich, *Derzhavin,* 5–28. Moscow: Kniga, 1988.
———. "Posleslovie." In V. F. Khodasevich, *Derzhavin,* 267–84. Moscow: Mysl', 1988.

Index